The Medieval Kitchen

THE Medieval

Original drawings by Patricia Glee Smith

ODILE REDON

FRANÇOISE SABBAN

SILVANO SERVENTI

Kitchen

RECIPES

FROM

FRANCE

AND

ITALY

Translated by Edward Schneider

THE UNIVERSITY OF CHICAGO PRESS

CHICAGO & LONDON

ODILE REDON is lecturer at the University of Paris VIII
Vincennes à Saint-Denis.
FRANÇOISE SABBAN is lecturer at l'École des Hautes Études en
Sciences Sociales in Paris.
SILVANO SERVENTI is an independent researcher.
GEORGES DUBY (1911–1996) was a member of the Académie
française and for many years held the distinguished chair
in medieval history at the Collège de France.
Originally published as *La gastronomie au Moyen Age: 150 recettes
de France et d'Italie,* © 1991, 1993, Éditions Stock

The University of Chicago Press, Chicago 60637
The University of Chicago Press, Ltd., London

© 1998 by The University of Chicago
All rights reserved. Published 1998
Original drawings © 1998 by Patricia Glee Smith
Printed in the United States of America
07 06 05 04 03 02 01 00 99 98   1 2 3 4 5
ISBN: 0–226–70684–2 (cloth)

Library of Congress Cataloging-in-Publication Data
Redon, Odile.
 [Gastronomie au Moyen Age. English]
 The medieval kitchen : recipes from France and Italy / Odile
Redon, Françoise Sabban, and Silvano Serventi ; translated by
Edward Schneider ; original drawings by Patricia Glee Smith.
  p. cm.
 Translation of: La gastronomie au Moyen Age.
 Includes bibliographical references and index.
 ISBN 0-226-70684-2 (alk. paper)
 1. Cookery, French—History. 2. Cookery, Italian—History.
3. Cookery, Medieval. 4. Food habits—France—History.
5. Food habits—Italy—History. I. Sabban, Françoise.
II. Serventi, Silvano. III. Title.
TX719.R3755   1998
641.5945'0902—DC21   97-31785
                                      CIP
Photos courtesy of the Bibliothèque Nationale de France, Paris.

This book is printed on acid-free paper.

Contents

Foreword

Georges Duby

To open this book is to set your mouth watering. You will grow hungry just scanning the table of contents and coming across dishes such as *Bourbelier* (Roast Wild Boar in Spiced Sauce), San Vincenzo's Day Grilled Eel, or Chicken *Ambrogino* with Dried Fruit. For the reader, the rich, subtle language of the recipes in this book will be a feast in itself; it will fill you with a sense of well-being.

But this book has other virtues: it responds to our fierce, gnawing urge to flee the anemic, the bland, fast food, ketchup, and to set sail for new shores. It affords a change of scenery. It brings you unfamiliar flavors: the light richness of almond milk; the elegant touch that a drop of rose water or a pinch of grains of paradise can add to dishes that somehow still remain rustic; the unexpectedly interesting flavor of borage; or the mingling of sweet and sour and the many pies and tarts that link the cooking of our distant ancestors to the most elegant of the modern world's exotic cuisines, such as Iranian, Chinese, and Moroccan. Will raising the curtain on these combinations create new fads? Will specialized restaurants be opened to challenge those where the snobs faint with delight at dishes that are claimed to follow the foodways of Thailand, or Zanzibar, or Monomotapa? It is my impression that these are already on the way. Let us hope that their owners will turn to this book rather than to any other: Here, great serious-mindedness is fused with lusciousness. It would also be good for our great chefs to pick up a copy and study it; it will prove a valuable stimulant for the creative imagination.

Like the task of unearthing Baroque music years ago, that of revealing medieval haute cuisine has been undertaken by highly skilled connoisseurs. Odile Redon, Françoise Sabban, and Silvano Serventi are blessed with lively minds and the most refined of palates. They are the kind of people who can tell you the name and vintage of any wine from its bouquet, and detect a scrap of orange rind simmering in a beef stew. Beyond flavors and aromas, they are sensitive to the aesthetics of presentation and to the serene, slow rites of the feast that every fine meal should be. Their sensuality, their love of food, and their joyful approach to life all enable them to choose the most delectable way of introducing each recipe. There is good old-fashioned technical language as well: they use the language of the kitchen, for they are good cooks—and I am speaking from personal experience. How can I ever forget the delicate rabbit baked in pastry that Françoise Sabban prepared for us, cleverly forming the crust into the shape of the tender young beast, as Guillaume Tirel—or Taillevent, as he was called—did for Charles V the Wise?

Furthermore, her writing, and that of her two colleagues, inspires readers to step up to the stove, where this volume will counsel them with care and in great detail. The pages that follow will not only make you dream; you will find that they constitute an altogether practical manual that explains when the necessary ingredients are in season and how to find them; that accurately sets out proportions and cooking times, which the original texts often neglect to mention; that even tells you when to make use of your freezer and when you can substitute an electric blender for a mortar and pestle.

The three authors are artists. They are also scholars and historians by profession. They delved into rare editions and even unpublished manuscripts to find the documents they issue here in original form, then used all their expertise to provide the most faithful possible interpretations. By making them widely available, they are helping to show us a very different Middle Ages from the one we had imagined—to which we would never have ascribed such refinement when it came to nourishing the body.

This, of course, is a very aristocratic Middle Ages. This is not a history of ordinary eating, like the studies by Massimo Montanari and Louis Stouff, based on more prosaic, less enchanting sources such as account books and legal contracts. The cooking treatises excerpted here form part of the most priceless libraries, gathered for royalty (even if some are claimed to be the work of an upstanding bourgeois householder), or at least for the aristocracy, to glorify court banquets and knightly feasts. We stand before them as we stand before the Duc de Berry's book of hours), at the apex of a culture. That is certainly true of France, fount of the arts—or rather of Paris, already the City of Lights—and, above all, true of brilliant Italy, open to trade in every form at a time when the Mediterranean was one of the great crossroads of the world, and when the foods of Germany clearly had far less appeal.

This, moreover, is the late Middle Ages: the fourteenth and fifteenth centuries. The great insight of the principles laid down by a Maestro Martino or a Maître Chiquart is less surprising when seen against the backdrop not of the eleventh-century Bayeux Tapestry or the twelfth-century *Pèlerinage de Charlemagne* but of Henri de Mondeville's treatise on surgery, the logic of William of Ockham, the polyphonic virtuosity of the music of the *ars nova*, or the frescos of Pisanello or Matteo di Viterbo, all dating from the fourteenth and fifteenth centuries. It is reasonable to consider that the art of cooking had been much refined since the days of Saint Bernard, as had armor and the decor of noble dwellings. Who on the other hand would say for certain that Philippe Auguste gorged himself on rotting meat that had been massively peppered to make it less disgusting? Or that his knightly comrades, taught by Chrétien de Troyes and André le Chapelain to exercise such grace and cleverness in the pirouettes of courtly love, were any less mindful of finesse and rigor when it came to the smoothness of sauces or the golden color of the pastries they relished as they laughed in the company of their fair damsels?

Preface

A book of medieval cooking is like an invitation to a journey, a journey in time that might yet recall an adventure in a distant land. If you accept the invitation you will enter a world of unknown sensations. First of all, you must forget the tomato—difficult in the case of Italian cooking—and you must eliminate the potato, that welcome refuge of French housewives, because it was only lately that these products came to the European continent from the Americas. For the same reason, you must banish peppers and chilies, to which Europe has grown used only through a relatively recent acquaintance with these exotica. Your polenta will not be made of corn, and you will have no coffee to sip after dessert; and there will certainly be no smoking. On the other hand, you can drink all the wine you want—but preferably thinned with water. You will seek a subtle balance between spices, to avoid overpowering the saffron with pepper, or the cinnamon and ginger with cloves. You will be clouded in the scent of rose water, and you will think nothing of showering a chicken with sugar or stuffing an eel with dried figs. Your sauces will no longer be made with cream; instead, it is their acidity that will rouse your palate. The day you "cook medieval" is the day you escape. But escape to where?

We could have decided to traverse the whole of Western Europe, because, as we shall see, in medieval cooking all those countries share common elements. But there are differences, and we have opted to confine ourselves to France and Italy. These two countries are neighbors, along the Alps and the Mediterranean coast, through a culturally mixed region: Italian and French, or Provençal. And the oceanic plain of northern France was already centered on Paris and had different cultural and environmental associations. To be sure, we do not rule out the occasional foray further afield, but this already vast territory is sufficient proof that cooking—while depending on local offerings and hence on climate and farming traditions for most meats and vegetables—aspired to more distant quests, and was able to carry them out: food traveled. We all know that spices, as costly as they were light to transport, came from the East. But almonds, citrus fruits, and wine also came north in response to a gastronomic demand. Recipes too traveled, and some unquestionably came from abroad—even if, on weak evidence and on the basis of analogies with modern cuisines, the Arab roots of medieval Western cooking have sometimes been exaggerated.

The cuisine we are reviving in this book is that of the fourteenth and fifteenth centuries, a period during which medieval cooking matured, following a total break with the gastronomy of antiquity, in contact with—not dependent on—Arab cooking, via the Iberian peninsula and Sicily. It is not easy to find traces of this medieval cooking in modern practice or in that of any time in the recent past: you will see that there is no confusing medieval cooking with traditional regional cuisines. This is because in the seventeenth century cooking underwent as radical a change as it had in the seventh to eleventh centuries. This was marked by the abandonment of oriental spices (except pepper), by an enhanced status for native aromatic vegetables and herbs, and by greater diversity in cooking fats and the ways they were used. This second change still influences our modern-day tastes; the arenas were France and Italy, another reason for limiting ourselves to those places.

As historians, we give our culinary activities a historical orientation. Perceptive writers have spoken of the seigniory as a refined political and economic structure that forms the very framework of medieval society, and of scholasticism as an intellectual discipline capable of structuring a lofty culture, yet they refuse to grant that the Middle Ages would have been able to develop anything but "defensive" culinary tastes: that famous need for spices to conceal the stench of rotting meat. To us, such interpretations seem lazy and marked by a rejection of the artifacts of life and of the everyday aesthetic choices we all make. Why should the European Middle Ages, so inventive in other spheres, have been incapable of creativity here? There is a great deal more to be said about human foodways in France than was said in the days when study was limited to *le pain, le vin et le companage*—"bread, wine, and what goes with the bread."

Acknowledgments

This work owes a great deal to friends who spared no effort to be of help. Some gave us the benefit of their knowledge, such as Bruno Laurioux, specialist in medieval culinary manuscripts; Mireille Demaules, who checked the translations from Old to modern French; Bernadette Grandcolas, who reread our manuscript with an editor's, and a cook's, eye; and Mary and Philip Hyman, who opened their library to us and gave us the benefit of their expertise in assembling our manuscript. We thank them all most warmly, along with Carole Lambert and Allen Grieco, who generously passed on the results of their work.

Other friends—and sometimes the same ones—tested our adaptations of the medieval recipes in their own kitchens: Claude Arnould-Redon, Bernadette Grandcolas, Allen Grieco, Sophie Lehry, Marie-Christine Pouchelle, and Hélène Sabban. We thank them.

But this book is also the result of long years of study and cooking in reconstructing historic banquets on various festive occasions. Here we had the help and cooperation of many people, in particular Jean-Louis Flandrin, who opened the way to this area of research, and Elisabeth Deshayes and Rémi Ledoux, who were often by our side at the stove.

Our thanks go also to:

Pietro Clemente, Dinora Corsi, Lorenzo Sensi, and the officers and members of the Contrada de la Selva, Siena.

Chiara Frugoni, Department of History of the University of Pisa; and Mario Carta, restaurant La Cerreria, Pisa.

Anna Maria Nada Patrone and the members of the Gruppo Santostefanese di Storia e Archeologia, Santo Stefano Belbo (Cuneo), and in particular Antonietta Zarzetto.

The teachers and students of the Collège d'Enseignement Secondaire of Goussainville.

The organizers of the Maison pour Tous, Élancourt.

The members of the theater company l'Unité et Cie.

Claudine Lavail, curator, medieval section, Musée de Bretagne, and the officers of the Centre de Formation des Apprentis du Commerce et de l'Industrie Hôtelière, Rennes.

The organizers of the Centre de Formation et d'Études de l'Éducation Surveillée, Vaucresson.

The organizers of the Association pour le Festival d'Histoire de France, Guyancourt.

Abbreviations

Note: Full citations of the following works may be found in the Bibliography.

Bo   "Le 'Registre de Cuisine' de Jean de Bockenheim"
Bü   New York, Pierpont Morgan Library, MS Bühler 19
Ch   Chiquart, Maître, *Du fait de cuisine*
Ds HB "Diversa Servicia"
Fc HB "Forme of Cury"
Fr   Frati, Ludovico, editor, *Libro di cucina del secolo XI*
Gu   Guerrini, Olindo, editor, *Frammento di un libro di cucina del sec. XIV*
Hi   Hieatt, Constance, editor, *An Ordinance of Pottage*
Lc   *Liber de coquina*
Ma   Martino, Maestro, *Libro de arte coquinaria*
Mo   Morpurgo, Salomone, editor, *LVII ricette di un libro di cucina del buon secolo della lingua*
MP   *Le Ménagier de Paris*
Ni   Nice, Musée Masséna, Bibliothèque de Cessole, ms. 226
Tr   *Tractatus de modo preparandi et condiendi omnia cibaria*
VT Scul *The Viandier of Taillevent*, edited by Terence Scully
        BN   Bibliothèque Nationale de France
        Maz   Bibliothèque Mazarine
        Vat   Vatican Library
VT XV *Le Viandier de Guillaume Tirel dit Taillevent*, edited by Jérôme Pichon and Georges Vicaire
Za   Zambrini, Francesco, editor, *Libro della cucina del secolo XIV*

Histories and Tales from the Kitchen

Literature unfolds more often in banquet halls, those settings for spectacular consumption, than in the kitchens where celebratory masterpieces and daily meals alike were laboriously prepared. Yet it is to the kitchen that we want to transport you as we follow the trail of a different literature, the literature of cookbooks, with which you are about to become acquainted—which is first and foremost a technical literature. But as we lead you to the kitchen, we will not be shedding our historian's function altogether, and you may encounter detours that you think too remote. So do not hesitate to choose your own itinerary and skip a section (although you will undoubtedly find yourself returning to it later to clarify some question).

WRITINGS ON COOKING

The Middle Ages did not invent the cookbook. At least one has come down to us from antiquity: the famous treatise of Apicius, a composite put together late in the fourth century A.D. to which any discussion of Roman cooking must refer. After that, we must await the beginning of the fourteenth century before the arrival of the medieval cookbook, whose content owes virtually nothing to its ancient precursor.

We now know of more than one hundred culinary manuscripts of the fourteenth and fifteenth centuries, many of which have been discovered, catalogued, studied, or published in recent years.[1] In this group, some ten manuscripts (written in French or Latin) belong to the French cultural zone and a similar number to the Italian.

A manuscript collection of recipes can take the form of a scroll *(rotulus):* a smaller version of the ones always being unfurled by a herald in children's books. One example is the oldest version of the book known as *Le Viandier.* The scroll is probably the most ancient form for our cookbooks. There are also small, easily held volumes akin to a modern book, or codex; this is the format of the treatise in Venetian dialect published in 1899 by Ludovico Frati. The original codex, at the Biblioteca Casanatense in Rome, measures 12.2 by 8.2 centimeters (4.8 by 3.23 inches). It is written in a highly legible

---

1. This is the work of Ingemar Boström (Italy), Rudolf Grewe (Catalonia and Scandinavia), Constance Hieatt (England), Carole Lambert (France), Bruno Laurioux (France and Italy), Alix Prentki (Germany) and Terence Scully (France and Savoy). See the Bibliography.

hand, well spaced on the page, and the recipes are organized alphabetically by title.

More often, such treatises were incorporated into a complex codex, or miscellany, where they form part of a grouping that can be more or less homogeneous. Marianne Mulon's 1971 edition, *Deux traités inédits d'art culinaire médiéval,* contains two good examples: these manuscripts at the Bibliothèque Nationale de France in Paris (lat. 7131 and lat. 9328) provide two of our sources: the *Tractatus de modo preparandi et condiendi omnia cibaria* (Tr)[1] and *Liber de coquina* (Lc), which are found together with a number of other treatises—on medicine, hunting, and agriculture for example—in a grouping devoted to nature sciences. Indeed, we shall see that the purpose of recipe collections relates as much to medicine as to cooking, and that in many respects medieval cooking is also a system of health through diet.

Finally, many texts come down to us in mutilated form, incomplete, or bound together with other works in volumes assembled later. These include the important fragment in the Biblioteca Riccardiana, Florence, edited in 1890 by Salomone Morpurgo (Mo).

By definition, cookbooks contain recipes; these can be organized in various ways, in line with a logic that is not always obvious. Still, we can note three kinds of organization. The first, alphabetical, is unusual; it is used in the *Libro de cucina* (Fr). Two others are more common. One categorizes the entries by principal ingredient (vegetables, meat, eggs, fish, and so forth) constituting a kind of culinary encyclopedia. An example is the *Liber de coquina* (Lc). The other organizes the recipes by type of dish: roasts, *potages/brouets,* sauces, fritters, pies *(torte/tourtes)* and so forth—an example here is Maestro Martino (Ma)—and outlines a culinary art or an art of dining. But these last two systems were rarely applied with perfect consistency, and there are frequent overlaps.

There can be two or more manuscripts of the same work, for example Maestro Martino's *Libro de arte coquinaria,* but most often we find families of books: books that are similar in content but that differ in organization or language. For instance, the Tuscan-language volume edited by F. Zambrini (Za), which is of the "encyclopedic" type, is very similar to the *Liber de coquina,* to the extent that, at some points, one seems to be a translation of the other (but which is the original?). Then, there are many common elements (principally, quantities for twelve wealthy food-lovers) in four Italian books or fragments: the books in Tuscan edited by Guerrini

---

1. The parenthetical references to cookbooks cited in this text are explained in the List of Abbreviations; page references are to the edition cited or, in the case of unpublished manuscripts, to the folio number.

(Gu) and Morpurgo (Mo), the one in Venetian or another northeast Italian dialect edited by Frati (Fr), and an unpublished manuscript in the Bibliothèque de Cessole in Nice.[1] These, however, are written in different dialects and the texts are laconic to varying degrees. Nor are they organized according to the same principles.

The various French books known as *Le Viandier* are successive re-arrangements of an early text dating from the end of the thirteenth century, which comes down to us in the form of a scroll; this was edited by Paul Aebischer in 1953. But since a fourteenth-century codex attributes the work to Taillevent, the paternity of all works entitled *Le Viandier*[2] lies with Guillaume Tirel, "Taillevent," cook to King Charles V then to Charles VI. Yet Taillevent may not have even been born when the first text was assembled; we must remember too that *viandier* ("provisioner") is a generic term, clearly derived from *viande,* which means "meat" in modern French, but which in old French referred to anything consumed to sustain life: provisions (the word for meat was *chair*).

Some recipes—or rather recipe names—are found with little modification in nearly all the books, whether French, Italian, or others. But quite different preparations can be concealed under the same name, such as *blancmangers, sauces camelines,* and *escabèches.* The latter term derives from Arabic sources as *sikbâj,* a word of Iranian origin. It is as though the dissemination of words ran parallel to that of culinary practice, but remained relatively independent of it.

This leads us to the question of authorship. Most of the books are anonymous; others bear the name of the chef—the *maître queux*—of some noble or royal kitchen. We have already mentioned Taillevent, alias Guillaume Tirel, cook at the French royal court toward the end of the fourteenth century; Maître Chiquart (Ch), who in the early fifteenth century served Duc Amédée VIII de Savoie; and Maestro Martino of the mid-fifteenth century, who cooked in Rome at the residence of the Patriarch of Aquileia. But we must not therefore assume that all cookbooks were aimed at a princely

---

1. We have not used the latter (ms. 226 in the Bibliothèque de Cessole in the Musée Masséna, Nice), edited by Giovanni Rebora in Miscellanea storica ligure XIX (1987), 1990, pp. 1530–60, which seems to be from central Italy. We thank Professor Gabriella Giacomelli of Florence, who helped us determine the languages of the various manuscripts.

2. Since several different texts are entitled *le Viandier,* we have had to refer to two editions. We have therefore used the following system of citations: "VT" (*Viandier de Taillevent*), followed by "Maz" (manuscript in the Bibliothèque Mazarine), "Vat" (Vatican Library), or "BN" (Bibliothèque Nationale de France), then by "Scul" (for Terence Scully, whose edition collates these three sources), and finally by the page of that edition, for example "VT Maz Scul 32." For the fifteenth-century editions, we have used "VT" followed by "XV" and the page number of the Pichon edition, for example "VT XV 40."

readership. One well-known example will prove the contrary. At the end of the fifteenth century, a Parisian bourgeois, getting on in years and possessed of a young, inexperienced wife, resolved to write her a book of advice: a guide to moral conduct, to domestic management—and to cookery. In the latter area, *Le Menagier de Paris*[1] took its inspiration from the more regal *Le Viandier.*

Both the bourgeois author and the royal chef convey practical knowledge in their recipes: each one sets out, sometimes using the same titles, a method of producing, through the transformation of animal- or vegetable-based ingredients, an edible article defined by its "goodness" in general as well as by its shape, color, and flavor (or flavors). The roots of this knowledge lie in an oral tradition passed down from mother to daughter or from master to apprentice, as well as in a written tradition: for each book contains recipes found also in others, to a greater or lesser extent similar in form and name. At the same time, we cannot eliminate the possibility that some recipes were invented or totally remade thanks to the creativity of an inspired cook.

Who read these cookbooks, and who used them? Those written in Latin were less broadly accessible. Perhaps they were kept in the master's library to enable him to select tasty, visually attractive food that would be healthy and proper to the season, to the ecclesiastical calendar (meat or fish) and to whether the meal was for an everyday or a special occasion. The master could use it to give orders to his cook. The books written in the vernacular French or Italian were undoubtedly more comprehensible, especially to professionals—the so-called *queux,* from the Latin *coquus* ("cook")—but not necessarily to housewives. Yet they provide recipes that cover a wide spectrum of cost of ingredients, fuel requirements, kitchen equipment, and time and difficulty of preparation. Books such as the *Liber de coquina* (Lc) or the Tuscan-language treatise (Za) explain the simplest ways to cook garden vegetables or even wild greens, alongside complex, fantastical concoctions such as a six- or seven-story *torta parmigiana,* a stuffed calf, and a pie containing live birds. While we obviously have no books about the cooking done by ordinary people, we still find recipes that it would have been possible to prepare either in a simple cottage—if only occasionally—or as part of the austere daily menu of a wealthier household, in a society whose average levels of consumption remained far below today's.

COOKING AND SOCIETY

Cooking is a cultural activity. That is, it unquestionably obeys geographical dictates when it comes to supplies, as well as norms, rules, and customs

---

1. Thus in the source; we have modernized it to *Ménagier* in the remainder of this book.

inherited and adapted by the society in which it is practiced. In the European Middle Ages, people generally opted for cooked food, although raw vegetables were not ruled out: salads and fruits were commonly eaten, although a completely "natural" diet of water and raw, unseasoned plants was the province of those who chose to marginalize themselves from society in one way or another, such as hermits or mystics.

Clearly, the degree of dependence on local conditions varied. A wealthy Florentine banker or the Duc de Savoie could choose the food that appeared on his table from a rich marketplace, while, come what might, the peasant in the mountains of any Mediterranean country would be eating his chestnuts, possibly trying to make them into flour, then into bread (however bad the inevitable results)—for the need for bread is a leitmotif of the French and Italian medieval diet, one that in fact persisted until fairly recently.

Dietary inequality has always existed, and we shall not dwell here on the statistics. We want rather to show the specifically culinary ways in which this inequality manifested itself. But we have already hinted at the first obstacle in our path: the recipes of the poor, of peasants, were not written down; to identify their cooking we have to make do with textual or archeological signs, while it is relatively straightforward to learn about less modest cooking through the collections of recipes of which we have spoken, through the account books of convents and noble and aristocratic households, and through the journals kept by members of the bourgeoisie. It will therefore be easier to proceed by setting out a series of contrasts.

The Peasant versus the Lord

The first contrast is that between the peasant and the lord, or the ruler. In times of famine, this could be brutal, as it was in 1315 and 1316, when all of Europe was pounded by a wheat crisis. The lord, who always had reserves in his barns and granaries, continued to eat normally or perhaps a little less, while the villein had to fall back on wild plants—that is, on a noncuisine—or had to try a variety of methods to treat plant products otherwise considered to be poisonous. But in times of what would have been viewed as abundance, there would certainly not have been a vast difference between the table of a minor village squire and that of his subjects: they all ate vegetables, lots of bread, and meat, generally boiled. Here, the difference was in the quantity; to find different *ways* of cooking we must shift the terms of the comparison to that between the village squires on the one hand and the great lords or territorial rulers on the other.

We can focus on a daily culinary routine only when studying the tables of the Duc de Savoie, the Dauphin de Viennois, the Comte de Foix, the Duc de Bourgogne, or their peers, or those of the King of France, the pope, or the emperor: only the powerful left any quantity of household records for us to explore. And another difference arises among the strata we have described: the number of feast days celebrated. The peasant had to wait for Carnival time, Easter, and the holy day of his village's patron saint, while his lord would seize on every possible family, military, or political event. At a princely court, there would have been a succession of at least monthly banquets.

The Normal Day versus the Feast Day

A second contrast, then, is between the normal day and the feast, clearly apparent from the account books of all noble and bourgeois households. Purchases become enormously inflated: quantities of meats of different kinds—young animals (the most highly prized), calves, lambs, or kids; and poultry, especially capons, whose flesh enjoyed the greatest esteem. Several days in advance, there would be hunting and bird-catching to stock up on game; the hunt was linked to recreation and gift-giving as much as to commerce. Eggs, flour, and cheeses were indispensable for many preparations and arrived in the kitchen in great quantities. Supplies of spices were acquired or renewed.

This distinction between normal days and feast days can be noted in every kitchen, but, as we have said, feast days were observed in different ways and with varying degrees of frequency. For certain religious holidays, the menu was ritualized. Lasagne at Christmas, the grain known as *farro* at Carnival, eggs and cheese at Ascension, goose on All Saints' Day, macaroni at Mardi Gras, pork on the Feast of Saint Anthony, lamb at Easter: this is the list suggested by the late-thirteenth-century poet Simone Prudenzani of Orvieto ("Il Saporetto," p. 134).

Meat versus Fish

Holidays fall into an annual pattern, but now let us look at other patterns that intersect with them over the weeks and the years: normal days and days of abstinence, meat days and fish days. The Church dictated abstinence from meat and all other animal products every week on Wednesdays, Fridays, and Saturdays, on the eve of festivals, and during the forty days of Lent. Of course, these days could coincide with festivals of other kinds; an example of how menus could be adapted may be found in our discussion of *Tredura* (recipe 18). Here is another: when Messire Sozzo Bandinelli assembled a brilliant court at Siena to celebrate his son Francesco's accession to knighthood on Christmas Day 1326, the festivities were to last the whole preceding week, with tournaments, exchanges of gifts, and banquets. The record contains the menus of three meat banquets (with 92 guests on Thursday the eighteenth, 80 on Tuesday the twenty-third, and 600 on Christmas Day), and one for a day of abstinence (120 guests on Wednesday,

Christmas Eve). Days of penitence did not require forswearing banquets; it was enough to replace meat with fish. Moreover, as in other literary texts, the chronicler mentions only the dishes reflecting festivity, abundance, and knightly courtesy—in a word, the meat and fish dishes—from among all the foods appearing on the banquet table.

At Siena in that December of 1326, the number of courses, as they appear in the chronicler's simplified version, varied from three to five (on the great day itself). At all the meat banquets, boiled veal, roast capon, and game meats were served; for the Christmas feast the vast quantity and variety of game are described in detail. Each day's menu is distinguished by a particular dish: ravioli and *ambrogino di polli* (recipe 30) for the Tuesday; blancmange for Christmas Day; *pastelli* on the Thursday. The banquets always ended with candied pears served with *treggea* (sugared almonds), and were always preceded and followed by *confetti:* sugarcoated whole spices.

The meatless Christmas Eve menu was no less gala, with four courses. First, following the *confetti,* came marinated tench and plates of chickpeas with smoked tench. In the second course a *torta sangalganese* was brought to the table, then roast eels, and finally a compote with *treggea,* followed by the unvarying candied pears and *confetti.* The notion of penitence— rather feebly for a family that prided itself on having given the Church (a century and a half before, it is true) the great reformer Pope Alexander III—was confined to that plate of chickpeas and to the mild privation of a meatless feast. The *torta sangalganese* was no doubt a Cistercian monastic delicacy, its name referring to the great Abbey of San Galgano in the territory of Siena.

Clergy versus Laity

This meatless menu leads us to another contrast, that between laymen and ecclesiastics. It is a complex one, because it spans socioeconomic differences. We can say that, owing to the prohibitions mentioned earlier and to the specific penitential rules applying to monasteries—rules which were actually followed in the strictly observant ones—the clergy are depicted as fish eaters. But, although the country parson, with his ill-phrased sermons, had to make do with a handful of bony little fish, or even with dried fava beans or chickpeas, a better-off priest or a canon in a well-endowed establishment could expect eels—and painstakingly prepared to boot (see recipe 63).

A fable found in several medieval collections of short tales contains a good illustration of this ecclesiastical hierarchy defined by degree of dietary penitence: "The little fish shall grow big" (reproduced in *Tables florentines,* p. 109). An abbot who flaunted his austerity ordered his steward to buy him only the smallest, cheapest fish in the market. His public relations campaign gained him elevation to the post of Bishop of Paris, upon which he proceeded to demand nothing but the finest foods. As he explained to his steward, he had used the tiniest fish as bait to catch the biggest. Indeed, anticlerical satires inevitably identify fat eels with the rubicund faces of monks and canons.

This is no innocent satire, for fresh fish was costly and not always easy to find, much less to purchase: fishing was an uncertain business. Thus, both during and outside Lent, the dietary hierarchy was more burdensome in terms of fish than of meat, and the intermittent but frequent obligation to eat a fragile and expensive product that was often mediocre in quality—or to make do with the ever-abiding dried herring—prejudiced ordinary people against the clergy. At least for the Church, even a sumptuous fish retained the odor of penitence: this "cold, moist" food of watery origins was a defense against the excesses of the flesh—at least so long as it was not warmed up with fiery spices.

City Eating versus Country Eating

The contrast between urban and rural diet is perhaps the best documented in literature, thanks to the tradition of the *satire du vilain*. But this is a one-way narrative: the town writing of the country. This imbalance is only exacerbated in other kinds of documentation.

The city is portrayed as a place of abundance and variety. That is the case of Paris, capital of one of the greatest kingdoms of Christendom, and it is also true of the most powerful Italian republics. Like those of Paris, the wealthy Florentine bourgeoisie brought to the city the produce of their urban and country properties and storehoused their supplies of wheat, oil, meat, and fat pork—all the basic ingredients. In normal times, the markets of Paris, Florence, Milan, and Venice overflowed with all the produce needed for good seasonal cooking, and all the necessary spices could be purchased from the spice merchant already ground or preserved. Some dishes, such as sauces and savory pies, were sold ready to eat; and householders could have the *fournier* cook their roasts as well as their loaves in his bread-oven. Everyone (at least in Tuscany and at least in a good year) ate, or wanted to eat, white bread, and the authorities made an effort to ensure good supplies of it.

Thus well-fed urban authors had a good time contrasting the abundance of the city with the chronic shortages of the countryside, where it was almost always necessary to make do with local produce, where a bad harvest meant bread even darker than usual, if there was any bread at all, and where even the lord of the manor was lucky to get hold of some pepper and would never even dream of richer spices.

The city-dweller imagined the peasant as eating a great deal of bread soaked in some sort of broth, and as a garlic-lover: in short, as a creature incapable of practicing the arts of the table that by the end of the Middle Ages had become an essential element of urban civility. To drive a young country-dweller from the town, the Sienese writer of tales Gentile Sermini has the cook in his story say:

> A man raised in the country is in the habit of eating two or three times of a morning, then having a snack and finally dining in the eve-ning upon a gosling with oft-reheated platters of beans or cabbage, and *acque pazze,* or water flavored with root vegetables and garlic. He fills his bowl with long slices of bread which he cuts by holding the loaf against his chest, has a nibble, then soaks the bread a few times more. When his hands are greasy, he has no idea what to do, for he is used to wiping them on his chest or his side to avoid soiling the white napery or his clothes. Anyone but a villager will be pained by his manners.
>
> It is his custom to devour everything in his big bowl before taking even a mouthful of meat; then he grabs everything together: meat and sauce and huge slices of bread. Sometimes he soaks all of his fingers in this, letting it dribble down his chest. He doesn't merely lick his fingers: he looks like he is sucking *fiedoni* [a kind of pastry with a soft filling]. He prefers to eat capon, pheasant, and partridge with coarse garlic or with ancient salt pork, as though he were still living in the country. When he eats a leek, he always starts by sinking his teeth into the leaves, repeatedly dipping the bitten end into the salt dish. (Sermini, 2: 442)

In the late Middle Ages, the cities of northern and central Italy were places of great wealth and high culture. (This was true of Paris as well, but in a rather different way.) In the kitchens of their wealthy citizens, as well as in those of nobles and high churchmen, a culinary art was developed as widely roaming as the merchants, scientists, and men of culture of the day. This was not the culinary art of everyone, only of those who always or nearly always ate white bread and who could select the meat and fish they preferred. Social inequality in diet was cloaked in the scientific mantle of dietetics, which advised manual laborers, artisans, and peasants to eat heavy meats or other coarse foods, including pepper and black bread—which are hard to digest, to be sure, but which maintain one's strength for work—while reserving for the leisured classes delicate poultry, which provides nourishment without weighing down the body or fogging the brain.

Sermini's fierce description brings us to the table for a depiction of non-civility. Let us now see how meals were arranged in a setting of civility, in the homes of the aristocrats and bourgeois who chose their food and had it cooked for them. For we know hardly anything more concerning the peasantry.

The Order of a Meal

Menus today are composed of several savory and sweet dishes served one after the other in a predetermined order. All guests eat the same dishes; in a formal meal, these are served to them individually. This sort of service did not become widespread until the end of the nineteenth century; earlier, the progress of a meal was conceived in a completely different way, whose subtleties are not always easy to grasp.

For France, we have a few fourteenth-century menus, where the stages of the meal are named using terms that suggest that the foods were served in a relatively fixed order. Great banquets comprised several successive courses, each of them involving a group of various dishes placed simultaneously on the table. This was comparable to the range of choice offered on a modern restaurant menu, but with all the foods actually placed before the diners, course after course. For each guest, however, the choice was confined to the dishes that were within reach. Thus, there was a de facto hierarchical selection of dishes: more or less refined foods as the case might be, depending on where the diner was seated.

The menu was organized around the pivot point of the roast, which was preceded by one or two courses and followed by one, two, or three more. The progression of foods without doubt reflected dietary principles: if the stomach is like a stew pot in which the various foods are "cooked," the "mouth" of that organ must be "opened" with fresh seasonal fruits such as melon, cherries, strawberries, or grapes, or with salads dressed as modern ones are with salt, oil, and vinegar: in other words, with items containing acids. Now the stomach was ready to receive dishes with sauce— known as *potages* and *brouets*—which, it was thought, required a long "cooking" time.

Then came roasted meats accompanied by various sauces. After the roasts, the host would have felt obliged to provide a sort of intermission or entertainment often known as an *entremets*. The *entremets*—a word which in France referred also to a whole range of sweet and salted preparations served at this point in the meal (and which today designates sweet desserts)—could be any one of many widely varied entertainments: music, dancing, acrobatic acts, or mock combats. Another element in these interludes could be food in masquerade, such as pies containing live birds, or poultry covered in golden feathers, or other roasted birds with their own plumage replaced.

The meal proper resumed with *desserte*—like our modern dessert, with one or more sweet dishes—and continued with the *issue de table* (literally "departure from the table"): cheese, candied fruits, and light cakes, often served with hypocras (a sweet, spiced wine) or sweet malvoisie or malvasia wines. All these things, eaten just before rising from the table, were intended to "close" the stomach and activate the process of "cooking": digestion. Finally came the *boute-hors*, which as its name suggests, was eaten in a different room. It consisted of *épices de chambre*—"parlor spices" as we might call them—such as *dragées* and candied coriander seed and gingerroot, chewing which aided the digestion and sweetened the breath.

Meals for those of more modest rank had fewer courses and in general a smaller choice of dishes, but they followed the same principle. The author of *Le Ménagier de Paris*—on whose description of a dinner given by Monsieur de Lagny for "*Monseigneur de Paris,* the President, the Procurator and King's Counsel" we have based our description of a typical banquet—also tells us of a number of simpler menus, but with the same structure.

The logic of Italian service is far harder to follow, because very few menus have come down to us, and it is difficult to discern the stages of the meals these represent. Yet supplementing them with other documents, such as sumptuary laws (intended to limit the extravagance of aristocratic banquets) and literary sources, shows that for Italians the notion of a meal was similar to that of their French neighbors. Like banquets in France, those of the Bandinelli family of Siena, which we have briefly described, were composed of a series of courses, each offering a variety of dishes. In his poem "Il Saporetto" (p. 123), with its gastronomic flavor, Simone Prudenzani of Orvieto describes a rich feast whose structure does not differ from that of a French menu. The meal begins with ravioli and lasagne in broth, and with soups described as in the French style; boiled meat and rich game stews come next, then roast game birds, followed by *torte* and other savory meat pies. Dried fruits and spices conclude the meal.

The same succession and the same dietary principles are ubiquitous: meats with sauces precede roast meats, and dried fruits close the stomach's "mouth," with spices assisting in digestion. In describing an informal supper in the countryside, consisting of salad, lasagne, and an omelette, the writer of tales Giovanni Sercambi of Lucca shows us that even far from a great banqueting hall, a well-conceived meal would begin with a food containing acids, to "open" the stomach (tale 123).

There are thus no fundamental differences to be seen between France and Italy in the order of a meal, although the French appear to have been more determined to structure the menu, as we can see in their use of a specialized vocabulary, which, with words such as *desserte* and *boute-hors,* makes it easier for us to follow the sequence of the meal.

In princely houses, service was provided by a horde of servants directed by a *maître d'hôtel* chosen from among the nobility, who was also in charge of supplies and the choice of menus and their preparation by the cooks. *Échansons* were responsible for the service of beverages, and the *écuyer tranchant* (also a nobleman) presided over the carving of meats at the high table. At the other tables, where those of lesser grandeur were seated, meats would have been sliced by the guests themselves, for the art of carving was part of the education of a nobleman, or any man of good breeding.

Distinguished Guests; Etiquette

Great banquets were governed by strict protocol, which determined the placement of the tables as well as the seating of guests and the degree of refinement of the food placed before them. The tables were covered with cloths and usually arranged in a U; guests were seated around the outside of the U so that they could enjoy the entertainment that took place in the middle. The central table, sometimes called the high table because it was set up on a platform, was reserved for the ruler and his guests of honor. Other distinguished guests were seated closest to the ruler, while those of lesser rank found themselves at the other end, all in strict conformity with the social hierarchy.

Tuscan literary tradition has it that Dante himself fell victim to this protocol. According to Sercambi, Dante was invited by King Robert to the Neapolitan court and, like the poet he was, arrived carelessly dressed. It was dinnertime and, owing to his appearance, he was seated at the tail end of the table. Since he was hungry, he ate anyway, but as soon as the meal was over he left town. Appalled at having mistreated the great poet, the king dispatched a messenger and invited him back to court. This time Dante arrived richly attired, which caused the king to seat him "at the top of the first table, right next to his own." Service had hardly begun when the poet began tipping meat and wine all over his fine clothes. The king was astonished, and asked why he was behaving in this way. Dante replied, "Your Majesty, I know that in paying me this great honor you are in fact honoring my clothes, and I wanted those clothes to benefit from the food that is being served. And I shall tell you frankly that I had no less genius or common sense when I came the first time, when I was seated at the tail end of the table because I was poorly dressed. Here I am again, with the same degree of genius, but this time well dressed, and you have had me seated at the top of the table" (Sercambi, tale 71).

Good Manners for Living and for Eating

The ritual of the medieval meal was governed both by moral considerations and by material constraints. Even at the tables of the greatest in the land, guests did not necessarily have their own place settings. Strangers often had to share a bowl, a glass, and a trencher (a piece of bread, wooden board, or pewter plate for solid food). This demanded of the two diners mutual consideration and a respect for the Christian and humanistic ethic of temperance: to eat little; not to grab for food; not to choose the best pieces.

It was the rule to wash one's hands before going to the table: a symbolic act, to be sure—which has survived in the celebration of the Eucharist during Mass—but one that also indicates a concern for hygiene, as most foods were picked up with the hands. For liquid foods and sauces, a spoon (usually one per person) was used to dip into the bowl shared with a neighbor, or even into the serving dish. Meats and other solid foods were cut up on the serving platter; it was good form to offer a portion to the comrade with whom you were sharing a *tailloir* (a wooden or metal platter; the word is like the English "trencher"), especially if she was a woman, who would not be expected to have mastered the art of carving. The morsels were then placed on the *tailloir,* picked up delicately with three fingers, and lifted to the mouth.

That is because the fork was not yet used for this purpose—except in Italy, where it was in use from the late fourteenth century, even in taverns, for eating pasta. A tale by Franco Sacchetti depicts two people sharing the same platter of steaming-hot macaroni, one wolfing it down and the other remaining hungry (*Tables florentines,* p. 21). Could not the early spread of the fork in Italy be connected with the consumption of pasta, which was already typical of that land? What other tool, apart from chopsticks, could be better for eating noodles? And the author of one of our recipe collections, which probably predates Sacchetti's story, suggests eating lasagne with a pointed stick (Lc, and recipe 6), which amounts to a preliminary design for the fork. But we must also link the use of forks to the generally more highly evolved customs of urban Italian society, who were less frozen in terms of social hierarchy and therefore more willing to accept new practices. From the fourteenth century on, the Priors (as members of the government were called) of Florence had their own individual napkins and cutlery, including a fork. This was a level of luxury that did not spread to the rest of Europe for another two or three hundred years. We recall that Henri III (1551–89) and his favorites were savagely taunted for preferring to eat with forks, and, at the very dawn of the Enlightenment, Louis XIV always displayed regal scorn for that intermediary between him and his food, which diminished his dining pleasure.

Most of the time, guests had no napkins, and they wiped their inevitably greasy fingers on the tablecloth. But to suck on your fingers was to commit an impermissible transgression of the rules of behavior. Similarly, it was not considered decent to put back a piece of meat that had been in your mouth, to spit by the side of the table, or to blow your nose in the tablecloth. A whole literature in prose and in verse—including treatises on civility, family records, and texts on table manners—reminded upper-class children of the basic principles that distinguished the behavior of a patrician from that of a peasant.

Good manners extended also to drinking. A guest of modest rank would not raise his glass before a person of higher station, or drink before his host had invited him to do so. You were to wipe your mouth before drinking; not to make gulping noises; not to empty your glass at one draft, but rather to drink slowly, taking small mouthfuls. Here again we find a concern for temperance—even more so in the case of wine, an intoxicating beverage that was to be drunk in moderation, and was always mixed with water. It is hard to imagine a banquet, or even a simple meal, without wine, especially in countries with a tradition of wine-making, such as France and Italy.

The Customs of Drinking

Grape growing began in the Mediterranean, and by the Middle Ages had spread to the most northerly of French lands: Lille, Caen, Beauvais, and Rennes were surrounded by vineyards, and "French" wines—those produced in Ile-de-France and in Champagne—enjoyed a reputation for excellence. When weather favored a good harvest, wine appeared on every table. Workers, students, artisans, and of course the wealthy bourgeoisie and landowners all drank wine—and in plenty. Individual consumption rarely fell below a quart a day, and often exceeded half a gallon, which illustrates the limited influence of the moralists and physicians who tirelessly preached moderation. Consumption was just as high, and certainly more consistent, in Italy, where production in the central and southern regions was obviously less dependent upon the weather.

While in these two wine-producing countries this was a "democratic" beverage, there was, as there is today, good and bad wine on the market. When supplies were sufficient, ordinary townspeople could afford low-quality wines produced locally using high-yielding grape varieties. Peasants, who were in general more underprivileged, often had to make do with cheap stuff squeezed out of the leftovers of the harvest, which had already been crushed once to make the first-pressing wines for the master and for the more affluent. Sometimes this was little more than vinegar mixed with water, as it was for the Tuscan peasants lauded by the hero of a tale by Franco Sacchetti. Visibly moved by the golden clarity of a glass of Trebbiano, he passionately praised them for having labored all the year to produce such a wonder for the sole delight of the gentlefolk of Florence (*Tables florentines*, p. 145).

Trebbiano was without doubt the favorite wine of the Tuscans, but, like most other Italian wines of the day, its fame hardly spread beyond the regional borders. Only Falerno enjoyed a certain standing on the other side of the Alps, but this was undoubtedly a vestige of the ancient glory associated with the fame of the Falernian wines of classical times. It was scant competition for the wines of France, which from the fall of the Roman Empire dominated the northern European market.

In the fourteenth century, the wines of Bordeaux and Burgundy were de rigueur on every aristocratic or bourgeois table in northern Europe. These were white, *clairet* (light red or pink), or red wines, low in alcohol, which were drunk young, preferably in their first year. This was for reasons of storage, to be sure, but also because that was the prevailing taste. On the other hand, the Italians do not seem to have been great fans of French wine, for they imported hardly any, but relied on their local output, preferring the heavier wines they produced. Yet they shared the infatuation of their northern neighbors with the sweet wines of Greece.

All of western Christendom imported sweet wines from Crete, Tyre, and Cyprus. But malvasia grapes were grown in Liguria, southern Italy, Sicily, and Sardinia; in these places, the sweet wine of that name was available to the minor bourgeois, the artisan, and the wealthy peasant alike. No celebratory dinner was complete without a final glass of malvasia, duly accompanied by a *cialdone*—a type of waffle for which, unfortunately, no recipe has come down to us.

The wines of Cyprus enjoyed a fine reputation in France, but they were costly, and only the wealthy could afford them. Moreover, we do not know at what point in the meal they would have been served. For the *issue de table* the French seemed to have preferred hypocras, a wine sweetened with sugar or honey and strongly spiced (see recipe 149). It too was associated with a sort of waffle, known as a *métier*.

Such pairings are a notable exception: in the Middle Ages we do not find the near obsession with matching wines and foods exhibited by many modern gastronomes. People chose their wine on the basis of their social standing, their occupation, their age, and their constitution. Whites and *clairets*, lighter and more delicate, were more appropriate for the higher classes, who were themselves more "delicate" and "refined" and who made more use of their brains than of their muscles. Red wines were more nourishing and had benefits for manual laborers. This was just as well, for they were also the cheapest. Young people were to opt for young white wines, which they would dilute with water according to their constitution, while for the elderly, physicians prescribed aged red wines drunk undiluted, which warm and nourish the body and which drive out melancholy.

In the Hippocratic tradition, wine is considered a food and, as Aldobrandino da Siena wrote in *Le régime du corps*, "For the man who drinks such wine in moderation, in accordance with the needs and capabilities of his nature, and in accordance with custom, with where he lives and with the season, it will give him good blood, good color, and good flavor; it will strengthen all bodily virtues and make a man happy, good-natured, and well-spoken" (p. 19).

THE PRACTICE OF COOKING
Kitchens, Chefs and Cooks

The space for which we now use the word "kitchen" bears no resemblance to that of the Middle Ages. Then, only in aristocratic dwellings or in the great bourgeois houses of the cities was the kitchen a separate room, possibly even detached from the rest of the residence. Villagers and artisans ate and cooked in a common room that was often filled with smoke, whose hearth was used for heating, lighting, and preparing food.

In every instance an open fireplace was the focus of culinary activities and the place where all cooking took place, apart from that requiring an oven. But ovens were not domestic appliances, and towns and cities controlled their construction with a view to saving on fuel, which was expensive, and to minimizing the risk of fire. In towns, ovens were owned by a lord or by a professional *fournier,* or oven keeper; in the countryside they were the property of the lord or of a rural community. They were first and foremost for baking bread; they were not indispensable for pastries, which were sometimes cooked in containers placed on the floor of the fireplace surrounded by the embers.

Thus, cauldrons, crocks, *oules* (pots for the dishes known as *potages*), frying basins *(casses)* and frying pans, grills and spits were all exposed to the open flame, which the cook knew how to control, making it gentle or overpowering as required. A few embers were enough to cook a terrine (see recipe 85, for a Crustless Lamb Pâté); a quick flame would lick the tender skin of quail duly prepared for roasting; a good, strong fire would help reduce a meat broth to aspic. In this perilous exercise, fireplace trammels, hooks, strings, tripods, and a variety of containers with legs were critical adjuncts to a subtle contract with a fire that, if a little too strong or smoky, could ruin a sauce or a soup beyond repair. The repeated instructions in culinary treatises on how to overcome these perils testify to how constant a concern this was for cooks.

As we see again and again in the pictorial record, close by the fireplace— where busy hands would be skimming the broth, stirring the frumenty with the big wooden spoon that was the special symbol of a cook, or basting the roast with the juices that fell into the dripping pan—a *broyeur,* or the cook herself, would, with great exertion, be pounding a pestle in a big mortar set on the table or even on the floor. They would then have to strain the sauce or the almond milk through a bag, sieve, or cloth; filter the broth that would enrobe a fish in limpid aspic; or sift the finely ground spices that would season the flavorful sauce of a *brouet*.

While preparing a meal always required great stamina, the variety and organization of the tasks would vary greatly from place to place. In a team of cooks working in a royal or noble kitchen, the work was divided among specialists who were in turn assisted by numerous obedient helpers: from the *hâteur* (from the obsolete word *hâte,* meaning a spit or roasted meat), who was in charge of roasting, to the *potier,* who saw to the pots and dishes, everyone had his own job to attend to. The *saucier* simmered the sauces; the *potagier* peered into the pots of *potage;* the *broyeur* manned the mortar; and, of course, the *souffleur* fanned and maintained the fires.

The woman cooking for a bourgeois household, or working with her daughters to keep her own house, would be able to do it all—but would be cooking on a far more limited scale. Yet her abilities would have far exceeded those required of a modern-day cook. Besides the actual preparation of food, she was in charge of the household supplies of wood and water. And no one paid her overtime when, knife in hand, she disjointed or boned a chicken she had just plucked, or skinned a hare or an eel, or emptied and cleaned a length of entrails, or scalded a piglet to remove the fine hairs from its skin.

From Caterer to Table; From Market to Kitchen

Yet, for the Parisian housewife, a number of services were available to ease her task. Once the *fournier* had roasted her goose to perfection, she could entrust the bird to the *oyer* (goose roaster) to carve it with professional skill. She would take it "to the *oyers* at Saint Merri or at the carrefour Saint Séverin or at the Porte Baudés, where said *oyers* cut and dismember [it], leaving it in fine pieces and ensuring that each piece includes skin, flesh, and bone—and they do it most obligingly" (VT Vat Scul. 87).

Other food trades would offer their services if you needed a gravy for your roast or if you wanted to organize a banquet. The baker would supply trenchers as well as table bread, whose whiteness was a sign of times of plenty and of high social status (poor people bought black bread and bread baked with a mixture of flours). The *oubloyer* would provide waffles and the dozens and dozens of *oublies* (thin wafers) that were obligatory for the rites of a great feast. The *saucier,* already the everyday supplier of garlicky *aillée* (see recipes 99 to 102), mustard, and *cameline* (see recipes 106 and 107), had to outdo himself on banquet days. For his part, the *épicier* was expected to deliver *épices de chambre* as well as the precious, exotic spice powders that lent their flavor and aroma to the great dishes of the era.

Supplies might seem scanty compared with the abundance of our markets, which overflow with produce imported from all over the world, but the medieval cook had considerable options, including many items that have since disappeared. But everything depended on the weather, on the rotation of the seasons, and on the vagaries of a precarious market.

As they are today, many animals were raised for food. Hogs and poultry were often kept domestically, while the commonly eaten lamb, kid, veal, and beef were purchased from the butcher.

Game enriched and added variety to the menu. Many of the birds we admire in zoos or plying the calm waters of our lakes ended up in the cooking pot: herons, bitterns, and swans, for example. Many game birds and animals were cannily aged and cooked in spiced sauces, but only roasted swans and peacocks would have been brought to the princely banqueting table decked in their own plumage and spitting fire from their beaks.

Fish—fresh, salted, or dried—was viewed as a meat substitute for the times of abstinence dictated by the liturgical calendar and had an important place in the medieval diet. Bream, shad, carp, trout, salmon, pike, eel, tench, sturgeon, and lamprey were fished in fresh water, and from the sea came sole, mackerel, gray mullet, skate, cod, conger eel, red mullet, tuna, turbot, brill, and plaice. But fresh supplies of this fragile food were always uncertain and posed a host of problems that towns and cities tried to deal with in various ways. Siena had a contract with Perugia guaranteeing its supplies from Lake Trasimeno, while the Paris market depended on relays of special coaches, *chasse-marées,* to bring fresh fish from Dieppe as quickly as possible.

To be sure, the range of fruits and vegetables was more limited than today's. At the same time, it included a variety of greens, salads, wild berries, and medicinal and other herbs whose flavors are forgotten but whose names still have resonance: pennyroyal, borage, purslane, hyssop, groundsel, fennel blossoms, cabbage sprouts, marjoram, red chickpeas, fava blossoms, parsley roots, elder flowers, cornel berries, and more. These were found alongside other more familiar garden produce including beets, leeks, cabbage, spinach, turnips, apples, pears, chestnuts, grapes, cherries, and melons. In certain parts of Italy local fruits were in great supply, especially pomegranates with their lovely, decorative seeds, and sour citrus fruits such as Seville oranges, lemons, and limes. When exported to the North, these were a luxury reserved for the kitchens of the greatest households.

With the liturgical year's alternation of feast and fast and with the succession of the seasons, fresh produce was often supplemented by conserves. Goose, pork, beef tongue, herring, cod, whiting, trout, salmon, oysters, cuttlefish, whale meat, and blubber, whether brined or dry-salted, provided valuable reserves. Those irreplaceable legumes—peas, fava beans, lentils, *fasoles* (an Old World bean of African origin related to the black-eyed pea) and vetches, as well as winter squashes, were dried and highly esteemed all year round. Dried nuts and fruits, such as almonds, walnuts, hazelnuts, raisins, and figs, brightened the winter monotony. *Confitures*—spiced vegetable or fruit mixtures cooked with honey, sugar, or grape must, different from modern fruit preserves but closely related to present-day Italy's *mostarda*—began to enjoy a popularity that did not fade in the following centuries. Vinegar and unripe grapes (whose juice and whose seeds preserved in salt were both called verjuice—*verjus*—and were flavorings of paramount importance) could be kept in store for several months. Cooks also used young wine, produced within the past year, and took care to have it in good supply.

Treatises on cooking contain many recipes for eggs. Some of these are for ordinary dishes such as stuffed eggs, but others are rather more surprising: spit-roasted eggs and *œufs perdus,* broken directly onto the hot embers! Eggs were common, and most useful, especially for less stringent days of abstinence. Cheeses too were popular and had many uses, depending on their type: fresh, rich, soft, dry, aged, pressed in forms, or served as curds, they were eaten plain or mixed into stuffings. Some cheeses were already famous: there are references to brie, but it is unclear whether this was similar to the brie we know today.

Milk was highly perishable; it would have been used close by its place of production; city dwellers were highly suspicious of milk sellers, who would sometimes water the product. There is never any mention of cream, which appears to have had no independent culinary existence. Butter was rarely used in these recipes. It was sold more often salted than sweet; a number of authors describe how to eliminate the salt by clarifying the butter over low heat.

But the main difference between a medieval master cook and a modern-day chef lay in the wealth of spices in his cupboard. Pepper, long pepper, ginger, cinnamon, cassia buds, grains of paradise (melegueta pepper or Guinea pepper), cubeb *(piper cubeba),* cumin, nutmeg, mace, cloves, and many more were sold by the spice vendor whole, ground, or in blends. The medieval spice vendor was a tradesman of high standing and served as a well-trained middleman between the international spice trade and his own customers: cooks, apothecaries, and physicians.

Tasks and Skills
Chopping, Grinding, Filtering, and Straining

Certain tools were critical adjuncts to the tasks and procedures of the cook. First and foremost, knives were indispensable for cutting up meat and vegetables, and for making a vast range of chopped preparations: stuffings for large "surprise" creations; suckling pigs or breasts of veal filled with rich, aromatic mixtures redolent of spices; boned shoulders of mutton, the meat chopped, seasoned and re-formed around the bone; meatballs; fowl distended with "entrails" created by the cook; marbled, jade-colored fillings for vegetable and cheese pies. All of these demanded skill with the blade on a clean cutting board. Such knife work is the first sign of notably developed cooking. It is as though the practitioner becomes a creative artist through this process of cutting raw materials into small pieces and imposing upon them the will of the cook.

Another method of breaking up ingredients that had a major role in medieval cooking was grinding or pounding in a mortar and pestle: spices, almonds, bread, cooked or raw vegetables, and even meats all found their way into the mortar as dictated by various recipes. We know from the texts that grinding had to be carried out to perfection, yielding the finest of powders and the smoothest of purees. The quest for fineness was not haphazard: it had import both for the cook and for the discerning diner. To achieve a thick, aromatic almond milk, every drop of essence had to be extracted from the blanched almonds, swollen from their water bath. Only finely ground spices would release their volatile flavor and aroma when added at the last moment to a sauce or *potage* on its way to the table. Parsley mashed and bruised by the pestle would yield the fresh flavor of crushed herbs—a flavor that mere chopping could never bring out.

The rationale for precision and refinement did not stop in the kitchen. While clear flavors and mouth-filling aromas were the objective, the last thing a diner wanted was the feeling of a grainy residue on the tongue. Filters, then, were the essential ally of the mortar and pestle. Made here of loosely woven fabric, the strainer, or *étamine,* would clarify a turbid liquid and make the results of the grinding process perfectly smooth. Hypocras was made with a decoction of wine, honey, and spices, strained several times until every particle of residue was eliminated. Almond milk—a vegetarian milk that was a basic element in cooking for times of abstinence, and that was also a common ingredient of meat *potages*—had to be free of the powdery debris of ground almonds, which was always removed by straining. Bread—dried, grilled, or even charred—would be soaked in broth, vinegar, or verjuice and cooked with sauces to thicken them; it too was almost always crushed and made into a panade, then sieved. In their attention to this detail, medieval cooks were no different from modern chefs, for whom the modern equivalent—the conical sieve or *chinois,* which strains out the tiniest fleck of scum and the merest hint of congealed fat—is essential for completing a sauce.

COOKING

But the defining processes of medieval cuisine lay in the cooking itself. The process of cooking was based on a genuine system, the keys to which are not readily discerned. Indeed, nineteenth-century descriptions of the "abominable ragoûts" and "appalling salmagundis" in which our forebears delighted were long accepted as gospel.

No, despite what we often hear even today, not all meat was boiled before being fried or roasted; not all roasted foods were necessarily bathed in sauces to lose all their flavor in hours of recooking. To the contrary, it is clear from close study of the verbs designating various cooking procedures that these words distinguished all manner of operations that took place before cooking and that required the use of fire, but that are no longer common today. Such precooking was mainly for meats—to cleanse them, firm their texture, and lightly brown them—but was used also for certain green vegetables, to set their color or remove their bitterness before final cooking or preparation.

Special care was devoted to preparing those meats that were suitable for roasting—the tenderest and most highly prized—whose merits would be brought out by cooking. Thus, while poultry was customarily plucked after soaking in hot water, it was recommended that smaller or more delicate birds be dry-plucked. And the cook was advised to wait for a shoulder of lamb roasting on the spit to render its external fat before larding it with parsley, to prevent the delicate herb from burning and thus losing its flavor (see recipe 47). Similarly, veal would be half-cooked in water—parboiled, or *pourbouli*—before being larded and roasted. Kids, lambs, geese, partridges, and so forth would be *refait*—literally "renewed": plunged into simmering water for a few moments to cleanse and slightly firm the flesh, which made it easier to lard the meat if necessary and which, above all, prevented the cooking from drying out the surface of the food.

For medieval *potages*—which were akin to modern-day stews, stew-soups, and soups—the characteristics of the meat itself were less important than attaining a blend of flavors and textures. A number of cooking methods could be used successively for a single ingredient, or variously for several components that would then be combined to complete a dish. In fact, there is nothing surprising about browning your pigeons in fat before adding them to the broth in which they were to simmer. And what is wrong with following our authors' advice to "parch" *(hâler)* your hare on the grill before adding it to a civet in the usual way? The creature loses excess moisture and browns gently, without the risk of burning the lard in the stew pot to achieve the same result.

Yet it is certainly quite odd by modern culinary lights to cook a capon in red wine, cut it up, and then fry the pieces before serving them with the cooking broth reduced to a sauce flavored with spices, thickened with the liver and the white meat pounded into a paste and with powdered almonds. Like other similar dishes, this one (*Brouet* of Capon, recipe 35) is a harmonious composition, where the flavor and texture of the meat itself are mingled with the aroma and savor of a vivid sauce, making a unified impression as the dish gives the tongue a momentary surprise with its supple crispness. Just think of the juicy yet crunchy chickens or ducks cooked by the Chinese technique of first steaming, then deep frying: you will quickly get the point of this fondness for achieving taste through texture by means of techniques that go far beyond simple, light cooking methods that have greater respect for the nature of the meat in question. We confess that we have lost both the desire for such culinary intricacy and the very notion of it, and that it is no longer of interest. Yet as historians we cannot offer a value judgment and leave it at that: it is our job to highlight the gap between today's gastronomic system and that which informed medieval culinary practice.

SEASONING

Given the important place of spices, it has also been said that medieval cooking was first and foremost about seasoning. True, the way that recipes were presented in certain medieval texts, especially those written in French, was based on the presence or absence of spices: *potages* were even defined as being "with" or "without" spices, and each category of dish included versions for invalids, free from strong spices. Spices were included in virtually all foods on the menu, from beginning to end. But which ones, and how many, depended on the other ingredients. They were rarer with vegetables and in subtly flavored dishes; then, only saffron might be used, as much for its golden color as for its aromatic flavor.

In any event, spices were almost always added to dishes by the same technique: first powdered, the spices were most often dispersed in liquid or in the sauce, which was then strained before being added to the rest of the dish toward the end of the cooking time. Although a beef tongue or a roast might sometimes be studded with whole cloves, that spice, like any other, would generally be added to sauces and foods in ground form.

To be sure, this specifically medieval technique did not rule out seasoning liquids as they boiled, but it denoted a style of seasoning that gave pride of place to clean, clear flavors not diminished by cooking, and demonstrated a high mastery of the art of combining and harmonizing flavors.

DISPERSION AND LIAISON

Spices gave structure to the flavor of a *potage* or a sauce, but they needed a medium, a support and a liaison to make their presence felt. They were dispersed in broths and other liquids, principally wine, verjuice, vinegar, and sour fruit juices. Much stress has been placed on the importance in the Middle Ages of cooking in an acidic medium and on the predilection for sour flavors, sometimes moderated by the sweetness of sugars. Besides this undeniable taste for the sharpness that is part of the appeal of mustard and, to a lesser extent, garlic, there was also a wish to preserve foods: it was known that vinegar, wine, and verjuice, combined with spices, were the best of preservatives. Meat in aspic, prepared in certain recipes with undiluted wine, was viewed as a meat preserve, as was the Italian *schibezia* (recipe 61), akin to *escabèche,* in which spices and vinegar were crucial ingredients to use with fish—and sometimes with meat—that the cook wished to store for a time.

But acidic flavors lacking in body would offer only the appetite-opening bitterness of a thin, quickly swallowed sauce. Medieval cooks liked to thicken their liquids: the *potage* in which the solid foods—*le grain*—had simmered; the diverse, colorful sauces that enhanced roasted meats; and even *entremets* made from milk, cereals, and dried or fresh fruit. They had to know not only how to produce properly cooked foods, but also how to modify, transform, and manipulate the liquids that flowed from meats or that were added in the course of preparation: to produce a new substance by means of thickening.

Through reduction and concentration, lengthy boiling would sometimes suffice, but more often liaisons were used. Paramount among these was white bread: its crumb—dried, toasted, or charred on the grill—would add the desired color as well as consistency. It would be soaked, sieved, and added at the very moment when an already flavorful sauce needed body. With brief boiling, the bread would lose its texture and would disperse in the liquid, which would become smooth, shiny, translucent, and creamy. When this was added to milk or stewed fruit, gentle heating would marry the elements to create a cream, which when cooled could become a flan or custard.

Eggs—most often the yolks alone—shared this role of thickener; they were also a coloring agent, as was saffron. To a lesser degree, livers (especially chicken livers), the breast meat of capons, powdered almonds, almond milk, and rice were also well-known thickeners for the medieval cook. The author of *Le Ménagier de Paris* included starch, probably wheat starch, along with flour on his list of thickeners of *potages;* while it was sometimes employed, this would have been rare. Indeed, while medieval cooking would be unthinkable without its liaisons (*sauciers,* who sold ready-made sauces, were known also as *lieurs*), neither flour nor dairy products such as cream and butter were used for their ability to thicken a liquid and make it creamy.

The singularity of medieval cooking lies in the thickeners it uses. From the seventeenth century on, in France, flour and fat would become the indispensable foundation for roux and thickened liquids.

Pork Fat and Almonds

The procedures of cooking are not mere techniques to make food edible. They can also create paradoxical marriages and harmonies, while separating things that in certain circumstances should indeed be sundered. Almonds fried in melted pork fat as a crisp, golden garnish for a soft blancmange provide a good example of the successful uniting of two antithetical symbols, one of plenty and celebration, the other of abstinence and penitence.

Historians, notably Louis Stouff for Provence, have shown that pork fat was the fat universally used in the Middle Ages. Olive, walnut, and poppyseed oils, depending on taste and on the region, were used in salads and as a substitute for pork fat on days of abstinence and during Lent. Pork fat in all its forms—fresh and salted pork belly and fatback and lard—was used to cook and fry, and to enrich flesh by larding it with strips of fat, or lardoons. Nor was it unsuitable for use with fish when served on meat days; pork fat grated into a trout pie added the richness needed for this kind of dish, which could easily be dry. The aroma of pork fat pervades all of medieval cooking. On the other hand, there are few references to beef fat, and even fewer to calf's fat—while beef marrow, collected at the time of slaughter, was a short-lived treat, used in fritters, patties, or stuffing. As for butter, it is rarely mentioned in our texts and seems to be of little importance, except in sources that speak of northern customs—although it is sometimes given as an option in place of cow's udder or pork fat in some of the savory pies described by Maestro Martino. It was not until the sixteenth century that butter achieved any importance in cookbooks.

Almond milk deserves special mention in terms of the quest for vegetarian substitutes for animal products when the ecclesiastical calendar obliged a cook to be imaginative. Not only was almond milk used as a substitute for fresh cow's or sheep's milk, but there were occasional attempts to turn it into the by-products that were made from its dairy equivalent. Was anyone really able to get almond milk to curdle into cheeses, or to turn it into butter or ricotta, as recipes from Martino and other sources suggest? These endeavors are surprising, since on meat days there seems to have been no inordinate fondness for regular milk. But almonds yield a nearly perfect milk: unlike the animal product, it does not readily spoil. So no matter what the time of year, almond milk and almonds themselves—whole or powdered, blanched or not—were used in all manner of sauces and in both savory and sweet recipes.

Religious requirements alone are not at the root of this taste; nor do culinary needs explain it entirely. Almonds are without doubt a remarkably versatile ingredient for the cook in the form of nut, thickener, milk, sauce, paste, oil, and cooking liquid. They had no rival, and fulfilled all their functions unfalteringly. But more than anything else, the almond is beautiful and it is white; in a culinary system that gave an important place to aesthetics and to the symbolism of colors, the dry fruit of the almond tree deserved its high status.

THE AESTHETICS OF COOKING

It is obvious that satisfying a biological need is not the sole objective of cooking, for it also aims at giving pleasure, which in the Middle Ages was transmitted primarily through the senses of sight and taste. It is surprising that our cooks mention odors so rarely—except in terms of eliminating the smell of smoke—as they were always using highly aromatic ingredients such as powdered cinnamon and cloves and rose water.

The eye was the first organ to "taste" savory pies, whose crusts were supposed to be impressive and beautifully browned—even adorned with historical or legendary figures molded in pastry by the *pâtissier*. Pastry provided an aesthetic way to serve any food, from wild greens to the noblest of fowl. This was a great innovation compared with the cooking of antiquity. It also offered pleasure born of surprise, for the crust concealed what was actually to be eaten. In addition to developing flavors, medieval cooking aimed also at presenting an artificial reality—from peacocks reclothed in their own plumage to masquerades such as pies that when opened proved to be nothing more than cages for live birds, a most refined form of *entremets*. The golden-brown roast too gratified the eye before satisfying the taste; in the pleasure given by browning, a pleasure produced through intimacy with the embers, we see a kind of tribute to fire.

The Pleasure of Color

Colors too engaged the eye. They often defined dishes and were an element in a cook's choice of allied ingredients. A request for white called for a foundation of rice and almonds, a complementary use of poultry flesh and seasonings of ginger and sugar. Cooks were enticed by variety, and advised using white on one side of a platter only, contrasting it with yellow by dividing a dish and adding egg yolks and saffron to the other half. If two capons were to be served, one could be coated with a white sauce and the other with a yellow sauce. Colors could be brought into play most readily in sauces, whose main function was not to nourish, but only to add flavor and to spark the appetite; thickened yet flowing, they would be served in the deep dishes known as *écuelles*. Diners could choose—by the presumed flavor, or by the perfectly obvious color—among black (as in "Saracen" sauces), white, camel's-hair tan (cameline sauce), blue, yellow, pink, or green.

To achieve these colors, our treatises used natural products as base ingredients, such as the leaves used in herb and green vegetable pies (chard, spinach, and so forth) or the herbs used in green sauces (such as parsley and basil). They also pressed spices into service, as we noted in our comments on the color white: cinnamon for a camel's-hair tan (in combination with golden raisins) and saffron for yellow (one recipe claims that there is a kind of saffron that adds no color, but we have not identified it). Pink garlic sauce (*Agliata pavonazza*, recipe 101) was colored by red grape juice, sky-blue sauces by blackberry pulp, and black by dark raisins, prunes, chicken livers, and darkly toasted bread.

But cooks were not repelled by artificial colors, especially to achieve subtle shades of red and pink. The reddish secretion of sandalwood (*Pterocarpe officinal*) would add an old-rose color; it was frighteningly named *draco* ("dragon") and dragon's blood, but also *sandoli* and cochineal cedar. One English recipe, entitled "Sanc-dragon," uses it to vividly color a rice pudding. The root of alkanet, or dyer's bugloss (*Buglossa anchusa* or *Alkanna tinctoria*), yields a luminous red. Archil or dyer's moss *(Rocella tinctoria)*—sometimes known in our sources as *tournesoc* or *tournesol*—when properly used could fine-tune reds, which could otherwise run to purplish, violet, or even blue. Deep down, the medieval cook was an alchemist—in a quest for color rather than for gold.

Shape and Texture

Thickness and fluidity; smoothness and coarseness: these too can be accentuated by color. As we have said, the function of medieval kitchen equipment was to attain refined textures, but it was not used according to any single principle. The thickness of a liquid was something to be determined by the cook; while broths were often thickened and creamy sauces strained smooth, sometimes what was wanted was a thin, clear sauce or one that was of uneven texture.

Moreover, there was an understanding of the various degrees and kinds of consistency. The very finest demanded know-how and skill. Nothing scared the author of *Le Ménagier de Paris* (who was not a professional cook) more than a raw-egg liaison. For him it was the ideal, but he tried to suggest substitute techniques: bread for squash soup (recipe 3), or the yolk of a hard-boiled egg in his version of *Jance* sauce.

The cohesiveness of a broth or a creamy sauce can be detected by the eye no less than by the palate. In a *potage* the liquid coats the solid part—the *grain*—providing a contrast both in flavor and in appearance. You could recognize a successful sauce at first sight: it cloaked without concealing; it delineated the form of a dish; it softened the angles and concealed the imperfections. And it could in turn be decorated: sprinkled with a snowfall of sugar, with pomegranate seeds, with vermilion candied coriander seeds, or even—why not?—with precious stones or pearls.

People were fond of shapes that reproduced existing forms, shapes that the cook would create using malleable ingredients. Pies containing fillings or whole creatures are one example; others are tortelli or ravioli cut in the shape of horseshoes, rings, animals, or letters of the alphabet, and chopped fillings or omelettes that reproduce the contours of the earthenware vessels in which they were cooked.

But nothing gave more delight than broths transformed into quivering, clear aspics imprisoning meats or fish (see recipes 123 and 124). The cook would color these transitory crystalline confections with all the dyes of his craft, adding fresh lavender and bay leaves and molding them in glass goblets of dazzling transparency.

A Taste for Sweetness . . .

Something that is most surprising to us about medieval cooking is its lack of interest in distinguishing sweet dishes from salty, even though in most cases one of these flavors dominates: adding a spoonful of sugar or a handful of raisins is not enough to change the basic character of a salty dish. The little bit of something sweet for the *issue de table*, which would become our modern dessert, took the form of fruit or sugared spices served at the end of the meal—although these were often served at the beginning as well. And every *brouet,* every sauce, every savory pie could contain sweet along with salty ingredients. Sweet and salty were simply not culinary categories.

Contrary to popular belief, Western cooks in the Middle Ages rarely used honey as a sweetener, in contrast to the practice in ancient Rome. But sugar was costly. In the Middle Ages, this "spice" was produced in Sicily and Andalusia, where sugarcane was grown. But it was also imported from farther afield, and its use in cooking came from the East, probably from India, as the Sanskrit origin of its name (*arkar,* meaning gravel or sand) indicates, passed on like so many other things via the Arab world. There are French references to medicinal uses of sugar from the early thirteenth century, but it was very rarely used in cooking until the fourteenth century, although Catalonia, Italy, and England were already using it a great deal, perhaps on the basis of Arabic treatises on nutrition. The Sugar Revolution did not come to France until the turn of the fifteenth century; it is reflected in the work of Maître Chiquart in the part-French, part-Italian region of Savoy.

You can, of course, sweeten without sugar, and sweet wines, plain or boiled grape must, and dried fruits such as raisins, dates, and prunes were widely used for that purpose. These were used to sweeten foods that were camel's-hair tan, brown, or black in color, while sugar gave the brilliance of snow (to use our authors' expression) to white dishes. Indeed, like other spices, it was often sprinkled over dishes in a snow-shower just before serving.

Most often, sugar and sweetness in general were combined with other flavors: salty, as noted; and, first and foremost, acidic, or sour.

. . . and a Taste for Sweet-and-Sour

In all regions a fondness for sour flavors seems to have come before the taste for sweetness. This was satisfied by locally produced liquids, most often vinegar or verjuice. We have already seen that sweet wines and grape must were used as sweeteners, so grape-juice products supplied indispensable sweet-and-sour harmonies in the music of flavors. Vinegar, of course, is wine that has been "spoiled," either intentionally or not, while verjuice is usually pressed from unripe grapes. Any juice from unripe fruits or from acidic leaves such as sorrel could serve the same purpose as verjuice. Lemons, limes, Seville oranges, oranges (which were all sour—oranges only later came from Spain in the sweet form we know today), and sour pomegranates were particularly sought after in Italy for their flavor, which was more subtle than that of unripe fruits. The marriage between sweet and sour was more advanced in Italy than in France; everywhere, it sooner or later became a constant element of medieval cooking, especially in its quest for delicate balance in its sauces.

The Selection of Spices

As we have already seen, another characteristic of medieval cooking that marks a sharp difference from that of today is the great use it made of a variety of spices, not just the ubiquitous pepper we use nowadays. Anyone who still believes that spices were used merely to mask the stench of rotting food need only read the recipes for their very precise combinations, their sense of dominating flavors, the limits they set on the options for a given dish, and their concern for the proper moment to incorporate the spices into a food. For roast crane, goose, or suckling pig, one collection of recipes suggests a sweet-and-sour sauce bolstered with marjoram and saffron; but it specifies that for river fowl the cook must avoid saffron, adding that "here, a good cook can use common sense and adapt to the local circumstances" (Za, p. 81). No, the point was not to conceal a flavor, but to create one that would please the master of the house and that could lend the name of its predominant spice to a sauce or a *brouet: cameline* (from *cannelle*, cinnamon) and *poivrade* (from *poivre*, pepper) are two examples.

The Italians remained devoted to pepper and were fond of saffron, which added color as well as aroma and which could be accommodated very well in vegetable cookery. They could even use locally grown saffron, less delicate perhaps, but cheaper than saffron from the East. The French were fond of combinations of ginger and cinnamon, with the former dominating. And in the fourteenth century, doubtless thinking of a blissful life eternal, they took up grains of paradise, or melegueta pepper, just as spicy as black pepper, but more expensive, which enabled the wealthy to keep it to themselves. This too was part of the point of these fragile, strongly flavored seeds, leaves, buds, flowers, pistils, and rinds, imported at vast cost from Africa and Asia: to stake out a social hierarchy in food preferences. Here again, theories of nutrition rationalized practice. They enabled the wealthy, under proper medical advice, to use the correct spices (which in the view of contemporary physicians were all "warm" and "dry" substances, apart from ginger and saffron, which were "warm" and "moist") to effect the strengthening and adjustment required by their respective temperaments.

Those who could not afford spices, even pepper, made do with the more humble flavors of the land: aromatic plants such as parsley, marjoram, fennel, hyssop, mint, and basil, and the even more rustic bulbs such as garlic, onion, and shallot. Garlic in particular, as we have noted, bore the odor of peasantry, but as you will see in the recipes was by no means barred from genteel tables. Nor was the onion, which often played a part in intricate preparations. Garlic had an especially prominent role to play in the sauce known as *agliata* or *aillée*, which was esteemed by one and all, judging by the large number of recipes for it (see recipes 99 to 102). In the various versions of *agliata/aillée*, the power of the garlic is always moderated and refined by other ingredients, including spices, and this sauce is not paired with boiled or roast meat, except as one of several options. Woe betide any host who tried to serve only garlic sauce at an aristocratic banquet. One newly married countess paid for such a lapse: setting herself up as mistress of the house from the very day of her wedding, she commanded the cook to make no sauces but garlic sauce. But her husband took vengeance: garlic and the countess both had to know their place as one modest pleasure among many (*Contes pour rire: Fabliaux des XIIIe et XIVe siècles*, pp. 198–99).

A Taste for the Exotic

As we have said, the Middle Ages was a time when food traveled. Noble courts moved from place to place, with or without their teams of cooks; aristocrats traveled; and national identity was far less rigid than it is today. Chiquart wrote in French, but lived in the Duchy of Savoy, a region with its feet firmly in an Italian world that was in cultural ferment. Maestro Martino worked in Rome, but leaned toward Catalan culinary arts and was inspired by the sophistication of French sauces. There is no lack of examples of tribute being paid to other places or other nations: *brouet d'Angleterre, torta ungaresca, chaudeau flament, torta francescha, potage des Lombards,* and *tourte pisane* constitute a huge map of Europe. And *brodo saracenico* (recipe 36), inspired by memories of Muslim Spain and the eastern Roman Empire, evoked the Arab world, at once nearby and distant.

Are these names to be taken literally, or as references to specific dishes? No one knows what made the *torta ungaresca* Hungarian in the minds of the authors of our Italian treatises, or why the *brouet d'Angleterre* should have seemed so English to the Parisian bourgeois who wrote *Le Ménagier de Paris*. We feel that their inclusion among ordinary recipes reflects the longing for a change of scene: words counted more than the facts about a foreign cuisine. Along with this evocation of faraway places summoned up by place names, a number of the dishes in these texts share titles that have phonetic similarities: *blancmangers* (blancmange puddings)—*blanmangieri, manjar braquo, blawmanger, blamang, blamensir; soupes dorées* (golden sippets—which came to be known as "French toast")—*suppa dorata, soppes dorre;* darioles—*diriola, darials; morterels* (a sort of hash of ground meat)—*mortarolo, martarolum, morterol, mortrowes*. These and more are ubiquitous. Beneath their common labels, we sometimes find near twins, but we also find poor imitations, little more than the faded image of a color or the faint whiff of a spice. So it is pointless to try to track down the family trees of these terminological similarities; it is better to view them as the reflection of a culture, of a set of shared representations and interests that go to form a coherent cultural pattern.

The spirit of the age was not limited by the precise borders that demarcated kingdoms, even within the boundaries of our little Europe. It bore the great international trade that vitalized Bruges, Barcelona, and Venice and that, wafting aromatic spices, intoxicated the people of the Middle Ages. This frenzy heightened the aspirations of those who wanted to see and be seen; from one end of Europe to the other, it created a life that was lived from trading port to trading port, through the intermediary of the Arab world, merchants, apothecaries, and spice dealers.

Europeans sometimes forget that there is more to the world than their continent: at the end of the Middle Ages they were not the only ones to be touched by this mania for spices, to inhale the scent of rose water, or to cook for the eyes as much as for the palate. The Chinese too—also customers of Arab traders—were engaged by this passion for goods from Arabia, India, and southern Asia, which were just as exotic and precious to them as they were to Westerners. The dietitian to the Mongol court at Beijing, who wrote a treatise presented to the emperor in 1330, used no fewer than twenty-four different spices in his cooking, and he tells us that saffron (or *zafulan* in the Chinese transliteration of the Arabic-Persian) illuminated dishes with a golden hue.

Not much would later remain of this orgy of foreign seasonings, either in China or in Europe. In China, five-spice powder is the sole vestige of a spice market that shut down as soon as the Mongol invaders packed up and left the country. And in France, with the gradual abandonment of the "medieval spice shop" (the disparaging term used by seventeenth-century cooks), and with the triumph of "natural" taste and of the native flavors of the following ages, all that survives, for better or for worse, is that impoverished four-ingredient mixture, *quatre-épices*.

This has been nothing more than a quick overview of a subject about which much remains to be learned. Here we think it important to stress the role of cities—Paris and the great towns of northern and central Italy—in the development of medieval culinary arts. Despite zones of deep poverty, the average standard of living was higher in the cities than elsewhere. Urbanites ate white bread; the markets were well supplied with agricultural produce, both local and from farther afield (almonds, citrus fruits, olive oil, and so forth); vendors could provide all spices; and aesthetic endeavor yielded masterpieces of architecture and painting—and, to our mind, of cooking as well.

Three treatises that were products of this urban context have drawn our special attention because of their general regard for good household management, because of the wide variety of their subject matter, and because of their exceptional gastronomic quality.

Le Ménagier de Paris (MP), the recipes of which are included in a domestic compendium written with fond solicitude by an elderly husband for his young wife, adapts the culinary arts of the nobility to the household of a gentleman—an *honnête homme*—while including more modest traditions. Like other, literary, texts, his writing shows that masters of the house, and men in general—not to mention professional cooks—were by no means banished from the kitchen, as it is too easy to conclude they were by extrapolating backward from the rigidity of nineteenth-century bourgeois society.

The second important source, the anonymous Tuscan treatise in the Bologna University Library, is available in a 1968 reprint of an 1863 edition by Francesco Zambrini (Za). To our mind, this text is closer to the medical tradition of recipe collections. Very often, it proves also to be realistic: it does not aspire, in the name of "art," to oust the simplest produce, such as all the various greens and herbs. Yet it was intended for professional cooks and does not reject pies filled with live birds or a whole garden made of dough and festooned with fruit of all kinds. It thus offers a wide range of culinary levels.

Finally, there is Maestro Martino (Ma). As we tested our recipes we found consistent confirmation of the excellence of his cooking, both his adaptations of "classic" recipes and his own inventions. His technical mastery was clearly complemented by enormous aesthetic and human sensitivity, manifested in his version of a pie filled with live birds—*pastello volativo*, or "flying pie":

> Make a very large pastry casing; and at the bottom you shall make a hole big enough to pass your fist through, or larger if you wish. The sides must be a little higher than usual. You shall bake this casing in the oven, filled with flour. When it is cooked, you shall open the hole in the bottom and remove the flour. You will already have prepared another small pie full of good things, properly baked and ready to eat, made to fit the hole you made in the large casing; you shall put it through that hole. Into the remaining space surrounding the small pie, you shall put live birds, as many as will fit. These little birds should be put in at the very moment you present [the pie] at table. When it has been presented to those seated for the banquet, you shall remove the lid, and the little birds will fly out. The objective is to amuse and entertain the company. But so that they do not feel cheated, you shall cut up and serve the small pie. (Ma 204)

Martino is the only cook whose recipe for this perfect example of an *entremets* is careful not to spoil the pleasure at the flight of birds with a frustrating sense of deprivation.

Moreover, we believe that he has an important place in the more extended history of the cuisines of Europe. Indeed, in the mid-fifteenth century he was recognized by the humanist Bartolomeo Sacchi, known as il

Platina, as the greatest cook of his time. By translating his recipes into Latin and incorporating them into a discussion of nutrition and medicine, il Platina made it possible for them to be disseminated throughout the ambit of Western humanism, where they were then translated in the sixteenth century into several languages, including French, Italian, and English. Unquestionably, the success of Italian cooking is secured by this pair, il Platina and Martino, more so than by Catherine de' Medici. The lengthy oral and written progression of a complex cultural practice carries greater historical weight than the random reminiscences of a nostalgic émigrée—even if she was a queen.

Medieval Cooking Today

We were just speaking of culinary "masterpieces." But while medieval frescos or other paintings, once properly restored, demand only that we train our intelligence and our senses, cooking—like music—requires an intermediary action: sounds do not endure over the centuries any more than a culinary composition. We can thus compare our practice of medieval cooking (with due account of the inevitable differences) to an archaeologist trying to duplicate prehistoric methods of cutting flint, to a musician striving to evoke the sonorities of the past, to an art conservator's patient search for the original state of a painting or a building. Parallel to our historical labors with texts and documents (which are in play here as well), we have been engaged in research using our hands and our senses. In public and in private, we have been preparing medieval recipes or complete banquets for a number of years, and we now feel it is time to pass on what we have learned.

In this book, we wanted to set out the documents on which our research was based (the recipes found in the medieval treatises), the cultural landmarks invoked to understand them (our introduction and our notes on the recipes), and the actual results of our work in the kitchen (our adaptations).

We have tested all the recipes in this book, adapting them to the size and equipment of a modern kitchen and to available ingredients; they will serve four to six. To make the recipes more useful, we have tried to use the language of today's cookbooks.

Our Selection of Recipes . . .

We have already explained why we chose three treatises (from Paris, Florence/Siena, and Rome respectively) as our most constant sources. We did not make use of every known book, and for the most part limited ourselves to manuscripts already published in modern editions. It was not always easy to choose from this range of sources; but, after reading the texts and in the light of our experiments in the kitchen, we set a few rules, or principles.

We tend to think that no recipe is uncookable, even if some may jar us by their (to us) unusual combinations of ingredients. In this process of negotiating with our prejudices, we drew the line at sweet creamy desserts made with fish broth, but fortunately not at eel pies with figs. We have not unearthed the artificial colorings used by our cooks, and have therefore been confined to the colors of herbs and fruits, and of saffron. After trying them, we rejected dishes whose taste we did not like. We were hesitant about other recipes because their complexity so obviously called for teams of chefs and helpers: a *torta parmigiana,* five, six, or seven tiers high, filled with ravioli (themselves stuffed) and other delights, would daunt even the most enterprising home cook. Some foods are impossible in our small kitchens simply because of their size: how could we ever squeeze in a whole calf (even if skinned) in order to stuff it with tender poultry?

We have tried to include foods in all the forms found in the Middle Ages; these forms helped us organize this book. For each kind of dish, we have tried to present various principal ingredients, so you can choose pies or tarts made from greens, cheeses, and fruits; pâtés made from meat, fish— or air (to hold live birds). Similarly, we wanted to provide lively, diverse variations on some of the recipes found most frequently, such as blanc-mange, mustard, and *sauce cameline.* Finally, it seemed a good idea to provide a sense of continuity by choosing a number of dishes whose names survive in modern cookbooks, even if the meaning of those names has changed. On the other hand, to reflect modern habits, we have tried to expand categories that we now view as important—such as desserts—but that were not essential in a medieval meal. To that end, we found recipes in English treatises, which earlier than other sources reflect a great fondness for sugar.

Some of these recipes are expensive, especially in what we are tempted to call their extravagant use of almonds. We have tried to balance the budget by including other, more modest, preparations for vegetables, fruits, fish, and sauced meats. But we cannot encourage you to economize on poultry: given that capons are excessively expensive, you can get good results with the best available free-range chickens. On the other hand, thanks to their affordable prices nowadays, spices no longer serve as an indicator of social class.

There is no asceticism in our historical outlook. We have given pride of place to recipes that yield flavors that are not merely acceptable but pleasurable to our modern tastes (which have developed over centuries of culinary evolution). In other words, we were looking for dishes that are *good* as well as historically significant. Quite apart from the feeling of surprise that is a part of pleasure, you can experience distant emotions, like those evoked by Tuscan tales, French fables, or courtly romances.

. . . and Their Arrangement

The problem of ordering the recipes was a difficult one, especially with the goal of simultaneously reflecting the original classifications and meeting the needs of the modern cook. Medieval culinary categories are far from clear, and are even harder to pin down when dealing with a larger geographical area. So we decided to draw on *Le Ménagier de Paris* for our overall scheme, because the arrangement of its recipes follows the order of a medieval menu and uses its terminology. Hence, you will find: *potages;* roast meats; fish; savory pies and tarts; sauces; eggs in various forms; *entremets,* fritters, and other fried foods; and sweetmeats and basic preparations. But in line with modern habits, we have subdivided these. For example, *potages*—foods cooked with liquid in a pot—have been divided into three groups: soups, pureed or chopped vegetable dishes, and meat dishes in sauce. With pastries too—pies and tarts—we have separated the salty from the sweet, which nowadays can be served as desserts.

There is additional information in the chapter introductions and in our comments on the recipes, for we wanted to ensure that there were frequent intersections between culinary and cultural material.

ADAPTING THE RECIPES

Adapting medieval recipes is always problematical, not so much in terms of ingredients (as we shall see later), but in terms of simply understanding the text. Many books, such as *Le Viandier* and the *Liber de coquina,* are rightly classed as crib sheets for professionals, and they merely toss off a bare listing of ingredients and techniques whose practical meaning is sometimes hard to figure out. Others are more detailed, because they were aimed at a readership that for one reason or another needed more information.

The author of *Le Ménagier de Paris*—the Parisian householder himself—tried to pass every detail on to his wife, because he assumed that she knew nothing. So he explains methods—sometimes suggesting several, in order of difficulty—and even deals with problems of shopping. Maestro Martino and the anonymous author of the fifty-seven recipes retrieved from the damaged manuscript edited by Salomone Morpurgo (Mo) were clearly kindled by a desire for aesthetic perfection, and they clarified their techniques by setting out the proportions of the ingredients and by explaining in detail the series of actions by which the food was transformed and decorated; these texts are themselves beautiful. All of this made the recipes easier to adapt. Like the two Italian sources, the text of Maître Chiquart exhibits a great concern for perfection—but to excess: rather than being helpful to ordinary cooks, it turns into a poem or a set of variations on a culinary theme. It is a sealed text, and it is difficult to pry out its reality.

We have always retained proportions when these are given in a usable form. But weight and volume measures cannot be converted unless you know their exact provenance—the place where the relevant reference weight (such as the *livre*) was actually produced. While nearly everywhere bearing the same names, medieval measures, like medieval recipes, varied a great deal from place to place. Often, recipes lack any quantities at all; this is one of the greatest obstacles to adapting them.

It has been our principle to consider each recipe as a document, illuminated, of course, by others and by our knowledge of the history of medieval cooking and of the milieu and society of the time. As far as possible we have followed the operations described in the texts without assuming that our failure to understand something meant that the scribe must have made an error. We did not permit ourselves to change one recipe on the basis of another, even if they had similar or related names: each recipe has its own meaning. From the books organized in an encyclopedic way, guided by respect for the text, we extracted and translated whole sequences, whose linkages indicate better than any isolated recipe the principles of transforming animal or vegetable ingredients in the kitchen. In these cases, we have adapted only one or two versions from among the many found in the original source (see recipes 19 and 44); the reader can try creating additional dishes from the medieval text itself. In our comments, we explain our interpretations and try as best we can to recreate the atmosphere in which the dish would have been prepared and eaten. That is why it is good to read them with the section "Histories and Tales from the Kitchen" fresh in your mind. Readers who wish to consult the original medieval texts will find them at the back of the book.

COOKING THE RECIPES

We accepted the texts for what they are, and we have refrained from passing judgment on the procedures they prescribe. We tried not to assess their place, value, or interest in the context of all the culinary actions required to cook a recipe.

For modern diners accustomed to medium-rare fish and *al dente* string beans, it will be hard to swallow the idea of cooking a single ingredient using several consecutive techniques. Many people who have tried to understand medieval cooking, from near or from afar, have considered this to have been simply a way of tenderizing fibrous meat or woody turnips. But we know that farmers worked at raising animals for meat, the best of which would have been reserved for chefs like Martino or Chiquart or for the kitchens of the Parisian bourgeoisie. Indeed, poultry was always specially fattened for market; nowadays, even in France, that wonderful white flesh is only rarely seen in the occasional old-fashioned capon or well-bred, free-range roaster. We have to face the fact that the sophisticated complexity of medieval cooking techniques arises from an approach and tastes that differ from those of today. A historian's curiosity demanded respect for the word as written, even though, had we been following a modern system of cooking, we might have automatically omitted some of the steps. The reader will see for himself that the game was worth the candle.

We undertook not to add to any preparation any ingredient that was not indicated in the text. There was one exception, however, to this general rule: salt. And we had to ease it so that we could make substitutions for unknown ingredients. It is known that mention of salt was often omitted from culinary texts of all periods. By salting dishes when they obviously should be salted, whether salt is mentioned or not, we are following the instructions of a number of sources to season to the taste of the guests or the lord.

Products that are unidentifiable, either because they have more or less disappeared or because they were everyday medieval preparations that were purchased ready-made, present an entirely different problem. We settled these problems—a dozen or so in all—one by one, as best we could in keeping with the spirit of the recipe. For each unknown or unavailable ingredient we substituted another that seemed close to it. For example, we replaced long pepper (very hard to find, except in some Indian groceries) with normal black pepper, and cassia buds with cinnamon.

But the substitutions were not always so simple. What were the ingredients of *échaudés* and *galettes,* the wafers used to thicken our dried-fruit *taillis* (recipe 134), or of the waffle-like *cialdoni* used as a base for the marzipan tart in recipe 136? And what were the various cheeses used to enrich fillings? We have made suggestions for each recipe, pending the discovery of additional documents enabling us to do better.

The ingredients of pastry doughs for pies and tarts remain an enigma; no medieval recipe survives. Since rich crusts are crisper, we have (for once) opted for the modern method and have most often specified *pâte brisée* (recipe 153). But we give readers the latitude to take another path and come closer perhaps to medieval practice.

Our search for verjuice (a conserve made from the juice or the seeds of unripe grapes) was most troublesome—and it was not always easy to find in the Middle Ages either. Stocks were laid in annually, but toward the end, so-called old verjuice had little merit and it would have been replaced by whatever substitutes could be found. In this book, we have favored lemon juice or cider vinegar diluted with water, although readers might follow *Le Ménagier de Paris* and various English sources, and try sorrel juice, wheat leaves, grapevine buds, or the juice of sour apples, plums, or pears. Those who have a trellis with a few climbing vines might try pressing their own verjuice and canning or freezing it. (See also Mail-order Sources, p. 266) This bitter, fruity juice of unripe grapes has a special flavor still favored in southwestern France to add zest to a dish of chicken or rabbit. Surely, it would be a fine idea to make the overproduction from poor wine grapes into verjuice, and to restore to grace this aromatic liquid that enjoyed deserved popularity right through the nineteenth century.

Finally, when a recipe presents alternatives, we have suggested the ingredient that is commonest today, or that was most to our taste. But a suggestion is not a command, and readers are free to make their own choices.

This, of course, is not the Middle Ages. Electricity is at our service; hot and cold water flow from the faucet; and while some of our merchants are not the equal of medieval *oyers,* the pork we buy at the butcher shop is free of bristles, and the fishmonger will skin your eels for you. Neither the weather nor the season has much effect on our diet; we live in a perpetual springtime, and we know nothing of the struggle with nature apart from the healthy fatigue of an occasional country walk.

Can we envision what cooking meant in the Middle Ages? In an era when almonds turn into marzipan at the touch of a button, could we make the time to achieve the same result with a mortar and pestle? Medieval chefs were certainly not lacking in fortitude, energy, skill, and know-how. Even if the workload was shared, there was no mechanical arm to turn the spit; some *hâteur* or apprentice had to stand there baking his hide so that a bleeding chunk of raw meat could become a golden-brown roast.

We are spared such physical exertions. Nowadays, we have blenders and electric rotisseries for allies; with their help we can take a step backward to another era. Simmering a frumenty or roasting a goose no longer presents any problems. But to cook is to take calculated risks, and the recipes in this book are not formulas that guarantee success. They demand talent and inspiration from the professional chef and the beginner alike: a dish cooked by an individual, at her own pace and in her own way, belongs to her.

So when we bid our readers to blanch their own almonds, prepare their own spice mixtures, grind their own mustard, roast their onions in the embers, and even (if they have the inclination) to spit-roast a suckling pig patiently over a real wood fire, it is not to overwhelm them, but to enable them through the heady uncertainty of experimentation to experience the true hands-on pleasure of cooking.

The joy of cooking and eating to your own taste may also be a way to thwart the internationalization of food that they are trying to impose upon us from London to Barcelona, from New York to Shanghai, on the pretext that it will free us from tedious drudgery.

PRACTICAL ADVICE
Equipment and utensils

Medieval cooking does not require any particular set-up; in fact, it will give you the chance, if you like, to light a fire in the fireplace and get to work with mortar and pestle or with a hand-cranked grinder. But for some of the more frequent procedures you will need:

—A blender or an electric meat grinder (or a manual model for more intrepid cooks)
—A good-sized stone or brass mortar, and a pestle

—A fine-mesh strainer made of metal, and a drum sieve or conical sieve *(chinois)*

—Cotton cheesecloth

Shopping

As we have said repeatedly, medieval cooking closely followed the seasons; you should remember this constraint when you go marketing. Another complication is to avoid anachronisms: we tend to forget the exotic origins of everyday foods, corn oil for example. So here is some basic advice. (You will find more advice in our comments on many of the recipes, and in Mail-order Sources.)

MEAT AND POULTRY

Buy the best—veal raised without steroids, prime or top choice domestic lamb, free-range chickens, and so forth.

VEGETABLES

Again, the best. The fresher the vegetables, the better the cooking, whether it is medieval or not. Keep away from new varieties, and New World plants such as tomatoes and peppers. Try to shop at a local farmers' market or a trustworthy greengrocer's rather than at the supermarket—although many supermarkets today have sections devoted to local and/or organically grown produce.

FRESH AND DRIED FRUIT

Go to the farmers' market and look for the most rustic varieties. Do not think for a minute that beautiful-looking fruit will necessarily have the best flavor. Be especially careful about the quality of your dried fruit. Only high-quality unblanched almonds will yield rich almond milk that will in turn impart great flavor to your food. Do not buy blanched almonds except in an emergency.

FATS AND OILS

Try to buy freshly rendered lard and fresh or salted fatback at a Polish, Hungarian, Italian, or other ethnic butcher shop. These are the fats most commonly used in medieval cooking.

If you have a good relationship with your butcher, you may be able to get hard veal fat and fresh beef marrow; in the United States it will be next to impossible to get beef-kidney fat. The few recipes that use these ingredients do not call for very large quantities.

You will want a good cold-pressed extra-virgin olive oil both for cooking and for dressings. For dressings, top-quality walnut oil will be useful as well.

Rather than buy mass-produced butter, try to find a flavorful butter (either unsalted or salted) churned by a local dairy; alternatively, fine French butters, from Charentes or Isigny, are sometimes available at a price (but make sure they are fresh). Above all, avoid anything marked "Light" (or, worse, "Lite").

Flour

Probably the closest thing to medieval flour is the stone-ground wheat flour sold in some organic-produce, health-food, or fancy food stores, or by mail order direct from the mill. Do not automatically choose the darkest, "whole-est" of wheat flours; they are harder to work with—and in any event the great cooks of the sixteenth century preferred white flours: the only ones good enough for royalty and the aristocracy.

The best choice is an unbleached, organic all-purpose or pastry flour (with an extraction rate of from 70 to 80 percent, which will yield a flour not quite so white as is common).

Sugar

Use crystallized or superfine white cane sugar. Remember that it is often used as a decoration, precisely because of its whiteness. For a few recipes, however, you will need some light brown sugar.

Milk

Unless you can get raw milk directly from a certified dairy (or keep your own cows!), you will need to settle for that modern invention, pasteurized whole milk. Some local dairies offer vat-pasteurized milk, which has better flavor. Under no circumstances use long-life or low-fat milk.

Cheeses

Fresh cheeses: The variety of fresh cheeses on the American market is narrower than that in France. Some markets offer French-style *fromage blanc.* Other possible alternatives are whole-milk farmer's cheese and cream cheese (preferably the "natural" kind made without gum stiffeners). Making your own *fromage frais* is not a particularly onerous task; several books on home cheese making can be found in good bookstores. Ideally, fresh cheese for cooking will have a butterfat content of from 40 to 80 percent. If the cheese you opt to use seems on the wet side (as *fromage blanc* generally is, and as farmer's cheese can be), drain it for a few hours in a fine strainer or in cheesecloth. Be sure also to take account of how salty a cheese is when you season your dish.

Grating cheeses: Home-grated *parmigiano reggiano* or another Italian *grana*-type cheese are the best options. But failing these, you can use well-aged Swiss gruyère or (better) sbrinzer, or French comté.

For each recipe, we will suggest the right cheeses in the list of ingredients.

WINES

Table wine: See "Some Menus" (below, p. 47).

Cooking wine: Good-quality dry wines, red or white depending on the recipe.

VERJUICE

Verjuice is hard but not impossible to find. Fancy food stores occasionally sell it. Several California producers will sell it by mail, and bottled sour grape juice is sometimes to be found in Middle Eastern groceries, where you may also find a concentrate that can be mixed with water as you need it. For the occasional treat, we reckon that it will be worth the expense. If you happen to be traveling in Périgord, in southwestern France, you will probably be able to pick some up there, as it is still used in the local cooking.

As a substitute, the juice of sour apples yields excellent results, as does the juice of Seville oranges if you can find them. Freshly squeezed lemon juice or apple cider vinegar, somewhat diluted (three parts juice or vinegar to one part water), also has good flavor.

VINEGARS

Use the best available wine vinegar, red or white depending on the recipe.

BREAD

A hearty sourdough bread, off-white in color, slightly tangy and moist: this will work perfectly to thicken sauces and *potages*. Avoid airy breads that *look* rustic but that are baked using fast-rising yeast and excessively white flour. If a recipe calls for toasted or grilled bread, you might try using good-quality packaged rusks from the supermarket.

ROSE WATER

This aromatic fluid is distilled from rose petals and water. Lebanese rose water has the best reputation, although Greek, French, Italian, and other brands are available as well. Middle Eastern groceries will be the best source. Return it to the store if its aroma has faded (as it will if it has been kept on the grocer's shelf too long).

SPICES

Obviously, the fresher the better. So do not store ground spices for too long: they will fade. But if you are planning to cook medieval dishes regularly, we advise you to prepare some spice mixtures and have them on hand.

Depending on the recipe, you will need whole or ground spices. You should therefore buy them in both forms, or buy whole spices only and grind them as needed in a little electric coffee-grinder. You can buy spices from groceries and spice merchants, of course, but also try Indian and Asian food stores. Mail order can be an excellent option as well.

Cinnamon: This is available everywhere, both in stick form (the rolled bark) and ground, and sometimes in "chunks." Cassia cinnamon *(Cinamomum cassia)* and "true" cinnamon *(Cinamomum zeylaicum)* are both available and can be used interchangeably, although cassia has a thicker bark in its stick form and a stronger, though less complex and refined, flavor than "true" cinnamon.

Cassia buds: These are the dried immature fruit of *Cinamomum cassia* and look like large cloves. They have a very pleasant cinnamon flavor and can be replaced by ordinary cinnamon. Under their Chinese name, *guiding,* they can be found in some traditional Chinese pharmacies, and mail-order spice merchants can supply them from time to time (ask, even if they do not appear in the catalogue). Or have your globe-trotting friends bring you some from Beijing or Hong Kong.

Ginger: Fresh gingerroot *(Zingiber officinale)* is now available in greengrocers and supermarkets, as well as in Asian markets, but it is the half-dried root that you will want for medieval cooking. For this, you can leave a chunk of fresh ginger to partially dry. You should also buy some ground ginger, which you can find in any grocery store.

Galangal: This aromatic root *(Alpinia officinarum)* is Chinese in origin and much used today in Southeast Asian cooking. It is rarely found in our texts, where it is called *garingal,* although it is used in hypocras (see recipe 149) and sometimes in aspics (could the word *galantine* have its roots in "galangal"?) You can buy fresh galangal in Thai or other Asian markets (do not confuse it with ginger: they look similar, but galangal is a thinner root and has a violet tinge). Its spiciness is similar to that of ginger, but its flavor is muskier and less lemony. Some spice merchants (including some on our list of mail-order sources) sell dried galangal, whole or ground, or you can dry the fresh root yourself. In a pinch, you can substitute ginger.

Pepper: Black pepper *(Piper nigrum)* is sometimes called "round pepper" in medieval sources to differentiate it from long pepper (q.v.). A number of varieties are available; Tellicherry peppercorns are considered to be the finest and most aromatic. It is best to buy whole peppercorns and grind them fresh, as needed, although pre-ground pepper, if fresh and of good quality, can be useful, especially in spice mixtures and in such preparations as hypocras.

    Some of our recipes refer to white pepper *(Piper album)*. This is the same peppercorn with its black shell removed. Like black pepper, it is readily available everywhere.

Long pepper: Not so readily available is the fruit of *Piper longum,* which is sometimes called for in our texts. This hard, black capsule, about three-quarters of an inch long and composed of many tiny seeds, has a very spicy flavor. You may find long pepper in Southeast Asian markets or, more likely, in Indian groceries, where it is sold inter alia as an ingredient of a honey-and-pepper tonic used in Vedic medicine. But until you find some, you can substitute regular black pepper.

Nutmeg: Everyone is familiar with the seed of *Myristica fragrans;* to this day it is widely, if discreetly, used in cooking of all kinds. Select large, heavy nutmegs and grate them fresh, as needed. Pre-ground nutmeg can be useful for spice mixtures, but make sure it is fresh and aromatic.

Mace: Mace is the dried aril (a fibrous cage-like covering) of the nutmeg. It is most often sold ground, although spice merchants should also carry whole, or "blade," mace. Its flavor is close to that of nutmeg, but has a hint of cinnamon about it as well. It is more orange in color than nutmeg.

Cloves: This is the dried bud of the tropical flower *Eugenia caryophyllata.* It is sold everywhere, whole and ground. Its flavor is most pervasive, so take care.

Grains of paradise, Guinea pepper, Melegueta pepper: These small seeds, black outside and white inside, are found in the fruit of *Amomum melegueta,* a plant of African origin. They have a very peppery flavor and can be purchased from some spice houses. They are extremely hard, and grinding them in a mortar and pestle or in a blender will take some patience (a spice- or coffee-grinder will do a quicker job). If need be, you may substitute Sichuan peppercorns plus a little black pepper, or, if these are unavailable, a mixture of allspice and black pepper, or black pepper alone.

Saffron: When you think of saffron, please do not think of the yellow powder sold to color paella, which is often adulterated. Think of saffron threads, the stigmas from the pistil of the *Crocus sativus* blossom. In the Middle Ages, it was grown in Europe, especially in Italy, but the most highly regarded saffron came from the East. Things have changed but little. While saffron is still grown in Europe, especially in Spain and Italy—and until recently in the Gâtinais in western France—the most prized comes from South Asia, specifically from Kashmir and Nepal. Sold by the gram (one twenty-eighth of an ounce), saffron is the most expensive of all spices. But it must be purchased in the form of threads if you want to be sure that it is genuine and if you want the flavor and color to blaze in your food. Fancy food stores, spice merchants, and Indian groceries are good sources.

Cardamom: There are six to eight cardamom seeds in each attractive teardrop-shaped capsule of *Amomum cardamomum* or *Elettaria cardamomum,* a plant native to Malabar and Ceylon; these capsules can be pale green or tan depending on variety and how they were processed. Note that black cardamom has an entirely different flavor and is not suited for these recipes. In Indian groceries, cardamom can be bought in the capsule, as whole seeds, or ground, and it is often found in fancy food stores and in some supermarkets. In India, cardamom is often chewed to sweeten the breath.

Some Menus

Any recipe in this book can be easily incorporated into a modern menu, but if one dinnertime you want to travel back to the Middle Ages here is some advice on organizing your meal according to medieval customs.

First of all, choose seasonal dishes; if you are Catholic, avoid meat dishes during Lent and on days of abstinence—and remember also to substitute vegetable oil for animal fats where necessary.

The order of your menu should follow the sequence *potage,* roast, *entremets,* which is the basis of the medieval meal, and the number of courses and dishes should be commensurate with the number of your guests. For four to six people, one dish per course will do, but with more company—eight, ten, or fifteen—do not merely expand each recipe, but increase the number of dishes per course, bearing in mind that each guest will not necessarily get to taste everything.

To illustrate our point, we have put together two basic menus for six persons, then adjusted them for larger numbers. Recipe numbers are indicated in boldface.

AUTUMN MENU FOR SIX

First course
Sweet Wine and Fresh Seasonal Fruit
Second course
Winter Squash or Pumpkin Soup (**3**)
Third course
Spit-roasted Hare (**53**)
Black Sauce, or *Poivre noir* (**108**)
Fourth course (*or* Entremets)
An Italian Blancmange from Foreign
Parts (**131**)
Issue de Table
Hypocras (**149**)
Cialdoni Wafers or Marzipan
Tart (**136**)
Boute-Hors
Cardamom and Anise Seeds

AUTUMN MENU FOR TEN TO TWELVE

First course
Sweet Wine and Fresh Seasonal Fruit

Second course
Winter Squash or Pumpkin Soup (**3**)
Sautéed Mushrooms with Spices (**21**)
Third course
Spit-roasted Hare (**53**)
Black Sauce, or *Poivre noir* (**108**)
Parsley-studded Lamb or
Mutton (**47**)
Pink Garlic Sauce (**101**)
Fourth course (*or* Entremets)
An Italian Blancmange from Foreign
Parts (**131**)
Cheese Fritters (**126**)
Desserte
Whole-Pear Pie (**97**)
Issue de Table
Hypocras (**149**)
Cialdoni wafers or Marzipan
Tart (**136**)
Boute-Hors
Cardamom and Anise Seeds

AUTUMN MENU FOR
FIFTEEN OR SIXTEEN

First course
  Grenache or similar Wine
  Fresh Seasonal Fruit
Second course
  Winter Squash or Pumpkin Soup (3)
  Sautéed Mushrooms with Spices (21)
  Limonia, or Chicken with
    Lemon (33)
Third course
  Spit-roasted Hare (53)
  Black Sauce, or *Poivre noir* (108)
  Parsley-studded Lamb or
    Mutton (47)
  Pink Garlic Sauce (101)
Fourth course (*or* Entremets)
  An Italian Blancmange from Foreign
    Parts (131)
  Cheese Fritters (126)
  Torta Bolognese, or Herbed Swiss
    Chard and Cheese Pie (81)
Desserte
  Whole-Pear Pie (97)
  Dariole, or Custard Tart (96)
Issue de Table
  Hypocras (149)
  Cialdoni wafers or Marzipan
    Tart (136)
Boute-Hors
  Cardamom and Anise Seeds

LENTEN MENU FOR SIX

First course
  Green *Porée* for Days of
    Abstinence (15)
Second course
  San Vincenzo's Day Grilled Eel (63)
Third course (*or* Entremets)
  Trout in Aspic (124)
Issue de Table
  Hypocras (149)
  Nucato, or Spiced Honey Nut
    Crunch (147)
Boute-Hors
  Wine and Spices

LENTEN MENU FOR
TEN TO TWELVE

First course
  Green *Porée* for Days of
    Abstinence (15)
  Sweet-and-Sour Fish (62)
Second course
  San Vincenzo's Day Grilled Eel (63)
  Poached Fresh Tuna with Yellow
    Sauce (70)
Third course (*or* Entremets)
  Trout in Aspic (124)
  Taillis, or Dried-Fruit Pudding (134)
Desserte
  Tiered Dried-Fruit Pie (98)
Issue de Table
  Hypocras (149)
  Nucato, or Spiced Honey Nut
    Crunch (147)
Boute-Hors
  Wine and Spices

LENTEN MENU FOR
FIFTEEN OR SIXTEEN

First course
  Green *Porée* for Days of
    Abstinence (15)
  Sweet-and-Sour Fish (62)
  Chickpea Soup (4)
Second course
  San Vincenzo's Day Grilled Eel (63)
  Poached Fresh Tuna with Yellow
    Sauce (70)
Third course (*or* Entremets)
  Trout in Aspic (124)
  Taillis, or Dried-Fruit Pudding (134)
  Pears in Greek-Wine Syrup (144)
Desserte
  Tiered Dried-Fruit Pie (98)
  Apple Jelly Candies (146)
Issue de Table
  Hypocras (149)
  Nucato, or Spiced Honey Nut
    Crunch (147)
Boute-Hors
  Wine and Spices

Wines

Among all the possible beverages, choose wine to accompany your medieval meal. And water it down—if you have the heart. For the first course, with the fruit, you could serve a sweet fortified wine of the Pyrenees region, such as a grenache from Banyuls or a muscat from Rivesaltes. This would not be out of keeping with the spirit of the age, as medieval hosts were quite happy to serve grenache at the beginning of a meal.

Potages, roasts, and *entremets* will work with a whole range of young, light wines.

Hypocras (recipe 149) was indispensable for the *issue de table,* except in summer, when it was "out of season." You can then quite happily substitute a rich, sweet wine such as a French malvoisie, an Italian malvasia, or a Hungarian Tokay.

We have no details as to the wine to accompany the spices in the *boutehors* course. But we think it might be hard to go back to a dry wine after the hypocras, and we advise you either to continue to serve hypocras or to choose a sweet wine, as in the *issue de table.*

These suggestions are based on the very scanty information at our disposal and in any event can give only rough guidance. Some modern wines have only the most distant relationship with those of the Middle Ages. While we urge you to avoid flagrant anachronisms such as sparkling wines, spirits, and drinks like anisette, at the same time we echo Aldobrandino da Siena in bidding you to enjoy wine in keeping with your normal habits.

Note on Presentation of Recipes

Each recipe begins with a translation of the original medieval text. (A key to the source abbreviations may be found on p. xvii.) The translation is followed by our comments, then by our rendering for the modern cook.

Soups and Pasta: Potages

In modern French, the word *potage,* like the English "soup," has given way to a whole elegant vocabulary of variations: broths, creams, bisques, and chowders, to name only a few. But they all boil down to the soup that we serve our families when the winter's cold seems to demand some kind of restorative warmth.

In the Middle Ages, the word *potage* was broader in meaning. It was used for diverse foods ranging in consistency and ingredients from a few crusts of bread soaking in light broth to substantial dishes of stewed venison with very little sauce. *Potages* were cooked in pots (though other foods were too). They were served in the deep plates known as *écuelles* and eaten with spoons. As part of a complete meal, *potages* were brought out during the first *service.* In general, these dishes were the result of a balance between a liquid (known itself as the *potage*) and a solid component (known as the *grain*). Garden vegetables, small birds, huge cuts of meat: anything could find its way into the pot, combined with milk, eggs, and, at times, cereals.

These dishes are omnipresent in medieval cookbooks. They constitute 40 percent of the recipes in *Le Ménagier de Paris,* to the point where the author felt it necessary to organize them, grouping them under a number of headings: "Ordinary *potages* without spices, not thickened," "Other *potages,* with spices and not thickened," "Other *potages,* thickened, and with meat" and "Other *potages,* thickened, without meat." This attempt to clarify matters for his young wife, a tyro in all matters domestic, would be admirable if the recipes under the various headings did not all too often undermine this sensible structure.

The category of *potage* deserves further clarification. These substantial vegetable dishes and meats cooked in sauce did not serve only to take the edge off a banquet-goer's appetite; they could sometimes replace an entire meal—more than sometimes for the peasant, but also occasionally in households that wanted for nothing. Take the "Extemporaneous Soup" *(Souppe despourveue)* found in recipe 10: isn't this the kind of thing you would hustle to prepare when guests dropped in unexpectedly? A little broth (always on hand), quickly warmed up and poured over a few *soupes,* or "sops, or sippets" of bread, would do the trick. The very French custom of adding a chunk of bread to the soup survived well beyond the Middle Ages, to the extent that *soupe* came to refer to the entire dish, as though the identity of the *soupe*—the bread—had dissolved in the broth and lent it its name. The Frenchness of this habit was noted in neighboring countries, especially Italy, where they viewed this method of soaking *soupes* of bread—called *zuppe* in Italian—as a French custom.

The Italians had customs of their own: variations on pasta gave substance to their *minestre* (the Italian equivalent of *potages*). These lasagne, macaroni, and ravioli became so important that, after having been cooked in and served with the broth, they would be placed alone on platters; to this day, that style of eating bears the odd name *minestra asciutta,* or "dry soup."

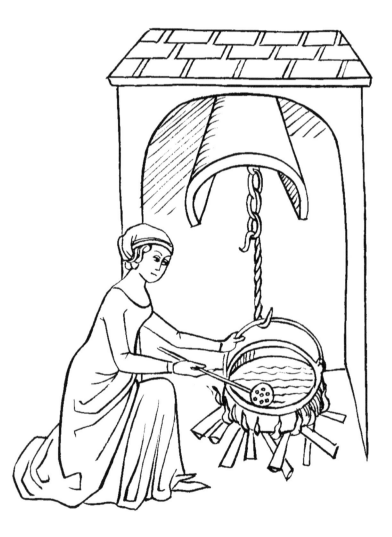

Soups and Pastas in Broth
1. Split-pea or Dried Fava Bean Soup

retonnée of new peas or fava beans.   Cook them until they break apart and drain them. Then take very fresh cow's milk—but tell whoever sells it to you that you do not want it if she has added any water, for they very often dilute their milk with water. If it is not extremely fresh, or if it contains any water, it will curdle. And first boil the milk before adding anything to it, because it would curdle then as well; then, first crush some ginger to arouse the appetite and some saffron for its yellow color. Although you can thicken [the soup] with beaten egg yolks, and the yolks color the soup nicely while thickening it, the soup, however, will curdle more readily with that liaison than with [a liaison] of bread and with saffron as a coloring. So those who want to make a bread liaison should take white bread, not leavened, soak it in milk or in meat broth, then mash it and put it through a sieve. And when your bread has been sieved, add it to the peas and add your spices without sieving, and boil it all together. When this is cooked, then add your milk and the saffron. For another liaison you can also use crushed, diluted peas or fava beans. But you can use the liaison you like best. And if you use a liaison of egg yolks, you should beat them, strain them, and pour them into the milk off the fire, once it has thoroughly boiled with the new peas or fava beans. The safest way is to pour a little milk into the bowl containing the beaten egg yolks and to mix them in little by little with sufficient milk to dilute the egg yolks thoroughly. Then pour the contents of the bowl into the soup, still off the fire, and in that way it will not curdle. If the soup is too thick, lighten it with meat broth. When it is ready, you should prepare some pieces of young chicken, veal, or goose giblets, first cooked then fried, and place two or three in each bowl, then pour in the soup. (MP 159)

The "new peas" in this recipe are not our usual green peas, which are the immature fruit of *pisum sativum* and which were an Italian novelty that flabbergasted the court of Louis XIV. Their appeal was, and still is, that they melt in the mouth and bear no resemblance to legumes or pulses. *Pois nouveaux* in the Middle Ages were picked at maturity and were probably more floury. So we suggest making this *cretonnée* with split peas, which are dried peas whose outer skin has been removed and which cook quickly. *Cretonnée* is a creamy soup served with *petite oé*, little chunks of cooked poultry or veal crisped in a skillet. Some people think the medieval term *petite oé* means gosling, or small goose, but it actually refers to goose giblets (see recipe 58).

This recipe's detail and its warnings to be careful show that the author was not a professional cook. He was timid about using egg yolks as a thickener, which is indeed tricky, and therefore gives us several options for thickening the puree of peas. Two of them—bread and crushed peas respectively—are foolproof. The third, which uses egg yolks, is more dangerous. In our version, we suggest this third option; while supposedly the most difficult, it yields the smoothest soup.

The original recipe comes from *Le Ménagier de Paris*, a study of domestic economy written toward the end of the fourteenth century by a Parisian bourgeois to instruct his young wife about household matters. It reflects the author's concern for good management; his mistrust of unscrupulous vendors who thought nothing of watering their milk, thus rendering it unusable, seems fair enough in a head of household who needed to husband his resources.

12	ounces split peas (350 g)
2	cups milk (500 ml)
3	egg yolks
½	teaspoon ground ginger
1	pinch saffron threads (optional)
1	cup (or more) leftover cooked chicken (preferably dark meat) or veal, or chicken livers, cubed
1	tablespoon good lard

Carefully wash the split peas, taking care to remove any stones, and leave them to soak in cold water for an hour. Cook the peas in 2 quarts (2 liters) of water until they are very soft and can be crushed with light pressure. Add salt to taste and drain.

Bring the milk to a boil; add the ginger and saffron. Remove from the heat. In a small bowl beat the egg yolks with a whisk and pour them through a strainer into another bowl large enough to hold the milk. Slowly pour the hot milk into the beaten yolks, whisking constantly.

In a heavy skillet melt the lard over medium-high heat. Add the cubes of cooked meat and sauté until crisp and golden brown. Sprinkle with salt to taste.

Reheat the peas over low heat, stirring to prevent them from burning. Slowly stir in the yolk mixture and heat until slightly thickened. At this point do not allow the soup to boil. Check for salt.

You can either put the cubes of meat into the soup tureen just before serving or bring them to the table and let your guests help themselves.

2. Herb Soup

enestra of greens.   Take Swiss chard leaves and a little borage; cook them in boiling clear water until the water comes back to the boil; then drain them and chop fine with a knife. And take a little parsley and raw mint and chop them along with the greens. Then pound everything in a mortar, and add to a pot with rich broth and boil briefly. If you like, you can add a little pepper. (Ma 146)

This is an excellent recipe for an "herb"—leafy vegetable—soup; its slightly minty aroma will take you by surprise. We recommend using beef rather than chicken broth, because its flavor goes better with the slight bitterness of the greens. People have been picking borage for a long time; it still grows wild in the French countryside and is sold at markets in certain parts of Italy, where it is grown for its coarse, fuzzy leaves, which are indispensable for filling a Genoese variation on ravioli. If you should encounter any wild borage, use it by all means. In seventeenth- and eighteenth-century France and England, its pretty blue flowers were used along with golden nasturtiums and other blossoms to adorn salads. Harrods department store in London still sells them for that rustically gentrified purpose, as do many farmers' markets in U.S. cities. But in this recipe, you can replace borage with spinach or any other salad green that can be cooked.

This pleasant but very simple mixed-greens soup does not show off the great talent of Maestro Martino, the author of the *Libro de arte coquinaria*, from which we have drawn many of our recipes. As you go through this book you will get a better idea of the genius of this great chef, who plied his trade toward the middle of the fifteenth century at Rome, in the service of the Patriarch of Aquileia.

rim and wash the chard. If you are using broad-stemmed chard, use only the leaves and save the stems for another dish. Wash the borage—or the spinach or other "herbs." Cook these greens in boiling salted water for 5 to 7 minutes, uncovered (which will help keep them bright green). Drain, then press in a sieve to squeeze out as much water as possible; chop finely with a knife or in a food processor. Set aside.

Coarsely chop the parsley and the mint, and puree first one then the other in a blender—or mince to a puree with a knife.

6 **cups beef broth** (1½ liters)
1 **generous pound Swiss chard leaves** (500 g)
A good handful of borage leaves (or spinach, romaine lettuce, arugula, or other greens)
1 **bunch parsley**
1 **bunch fresh mint**
 freshly ground black pepper
 salt

Do not puree the mint too far in advance, lest it turn dark and lose its aroma.

Bring the broth to the boil and add the cooked greens, plus about 3 tablespoons parsley puree and 2 or 3 tablespoons mint puree to taste. Return to the boil, and turn off the heat; add salt and pepper to taste.

The uncooked parsley and mint are what add the fresh flavor to this soup; you can adjust the quantity to taste. The cooked Swiss chard and other greens give the soup its body.

3. Winter Squash or Pumpkin Soup

quash.   For squash, peel them and cut them into slices. Remove the seeds if there are any and cook them in water in a pan, then drain them and rinse in cold water; squeeze them and chop them finely; mix with some beef and other meat broth and add cow's milk, and mix half a dozen egg yolks, put through a sieve, into the broth and milk; on fast days [use] the cooking water from [dried] peas, or almond milk, and butter. (VT XV 181)

We've chosen the Lenten version, which unites the delicate flavor of almond milk and butter to the sweetness of the squash.

The cucurbits are a large, rich family including cucumbers, melons, and squashes. But the Old World knew neither the winter squash *(Cucurbita pepo)* nor the pumpkin *(Cucurbita maxima)*, both of which were brought from the Americas. If we can trust the title of the recipe, *Congordes,* and if we think of the depictions of squash *(zucche)* harvests in the many manuscripts comprising the *Tacuinum sanitatis*—a medical treatise of Arab origin that lists the medicinal properties of various foods—the cook is probably dealing here with gourds *(Lagenaria vulgaris)*. These came originally from southern Asia, and were well known in Western Europe in the Middle Ages. But without fresh gourds to hand, you can prepare this soup with winter squash or pumpkin.

This recipe comes from *Le Viandier,* a best-seller of the time, according to Bruno Laurioux. It is attributed to the cook to Charles V and Charles VI, known as Taillevent, though it was actually put together long before, toward the end of the thirteenth century. This is proven by a manuscript that probably predates Taillevent. We chose recipes from *Le Viandier* using four manuscripts of the text, collated and edited by Terence Scully, and from the printed version published in the fifteenth century, less well arranged but often richer in content because, in fact, it includes recipes that have no connection with *Le Viandier.*

5½ **pounds winter squash or pumpkin** (2.5 kg)

4 **cups almond milk** (1 liter) **made with a little more than 4 cups of water and ⅔ cup almonds** (100 g) (recipe 151)

4 **tablespoons (2 ounces) butter** (60 g)

Salt to taste

Peel the squash and remove the seeds. Cut it into 1-inch (2-cm) chunks and cook in boiling salted water for about 10 minutes. The squash must remain firm and must not fall apart; you will need to be vigilant, as cooking time will vary with the variety of squash or pumpkin you use.

Drain, and press gently in a sieve to remove excess water. Chop to a coarse puree with a knife or in a food processor. Place the puree into a saucepan, add the almond milk and butter, and bring to the boil. Check for salt before serving.

4. Chickpea Soup

Brodo of red chickpeas.   To make eight platefuls: take a *libra* and a half [1 *libra* = about 10½ ounces (300 g)] of chickpeas and wash them in hot water, drain them, then put them in the pot in which they will be cooked. Add half an *oncia* [1 *oncia* = about 1 ounce (30 g)] of flour, i.e., "flower" [of wheat], a little good oil, a little salt and about twenty crushed peppercorns and a little ground cinnamon, then thoroughly mix all these things together with your hands. Then add three measures of water, a little sage, rosemary, and parsley roots. Boil until it is reduced to the quantity of eight platefuls. And when they are nearly cooked, pour in a little oil. And if you prepare this soup for invalids, add neither oil nor spices. (Ma 147)

Medieval cooks had the choice of red or white chickpeas, as the author of *Le Ménagier de Paris* teaches his bride. If you do not care for chickpeas, this soup may change your mind. It is rich, aromatic, and hearty, and would make an excellent winter dinner all by itself. In theory, it should be made with "Hamburg parsley," a plant grown for its bulbous root rather than for its leaves.

This was common in the Middle Ages and is still used in Slavic and Germanic countries to flavor borschts and broths. You can use parsley stems or a root vegetable such as parsnip.

ry to get chickpeas that are no more than a year old. The day before, pick through the chickpeas for stones and debris, and wash them. Soak them in warm water overnight.

The next day, whisk together the flour, oil, pepper, and cinnamon in your soup pot. Drain the chickpeas and add them to the pot; mix well with your hands. Add cold water to cover. Bring to the boil, skimming any gray scum that may rise to the surface of the water.

1¼ cups dried chickpeas (200 g)
1 tablespoon flour
2 tablespoons extra-virgin olive oil
10 black peppercorns, coarsely crushed
¼ teaspoon ground cinnamon
fresh sage
parsley or parsnip
salt

Add a generous sprig of sage, a branch of rosemary, and a handful of parsley or one parsnip, diced. Simmer for 2 hours over very low heat, until the chickpeas are very tender. When done, add salt to taste. It is hard to predict how long the soup will take to cook; much depends on the quality and freshness of the chickpeas.

5. Zanzarelli

o make zanzarelli. To make ten platefuls: take eight eggs, half a *libra* of grated cheese, and breadcrumbs, and mix these things together. Then, take a pot of meat broth colored yellow with saffron and put it on the fire; and when it begins to boil put in this mixture and stir once with a spoon. And when it seems to have thickened, remove the pot from the fire and serve up, then sprinkle with spices. (Ma 137–38)

Your Roman friends will love this soup for its somewhat rough, thick richness, like that of stracciatella, a very popular soup in the Italian capital. Indeed, its ingredients are more or less the same as those of zanzarelli, apart from the spices.

From the cook's standpoint, this is an interesting recipe, because the eggs do not play their usual role as a creamy thickening agent; to the contrary, you want them to "curdle," which gives the soup a special graininess that harmonizes well with the graininess of the breadcrumbs and the grated cheese.

2 quarts chicken stock (2
liters)(recipe 152) (this is more
than normal, because this soup
is so good that everyone will
want seconds)

8 eggs

1¼ cups (7 ounces) freshly grated
parmesan cheese (200 g)

3 ounces dry bread, grated fine;
or 1 cup dry breadcrumbs
(80 g)
saffron threads
mixed ground spices
(cinnamon, ginger, nutmeg,
black pepper, etc.)

Mix the parmesan, breadcrumbs, and eggs to form a soft paste. You can vary the proportions depending on your taste and on the desired consistency of the final soup.

Bring the stock to the boil and add half a dozen threads of saffron. Turn off the heat and let steep for a few minutes, until the broth takes on a nice golden color from the saffron. Return to the boil and add the egg mixture all at once. Stir vigorously with a wire whisk and bring back to the boil for a moment, until the liquid separates: as the eggs cook, they will change the soup's appearance from creamy to slightly granular.

Remove from the heat. Check for salt, ladle into individual soup plates, and sprinkle generously with the spice mixture.

6. Lasagne

Of lasagne.   To make lasagne take fermented dough and make into as thin a shape as possible. Then divide it into squares of three fingerbreadths per side. Then take salted boiling water and cook those lasagne in it. And when they are fully cooked, add grated cheese.

And, if you like, you can also add good powdered spices and powder them on them, when they are on the trencher. Then put on a layer of lasagne and powder [spices] again; and on top another layer and powder, and continue until the trencher or bowl is full. Then eat them by taking them up with a pointed wooden stick. (Lc 412)

> This recipe is interesting from several points of view—not because lasagne were an innovation in the fourteenth century, but because of the unusual method it sets out. Pasta was common in medieval Italy and we are obliged to shatter a beloved myth by noting that Marco Polo had nothing to do with this popularity: we find references to *maccaroni* (*maccheroni* in modern Italian) in texts dating from before his lifetime. Lasagne, which are cut from a sheet of pasta formed with a rolling pin, are the likely successors of the *laganae* of Roman times, for which the late fourth-century treatise of Apicius includes two recipes, although these yield quite different results, as one is boiled and the other baked. The mixture of wheat flour and water known as pasta is also defined in part by its being cooked in moist heat: boiling water in the West and steam or boiling liquid in China.
>
> While lasagne are the culmination of a pasta-making tradition dating back to antiquity, the origin of macaroni and vermicelli, first mentioned in medieval Italian cooking treatises, is far less certain. Ravioli and tortelli too are in a

separate, poorly defined category (see recipe 8). Forming macaroni and vermi-celli uses a technique newer than that of rolling out a sheet of dough: the dough is shaped with the fingers into little rods or worm shapes; you make the hole in macaroni by inserting a metal wire lengthwise into the dough and roll-ing it back and forth on the table. Making a dish of macaroni took lots of time and patience. Another innovation was that these new pastas were often preserved by drying, which was not true of lasagne.

To return to our lasagne, the recipe we have selected is distinctive for its use of a "fermented" dough—*pastam fermentatam* in Latin—that is, a leavened dough. There is no room for doubt that leavening is used. In a prior recipe *fermento* is added to a fritter dough precisely to make it "grow" *(ut crescat)*.

Other Italian books contain recipes for lasagne made of flour and water and boiled in meat broth for meat days, or in almond milk for days of absti-nence. In this recipe, our lasagne are simply boiled in salted water.

Another of the unusual elements that made us choose this version in the *Liber de coquina* is that it is the only one to explain clearly how lasagne are made—by rolling out the dough and cutting it into squares three finger-breadths a side—and how they are eaten: with a little pointed wooden stick. We can quite see the need for a tool with which to eat hot lasagne without burning our fingers. But the fork was on the way! (See above, p. 13.)

It is only natural to wonder why these lasagne are made from a leavened dough, similar to bread dough, rather than from a simple mixture of flour and water. Remember that in Italy today lasagne, like other fresh pastas, are made from flour and eggs. We have found, in fact, that a leavened dough, when boiled, has a slight springiness that is lacking in an unleavened dough; this consistency comes close to the *al dente* texture of perfectly cooked pasta.

In any event, these lasagne are plain but not dry—"light" in today's jar-gon—and are well worth trying. We think that, despite its apparent simplicity, the flavoring of freshly grated parmesan cheese (be generous), spices, and freshly ground pepper is among the finest ways to serve pasta.

issolve the yeast in a little of the water. Leave to proof for 10 minutes, then mix into the flour. Dissolve the salt in the remaining water and add to the flour mix-ture to form a dough that is not too stiff. Knead for about 10 minutes as you would a bread or pizza dough. The dough should be smooth and elastic; it should reveal many tiny holes when you cut it with a knife.

Cover the dough with a towel and leave to rise in a warm place for about an hour.

Grate the cheese and prepare the spice mixture; set aside. Toward the end of the

For the dough

3 **cups flour** (375 g)
1 **cup tepid water** (25 cl)
1½ **teaspoons salt** (7 g)
1½ **teaspoons active dried yeast** (8 g) **or ¾ ounce fresh baker's yeast** (20 g)
⅔ **cup freshly grated parmesan cheese** (100 g)
     freshly ground black pepper

For the spice mixture

½ teaspoon ground cardamom

½ teaspoon freshly grated nutmeg

⅛ teaspoon freshly ground black pepper

⅛ teaspoon ground cinnamon

rising time, bring a large pot of well-salted water to the boil; add a few drops of oil to prevent the lasagne from sticking to one another. Preheat a baking or gratin dish in the oven or by filling it with boiling water (being sure to dry it thoroughly before using).

Punch down the dough, knead it back into a ball, and roll it out to an even thickness of about ¹⁄₁₆ inch (1.5 mm). This dough has a tendency to stick, so flour your work surface well. Unless you have a great deal of space, you will probably have to divide the dough into 2 or more pieces for rolling and cutting. Cut the sheet or sheets of dough into 2-inch (5-cm) squares.

Cook the lasagne in the rapidly boiling water; stir as you add them to keep them from sticking. They are done when they rise to the surface of the water; this will take a mere 2 or 3 minutes. Taste one to make sure it is cooked; it should not taste of flour and should be elastic but not too soft.

Remove the lasagne with a skimmer or slotted spoon; do not drain them completely dry. Place a layer of lasagne in the preheated baking dish, sprinkle it generously with grated parmesan, a good pinch of spices and 2 or 3 grinds of black pepper. Repeat until you have run out of lasagne. Finally, top with plenty of parmesan and sprinkle with spices and pepper.

Serve immediately in heated soup plates.

7. Meat Ravioli in Broth

Ravioli for Meat Days.   To make ten platefuls: take a half *libra* of aged cheese and a little of another fat cheese and a *libra* of fat hog's tripe or calf's head, and cook it in water until very tender. Then chop it well and take nice herbs, thoroughly chopped, and some pepper, cloves, and ginger; and if you add the chopped breast of a capon, so much the better. And mix all these things together. Then make the dough very thin and enclose the mixture in the dough as it should be. And these ravioli should be no larger than half a chestnut; and cook them in a broth of capon or good meat, colored yellow by saffron when it boils. And let them boil for the time [it takes to say] two paternosters. Then serve and put on top grated cheese and sweet spices mixed together. You can make similar ravioli with breast of pheasant, partridge, and other birds. (Ma 144)

> This recipe demands inspiration and patience, but the results are worthy of a great chef. The flavor depends on the choice of meats and herbs. We have made these ravioli a number of times for banquets great and small, varying the ingredients on each occasion. In this version we mix fresh cheese, unsmoked salt pork, chicken breast, parsley, and a little fresh mint: in all a thoroughly classic combination, but with an unexpected delicacy thanks to that touch of mint. Another excellent idea is sprinkling the ravioli at the last minute with grated parmesan flavored with sweet spices. And remember that these ravioli should be no larger than a half-chestnut—not that they will be any less tasty if your calibrations are off!

Make the chicken broth in advance; re-move one chicken breast when it is cooked and set aside for the stuffing. Skim the fat from the broth and strain out the meat and vegetables.

In another pot, boil the pork for about an hour and a half (do not presoak). When it is tender, chop it finely in a meat grinder or food processor or by hand; also chop the chicken breast, the parsley, and the mint (you can use more or less of these herbs, to taste). Combine these ingredients and add the fresh cheese. Season with the pepper, the cloves, and the ginger. Add grated par-mesan to taste and according to how salty the stuffing is already (you can poach a nug-get of stuffing and taste it for seasoning). Reserve 6 tablespoons parmesan for gar-nish. The stuffing must be highly seasoned, quite firm, and thoroughly amalgamated.

Make a pasta dough using the flour and eggs. Divide the dough into pieces about the size of an egg; keep them wrapped in a towel or in plastic wrap. Preferably using a roller-type pasta machine, roll the dough into very thin, almost transparent strips.

As each strip is rolled out, place it on a lightly floured board and drop rounded tea-spoons of stuffing evenly spaced, about an inch from one edge of the strip of pasta. Fold the other edge over the stuffing, press-ing firmly around each ball of stuffing to seal well. If you feel that the dough is not sticking, moisten it very slightly with water.

6 cups chicken broth (1½ liters) (recipe 152)

For the pasta dough

1½ cups flour (200 g)
2 eggs

For the stuffing

11 ounces lean salt pork or pancetta in one piece (300 g)
1 scant cup parmesan cheese, approximately (150 g)
scant 4 ounces fresh cheese (such as farmer's cheese) (100 g)
1 skinless, boneless chicken breast, poached (from when you make the chicken broth)
3 tablespoons chopped parsley, or to taste
2 tablespoons chopped fresh mint, or to taste
¼ teaspoon freshly ground black pepper
1 pinch ground cloves
scant ¼ teaspoon ground ginger
7 to 9 threads of saffron
2 heaping tablespoons sweet spice mixture (recipe 150, variation 2B)

Cut into square ravioli with a pastry wheel, a knife, or a cookie or ravioli cutter. The smaller the ravioli, the nicer the dish.

About 15 minutes before serving, bring the broth to the boil and add the saffron; turn off the heat and steep until the liquid has taken on a nice golden color. Return to the boil and slip the ravioli in from the edge of the pot (one by one, but in rapid succes-sion). They will probably take 5 to 7 minutes to cook, but watch them carefully, keeping them immersed with a skimmer. Theoretically, they are done when they float to the surface, but taste one to be sure. Pour the ravioli and broth into a large tureen and serve. Mix 6 tablespoons grated parmesan with 2 tablespoons sweet spices and serve in a small bowl; diners can sprinkle their ravioli with this mixture to taste.

8. White Ravioli or Dumplings with Sugar

White ravioli.   Take some good provatura [cheese] and pound it well, then, while continuing to pound, add a little butter, some ginger, and some cinnamon. For one provatura add three well-beaten egg whites and an appropriate amount of sugar. Mix all these things together. Then make ravioli the length and thickness of a finger. Then roll them in good flour. Note that these ravioli should be made without a dough [*marginal note:* but if you want to make them with a dough, do so]. Boil them gently so that they do not break. Remove them when they have boiled and place them in bowls with sugar and cinnamon. You can color them yellow with saffron. (Bü 5rv)

> We found this recipe in an unpublished manuscript in New York's Pierpont Morgan Library. Scholars think it is of Neapolitan origin. It contains many recipes similar to those in Maestro Martino's *Libro de arte coquinaria*—which however contains no *ravioli bianchi*. For various linguistic and structural reasons, including the menus that follow the actual recipes, we think that this anonymous manuscript postdates Martino's work.
>
> This recipe explicitly refers to ravioli in the sense of a stuffing wrapped in dough, but the dough is omitted here, as it is in modern *ravioli nudi*—naked ravioli. In medieval Italian cooking sources there are nearly thirty recipes entitled *Ravioli*; in general the term refers to foods made with a dough, as in Meat Ravioli in Broth (recipe 7) and Maestro Martino's Egg Ravioli (recipe 120). This shows that the names of dishes do not have a precise meaning, notably in the case of ravioli, whose evolution took two divergent paths in the fifteenth century: stuffed dough cooked in moist heat and served at the beginning of the meal sprinkled with grated cheese and spices; and stuffed dough deep fried and served at the end of the meal sprinkled with sugar or drizzled with honey, a category that overlaps with fritters. This recipe, in which the ravioli are boiled but sprinkled with sugar, may indicate some evolutionary vacillation.
>
> *Ravioli bianchi* were served as a first course at a banquet given by Sozzo Bandinelli on December 23, 1326, for the knighting of his son. (We have already spoken of this dazzling knightly court; see p. 6). Nothing, however, is stopping you from serving them for dessert; after all, they are sweet.
>
> In southern Lazio and in Campagna you still find a cheese known as provatura, made of pulled curd, like mozzarella. But it is not certain that this is the *probatura* of the fifteenth century. In any event, the use of this cheese confirms the southern origins of the Bühler manuscript.

1¼ **pounds mild, reasonably soft white cheese such as a very young French or Swiss tomme, or farmer's cheese, or mozzarella** (600 g)

1½ **tablespoons butter, at room temperature** (20 g)

In a mortar or in a food processor, mash together the cheese, butter, ginger, half the cinnamon, all but 2 teaspoons of the sugar, a pinch of salt, and the saffron, if using. When the mixture is very smooth, work in the egg whites. Forming the ravioli will be much easier if you chill the mixture in the refrigerator for a while.

Mix together the remaining sugar and cinnamon, and set aside. Put some flour for dredging in a shallow soup plate or a pie pan.

Fill a broad pan with water and bring to the boil. Lower to a simmer.

Make the ravioli: for each, shape a heaping tablespoon of the cheese mixture into a finger-sized cylinder. Dredge in flour and set aside on a floured cookie sheet or tray.

2 egg whites, lightly beaten
4 tablespoons sugar (60 g)
   flour for dredging
½ teaspoon ground ginger
1 teaspoon ground cinnamon
   salt
   a few threads saffron, crumbled
   (optional)

Gently drop the ravioli into the barely simmering water one by one. Do not crowd the pan or let the water boil vigorously, because these ravioli are fragile and can easily break. When the ravioli float to the surface, remove them with a skimmer or slotted spoon, draining well.

Serve 3 or 4 ravioli per person, sprinkled with the cinnamon-sugar mixture. Serve cold or warm (not hot).

9. Cheese Gnocchi

If you want some gnocchi, take some fresh cheese and mash it, then take some flour and mix with egg yolks as in making *migliacci*. Put a pot full of water on the fire and, when it begins to boil, put the mixture on a dish and drop it into the pot with a ladle. And when they are cooked, place them on dishes and sprinkle with plenty of grated cheese. (Gu 33)

Nowadays the word "gnocchi" generally means either boiled balls of dough made of flour, mashed potatoes (or even pumpkin) and eggs, or discs of cooked semolina browned in the oven. Nothing like either of these things seems to have existed in the Middle Ages, which is hardly surprising given that the potato did not arrive from the Americas until centuries later. These gnocchi are miniature dumplings made of flour, fresh cheese, and egg yolks and are cooked in boiling water. The gnocchi in another Italian source are made of flour, bread, and eggs.

But you won't be any the worse for sticking with these gnocchi, even for nonmedieval meals: they are easy to make, light, and tasty. Try them with a rich rabbit stew, or indeed as an accompaniment to some of our meat-based medieval *potages*.

The text from which we took these gnocchi was edited in 1887 by Olindo Guerrini. In the nineteenth century, it was a custom for scholarly Italians to edit a short text as a wedding gift, preferably a literary or historical curiosity. Weddings thus gave serious gentlemen the right to contemplate workaday matters. At a time when history had room only for politicians and soldiers, cookery could be nothing more than a curiosity. Guerrini presented his edition of this culinary treatise to his friend and fellow professor at the University of Bologna, Giosuè Carducci—who was also a poet and a future Nobel Prize winner (in 1906)—on the occasion of the wedding of his daughter Laura.

This text is contained in a codex in the library of the University of Bologna, where it precedes the treatise edited by Francesco Zambrini (Za). They are at the end of the volume, which, contrary to tradition for such manuscripts, contains only literary and spiritual texts. Like the other text, Laura Carducci's gift book was written in Tuscan, although the editor modified the spelling. It is one of the collections written for twelve servings, like the texts edited by S. Morpurgo (Mo) and L. Frati (Fr) and like the unpublished manuscript in the Bibliothèque de Cessole, Nice (Ni).

1¼ **pounds cream cheese** (600 g)
1½ **cups flour** (200 g)
6 **egg yolks**
6 **to 8 tablespoons freshly grated parmesan cheese**
salt

Mash the cream cheese into a creamy paste; if it is too stiff, force it through a sieve. With your hand, mix in the flour. Add salt to taste and blend in the egg yolks, one by one. Continue kneading to form a smooth mixture, neither too firm nor too soft.

Bring a large pot of salted water to the boil and lower the heat to a simmer. Put the cheese mixture on a plate, and drop half-teaspoonfuls of the mixture into the simmering water. It is quicker for two people to do this simultaneously.

Cook for a few minutes, until the gnocchi rise to the surface of the water. Drain and turn into a heated serving dish. Sprinkle generously with grated parmesan and serve immediately.

10. Extemporaneous Soup

Bare-Bones Soup. Take some parsley and fry it in butter, then add boiling water and bring to the boil. Salt, and put your slices of bread [in the plates] as for pea broth. For meat days, take some meat broth and have ready some bread soaked in the lean portion of this meat broth, then mash it and [add] six eggs. Strain and mix with broth in a pan with spices, verjuice, vinegar, and saffron. Remove when it comes to the boil, and serve in soup plates. (MP 145–46)

Water, a little parsley, a lump of butter, a few slices of bread, a couple of eggs, a drop of vinegar, and some spices: this excellent soup has a mild sourness that will remind you of sorrel soup. In keeping with its name (which implies both minimal ingredients and a certain suddenness), extemporaneous soup can be prepared on short notice. Indeed, we suggest the simplest version, using water, but enhanced with a final treatment usually reserved for meat broths. In hostelry kitchens, there was always a supply of this precious liquid to put together a soup, even for unexpected guests.

𝔖oak the bread in water. When it has softened, squeeze it out and mash it with a pestle or a fork. Beat the eggs and mix into the bread. Press the mixture through a coarse sieve or puree in a food processor and stir in the spices, vinegar, and verjuice.

Melt the butter in a saucepan over medium heat and gently sauté the parsley. Add one cup of water per person and bring to the boil. Add the bread mixture, return to the boil and cook briefly. Add salt to taste and serve.

Per portion

2 tablespoons finely chopped parsley
2 tablespoons butter (25 g)
½ slice country bread
1 egg
½ teaspoon wine vinegar
½ teaspoon verjuice or the juice of half a lemon
a pinch of ground ginger
a pinch of freshly grated nutmeg
a pinch of ground cloves
salt

11. Almond-Milk Soup

𝔄lmond milk.   Parboil and skin your almonds, then put them into cold water, then crush them and moisten with the water in which you have cooked your onions, and strain through a sieve: then fry the onions and put in a little salt, and boil on the fire, then add your sippets [of bread]. And if you are making almond milk for invalids, do not add any onions, and instead of moistening the almonds with the onion water as mentioned above, put them in and moisten them with plain warm water and bring to the boil, and do not add any salt, but plenty of sugar to the drink. (MP 241)

> This soup—whose "invalid" version omits the onions and is instead sweetened with sugar—is most delicate. There is a perfect marriage between the subtle flavor of the almonds and that of the onion-cooking water. Nearly all medieval cooking treatises include a chapter on preparations for invalids. They suggest food without strong spices, light foods such as almond milk, or health-giving dishes such as a restorative chicken broth—a true poultry elixir. In this recipe, the sugar is used for its medicinal powers; it was a rare and costly ingredient and, like spices, was imported and sold by apothecaries.

𝔅ring the water to the boil; meanwhile, peel and rinse the onions. Add them to the boiling water and simmer for 20 minutes. Remove with a skimmer and set aside both the onions and the cooking water.

Meanwhile, parboil the almonds for 10 seconds; drain them, put them into cold water to cool, and pinch each nut between thumb and forefinger to remove the brown skin. Dry the nuts and grind them in a food

1⅓ cups almonds (shelled but not blanched) (200 g)
10 ounces onions (3 medium onions) (300 g)
2 quarts water, approximately (2 liters)
2 or 3 thin slices country bread
2 tablespoons butter (25 g)
salt

processor. Gradually add 6 cups (1½ liters) of the water in which the onions were cooked; if less than 6 cups remains, make up the difference with plain hot water. Continue processing until you have a uniform, white liquid. Strain this through a cotton cloth or a very fine sieve into a pan, squeezing to obtain as much almond milk as possible.

Chop the boiled onions and sauté them in the butter until golden. Add salt to taste.

Bring the almond milk to the boil and remove from the heat. Stir in the onions and pour into a tureen over the slices of bread.

PORÉES/PORRATE AND VEGETABLES

Porées (*Porrate* in Italian sources) were made from "leaves"—*feuilles*—as green vegetables were called: chard, spinach, watercress, leeks, and so forth. They were a classic of medieval French cooking. One of the cook's major concerns was to give them (or to preserve) a given color: green, black, or white. Since we do not have measurements for the liquids that were added to these recipes, we do not know the exact consistency of these preparations. Were they clear, like the herb soup in recipe 2, or quite thick, like hashed vegetables? In any case, they were served in the deep plates known as *écuelles,* and were eaten with a spoon. As we shall see in these recipes, their density could vary quite a bit.

12. White *Porée*

White *porée* is so called because it is made with the white of leeks [served] with pork loin, andouille, or ham on meat days in autumn and winter. And note that no fat other than that of hog is suitable for this.

First, pick through, wash, slice, and *éverder* [see recipe 14 for an explanation] the leeks if they are young, i.e., in summer; in winter, when they are older and tougher, it is better to boil them than to *éverder* them. And if it is a time of abstinence, after having prepared them as indicated, you must put them in a pot with hot water and cook them; also cook sliced onions, fry them, and then fry the leeks with them; then cook everything in a pot with milk, whether it is a meat day or a day of abstinence; but if it is Lent, substitute almond milk. And if it is a meat day, when the summer leeks have been *éverdés* or the winter leeks boiled as indicated above, put them to cook in a pot together with the water from salt meat or with pork and pork fat.

Note: Sometimes a bread liaison is made for the leeks. (MP 139–40)

> This recipe shows clearly how the seasons and the days of the year were differentiated for culinary purposes. The broad distinction between meat days and "fish days"—the days of the week when meat would be replaced by fish—is overshadowed by the season of Lent, when all products of animal origin were forbidden. An interesting gradation can be seen: meat broth and cow's milk for meat days, cow's milk alone for days of abstinence, and only almond milk for fast days and during Lent.

In our interpretation of this recipe, we will imagine that it is winter, and that we must therefore cook with "older and tougher" leeks.

Slice and carefully wash the leeks, white part only. Cook in boiling salted water for a few minutes. Drain and reserve.

Peel and slice the onions. Sauté over low to medium heat in 2 tablespoons oil until they are very tender but not browned.

Meanwhile, soak the bread in 2 cups of warm milk.

Place the remaining milk in a saucepan and add the leeks and the onions.

4½	pounds medium leeks (2 kg)
6	cups milk (1½ liters)
3	medium onions
3½	ounces dry country bread, crusts removed, about 2 large slices (100 g)
2	tablespoons oil
	salt

Mash the bread with a fork, and press through a sieve. Add this panade to the saucepan. Cook over low heat for 20 minutes or half an hour, until the mixture is nice and thick.

Add salt to taste. Thin with a little more milk if the *porée* is too thick.

Serve like a soup.

13. White *Porrata* with Almond Milk

White *porrata.* If you want to make a white *porrata* for twelve persons, take two *libre* of almonds and an *oncia* of good, well-pounded ginger; take four bunches of leeks and put them to boil, and when they are properly cooked, especially the white parts, remove them from the water and chop them. Then take the almonds, thoroughly washed and thoroughly skinned, and mixed with a little water and well strained; put them to boil with the leek and cook it well, and add some of that ginger. This dish must be white and quite thick. Sprinkle the servings with spices. (Mo 21)

This text is from a treatise in Italian-Tuscan, from which 57 recipes survive as part of a composite manuscript in the Biblioteca Riccardiana in Florence; these were edited by Salomone Morpurgo in 1890. This treatise is among the collections mentioned in the introduction whose recipes are formulated for twelve portions. It is of special interest because it provides more detailed instructions than the others and sets out to be specific about the proportions of the various ingredients.

1½ pounds leeks (700 g)
 2 cups almonds (300 g)
 2 tablespoons ground ginger
     (12 g)
     salt

For the spice mixture
¼ teaspoon ground cardamom
¼ teaspoon freshly grated nutmeg
¼ teaspoon ground cinnamon
 1 pinch ground cloves

Cook the leeks (white part only) in boiling salted water; drain and put through a food mill or puree in a food processor. Blanch the almonds by placing them in boiling water for a minute; drain and remove the skins. Dry the almonds, then grind to a powder in a blender, in batches if necessary. Mix the almonds with enough warm water to yield a thick liquid. Strain into the leeks, pressing to extract as much liquid as possible. Add the ginger and simmer until the *porrata* is thick.

Serve hot as a vegetable side dish, sprinkled with the spice mixture.

14. Green *Porée* with Swiss Chard

Chard *porée.* A *porée* of chard that is washed then cut up and boiled will stay greener than one that is first boiled then chopped. But it will stay even greener if it is trimmed, washed, cut up, and soaked in two changes of cold water, then, after drying it by handfuls, put into the pot to boil with broth, fat pork, and mutton broth; when it has cooked a little and you wish to serve it, top it with trimmed, washed, and chopped parsley and a little young fennel; bring to the boil only once. (MP 141)

> The point of this process is to retain the green color of the dish. But how are we to interpret the recipe if we take the verb *esverder* to mean "boil," as writers often do? Here, in fact, the chard is to be *éverdée* in cold water, not in boiling water as is more common. Hence, we should understand this word in its literal sense of "removing the greenness," or whatever is bitter or underripe, no matter whether it is soaking or boiling that is used to achieve this. And in fact, if you chop the uncooked chard and soak it as the recipe directs, the soaking water will turn green, as though you had indeed "removed the greenness" from the chard. We cannot claim that this procedure really helps the chard retain its color when it is cooked, but when we tried it our *porée* certainly was a magnificent green.

Trim the chard of its fleshy white stalks. Wash the leaves thoroughly and cut them into fine strips. Soak in cold water; rinse in a change of water and drain. Dry carefully.

Meanwhile, put the pork and broth into a pot and bring to the boil. You could also add a few lamb bones if your butcher can spare them. When this reaches the boil, add the chard and cook for about 15 minutes. Remove from the heat, add the parsley and fennel, check for salt, and serve hot.

3¾ pounds Swiss chard leaves (or young, fine-stemmed chard) (1.7 kg)

7 ounces salt pork belly or blanched pancetta, cut into matchstick pieces (200 g)

2 tablespoons minced parsley

1 tablespoon minced fennel

4 cups meat broth (1 liter)

salt

15. Green *Porée* for Days of Abstinence

Green *porée* for fish days.   Trim, cut up, and wash it in cold water without cooking it; then cook it in verjuice and a little water, adding salt. It must be served boiling hot and good and thick. And at the bottom of the bowl, under the *porée,* put some salted or fresh butter, or cheese or curd[?], or aged verjuice. (MP 142)

> This is the same *porée* as recipe 14, but thicker and without the meat broth or pork: for those with delicate systems!

3¼ pounds Swiss chard leaves
     (1.5 kg)
⅔   cup verjuice (20 cl) or ⅓ cup
     cider vinegar (10 cl) mixed with
     ⅓ cup water (10 cl)
⅔   cup water (20 cl)
2   to 6 tablespoons butter
     salt

Wash the chard, then cut into fine strips. Soak in two changes of cold water. Add the verjuice (or vinegar) and water to a pan, add salt, and bring to the boil. Cook the chard over low heat for 20 to 30 minutes. When completely cooked, drain thoroughly.

Put the chard into a warmed serving bowl; stir in anywhere from 2 to 6 tablespoons butter, until the dish seems nice and creamy. Check for salt and serve.

16. Watercress *Porée*

Lenten watercress *porée* with almond milk. Take your watercress and cook it in boiling water with a handful of chopped Swiss chard. Then fry it in oil and boil it with almond milk. On meat days, fry it in pork fat and butter until cooked, then moisten with meat broth; or [serve with] cheese and serve immediately, for it will burn. But if you add parsley, it does not need to be *éverdé*. (MP 140)

We offer two variations for this watercress *porée*, one Lenten version, which we interpret as a soup, and the other for normal days, which we give as a vegetable dish with fresh cheese.

A. *As a soup for Lent*

4   or 5 bunches watercress
     a good handful Swiss chard
     leaves
1   quart almond milk (1 liter)
     (recipe 151)
1   tablespoon oil
     salt

Trim and wash the watercress and chard. Chop the chard. Cook all the greens in boiling salted water for about 8 minutes. Drain and thoroughly dry. In a saucepan or casserole, sauté the greens in a tablespoon of oil, then add the almond milk. Bring to the boil and simmer for a few minutes. Check for seasoning and serve.

B. *As a vegetable dish*

4   or 5 bunches watercress
     a good handful Swiss chard
     leaves
2   tablespoons butter
½   cup *fromage blanc* or farmer's
     cheese (100 g)
     salt

Prepare and cook the vegetables as in version A. When they are dry, sauté them in butter, then add the cheese. Mix well and cook over very low heat for a few minutes. Check for salt and serve.

17. Black *Porée*

Black *porée* is one made with thin slices of salt pork; that is, the *porée* is trimmed, washed, cut up, and boiled, then fried in the fat of pieces of salt pork; it is then moistened with boiling water . . . ; you should place two pieces of pork upon each bowl. (MP 142)

> We have had the white of almond milk; now, the "black" resulting from frying in pork fat.

Wash the chard, then cut into fine strips. Add the chard to a large pot of boiling salted water; when the water returns to the boil drain the chard and dry it well.

    Meanwhile, cut the pork into small matchstick pieces and put it into a heavy-bottomed saucepan or casserole over medium-low heat; cook gently to render the fat, but do not let the pork brown. Add the thoroughly dried chard to the pork and cook, uncovered, for 15 to 20 minutes, stirring occasionally. Add the water, bring to the boil, and simmer for 10 minutes. Check for salt, and serve.

3¼ **pounds Swiss chard leaves** (1.5 kg)

7 **ounces very fatty salt pork belly** (200 g)

4 **cups water** (1 liter)

salt

18. *Tredura* (Hashed Leeks)

Tredura. To make *tredura*, take whites of leek and boil them, whole, then chop them well with a knife; then fry them with the fat of meat you have cooked; take bread and grate it, and soak it in hot water; take a piece of meat, and chop the bread and the meat with a knife; then take beaten eggs and plenty of saffron, beat together, and pour over the fried leeks with plenty of spices; and it will be good. (Fr 62)

> This recipe is from a lovely little cookbook written in the fifteenth century in a dialect belonging to northeastern Italy—the Veneto (edited by Ludovico Frati in 1899). But the recipes are neither typical of nor exclusively from that region. As we've said, food traveled! We note that the dish known as *tredura* or *tridura* was part of the Florentine tradition. At Florence, the Tosinghi, Visdomini, Aliotti, and Ughi families were guardians of the cathedral, and the bishop had the obligation to make them a ritual offering on high holy days, around Christmas and Easter, and on Saint John's day, June 24 (John the Baptist was the patron saint of the city). In a manuscript in the Archivio Arcivescovile at Florence, the notary Ser Lorenzo Tani describes the Saint John's Day ceremonies for 1356:
>
> > We took planks of planed pine with two handles at each side, and we placed upon them these foods, to wit: first, as a boiled dish, upon each platter a piece of salted pork of four *libre* and a plate of *tridura*. And as a roast, upon each platter a roasted shoulder of mutton. All the platters and plates were white

and new. Upon each plank we arranged a row of roasts and a row of boiled meat, with the *tridura*. At each end of the plank, we stationed a servant who took hold of the handles. And thus they marched one behind the other, and Ser Manno and I along with two domestics.

When we reached the door of the bishop's palace, there were Niccolò and Guccio degl'Ughi. To each of them we gave a platter of boiled meat and one of roast, and a plate of *tridura*. It is true that we did not give them either the platters or the plates, but they had their own platters and their own plates, and we tipped ours into theirs and kept our own. Then, Ser Manno went off with some of those planks and, with one of the domestics, he went by way of the Via di Neta and Piazza San Giovanni. And from San Michele he entered the courtyard of the Visdomini; he halted upon the benches in the loggia and called out by name to summon the Visdomini (those who had to pledge an oath of loyalty to the bishop)—who came in person and who sent a servant or domestic. To each he gave a platter of boiled meat and one of roast and a plate of *tridura*, keeping for himself the platters and plates, as stated above. After this disbursement, he went to the Aliotti and did the same.

I went with another domestic and with other planks . . . and I did the same (at the homes of the Ughi and the Tosinghi). (Benefitiali di Ser Lorenzo Tani, fo. 70v–71v)

By custom there were similar offerings on the two days following Christmas, Holy Thursday, and Easter Monday and Tuesday. The boiled meat was normally pork (fresh or salted) and the roast was of fresh pork, and there were also meat pies, except on Saint John's Day, when the bishop was obliged to provide only shoulders of mutton for the roast, as we have seen in Tani's description.

There also had to be a meatless version for Holy Thursday and for when December 26 or 27 fell on a Friday. The Holy Thursday offering would include a "platter of tenches weighing 18 *oncie* and an eel of 15 *oncie* made into a pie." On Fridays, eggs and dairy products were acceptable, and if December 26 fell on a Friday the bishop would offer "a half-cheese from Pisa weighing two *libre*, cooked, with *tridura* and a quarter of an egg-and-cheese *torta* containing fifty eggs" (Lami, *Sanctae Ecclesiae Florentinae monumenta*, III).

2¼ **pounds leeks (1 kg)**

7 **ounces salt pork belly or pancetta (200 g)**

  scant 4 ounces dry country bread, about 2 thick slices (100 g)

3 **eggs**

  good pinch saffron (about 15 threads)

  salt

Soak the bread in hot water. Trim and wash the leeks, then cook them in boiling water along with the pork. When the leeks are done, remove them and chop them with a knife; if necessary, continue cooking the pork until tender. Remove the fatty parts of the boiled pork, dice them and place them in a skillet over medium heat. When the fat has rendered, add the leeks and sauté until very lightly browned.

Squeeze the moisture out of the bread and mash it into a pulp. Dice the lean parts of the pork and add the bread, eggs and saffron. When ready to serve, add this mixture to the leeks and warm through without boiling; check for salt.

Sprinkle the serving platter or individual servings with some of the spice mixture to taste.

For the spice mixture

¼ teaspoon ground ginger

¼ teaspoon ground cinnamon

¼ teaspoon ground nutmeg

19. "Little Leaves" and Fennel

Of little leaves. Take spinach and chard; pick them over well and boil them. Then remove them and chop them very well with a knife; then take parsley, fennel, anise[?], onions, chop them and mash them with a knife, and fry them well in oil; take other "little herbs" and fry them all together, and add a little water and bring to the boil; add pepper and spices and serve.

In this way you can add beaten eggs, boneless fish flesh, meat of mutton or pork, or salted meat; vary it by the lights of a good cook. You can take marjoram, rosemary, parsley with good spices, with cloves. These herbs, finely pounded in a mortar, if chopped fish or meat is added, can be made into [sausages such as] *mortadelli* or *comandelli* and many other things; to make this, you can use cultivated plants, or wild ones if you cannot get garden plants.

The same dish with borage

Take borage, spinach, and chard, and other similar plants; put into cold water and boil, then discard the water; chop them thoroughly with a knife; put them back to cook in almond milk and, by putting in some chopped tench flesh, you can serve it to your master during Lent with spices and saffron, with sugar added.

As above

You can also take whole fennel, boiled and cooked with cinnamon, pepper, and saffron; add beaten eggs and chicken flesh or other meat, or what you will.

As above

You can also take aromatic "little herbs," boiled, chopped, cooked with breast of chicken, pounded in the mortar, and added to the greens. You can give them to your master and to invalids to loosen the bowels.

As above

Take white fennel, finely chopped, and then fry with a little finely chopped white of leek, with an egg or some pork fat; add a little water, saffron and salt, and put it to boil; if you like, add some beaten eggs.

As above

Take well-washed fennel and boil it; discard the water and fry with oil or pork fat and salt, and serve. (Za 3–6)

The point of this sequence is clearly to take advantage of the vegetables that are in season. In this sixteenth-century Tuscan book (edited by Francesco Zambrini), as in the similar Latin source (Lc, edited by Marianne Mulon), these recipes are found in the chapter that gives ways of cooking what we now call green vegetables (*herba* in the Latin source), such as cabbage, leeks, purslane, and lettuces, and dried legumes such as fava beans, lentils (see recipe 24), dried peas, and chickpeas. In recipes 20 and 21 below you will find ways to cook asparagus and mushrooms. For the cook this is not so much a question of culinary research as of adapting to what is in the market—or in the garden. This is an unassuming kind of cooking that is most characteristic of recipe collections associated with treatises dealing with agriculture or with health and diet. Moreover, the author notes the curative uses of herbs and leaves (such as those which "loosen the bowels"). *Le Régime du corps*, written in the thirteenth century (in French) by Aldobrandino da Siena, in its third part, on diet and health, entitled *Des simples choses qu'il convient à oume user* ("Simple things that anyone may use") includes a chapter devoted to "all manner of herbs." There we read that chard and spinach are suited to hot temperaments, are very nourishing and effect relaxation, while fennel is nutritionally worthless, but could have some curative value as a diuretic and against bladder stones.

We suggest two adaptations, but we encourage you to read the original text and create your own versions in accord with the season, your preferences, and your dietary requirements.

A. *Hashed chard and spinach with aromatic herbs*

1½ **pounds spinach** (700 g)
1½ **pounds Swiss chard** (700 g)
 1 **large onion**
    a bunch of mixed herbs: parsley, fennel leaves, coriander (cilantro), dill, marjoram, rosemary, basil, hyssop, or any other fresh herbs. Avoid tarragon and thyme; these were not found in medieval cooking, although they were grown in gardens.
 2 **tablespoons olive oil**
 1 **pinch freshly ground black pepper**
 1 **pinch ground cloves**
¼ **teaspoon freshly grated nutmeg salt**

Thoroughly wash the spinach and the chard; remove the stems. Cook the chard leaves and then the spinach in boiling salted water for about 10 minutes; drain thoroughly and chop with a knife.

Chop the onion together with all the herbs and sauté in the olive oil until the onion is translucent. Add ¾ cup of water, then the chopped greens, and finally the spices and salt to taste.

Mix well and cook gently for a few minutes. Serve hot or warm, either by itself or with eggs, meat or fish.

B. *Fennel and leeks with saffron*

Wash the fennel. Thinly slice the white bulbs (do not use the stems or leaves). Do the same with the leeks. Cut the pork into small pieces and cook in a casserole until it begins to brown. Add the fennel and leeks and stir. Add ¾ cup of water and some salt (only a little, because of the salt pork).

Cook, covered, over low heat for about 30 minutes, depending on how soft you like your vegetables. Meanwhile, beat an egg with the saffron and set aside to infuse. Just before serving, stir some of the hot juices from the vegetables into the egg and saffron mixture, then, off the heat, pour the egg mixture into the pan of vegetables and mix well. Serve hot or warm.

2¼ pounds fennel (1 kg)
generous 1 pound leeks (500 g)
2 ounces salt pork belly or blanched pancetta (50 g)
1 egg
1 pinch saffron (a dozen or so threads)
salt

20. Asparagus with Saffron

Of asparagus.   Take the asparagus and boil it; when it is cooked, put it to cook with oil, onions, salt, and saffron, and with ground spices, or without. (Za 8)

Our Tuscan-language treatise is the most diverse source of vegetable recipes (see recipe 19); indeed, it is the only one to mention asparagus, which are prepared in the simplest imaginable way—but what flavor! Barely tenderized in boiling water, then gently cooked in a drop of extra-virgin olive oil with a little green onion, saffron, nutmeg, and pepper, these asparagus are barely recognizable when you think of the waterlogged vegetable that we French always seem to be eating with mayonnaise.

Carefully peel the asparagus and break off the woody, fibrous ends of each spear. Wash, then cook in boiling salted water for about 10 minutes (or steam them). They should not become droopy, but should remain slightly crisp.

Heat the olive oil in a skillet and gently cook the onions until translucent but not browned. Add the asparagus and the saffron. Lower the heat, cover the skillet, and cook gently for about 7 minutes. Turn the asparagus, and season with salt, pepper, and a little nutmeg. Continue to cook, covered, over low heat for another 10 minutes or so. Serve when the asparagus is just turning golden.

2¼ pounds fairly large asparagus (1 kg)
2 tablespoons olive oil
2 green onions, sliced (these and asparagus appear more or less simultaneously, in springtime)
freshly grated nutmeg
a small pinch saffron (7 or 8 threads)
salt
freshly ground pepper

21. Sautéed Mushrooms with Spices

Mountain mushrooms. Take mountain mushroom and boil them; and discard the water; then fry them with finely sliced onion, or with white of leek, spices, and salt, and serve. (ZA 24)

> Here is another recipe from our Tuscan book. We do not know exactly what wild mushrooms it refers to. Try this dish with ordinary cultivated mushrooms if you can find nothing else; they will be transformed.

generous 1 pound wild or cultivated mushrooms (500 g)
1 small onion
olive oil
1 pinch freshly ground pepper
1 pinch ground ginger
1 pinch freshly grated nutmeg
2 pinches ground coriander seed
salt

Trim and clean the mushrooms; if they are large, cut them in half or into quarters. Cook in boiling water for about 10 minutes; drain thoroughly.

Meanwhile, finely chop the onion and sweat it in a little olive oil until very soft. Add the mushrooms, raise the heat to high and sauté for a minute. Season with salt and the spices, lower the heat, cover the pan, and simmer for about 15 minutes. From time to time, check on the mushrooms and give them a stir. Serve when golden brown.

22. Fresh Fava Beans with Herbs

Fresh fava beans with meat broth. Take the fava beans and skin them with hot water, as is done for almonds, then put them to boil in good broth. And when they seem cooked, add to them a little parsley and chopped mint, and boil them with some good salted meat. And this *menestra* should be slightly green to look nicest. And you can do the same with peas and any other fresh vegetable, but note that they should not be skinned with hot water like fava beans; rather, leave them as they are, with their thin skins. (Ma 149)

> It is a bit gloomy to shell fava beans all by yourself, but with help it can go quickly. This dish tastes of springtime and is absolutely delicious. Maestro Martino once again demonstrates his vast talent with fresh vegetables—a talent the Italians have not lost. Similar dishes are still eaten in season around Rome and Naples. Nowadays they often add a handful of pasta, and why not? You might try it yourself if you are interested.
>
> Freshly shelled peas are excellent for this preparation.

Shell the fava beans and plunge them into plenty of boiling water for 5 seconds or so. Drain them and refresh in cold water. Use a paring knife (or your fingernail) to pierce the tough skin of each bean, and slip the bean out. Cut the pork into tiny dice.

Add the broth, beans, and pork to a saucepan or casserole, bring to the boil, and cook for about 10 minutes: until the beans begin to break up, but before they turn to mush. Add the parsley and mint. Return to the boil and cook for a few moments. Add salt to taste and serve.

2   cups beef or chicken broth (½ liter) (recipe 152)
4½ pounds fresh fava beans (2 kg)
4   ounces salt pork belly or pancetta (100 g)
1   tablespoon finely chopped parsley
1   tablespoon chopped mint (chopped at the last minute)
    salt

23. Puree of Dried Young Fava Beans

Potage of young fava beans.   Put your skinned, well-cleaned and washed fava beans on the fire, and when they begin to boil remove the water from the pot, and replace it with cool water to cover the beans by two fingerbreadths; add salt to your taste, and boil your dish, tightly covered, at a distance from the flame, because of the smoke, until that dish is thoroughly cooked and forms a sort of paste. Then put it into a mortar, and stir and mix it well and make it homogeneous; then return it to the pot and heat it. And when you wish to dress your platters or plates, serve your food with the following preparation: First cook thinly sliced onions in hot oil, add sage, and figs or apples cut into little pieces. And put this preparation, boiling hot, into the platters or plates already containing the fava beans, and bring to the table; some like to sprinkle spices over the top. (VT XV 206)

> This is an eye-opener: a delicious puree of fava beans with smothered apples and onions redolent of sage. Even as part of a modern meal—served with roast pork or duck—it will win gastronomic victories. It is especially good with the small yellow skinless fava beans (*féveroles* in French) you can sometimes find in Middle Eastern groceries and fancy food stores. *Le Ménagier de Paris* too includes several recipes for fava beans, which were eaten both fresh and dried; the author even points out that if you want to lend the flavor of fresh beans to a puree of dried favas you had only to cook it with a handful of young shoots of fava plants, which you were to sow monthly in order to have the shoots always available. From this we can gauge the importance of these beans in the medieval diet. Our puree would have been made with dried fava beans that had already been skinned (*fèves frasées* or *fèves frésées*); these were processed by boiling them just until their skin wrinkled, when it could be removed. This was done around Easter time.

1   **pound very small dried fava beans** (500 g)
1   **pound tart apples** (500 g)
4   **medium onions**
3   **tablespoons olive oil** (5 cl)
4   **or 5 leaves fresh sage** (optional)
    salt

A day in advance, wash the beans and leave them to soak in cool water; change the water once or twice if possible.

The next day, drain the beans and put them in a pot or casserole and add cold water to cover. Bring to the boil and drain. Return to the pot and cover with plenty of unsalted boiling water. Cook until the beans are very tender. Drain, and put through a food mill or puree in a food processor until smooth; add salt to taste.

Peel the onions and slice them into rounds. Peel and core the apples, and cut them into thin slices. Heat the oil in a skillet and sauté the onions over low heat. When they are half done, add the apples and the sage and continue to cook over low heat until the apples have fallen apart, 15 to 20 minutes or so.

When ready to serve, reheat the bean puree. Turn it onto a serving platter, and spoon the onion-apple mixture into the center.

24. Lentil Puree

Lentils another way.   Take some lentils, well washed and free of stones, and cook them with aromatic herbs, oil, salt, and saffron. And when they are cooked, mash them well; and put on top beaten eggs, cut-up dry cheese; and serve. (ZA 22–23)

This recipe, taken from our Tuscan-language treatise, is representative of a group of preparations for legumes—chickpeas, peas, fava beans, and *fasoles* (*faxoli, fasoli*, etc., in Italian: an Old World bean native to Africa and similar to the black-eyed pea)—using a liaison of beaten eggs and, generally, cheese. This, however, was a choice way to finish the dish: dried legumes could also be cooked more simply, with salt meat, aromatic vegetables, and herbs, or oil, as indicated in many recipes in this collection.

1   **pound green lentils (preferably the small Umbrian or French variety)** (500 g)
1   ***bouquet garni:*** **a selection of parsley, sage, rosemary, thyme, basil, etc.**
3   **tablespoons good olive oil**
1   **pinch saffron** (5 or 6 threads)
6   **tablespoons freshly grated parmesan cheese**
4   **eggs, beaten**
    salt

Over low heat, cook the lentils in 4 times their volume of water with the oil, saffron, and *bouquet garni*. Add salt when the lentils are done. If a great deal of water remains, drain the lentils. Put them through a food mill, crush them in a mortar, or puree in a food processor.

Mix the beaten eggs with the parmesan. Reheat the lentils, then remove from the heat. Add the egg mixture and mix well. The lentils will form a lovely, smooth, firm and very flavorful puree.

25. Pumpkin or Winter Squash Soup

To cook squashes, peel them as they should be, and then cook them with meat broth or water; add a little onion according to the quantity you want to make. And when they seem cooked, take them out and put them through a sieve or pound them very well; and cook them in a pot with rich broth and a little verjuice. And they should be slightly yellow with saffron; and when they are cooked, remove them from the fire and leave them a while to cool. Then take egg yolks according to the quantity and beat them with a little aged cheese, and add them to the squash, stirring constantly with the spoon so that they do not stick; dress your bowls, and top with sweet spices. (Ma 148)

> Another excellent recipe from Maestro Martino: a spiced pumpkin or winter squash soup flavored with onions and cheese and made creamy with an egg yolk liaison. Comparing it with similar dishes from French sources, we have to admit that it is vastly superior in refinement.

Peel and seed the pumpkin or squash, cut it into pieces, and cook it together with the onion in a quart (liter) of salted water until very tender. Drain and put through a food mill or puree in a food processor. Return to the pan, add the broth and verjuice or vinegar, and bring to the boil. Crumble the saffron between your fingers and add it to the pan.

Beat the egg yolks together with the parmesan. Remove the soup from the heat, then whisk in the egg yolk mixture. Reheat over very low heat; be sure not to let the soup boil again at this point.

Sprinkle with the spice mixture, and serve.

4½ **pounds pumpkin or winter squash** (2 kg)
1 **onion, sliced**
1¾ **cups broth** (40 cl)
2 **tablespoons verjuice, or 1 tablespoon cider vinegar mixed with 1 teaspoon water**
2 **tablespoons freshly grated parmesan cheese**
2 **egg yolks**
1 **small pinch saffron (4 or 5 threads)**
scant ½ teaspoon sweet spices (recipe 150, variation B)
salt

26. Roast Onion Salad

Of onion salad.   Take onions; cook them in the embers, then peel them and cut them across into longish, thin slices; add a little vinegar, salt, oil, and spices, and serve. (Za 90)

> This recipe appears at the very end of our Tuscan collection, after the recipes for invalids. It is clearly written in the hand of someone other than the scribe of the rest of the text. We searched in vain for this recipe in other cookbooks of the period, but it did not appear even in Maestro Martino. But a century later Bartolomeo Sacchi, known as il Platina, the illustrious librarian to Pope Sixtus IV and a learned epicure, would include it in his survey of gastronomy

and nutrition, aptly entitled *De Honesta Voluptate et Valetudine (On Honest Indulgence and Good Health)*. However, he replaced the vinegar with boiled wine.

Nonetheless, this unusual salad is succulent, especially if served just luke-warm. It provides an alternative to baked potatoes for fireplace cooking. This rustic salad is still served in certain parts of Spain and Italy, where they really know their onions.

2   **pounds medium red or other sweet onions, about 6 onions (800 g)**
    olive oil
    wine vinegar
    scant ½ teaspoon fine spices (recipe 150, variation A)
    salt
    pepper

If your fireplace is ablaze, roast the on-ions in the embers until they are very tender; if not, roast them in a 500-degree (250 degrees C) oven for about an hour in-dividually wrapped in aluminum foil.

Remove the onions from the oven, un-wrap them, and let them cool a while. The skins should be blackened and caramel-ized. When they are cool enough not to burn you, peel the onions and cut them into thin slices with a very sharp knife.

Put the onions into a salad bowl. Season with salt, pepper, and the spice mixture. Add a little olive oil and vinegar to taste. Mix and serve.

MEATS COOKED IN SAUCE
27. *Le Ménagier's* Civet of Hare

Civet of hare. First, split the hare through the breast. And if it is freshly caught, say one or two days, do not wash it, but brown it on the grill, that is, sear it over a good charcoal fire, or on a spit; then take cooked onions and lard and brown them in the lard with the pieces of hare, stirring the pot often, or fry it in a skillet. Then grill and char some bread and soak it in broth with vinegar and wine; and, having ground some ginger, grains of paradise, cloves, long pepper, nutmeg, and cinnamon, mix them with some verjuice and vinegar or meat broth, and set aside; then mash your bread and mix it with some broth, and put the bread, but not the spices, through a sieve; mix the broth, the onions and the lard, the spices, and the charred bread, and cook it all together, with the hare as well; take care that the civet be brown, sharp with vinegar, and moderately seasoned with salt and spices.

Civet of coneys, as above. (MP 169)

This is a fine recipe for civet of hare, which can also be made with a "coney": a rabbit, preferably wild. The dish is special for the perfect consistency of its bread-thickened sauce, and for its spiced, sharp taste. It will be popular with lovers of acidic, spicy flavors. Top-quality wine vinegar is a must.

reheat the broiler. Broil or toast the bread, break it up, put it into a bowl, and soak it in ⅓ cup each of vinegar, red wine, and broth. Arrange the pieces of hare or rabbit in an ovenproof dish and put under the broiler just to brown; turn and brown the other side.

Chop the onions. Over medium heat, melt the lard in a casserole and sauté the onions until lightly browned. Add the hare or rabbit and continue to brown for a minute or two.

Meanwhile, grind the grains of paradise, mix with the other spices, and blend with the verjuice (or lemon juice mixture) and the remaining vinegar (about 3 tablespoons).

Mash the soaked bread with a fork and add the remaining broth to the bowl; combine well. With a spoon or rubber spatula, press the bread mixture through a sieve to form a smooth paste, or panade.

Add the panade and the spice mixture to the hare, season with salt and cover the casserole. Cook over low heat for 90 minutes to 2 hours for a wild hare, or for 45 minutes to 1 hour for a domestic rabbit. If you find the sauce thickening too quickly, add a little hot broth.

Serve when the hare or rabbit is meltingly tender and the sauce thick enough to coat the meat.

1 **hare (or 1 rabbit), about 3½ pounds, cut into serving pieces (1.5 to 1.7 kg)**
3 **medium-small onions**
1 **tablespoon lard**
2 **slices country bread**
2 **cups meat broth (½ liter) (recipe 152)**
10 **tablespoons (5 fl. ounces) good-quality red wine vinegar (15 cl)**
⅓ **cup good red wine (10 cl)**
3 **tablespoons verjuice (5 cl), or the juice of half a lemon plus 2 teaspoons water**
1 **teaspoon ground ginger**
½ **teaspoon grains of paradise**
½ **teaspoon ground cinnamon**
1 **pinch ground cloves**
¼ **teaspoon freshly grated nutmeg**
¼ **teaspoon freshly ground black pepper**
salt

28. Civet of Hare or Rabbit

Civet of hare or other meat. Cut up the entire hare and, after washing it a little, cook it in water; then take the cooked liver and lungs and pound them well in a mortar, and when the hare is cooked, take spices, pepper, and onion and fry them in pork fat with the lung and grilled bread; and when all these things have been boiled together, bring to the table. Note that, when the liver and lungs are cooked, you must cut them up and pound them in a mortar with spices and grilled bread, and thin them with good wine and a little vinegar. And when the hare is cooked and fried with the onions, pour that sauce over the hare and let it cool until lukewarm, and serve. The same can be done with partridges, i.e., *starne* [another word for partridges]. (Za 43)

A reading of this text would suggest that it conflates two versions of the recipe.

According to its title, the recipe we adapt here was devised for "hare or other meat," while the body of the text says that it is suitable for partridges. It would be only reasonable for a cook to find it too roundabout to rewrite a text in order to explain it. But in later culinary writings it became common to sketch the general sense of a recipe before setting out the precise method. The *Liber de coquina,* which is related to the Tuscan volume from which this recipe is taken, gives a rather different method for a civet of hare or rabbit. If you have no hare, a nice rabbit will do.

It is surprising to be instructed to boil the rabbit first, but you will soon see that this diminishes neither its flavor nor its tenderness.

1 **large hare or rabbit, about 5½ pounds** (2.5 kg)
generous 8 ounces salt pork belly or pancetta (250 g)
4 **medium-large onions**
2 **slices country bread**
1¼ **cups light-bodied red wine** (30 cl)
3 **tablespoons wine vinegar** (5 cl)

For the spice mixture
¼ **teaspoon freshly ground black pepper**
¼ **teaspoon ground ginger**
1 **pinch ground cloves**
salt

Cut the hare or rabbit into serving pieces. Rinse it, and simmer it (including the liver and lungs) in salted water for about 30 minutes (longer for a hare), or until tender. Drain the meat, pat it dry, and reserve.

Cut the pork into ⅛-inch dice. Grill or toast the bread.

In a meat grinder or food processor, finely chop the cooked liver and lungs, and the toasted bread. Whisk in the spice mixture, the wine, and the vinegar. Place this mixture into a small, heavy saucepan and bring to the boil; simmer, stirring frequently, until thickened to a good sauce-like consistency.

Slice the onions. In a skillet, heat the salt pork until it begins to render its fat. Add the onions and the pieces of hare or rabbit and sauté until nicely browned. Add the sauce, bring to the boil, and simmer for half a minute. Serve lukewarm.

29. Sweet-and-Sour Civet of Venison

To make a game-meat civet, first cook the meat in water mixed with an equal amount of vinegar, and when it is cooked take it out of the broth so it can dry. When it is dry, fry it in good pork fat; and if you want to make two plates of this civet, take a *libra* of raisins and half a *libra* of almonds without skinning them and crush these things well. Then take a *libra* of bread cut into slices and dried at the fire, but not too burnt, put it to soak in a little red wine, and mash it with those things, then thin it with broth from the meat, and put it through a sieve into a pot, and put it over the embers, far from the fire, and let it boil well for a half hour; then add plenty of ginger and cinnamon so that it be mild or strong according to the collective taste, or to the taste of your master. Then take an onion and cook it in a pot and mash it well; mix it with the pork fat in which it was cooked and add it all to the pot containing the aforementioned things, letting it boil a little longer; then serve out that meat, and over it put some of this civet, and send it to table. (Ma 122)

> From this recipe we learn that the cook in service had to adjust the flavor of his dishes to his master's taste, and this civet would incline more toward the mild or toward the sour depending on the preferences of the lord of the domain. So you too can adjust the quantity of spices to your mood or your appetite. The amounts in our adaptation are a minimum that you can go far beyond.

Simmer the meat for 1½ to 2 hours in the vinegar mixed with 6 cups of water and seasoned with salt. The meat should be tender but not overcooked. Remove the meat and keep warm.

Meanwhile, crumble the bread and soak it in the wine. Chop the raisins and almonds in a food processor until they form a fairly smooth paste. Mash the soaked bread to a paste and add it to the food processor with the raisin mixture, then add 3 cups (¾ liter) of the meat cooking liquid. Press this mixture through a sieve or put it through the fine blade of a food mill into a saucepan, add the spices and bring slowly to the boil over low heat. Simmer for 30 minutes or until the sauce is smooth and thickened. Peel and slice the onion. Cut the pork into small strips; sauté a quarter of the pork in a skillet until the fat begins to render, then add the onion and cook over low heat until the onion is tender and translucent, but not browned. Pick the strips of pork out of the pan with a fork or a pair of tongs and add them to the sauce. Puree the cooked onions in a food processor and add them to the sauce as well. Simmer for a minute or two longer.

4½	pounds venison—a braising cut such as shoulder or neck (2 kg)
7	ounces unsalted pork fatback (200 g)
⅞	cup raisins (150 g)
½	cup unblanched almonds (75 g)
5	ounces country bread, lightly grilled or toasted (150 g)
6	cups good red wine vinegar (1½ liters)
1¼	cups red wine (30 cl)
1	teaspoon ground ginger
1	teaspoon ground cinnamon
1	medium-small onion
	salt

Render the remaining pork strips, add the venison, and brown it on all sides. Drain well and arrange on a serving platter. Check the sauce for seasoning. Add more spices if their flavor is not marked enough; the quantities given are on the scanty side.

Coat the meat with the sauce, and serve immediately.

30. Chicken *Ambrogino* with Dried Fruit

If you want to make a chicken *ambrogino,* take the chickens, cut them up, then put them to fry with fresh pork fat and a bit of onion, cut crosswise. When this is half cooked, take some almond milk, mix it with broth and a little wine, and add it to the chickens, first skimming off the fat if there is too much; add cinnamon cut up with a knife and a few cloves. When it is dished up, add some prunes, whole dates, a few chopped nutmegs, and a little crumb of grilled bread, well pounded and mixed with wine and vinegar. This dish should be sweet and sour; and be sure that the dates do not burst open. (Gu 20)

Could the name of this dish—*ambrosino* or *ambrogino* depending on the source—have anything to do with ambrosia, the food of the gods? There is indeed something divine about this complex recipe whose sweet, sour, spiced flavors and whose juxtaposition of two separate sauces generate rich harmonies on the tongue. The name appears on the menu of a feast given at Siena on Tuesday, December 23, 1326. It began with *ravioli bianchi*, boiled veal, and venison, after which the 90 guests were served *pollastri ad ambrosina aschibeci*, followed by roast capon and candied pears with *treggea* (sugared almonds) (*Cronache Senesi*, p. 445). The list is certainly impressive, but it was to celebrate the knighting of Francesco Bandinelli, a young man from one of the most eminent families of Siena—and this was but one of four banquets held during the week leading up to the celebration itself. The wording links the *Ambrogino* to the class of dishes known as *escabèches*, which is not surprising as it contains more than one of the traditional ingredients of these dishes: wine and onions (see recipes 61 and 62).

1 **chicken, 3½ to 4 pounds**
3 **ounces fresh pork fatback**
   (80 g)
2 **medium-large onions**
8 **prunes**
10 **dates**
2 **slices country bread**
   generous ¾ cup dry white wine
   (20 cl)
3 **tablespoons wine vinegar** (5 cl)
   scant ½ cup chicken broth
   (10 cl) (recipe 152)
   a 1-inch piece cinnamon stick,
   coarsely broken up with a
   heavy knife
3 **cloves**
1 **pinch freshly grated nutmeg**
   almond milk made from ⅓ cup
   almonds (50 g) and 2 cups
   warm water (½ liter) (see
   recipe 151)
   salt

Toast or grill the bread; remove and discard the crusts.

Cut the chicken into serving pieces and slice the onions; pat the chicken dry. Cut the fat into ⅛-inch cubes. Over medium heat, render the fat in a large skillet, then add the chicken and onions and cook until lightly browned.

Mix the almond milk with the broth and half of the wine. When the chicken is lightly browned, season it with salt to taste and add the almond milk mixture, the cinnamon, and the cloves, and simmer for about 30 minutes.

Pit the prunes and the dates. Break up the bread and mix it with the vinegar and the remaining wine. When the chicken is nearly done, add the prunes, dates, bread mixture, and nutmeg to a small saucepan. Cook over low heat, ensuring that the prunes and dates remain whole. When this sauce has thickened, salt to taste and remove the pan from the heat. Check both preparations for seasoning and flavor balance.

To serve, arrange the chicken on a serving platter, topped with the almond-milk sauce in which it cooked and surrounded by the prunes and dates from the second sauce. Pour the second sauce over the first.

31. Chicken with Fennel

Fenneled chicken.   Take the chickens, cut them up, fry them, and when they are fried add the quantity of water you prefer; then take "beards" of fennel, "beards" of parsley, and almonds that have not been skinned; and chop these things well, mix them with the liquid from the chickens, and boil everything, then pass through a sieve. Add it to the chickens, and add the best spices you can get. (Gu 45)

> This chicken recipe, with its tan and green sauce and its subtle flavor of fennel, is remarkable. It is another light dish that would not be out of place on the most inventive of modern menus.

Cut the chicken into serving pieces and pat dry. Melt the lard in a casserole over medium-high heat and brown the chicken. When it is golden brown, add the water and salt to taste. Lower the heat and simmer, covered, for 40 to 45 minutes or until tender.

Meanwhile, wash and thoroughly dry the herbs. Grind the almonds finely in a blender, then add the herbs and blend to a paste.

Remove the chicken from the casserole and keep it warm in a very low oven, covered loosely with aluminum foil.

1 free-range chicken
⅔ cup unblanched almonds (100 g)
a handful of fennel or dill leaves
a handful of parsley
2 cups water (½ liter)
scant ½ teaspoon fine spices (recipe 150, variation A)
2 tablespoons lard or oil
salt

Add the almond mixture to the casserole and reduce over medium heat until the sauce has thickened.

Arrange the chicken on a serving platter and strain the sauce over the chicken. Sprinkle with the spices to taste and serve.

32. Chicken with Verjuice

Gratonata of chickens. Cut up your chickens, fry them with pork fat and with onions; and while they are frying add a little water so that they cook nicely in the pan; and stir them often with a large spoon; add spices, saffron, and sour grape juice [verjuice], and boil; and for each chicken take four egg yolks, mix them with verjuice and boil this separately; and beat everything together in the pan, and boil everything together with the pieces of chicken; and when it boils remove it from the fire and eat it. (Za 69)

> This recipe will yield tender chicken coated in a mildly sour, golden sauce. It is worth searching for genuine verjuice (see Mail-order Sources) for its fruity, lightly acidic flavor and aroma. The verjuice and egg yolk mixture can be simmered briefly, and gives the sauce a wonderful, creamy consistency.

1 free-range chicken
1 medium-small onion
2 ounces fresh pork fatback
10 tablespoons (5 fl. ounces) water (15 cl)
10 tablespoons (5 fl. ounces) verjuice (15 cl), **or the juice of 1 lemon mixed with 3 tablespoons water**
4 egg yolks
½ teaspoon ground mace
½ teaspoon ground ginger
1 pinch cinnamon
1 pinch saffron threads
   freshly ground black pepper
   salt

Cut the chicken into serving pieces; pat dry and season with salt and pepper. Cut the onion into thin slices.

Cut the fat into ⅛-inch cubes and render over low heat in a heavy-bottomed casserole. Add the chicken and onion and brown on all sides; take care not to burn. Spoon excess fat, if any, out of the casserole, add the water, and bring to the boil. Then add one-third of the verjuice and the spices. Turn the heat to very low, cover the casserole, and simmer for 30 to 45 minutes, or until the chicken is done (check for doneness by piercing a thigh; the juices should run clear and the flesh should be tender).

When ready to serve, beat the remaining verjuice into the egg yolks in a small, heavy saucepan. Over low heat, bring just to the boil. The moment the verjuice mixture comes to the boil, add it to the casserole with the chicken, off the heat. Mix well and make sure the sauce has thickened. If not, heat the casserole over the lowest possible heat until the sauce thickens.

Check for seasoning and serve.

33. *Limonia,* or Chicken with Lemon

Limonia. To make *limonia,* fry chickens with fat and onions. And crush some skinned almonds, moisten with meat broth, and strain. Cook with the chickens and spices. If you have no almonds, thicken the broth with egg yolks. When the time to serve nears, add the juice of lemons, limes, or bitter oranges. (LC 402)

Recent studies indicate that the name of this recipe (*limonia* or *lomonia*, depending on the source) and the names of many others ending in *-ia* are certainly of Arabic origin (see also the next recipe). There is a connection here with the Arabic word *laymun*, the source of the Italian *limone* and the English "lemon."

Yet this recipe has been absorbed into the practices of the medieval European kitchen. While the use of almond milk may evoke the Arab world, this ingredient was commonly used in the western Mediterranean as well. The pork fat in which the chicken is browned, on the other hand, would not have appeared in the original recipe, as pork products are banned from Muslim kitchens.

Blanch the almonds and use the broth to prepare almond milk by the method explained in recipe 151. You will need about 1¼ cups (30 cl).

Cut the chicken into serving pieces and pat dry. Slice the onions.

Cut the fat into coarse dice and render in a casserole, then add the chicken and onions and brown on all sides over medium heat. Remove the chunks of unrendered fat. Salt the chicken to taste and sprinkle with spices.

Add the almond milk and bring to the boil. Lower the heat and simmer, covered, over low heat for 30 to 40 minutes. When the chicken is done, check for seasoning, then add the lemon juice. Return to the boil for a moment, then serve.

1 **free-range chicken**
1 **cup almonds** (150 g)
2 **cups meat broth** (½ liter) (recipe 152)
2 **medium-small onions**
2 **ounces fresh pork fatback** (60 g)
juice of 1 lemon
1 **teaspoon strong spice mixture** (recipe 150, variation C)
salt

The sauce will be quite liquid. If a thicker sauce is desired, use a little less almond milk.

34. *Romania,* or Chicken with Pomegranate Juice

Romania. To make *romania*, fry chickens with pork fat and onions, crush unskinned almonds, and moisten with the juice of sour pomegranates and sweet pomegranates. Then, strain and boil with the chickens, stirring with a spoon. Add spices.

You can also make a green *brodo* with herbs. (LC 402)

Like that of *limonia* (recipe 33), this recipe is probably of Arab-Persian origin, according to Maxime Rodinson, who observes (in a 1950 article entitled "Romania et autres mots arabes en italien") that the Arabic word for pomegranate is *rumman*. We note, however, as with *limonia*, that the use of pork fat is hardly orthodox for a Muslim dish.

While many recipes feature only the seeds of the pomegranate, for their visual beauty, here the juice is used as a principal ingredient. The pomegranate

(*Punica granatum*) originated in Persia and was known by the ancient Greeks and Romans. It was valued above all for its magnificent red flowers; in the Middle Ages its fruit inspired many painters and tapestry makers.

As the recipe suggests, both sour and sweet varieties were available. Sour pomegranates no longer come to market in the West; we have substituted a little lemon juice in this chicken dish, whose rosy color and gentle flavor will charm the eye as much as the palate.

1 **free-range chicken, about 3¼ pounds** (1.5 kg)
2 **fresh pomegranates**
1 **cup unblanched almonds** (150 g)
1 **medium-large onion**
2 **ounces fresh pork fatback** (50 g)
   juice of 1 lemon
½ **teaspoon strong spice mixture** (recipe 150, variation C)
   salt

Wash the almonds and dry them thoroughly. When they are completely dry, grind them to a powder in a blender. Remove from the blender jar and set aside (you need not wash the blender before the next step).

Cut the pomegranates in half and scoop out all their seeds into the blender jar. Puree the seeds and strain; this should yield 1¼ to 1½ cups of juice. Mix the juice and the ground almonds, and add the lemon juice. Press the mixture through a fine strainer; the result will be an almond milk made with pomegranate juice instead of water.

Cut the chicken into serving pieces and pat dry. Sprinkle with salt. Cut the fat into ⅛-inch dice and render it over low heat in a heavy-bottomed casserole.

Peel the onion and slice into thin rings. When the fat has rendered, brown the chicken and onion until evenly golden. If excess fat remains in the casserole, spoon most of it out before proceeding.

Add the almond-pomegranate juice and the spices. Bring to the boil, then turn the heat down as low as possible and simmer, covered, until the chicken is tender, 30 to 45 minutes.

Check for seasoning and serve.

35. *Brouet* of Capon

rouet of capons.   Cook your capons in water and wine; then cut them up and fry them in lard, then pound the meat of your capons and their livers, and almonds, and moisten with your broth and boil this; then take ginger, cinnamon, cloves, galangal, long pepper, and grains of paradise, and moisten with vinegar and bring to the boil; when serving, place meat in each bowl and pour the *potage* over. (MP 149)

We must take the word *brouet* in its broadest sense. Here we are not making soup, but cooking a dish of meat with sauce, using a most unusual technique, where the basic components are cooked independently: the capon goes through two successive cooking processes, and the accompanying sauce is made separately, using the broth in which the capon was simmered. The two elements come together only when the dish is served.

Capons—castrated, fattened roosters—are hard to come by and expensive, so we recommend using a good chicken, although nothing is stopping you from cooking your *brouet* with a real capon if you can find one.

Rinse the chicken inside and out, pull excess fat from the cavity, and place in a stainless steel or other nonreactive pot just large enough to hold it comfortably. Add the chicken liver, the 2 bottles of wine plus 2 cups (½ liter) of water, and a generous tablespoon of salt. Bring to the boil, carefully removing any scum that rises to the surface. Reduce the heat to very low and simmer for 30 to 45 minutes (possibly longer for a large capon) until done, but not overcooked.

Remove the chicken from the pan and drain well. Let it cool briefly, until you can handle it comfortably, then cut it into serving pieces. Take the meat from one side of the breast and place it in the jar of a blender, along with the cooked chicken liver and the almonds. Add 2 or 3 tablespoons of the broth in which you cooked the chicken, and puree. Gradually add additional broth to create a thick liquid. Pour it into a small saucepan and simmer until it thickens slightly; add a little more broth if it becomes too thick.

1 free-range chicken or capon, and its liver
⅔ cup unblanched almonds (100 g)
2 bottles good red wine (1½ liters)
   generous ¼ cup red wine vinegar (7 cl)
   lard for browning the chicken
¼ teaspoon ground ginger
¼ teaspoon ground cinnamon
1 pinch ground cloves
¼ teaspoon ground galangal (if available)
¼ capsule long pepper, ground in a mortar or spice grinder or grated on a nutmeg grater (or see p. 45 for substitution)
4 or 5 grains of paradise, ground in a mortar or spice grinder (or see p. 46 for substitution)
   salt

Mix all the spices with the vinegar. When the almond mixture reaches the consistency of a thick sauce, add the spiced vinegar and return to the boil. Taste for seasoning.

Over medium-high heat, melt some lard in a skillet (nonstick is best), and brown the pieces of poached chicken on all sides. Drain on paper towels, and serve with the sauce spooned over.

36. "Saracen" Chicken

Saracen *brodo.*   Take roasted capons, and pound their livers, with spices and grilled bread, in a mortar; and moisten this in the mortar with good white wine and sour fruit juices. Then cut up those capons and boil them with those things in a pan; and add dates, Greek raisins, prunes, whole skinned almonds, and an adequate quantity of pork fat; and serve. You can use a similar method for sea fish. You can put apples and pears in these *brodi.* (Za 32)

The adjective "Saracen" suggests Arabic descent, but let's be sensible. First of all, our cookbooks provide the largest number of "geographical" variations for *brouets* and *brodi* because they were a very common type of dish; it is fair to wonder whether it is the dishes themselves or merely their names that have exotic associations.

In this instance, the use of fresh and dried fruits with meat recalls the flavors of modern-day North Africa. The use of wine in a Muslim dish would be surprising; that of pork fat is clearly inadmissible, although it could have been added when the recipe was imported. So this remains an open question, which we raised earlier in "Histories and Tales from the Kitchen" and in our comments on the recipes for *Limonia* (recipe 33) and *Romania* (recipe 34). This *brodo* is dark in color; we might note a possible connection between the adjective "Saracen" and the dark complexion of the Moors.

You can prepare this recipe with leftover roast chicken.

1 free-range chicken or, better, a capon, and its liver
⅓ cup blanched almonds (50 g)
    scant ⅓ cup raisins (50 g)
10 dates
10 prunes
2 slices country bread
1 cup white wine (¼ liter)
1 or 2 lemons
1 orange (not too sweet)
1 ounce salt pork fatback, cut into ⅛-inch dice
1 apple
1 pear
    salt

For the spice mixture
¼ teaspoon freshly grated nutmeg
¼ teaspoon freshly ground black pepper
1 pinch ground ginger
1 pinch ground cloves

Salt the chicken and place the liver in the cavity. Roast it by whatever method you prefer. It should be nicely browned, but preferably not completely cooked or it could fall apart when you simmer it in the sauce.

Meanwhile, toast or grill the bread. Squeeze the oranges and lemons and mix their juice with the wine. Peel and core the apple and the pear. Rinse the almonds and, if necessary, the raisins and prunes as well.

When the chicken is done, carve it into serving pieces and reserve. Remove the liver from the cavity; place it a mortar or food processor together with the bread and the spices and pound or grind finely. Add the citrus juice mixture and mix well.

Pour this mixture into a medium-large saucepan or casserole and add the chicken, the fresh and dried fruit, the almonds, and the diced fatback. Bring to the boil and simmer for 15 to 20 minutes. Check for seasoning and serve.

You can adjust the amount of sauce by using more or less wine than indicated.

37. Squabs with Almonds and Spices

If you want smothered pigeons, take the pigeons, cut them up, put them in a pan with chopped pork fat, add spices and a little finely sliced onion; put it on the fire, brown until half cooked, and add 30 almonds with their skins and 30 skinned. Take the boiled livers, pound them well with a little grilled bread, mix with wine, strain, and add to the pigeons; add spices and sugar to the plates. (Gu 24)

The way spices are used in this recipe is unusual for Western medieval cooking. In *potages,* spices were generally added at the end of the preparation or strained with the sauce, probably with a view to maximizing their flavor and aroma. But here the meat is sprinkled with spices when it is browned in the fat and additional spices are added at serving time. This is typical of some oriental cooking, where, for stewed dishes, the meat is browned before liquid is added. Even if the title of the recipe is silent on the matter, might this method of cooking the pigeons not have been influenced by the high traditions of Arab-Persian cooking?

Quarter each squab; cut the fatback into small dice; peel and finely slice the onions. Thoroughly rinse the unblanched almonds, drain them, and leave to dry on a towel.

In a small pan, bring some salted water to the boil. Add the squab livers, lower the heat, and simmer for 5 minutes. Drain and reserve.

Add the fatback to a casserole and render it over medium heat. Add the squab pieces and brown them on all sides, about 5 or 6 minutes, then add the onions, 3 teaspoons of the spice mixture, and salt to taste. Add all the almonds to the casserole, lower the heat, and lightly brown the almonds, 30 seconds or so. Cover and cook gently over very low heat while you prepare the liver-wine sauce base. Do not let the squabs or the almonds burn.

Puree the livers and the bread in a blender; add the wine and blend until smooth. Press this mixture through a sieve into the casserole containing the squabs.

4 squabs, and their livers
4 ounces fresh pork fatback (120 g)
4 small onions, 4 ounces total (120 g)
1 slice country bread, toasted or grilled
1⅔ cups red wine (40 cl)
40 almonds, not blanched (½ cup)
40 blanched almonds (½ cup)
1 teaspoon sugar
   salt

For the spice mixture
2 teaspoons ground coriander seed
⅔ teaspoon ground ginger
½ teaspoon ground cinnamon
⅛ teaspoon freshly ground black pepper
1 pinch ground cloves

Bring to the boil, then lower the heat and simmer, covered, for about 10 minutes. The sauce will thicken and become rich-tasting, and will coat the meat nicely. When ready to serve, sprinkle with more of the spice mixture and taste for seasoning. Sprinkle with a little sugar; this will not sweeten the dish, but will soften the flavor of the spices and add balance to the sauce.

38. *Gravé* of Quails

Gravé of small birds or other meat. They should be dry-plucked; then take pork fat cut into square pieces and put it in a pan and melt the fat, and fry them [the birds] in it; then cook them in meat broth; then take bread toasted on the grill, or breadcrumbs, soaked in meat broth and a little wine; then take ginger, cloves, grains of paradise, cassia buds, and the livers, and pound them; then put your bread and broth through a sieve, and add the finely crushed spices without sieving them; and boil with your birds and a little verjuice;

Note: Those who have no broth may use the water from cooking [dried] peas;

Note: It should not be too thick, but rather light, so only bread and the livers should be used as a thickener. (MP 150)

Cassia buds, a very common spice in medieval cooking, are the dried immature buds of *Cinamomum cassia*. They look like large cloves and their flavor is more fine and delicate than that of the cinnamon bark we use nowadays. Still, they can be successfully replaced by ordinary cinnamon, as they rarely come to market outside China (although it is worth checking with the spice merchants in our list of Mail-order Sources, some of whom get them from time to time).

Some commentators have heard in the word *gravé* an echo of the English word "gravy." This etymological link makes for an appealing hypothesis, but unfortunately it is shattered by the existence of the word *grané*, which is clearly derived from *grain* (meaning the solid part of a dish), and which is used for similar kinds of preparations. So we remain puzzled by the exact meaning of the term.

6   quails, with their livers if possible (if quail livers are unavailable, substitute 2 chicken livers)

5   ounces fresh pork fatback (150 g)

3   cups meat broth (¾ liter) (recipe 152) or liquid from the cooking of split peas

1   generous slice country bread, slightly dry

scant ½ cup good red wine (10 cl)

scant ½ cup verjuice (10 cl), or the juice of 1 lemon diluted in 3 tablespoons water

½   teaspoon ground ginger

1   pinch ground cloves

1   teaspoon grains of paradise, ground (see p. 46 for substitutes)

¼   teaspoon ground cassia buds or cinnamon

salt

Grill or toast the bread, cut it into small pieces, and soak it in the wine mixed with an equal quantity of broth. Clean the quails and reserve their livers. If using chicken livers, cut each in thirds.

Cut the fatback into small dice and render it in a casserole over medium heat. Add the quails and brown on all sides, then add the livers and broth to cover. Salt to taste, bring slowly to the boil, and simmer for 10 minutes.

Meanwhile, mash the bread and press it through a sieve. Remove the livers from the casserole and puree them together with the spices. Add the verjuice or diluted lemon juice to the livers and combine with the bread mixture. Add to the quails and simmer, covered, for 10 to 15 minutes or until tender.

Check for seasoning and serve. The sauce should be rather light.

39. *Seymé* of Veal

Gravé or *seymé* is a winter *potage*. Peel onions and cook them all cut up, then fry them in a pot; now you should have your chicken split down the back and browned on the grill over a charcoal fire; and the same if it is veal; then you must cut the meat into pieces if it is veal, or in quarters if it is a chicken, and put it into the pot with the onions, then take white bread browned on the grill and soaked in broth made from other meat; then crush ginger, cloves, grains of paradise, and long pepper, moisten them with verjuice and wine without straining this, and set aside; then crush the bread and put it through a sieve, and add it to the *brouet,* strain everything, and boil; then serve. (MP 151)

> The recipe gives us the choice of chicken or veal; we have chosen the latter. Here, *seymé* is given as the equivalent of *gravé;* for the moment we have nothing to add on this matter of terminology.

Pre-heat the grill or broiler.

Peel and slice the onions, then steam or boil them until crisp-tender. Meanwhile, pat the meat dry and grill on both sides until golden brown. If using a broiler, place the meat in one layer on a baking sheet or in a shallow roasting pan and broil until golden brown, then turn and brown on the other side.

Grill or broil the bread, cut it into small pieces, and pour the broth over it. When it has softened, crush it with a fork and press it through a sieve into a bowl. Mix the spices with the verjuice and the wine and pour this through the sieve into the bowl.

Melt the lard in a casserole and sauté the onions until lightly golden; add the meat and continue to sauté for a minute or so. Add the spiced bread mixture and salt to taste. Bring to the boil, lower the heat, and simmer, covered, for about an hour. Check for seasoning and serve.

1¾ to 2¼ **pounds stewing veal, free of gristle and cut in large chunks** (800 g to 1 kg)

4 **medium-small onions**

2 **slices country bread, dry**

2 **cups meat or chicken broth** (½ liter) (recipe 152)

3 **tablespoons red wine** (5 cl)

6 **tablespoons verjuice** (10 cl) **or the juice of 1 lemon mixed with 3 tablespoons water**

⅓ **teaspoon ground ginger**

1 **pinch ground cloves**

¼ **teaspoon grains of paradise, ground** (see p. 46 for substitutions)

⅓ **capsule long pepper, ground** (see p. 45 for substitutions)

2 **tablespoons lard**
 salt

40. Haricot of Lamb

Héricot of mutton. Cut it into small pieces, then boil it for a moment, and fry it in lard, and fry with it some onions finely cut up and cooked, and moisten with beef broth, and add mace, parsley, hyssop, and sage, and boil it together. (MP 148)

Haricot de mouton is a classic of traditional French cooking—but there are no haricot beans in this early version. This is only natural, for the *Phaseolus vulgaris* is an American plant and was unknown in Europe in the fourteenth century. It was among the new things that Christopher Columbus brought back from the other side of the Atlantic.

The ancient Romans and Greeks cooked with the *phasiolus*, which in medieval France was known as the *fasole* or *faséole*. This was an African legume belonging to the family *Vigna* and was very similar to the New World *Phaseolus vulgaris*. The *fasole* has more or less disappeared, but you can easily find its descendant: the black-eyed pea.

So what is the meaning of these terms—*héricot, haricot,* or even *héricoq*—found in the titles of a whole series of medieval recipes for lamb or mutton stew? The most common theory is that *haricot* is derived from the verb *aricoter*—to cut into little pieces—which is apt for a stew made with small chunks of meat. One might, of course, wonder how the *Phaseolus vulgaris* came to be called a haricot bean. Could there have been a phonetic confusion between the French word for a mutton stew and another word of unknown origin referring to that plant? And could this have led to their subsequent union in a single dish? In any event, this hypothetical merger has been a great gastronomic success, judging by the lasting popularity of the recipe.

Even bean-free, this medieval stew is delicious. The combination of fresh herbs and mace gives it a fresh, vivid flavor.

1½   **pounds boneless shoulder or leg of lamb, cut into ¾-inch cubes (700 g)**

3   **medium-large onions**

3   **cups beef broth (¾ liter)**

1   **heaping tablespoon lard**

4   **tablespoons chopped parsley**

5   **or 6 leaves fresh sage, chopped**

¼   **teaspoon ground mace**

1   **tablespoon chopped fresh hyssop, or 1 teaspoon dried (or substitute 2 teaspoons chopped fresh mint)**

Peel the onions and cut them into ⅜-inch slices, then simmer or steam them for 5 to 7 minutes, until crisp-tender. Briefly plunge the lamb into boiling water, until it turns gray, then drain it well. Melt the lard in a casserole over medium heat; add the lamb and brown it lightly on all sides. Add the onions and sauté until lightly golden, then add broth just to cover, plus the herbs, the mace, and salt to taste. Bring to the boil, lower the heat and cook gently, covered, for an hour to 90 minutes. When the meat is very tender, check the sauce for seasoning and serve.

Parboiling the lamb might seem pointless, but it "cleanses" the meat and, rather than diminish its quality in any way, improves it.

December calendar page, preparation of pigs after slaughter. Book of Hours (Flanders, early sixteenth century). Paris Bibliothèque nationale, Ms. Smith Les. 38, fol. 12v°.

The essential gestures of the cook. Virgil, *Opera Omnia* (Ferrara, 1458).
Paris Bibliothèque nationale, Ms. lat. 7939A, fol. 48.

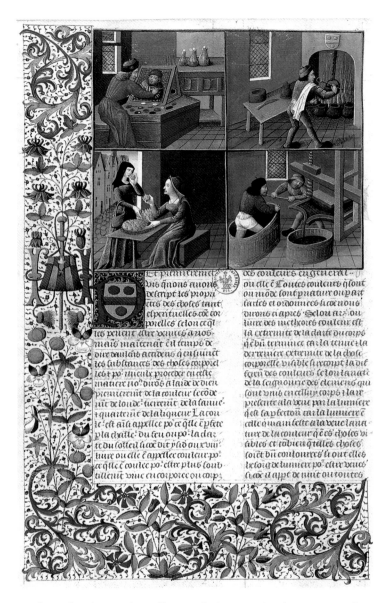

Colors, flavors, and smells. Bartholomeus Anglicus, *Livre des prepriétés des choses* (France, fifteenth century).
Paris Bibliothèque nationale,
Ms. fr. 9140, fol. 361v°.

Reheating the whey in order to make ricotta cheese. *Taquinum sanitatis* (1474). Paris Bibliothèque nationale, Ms. lat. 9333, fol. 60.

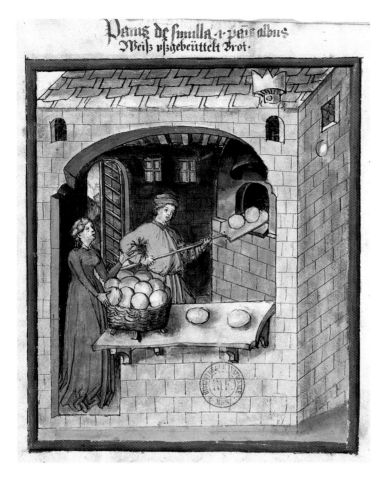

Community oven for baking bread. *Taquinum sanitatis*
(1474). Paris Bibliothèque nationale,
Ms. lat. 9333, fol. 61v.

Harvesting squash. *Taquinum sanitatis* (1474). Paris
Bibliothèque nationale, Ms. lat. 9333, fol. 19v°.

Picking green grapes for making verjus. *Taquinum sanitatis* (1474).
Paris Bibliothèque nationale, Ms. lat. 9333, fol. 83.

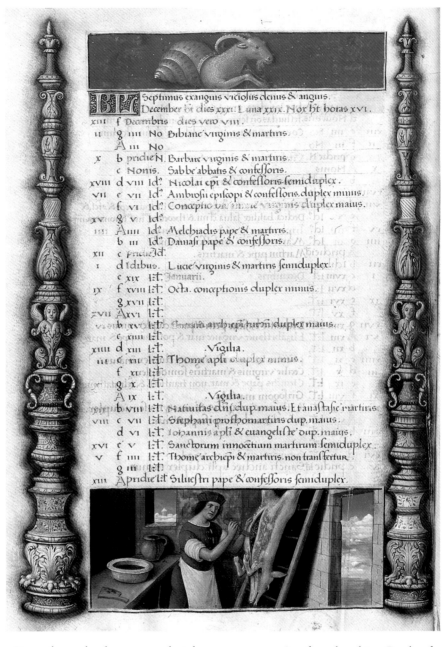

Septimus exanguis viciosus denus & anguis.
December h dies xxxi. Luna xxix. Nox ht horas xvi.

xiii f Decembris dies vero viii.
ii   g iiii No Bibiane virginis & martiris.
      A iii   No
x   b pridie N. Barbare virginis & martiris.
      c Nonis. Sabbe abbatis & confessoris.
xviii d viii Id? Nicolai epi & confessoris semiduplex.
vii   e vii   Id? Ambrosii episcopi & confessoris. duplex minus.
      f vi   Id? Conceptio virginis & virginis duplex maius.
xv   g v   Id?
iiii A iiii Id? Melchiadis pape & martiris.
      b iii   Id? Damasi pape & confessoris.
xii   c pridie Id.
i   d Idibus. Lucie virginis & martiris semiduplex.
      e xix   Kt. Januarii.
ix   f xviii Kt. Octa. conceptionis duplex minus.
      g xvii Kt.
xvii A xvi   Kt.
      b xv   Kt. Sueani archiepiscopi & martiris duplex maius.
      c xiiii Kt.
xiiii d xiii Kt.   Vigilia.
      e xii   Kt. Thome apli duplex minus.
      f xi   Kt.
      g x   Kt.
      A ix   Kt.   Vigilia.
      b viii Kt. Natiuitas dni. dup. maius. Et anastasie martiris.
viii c vii   Kt. Stephani prothomartiris dup. maius.
      d vi   Kt. Iohannis apli & euangeliste dup. maius.
xvi   e v   Kt. Sanctorum innocentium martirum semiduplex.
v   f iiii Kt. Thome archiepi & martiris. non transfertur.
      g iii   Kt.
xiii A pridie Kt. Siluestri pape & confessoris semiduplex.

December calendar page, a butcher prepares a pig after slaughter. Book of Hours (Use of Tours, late fifteenth century). Paris Bibliothèque nationale, Ms. lat. 886, fol. 9v°.

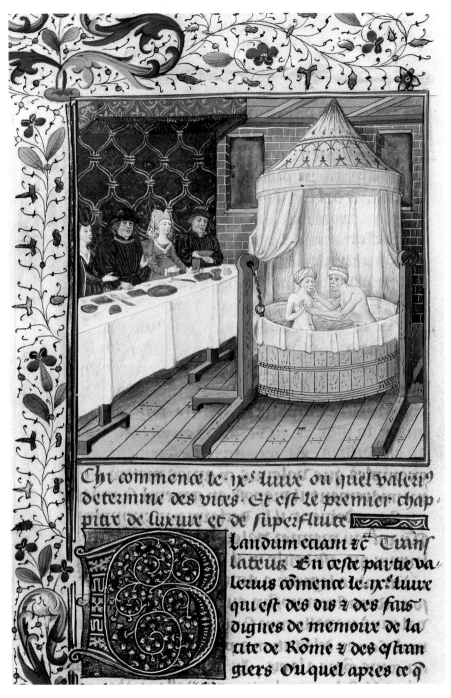

Chi commence le .ix.ᵉ liuue ou quel valeriᵘˢ
determine des vices. Et est le premier chappitre de luxure et de superfluite

Landum eciam ꝛc. Tranſ
latoꝛ. En ceſte partie va
lerius commence le .ix.ᵉ liuue
qui est des dis ꝛ des fais
dignes de memoiꝛe de la
cite de Rome ꝛ des estran
giers ou quel apꝛes ce ꝗ

At the baths, the pleasures of the feast and the flesh. Valerius Maximus,
Les faits et dits memorables. Paris Bibliothèque nationale,
Ms. fr. 6185, fol. 255.

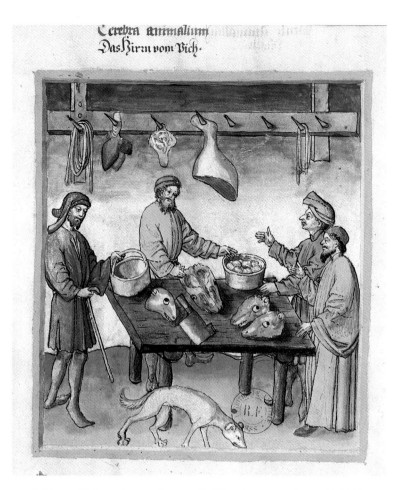

Selling offal at the market stall. *Taquinum sanitatis* (1474).
Paris Bibliothèque nationale, Ms. lat. 9333, fol. 75.

Gallanta.

Nature. f. 7.f. melior erca. sparata ai pull colubic. Juuamentu.
collere. nocumentiz. nerius 7 melancolie remotio noci ai uino re
cent octouferio.

A courtly summer banquet. On the menu: chicken and pigeon
galantine. Abu Khasim, *Observations sur la nature et les
propriétés des aliments* (Pavia or Milan, 1390).
Paris Bibliothèque nationale,
Ms. n.a.l. 1673, fol. 65v°.

A feast at Alexander's court. *La geste ou histoire du noble roy Alexandre* (France, fifteenth century). Paris Bibliothèque nationale, Ms. fr. 9342, fol. 13.

41. Lamb *Ausoerre*

Mutton *ausoerre*.   Cut the mutton into pieces, then wash it and cook it in water, then crush parsley and bread, and strain, and put it in a pot with spices. (MP 148–49)

We do not know the meaning of the word *ausoerre*. This dish is extremely simple and is perfect for the diet-conscious: like many other medieval *potages,* there is not an ounce of fat in its sauce, apart from what comes from the meat itself. Judging by its ingredients and method, this dish undoubtedly reflects everyday medieval cooking: boiled mutton, seasoned only with parsley and served in a bread-thickened sauce enlivened by a few spices. It appears only in *Le Ménagier de Paris*—whose author is forever reminding us not to take him for one of those great lords for whom price is no object.

Cut the meat into chunks and place in a casserole. Add water just to cover and salt to taste. Bring to the boil, lower the heat, and simmer, covered, for about an hour or until tender. Break up the bread in a bowl and add some of the cooking liquid; when the bread is soft, mash it with a fork.

Chop the parsley very finely and add it to the mashed bread; press this through a sieve (or puree in a blender) to form a creamy green puree. Add it to the casserole, stir well to blend and simmer for a few minutes to let the parsley flavor permeate the meat. Stir in the spices, check for seasoning, and serve.

- 1½ to 1¾ **pounds boneless stewing lamb, such as shoulder** (700 to 800 g)
- 1 **small bunch parsley**
- 1 **large slice country bread, crusts removed**
- ½ **teaspoon fine spice mixture** (recipe 150, variation A)
  salt

42. *Sardamone:* Lamb Sauté

Meat *sardamone*.   Take flesh of mutton, from the breast; cut it small and boil it well; and when it is boiled so that it no longer has a high odor, remove the water and fry the meat with pork fat; then add enough of that water so that little remains of the broth; and when this is cooked, add coriander and chopped carrots, with spices and sufficient saffron. If you have no coriander, add cumin; and eat it. (Za 69)

This Italian recipe for a lamb sauté appears in no French sources. The crushed coriander seeds and carrots added at the end of the preparation are unexpected, but the results are most successful in both flavor and appearance. Guests always like this very simple dish.

There is some doubt, however, about what kind of coriander is intended here. If, contrary to normal usage, the recipe means fresh coriander leaves, it is no less delicious or colorful for that.

2¼ pounds breast or neck of lamb, boned and trimmed (1 kg)

1½ ounces fresh pork fatback (40 g)

½ pound carrots (200 g)

1 teaspoon whole coriander seeds, or 1 tablespoon chopped fresh coriander leaves

3 or 4 threads saffron

1¾ cup water or broth (40 cl) (recipe 152)

salt

For the spice mixture

¼ teaspoon each ginger, cinnamon, nutmeg, and pepper, all ground

Cut the meat into cubes. Plunge it into boiling water for a moment, drain, and pat dry (although this parboiling is pointless with young lamb, which has no strong odor to remove).

Render the fatback in a casserole over medium heat and add the meat; brown lightly on all sides. Add salt to taste, then add the water or broth and simmer, covered, over very low heat for about 45 minutes or until tender (this will depend on the age and cut of the meat).

About 5 minutes before the meat is done, crush the coriander seeds (if using) and grate or finely chop the carrots. Toss the carrots with the coriander (seeds or leaves), the saffron, and about ½ teaspoon of the spice mixture; add this to the casserole and cook briefly. Check for salt and spices and serve.

43. Carbonata

To make *carbonata*, take salt meat layered with lean and fat, and cut it in slices, and put it in a pan to cook; do not let it overcook. Then put it on a plate and sprinkle it with a little sugar, a little cinnamon, and a little finely chopped parsley. And you can do the same to prepare salt pork[?] or ham, using orange or lemon juice in place of vinegar, whichever you prefer; it will make you drink all the better. (Ma 131)

Careful reading reveals that this recipe actually contains two versions: the normal one, made (it is implied) with vinegar; and a more refined version with citrus juice as the basis of its sauce. And that last phrase—"it will make you drink all the better"—leads us to presume that *carbonata* (found in French sources as *charbonnée* or *carbonnée*) was the ideal accompaniment to a drinking bout, because its saltiness increased thirst.

Carbonata is a quick and tasty dish for an evening meal. We suggest using sliced pancetta or high-quality dry-cured raw ham such as *prosciutto di Parma* or Smithfield or other country-type ham. If you can get some reasonably lean unsmoked bacon, it will add an extra touch of rusticity to the dish.

In an ungreased skillet, lightly brown the meat, then set it aside on a warmed serving platter. Sprinkle the sugar into the skillet, stir for a moment with a wooden spoon, then immediately add the fruit juice or vinegar. Bring to the boil, scraping the bottom of the skillet with the spoon, add the parsley and cinnamon, boil for a moment, taste for seasoning, and pour over the meat. Serve immediately.

12 thin slices pancetta, prosciutto (or other raw country ham), or lean, unsmoked bacon

1 teaspoon sugar
juice of 2 lemons or 2 bitter oranges, or 4 tablespoons wine vinegar (7 cl)

1 tablespoon finely chopped parsley

¼ teaspoon cinnamon

44. *Fegatelli:* Pork-liver Bundles

Tomacelli or *mortadelle.* Take the pork liver and boil it; then remove it and chop it on the table with a knife very vigorously, or grate it with a grater like dry cheese. Than take marjoram and other aromatic herbs, well pounded with pepper, and the liver; in the mortar moisten it with egg so it will be thick. Then take pork caul fat and wrap the mixture in little round mounds; and fry them individually in a pan with pork fat; when they are cooked, remove them and put them in another pan. And take spices, with saffron and pepper, mixed with good wine and pour this over [the *tomacelli*] in the pan, and boil them properly; eat them.

Fegatelli

Take the liver, cut it into pieces, and roast it on a spit; and when they are not completely cooked, wrap them in pork caul fat and cook them. When they are cooked, put them in another pan and pour over them the sauce described above; and it is better to wrap each piece individually in caul fat. (Za 73–74)

Fegatelli are to this day among the great delights of the Tuscan winter. You can buy them ready-made in the butcher shops of Siena and Arezzo—but in winter only. Uncooked liver is cut into walnut-sized cubes, seasoned with salt, pepper, and fennel seeds, wrapped in caul fat and threaded onto little wooden skewers, alternating with bay leaves and thin slices of bread, all ready to grill or roast.

And to highlight this regional culinary continuity, it is *fegatelli* rather than *tomacelli* that we have decided to adapt here. They are indeed best eaten in wintertime—and let us not forget that this was the traditional time for pig-killing and offal-eating. The main difference between the medieval recipe and current practice is the use of multiple cooking processes, which is entirely in keeping with the habits of the time.

scant 1¼ pounds pork liver
(500 g)

6 ounces pork caul (150 g)

1¼ cups light-bodied red wine
(such as Beaujolais) (30 cl)

a good handful chopped fresh
parsley and marjoram, mixed
(or a handful fresh parsley plus
1 teaspoon dried marjoram)

12 threads saffron, approximately

salt

For the spice mixture

¼ teaspoon freshly ground black
pepper

⅛ teaspoon ground ginger

1 pinch ground cloves

Preheat the grill or broiler to a moderate heat. Cut the liver into 1¼-inch (3 cm) cubes. Rinse the caul and soak it briefly in cool water (this will make it easier to handle); spread it out onto a clean towel to dry. Cut the caul into pieces large enough to wrap the cubes of liver.

Briefly grill or broil the liver, just to sear the outside surface; it will receive further cooking. Remove from the heat and sprinkle with salt. Put the chopped herbs on a plate and roll the cubes of liver in them to coat lightly. Wrap each cube in caul, securing it with a toothpick if necessary.

Return the wrapped cubes of liver to the grill or broiler and cook for 5 to 7 minutes, turning halfway through the cooking time; the caul will render its fat and turn golden brown.

Meanwhile, add the spice mixture to the wine in a stainless steel or other nonreactive saucepan and bring to the simmer. When the *fegatelli* are browned, add them to the hot spiced wine and simmer for about 5 minutes.

Serve hot or warm.

45. A "Vinaigrette" without Vinegar

Another *vinaigrette*. And for those who want to make *vinaigrette*, take pork livers and wash them, and then put them on a grill over good coals until nicely cooked; and when it is cooked, put it on a good surface and cut it into small dice; and then take plenty of onions, and peel and wash and cut them very small, and fry all of this together in excellent pork fat. And for the liquid of this *vinaigrette* take very good light red wine, the best you can get, according to the quantity of the liquid, and add beef or mutton broth in the necessary quantity; then take good white bread; cut it in nice slices and grill them on the grill until they are well browned; then put them to soak in the wine and broth. And when it is thoroughly soaked, take spices—white ginger, grains of paradise, pepper (but not too much), plenty of cinnamon—as much as necessary, as well as salt; and put it all carefully through a sieve, then bring it to the boil; when it has boiled, put in the fried meat. Then serve when required. (Ch 181)

> Apart from its name, this dish has nothing in common with a modern vinaigrette; it doesn't even contain any vinegar. Yet the other five known versions of the same recipe do indeed include vinegar among the ingredients, which could mean (as Terence Scully, who recently edited this text, appears to believe it does) that Chiquart simply forgot it. Did he forget, or was he making the

supreme distinction? By opting not to add vinegar to this preparation (which is, moreover, far more elaborate than other versions), perhaps the great chef was putting his personal stamp on a famous, but to his mind too ubiquitous, dish.

Despite its name, this "vinaigrette" is a *potage,* in the medieval sense of the word. It consists of a *grain,* or solid part, and a *potage,* or flavorful liquid, which are prepared separately and combined only when the dish is ready to be served.

Toast or grill the bread, cut it into small pieces, and put it in a bowl to soak with the wine and the broth.

Trim the liver and lightly grill it or broil it, turning once; it should not be fully cooked at this stage. Cut the liver into ⅜-inch (1-cm) dice and set aside.

Cut the fatback into ⅛-inch (3-mm) dice and render it in a skillet over low heat. Peel and slice the onions, and brown them lightly in the rendered fat. Raise the heat to medium, add the liver, and sauté until nicely browned.

Meanwhile, mash the soaked bread with a fork, or puree it in a food processor; you should have a fairly thin slurry of bread, wine, and broth. Add the spices and the salt, combine well, then press the mixture through a strainer into a sauce-pan. Bring to the boil, and simmer until thickened.

generous 8 ounces pork liver (250 g)

4 medium-small onions

6 ounces fresh pork fatback (150 g)

scant ½ cup good, light-bodied red wine (10 cl)

4 cups beef broth (1 liter) (recipe 152)

1 large slice stale country bread

½ teaspoon ground ginger

½ teaspoon grains of paradise, crushed or ground (see p. 46 for substitutes)

1 teaspoon ground cinnamon

black pepper

salt

When you are ready to serve, reheat the liver-onion mixture and add it to the sauce. Check for seasoning and serve.

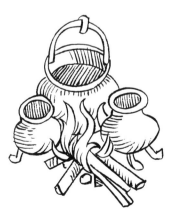

Roasted Meats

Roast meat is the happy result of an alliance between fire and human ingenuity. It was basic to the medieval meat menu. It was a sign of wealth, feasting, and gastronomic lavishness, for the naked flame will be kind only to the tenderest and most succulent cuts of meat—eaten only by those predestined for such luxury by their wealth.

But you would inevitably underestimate the importance and symbolic meaning of roasted meats if you tried to gauge this by their prominence in medieval cookbooks. None of our authors felt it necessary to explain step by step how to go about roasting, from skewering to carving. Even the author of *Le Ménagier de Paris*, generally more discursive and practically-minded than most of the others, is stingy with his details. In French sources, the chapters on roasts (where they exist at all) are most often limited to a tedious list of animals, sometimes followed by a brief note on the need for larding to prevent the meat from drying out, on precooking, on basting, or on the names of sauces traditionally served with the creature in question once it has been properly roasted. But how do you tell when it is done? We know from repeated injunctions that it should be browned, but should it be tender? Juicy? Blood-rare? We never learn any of this.

This lack of information, so vexatious for the historian, is undoubtedly the result of a universal familiarity with fires, hearths, and fireplaces. Meats were put onto spits (oven-roasting was rare), and placed before the fire in the hearth, where everyone could see them—and smell them. Professional chefs and cooks did not necessarily have a monopoly on this process: a hunter, or even a food-loving urban gentleman, could roast his little game birds all by himself. They would have known not only how to handle a spit, but also how to choose the right meats, drawing a clear distinction between those suited to the open flame and those best boiled. Let us consult Maestro Martino, here as elsewhere the most precise (and without any attempt at stylistic flourish):

> The gross flesh of the steer and the cow must be boiled.
> The flesh of the calf, i.e., the rear portion of the breast, is good boiled, and the loin roasted; the haunch in meatballs.
> All the flesh of the sheep is good boiled, apart from the shoulder, which is good roasted, as is the leg.
> The flesh of the hog is unhealthy in any preparation; but the loin can be roasted with onions when it is fresh, and the rest should be

salted or prepared as you think best.

All the flesh of the kid is good boiled or roasted, but the saddle is best roasted.

The same is true for lamb.

The flesh of the goat is good in January with garlic sauce.

Of the flesh of the hart, the foreportion is good in a *brodo* larded with pork fat, the loins can be roasted, and the haunches are good in a plain pie or in meatballs.

The flesh of the roe deer is good in the same preparations.

The flesh of the boar should be prepared in a *peperata,* a civet, or a *brodo* larded with pork fat.

All of the hare is good roasted, but the rear portion is the best, and the foreportion is good in sauce, as has been noted.

The flesh of the rabbit is better roasted than any other way, and the saddle is the best part.

The flesh of the bear is good in a pie.

And who today would disagree with Martino's wise advice?

46. Roast Kid with Sauce of Gold

Roast kid in sauce. Take a quarter of a kid, and prepare it carefully as it should be for roasting, and lard it and put in it plenty of peeled cloves of garlic, as though you were studding it or larding it. Then take good verjuice, two egg yolks, two finely crushed cloves of garlic, a little saffron, a little pepper, and a little rich broth, and mix all these things, and put them in a dish under the kid as it roasts; and baste it with this sauce from time to time. And when it is cooked, place the quarter kid on a platter and pour the sauce over it, along with a little finely chopped parsley. And this quarter kid should be well cooked, and eaten as hot as can be. (Ma 130)

Finally, a good recipe for kid, which is so often bland. When we fed this dish to friends, they could hardly believe it had come from a medieval manuscript and not from a book of cutting-edge modern cooking. You can often find baby kid in butchers with a Muslim or Greek clientele.

A leg or shoulder of kid, or half a young kid

2 ounces fresh pork fatback (50 g)

6 cloves garlic

salt

Preheat the oven to 425 degrees F (220 degrees C). Peel the 6 cloves of garlic and slice each one lengthwise into several strips. Cut the pork fat into small strips. Pierce the meat all over with a small paring knife, and insert strips of fat and garlic into the slits. Salt the meat generously.

Beat the egg yolks and blend them with the broth and the lemon juice; season with the pepper, the minced garlic, and the saffron. Pour this mixture into a roasting pan and add the meat. Roast for 45 minutes to an hour, to an internal temperature of about 150 degrees F (65 degrees C), basting with the sauce from time to time.

When ready to serve, baste once more with the sauce and sprinkle with the chopped parsley.

For the sauce
generous ¾ cup beef broth (20 cl) (recipe 152) **or chicken broth**
juice of half a lemon
2 **egg yolks**
¾ **teaspoon freshly ground black pepper**
4 **or 5 threads saffron**
2 **cloves garlic, minced**
1 **tablespoon chopped parsley**

47. Parsley-studded Lamb or Mutton

oast mutton with fine salt or with verjuice and vinegar. The shoulder should first be put on the spit and rotated before the fire until it has rendered its fat, then it should be larded with parsley, and no sooner, for two reasons: first, because it is easier to lard, and secondly, because if it is larded earlier the parsley will burn before the shoulder is roasted. (MP 177)

> What could be simpler than this shoulder of lamb larded, surprisingly, with parsley? Why didn't we think of it before? There is no better way to impregnate the juices of roasting meat with the herb's inimitable flavor and aroma. Serve the roast plain, just as it comes out of the oven, and let your guests season it to taste with salt—or with good vinegar or verjuice if they like sharp, acidic flavors.

reheat the oven to 425 degrees F (220 degrees C). Wash and dry the parsley, and pick through it, choosing about fifteen very leafy sprigs.

If you have a rotisserie, place the meat on a skewer. If not, place it on a rack in a roasting pan. Roast for about 20 minutes; then remove it, and use a paring knife to cut

A shoulder of lamb or mutton, about 3¼ pounds (1.5 kg)
1 **bunch parsley**
salt
wine vinegar or verjuice, optional

fairly deep holes into the flesh. Push a sprig of parsley into each hole. On the one hand, you should be careful not to burn yourself; on the other, work as quickly as you can so that the meat does not get cold.

Return to the oven for another 40 minutes, or longer depending on how well cooked you like your lamb. Turn off the oven and leave the door ajar; let the meat rest for about 15 minutes before serving.

Carve the meat, and serve on a warmed platter. Place dishes containing salt, vinegar, and verjuice on the table.

48. Roast Shoulder of Lamb with Pancetta

houlder of ram. Lard the shoulder of ram, place it on the spit and roast it, and sprinkle it with salt; carve it and serve it with green sauce. (Tr 388)

Rather than stud a lamb roast with the usual garlic (which not everyone adores), try larding it with good, fatty pancetta as they used to do in the Middle Ages. It adds flavor and succulence to the meat. And don't forget the famous green sauce (recipe 105), as the recipe prescribes.

A shoulder of lamb, about 3¼ pounds (1.5 kg)
6 ounces pancetta, sliced about ¼ inch thick (150 g)
salt

Preheat the oven to 425 degrees F (220 degrees C). Cut the pancetta into small strips and, using a paring knife to pierce the meat, insert them into the lamb.

Sprinkle the lamb with salt, and roast for about an hour and a quarter, either on a rack in a roasting pan or skewered on a rotisserie. When it is done, turn off the oven and leave the door ajar; let the meat rest for about 15 minutes before serving. Serve with green sauce (recipe 105), to which you have added the meat juices from the roasting pan.

49. Stuffed Suckling Pig

tuffed piglet. The piglet, slaughtered and bled at the throat, should be scalded with boiling water, then scraped: then take some lean pork, remove the fat and offal from the piglet, and cook them in water: then take twenty eggs and hard-boil them, and some chestnuts boiled and skinned: then take the yolks of the eggs, the chestnuts, good aged cheese, and flesh from a cooked ham, and chop this; then pound it with saffron and plenty of powdered ginger mixed with the meat; and if the meat becomes too hard, add some egg yolks. And do not open your pig at the belly, but through the side, making the smallest hole you can: then put it on a spit, and then fill it with your stuffing and sew it shut with a big needle; it should be eaten with yellow sauce if it is winter, or with cameline sauce if it is summer.

Note that I have also seen piglets larded, and they are very good. That is how they prepare them nowadays—and pigeons as well. (MP 178)

A true suckling pig should be only about two weeks old and should weigh no more than nine pounds (4 kg) or so. Judging by the amount of stuffing required, the piglet in this recipe would have been older and bigger. Note the care devoted to its preparation: the pig must not simply be slit open at the belly; it must be cleaned and stuffed through a small hole cut into the side, which demands considerable skill.

We have adapted the recipe for a suckling pig weighing about 13 pounds

(6 kg); you can adjust it depending on what your butcher can supply. But to be truly faithful to the original technique, you will need to keep your own pigs, or have a friend who does. For one thing, suckling pigs bought at the butcher have generally been slit open and do not often come with their offal. But if you can, order one in advance and get its lungs, liver, spleen, heart, and kidneys. As for the slit belly, you'll just have to sew it back up again to keep the stuffing in place as the pig roasts.

Bring a big pot of salted water to the boil; add the pork and the suckling pig's lungs, liver, spleen, heart, and kidneys, and simmer for about an hour (remove the liver after 20 minutes).

In separate pans, boil the chestnuts and hard-cook the eggs (both the chestnuts and the eggs should cook for 20 minutes from when the water returns to the boil). Shell and skin the chestnuts and shell the eggs, separating the yolks from the whites.

Clean the pig carefully with a damp towel, removing all remaining hairs, blood, and other debris. Salt it generously, inside and out, and set aside while you prepare the stuffing.

When the pork and the pig's offal are cooked, drain them well, let them cool for a few minutes, and grind them in a meat grinder or (in batches) in a food processor, along with the ham. Place the ground meats in a large mixing bowl.

	A whole suckling pig, with its lungs, liver, spleen, heart, and kidneys
2¼	pounds pork shoulder (chuck) roast (weight with bones) (1 kg), boned
1	pound ham
50	chestnuts
25	eggs
2	or 3 additional egg yolks if needed
10	ounces parmesan or aged Swiss gruyère cheese (300 g)
1	heaping tablespoon ground ginger, or more if needed
3	pinches saffron threads
	salt

Mash the hard-cooked egg yolks and the chestnuts, grate the cheese, and combine with the ground meats. If the mixture seems too stiff, add a couple of raw egg yolks to loosen it. Add plenty of salt (bearing in mind, however, that the cheese is salty), a heaping tablespoon of ground ginger, and 3 generous pinches of saffron threads, crushed between your fingers. Make a little patty of the stuffing and fry it in a small skillet; taste for seasoning, and add additional salt or ginger as necessary.

Preheat the oven to 400 degrees F (200 degrees C).

With paper towels, dry the cavity of the pig and sprinkle with salt once again if you think it necessary. With a trussing needle and cotton butcher's twine, tightly sew up the belly two-thirds of the way. Add the stuffing through the remaining gap; when the pig is quite full, finish sewing it up. Do not leave even a tiny opening.

Tuck the pig's legs under the body and set it in a roasting pan. Wrap its ears with aluminum foil to prevent them from burning. Roast for 2½ to 3 hours, checking its progress from time to time. It should be nicely browned.

In winter, serve with yellow sauce, or *poivre jaunet* (recipe 109), in summer with a cameline sauce (recipes 106 and 107).

50. *Porchetta,* or Inside-out Suckling Pig

Piglet.   To prepare a piglet nicely: first, ensure that it is properly scraped so that it is white and clean. Then open it right along the backbone and remove the insides, and wash it very well. Then take the piglet's liver and chop it with a knife, along with good herbs, and take some finely chopped garlic and a little good pork fat, and a little grated cheese, and a few eggs, and crushed pepper, and a little saffron, and mix all these things and put them into the piglet, reversing it as is done with tenches, that is, turning it inside out. Then, sew it up and tie it well, and put it to cook on the spit or on a grill. But cook it slowly so that both the meat and the stuffing will be cooked. And make a little brine with vinegar, pepper, and saffron, and take two or three sprigs of bay or rosemary, and frequently baste the piglet with the brine; geese, ducks, cranes, capons, chickens, and such can be treated in a similar way. (Ma 127)

> Here is that famous "inside-out piglet." This Italian recipe is completely different from the stuffed suckling pig in recipe 49. Here everything is reversed: the suckling pig is cleaned through the back and split open from top to tail, whereas the recipe from *Le Ménagier de Paris* instructs the cook to take great care to make only a tiny opening in the creature's side. But the most striking instruction is to turn the pig inside out. What exactly does this mean? Martino tells us to do this as with a tench. In fact, we have cooked a number of fish in this way (see recipes 68 and 69), by boning them and folding them over the stuffing flesh-side out. And they were excellent. But how do you turn a whole pig inside out? Opening the pig along the back (which is still the practice in certain parts of France such as the northern Lorraine, and which involves removing pretty much the whole backbone) would most likely make it possible to try something quite different from what we suggest in our version of the dish. Perhaps some of our readers are in a position to supervise the butchering of their piglet from start to finish; we hope they will try the original version of this recipe and let us know how it goes. For the rest of us, the recipe below still yields a delicious dish.

Wash the suckling pig inside and out, and wipe it thoroughly with paper towels or a cloth. Season it generously, inside and out, with salt and pepper. Wash, dry, and stem the herb mixture.

In a food processor or meat grinder, chop the liver, the fat, the garlic, and the herb mixture, in batches if necessary; combine in a bowl. Add the cheese and the eggs and season to taste with salt, pepper, and saffron. Fry a small patty of the mixture and taste for seasoning.

Stuff the pig according to the instructions in recipe 49, bearing in mind, however, that here the stuffing will not fill the whole cavity and is intended to flavor the roast—so do not be afraid to season it generously.

Roast according to the instructions in recipe 49. Prepare a basting liquid with the vinegar seasoned with salt, pepper, and a little saffron. Using a brush made from the bay and rosemary, baste the suckling pig often as it roasts.

1 suckling pig, 11 to 13 pounds with its liver (5 to 6 kg)
about 2 pounds fresh pork fatback (1 kg)
about 10 ounces parmesan cheese, grated (300 g)
about 5 ounces garlic, approximately 2 large heads (150 g)
about 7 ounces of a mixture of parsley and dill or other aromatic herbs (200 g)
about 6 eggs
2 cups good red wine vinegar (½ liter)
several pinches saffron threads
1 branch fresh bay leaves
1 branch fresh rosemary
salt
pepper

51. Cormary: Roast Loin of Pork with Red Wine

Cormary. Take finely ground coriander and caraway, pepper powder, and ground garlic, in red wine; mix all this together and salt it. Take raw pork loins, skin them, and prick it well with a knife, and lay it in the sauce. Roast it when you wish, and save what falls from the meat as it roasts and boil it in a pot with good broth, and then serve it with the roast. (Fc HB 109)

> In the Middle Ages, the English seem not to have loathed garlic, and they used it in quite a number of dishes, whereas the French and the Italians appear to have used it only in sauces. On the other hand, the French and the Italians loved mint, which they used often with all sorts of vegetables. How things have changed! The average Briton cannot stand garlic, while for the typical Frenchman mint has long been synonymous with nothing more than toothpaste (at least until the spread of Vietnamese cooking).
>
> In any event, this English recipe for pork roasted with garlic and spices is worthy of a place on the modern table. In the context of a twentieth-century dinner, we recommend serving it with a Puree of Dried Young Fava Beans (recipe 23), which is the perfect accompaniment.

1 loin roast of pork, bone-in, a generous 3 pounds (1.5 kg)
1 cup good red wine (¼ liter) scant ½ cup broth (10 cl) (recipe 152)
4 large cloves garlic, crushed
1 teaspoon ground coriander seeds
1 teaspoon ground caraway seeds
⅓ teaspoon ground pepper salt

In a glass or other nonreactive ovenproof dish, make a marinade with the wine, garlic, coriander, caraway, and pepper. Tie the roast neatly, pierce it all over with the point of a knife, and season with salt. Place the roast in the marinade, turning to coat all over. Marinate for a few hours or overnight, turning occasionally.

Preheat the oven to 350 degrees F (175 degrees C). Roast the pork for about 90 minutes, basting frequently. When it is done, remove the roast from the pan and let it rest in a warm place while you make the sauce.

Over medium-low heat, bring the pan juices to the boil and add the broth. Return to the boil, taste for seasoning, and serve with the meat.

52. *Bourbelier* of Wild Boar in Spiced Sauce

Bourbier of fresh wild boar.   First you should place it in boiling water and remove it forthwith, and roast it, basting it with a sauce made of spices, that is ginger, cinnamon, cloves, grains of paradise—and it is better if you add grilled bread soaked in wine, verjuice, and vinegar, and baste it with this; and when it is cooked, pour all [the sauce] over; it should be limpid and dark-colored. (VT Vat Scul 94)

> This recipe, highly typical of French culinary sources, is taken from the Vatican manuscript of Taillevent's *Le Viandier;* other texts give the name as *bourblier* or *bourbelier*. While *bourbier* means "quagmire," the author of *Le Ménagier de Paris* notes that *bourbelier* refers to the backbone. The same author tells us that the sauce is called *queue de sanglier*, or "boar's tail." In our version of the recipe we have specified young wild boar (up to around six months old), as does Maître Chiquart, cook to Duc Amédée VIII de Savoie, who advises preparing *bourbulleys*, as he calls them, with young boar. But in Chiquart's recipe, the meat must be washed, scalded in broth, and larded before being spit roasted. When it is nearly cooked, Chiquart instructs that the meat should be *boutonné*, or studded with cloves, and put back to roast until perfectly done. The sauce is prepared separately and served with the meat.
>
> Other sources of *Le Viandier* call for the cooked roast to be sliced and simmered in the sauce.

First make the basting sauce. Mix the wine, the vinegar, the verjuice, the salt, and the spices. Soak the bread in this mixture until completely sodden and soft; mash it with a fork. If you like, you can force the sauce through a sieve or puree it in a food processor, but this is not absolutely necessary, especially if you have done a good job mashing the bread.

Preheat the oven to 425 degrees F (220 degrees C).

Bring a large pot of water to the boil. Lower the meat into the water and remove it as soon as its color changes. This cleanses the boar of surface impurities and does nothing to diminish its flavor: quite the opposite.

Place the meat on a rack in a shallow roasting pan and roast for about 20 to 25 minutes per pound. Using a branch of rosemary as a brush, frequently baste the meat with the wine mixture.

When the roast is done, pour the remaining sauce over it and place the meat on a serving platter. Pour the sauce from the roasting pan into a sauce boat and serve with the roast. If there is not enough sauce, you can place the roasting pan over medium heat and deglaze it with water, scraping any caramelized juices into the liquid with a wooden spatula. This will yield a richly-colored sauce; taste it for salt before bringing it into the dining room.

1 **leg, loin, or rib roast of young wild boar, bone-in, 3¼ to 4½ pounds** (1.5 to 2 kg)

2 **cups good red wine** (½ liter)

1 **cup good red wine vinegar** (¼ liter)

1 **cup verjuice** (¼ liter) **or ⅔ cup cider vinegar** (15 cl) **plus a scant ½ cup water** (10 cl)

2 **ounces toasted country bread** (60 g)

1 **teaspoon ground ginger**

1 **teaspoon ground cinnamon**

1 **teaspoon grains of paradise, ground in a mortar or spice grinder** (see p. 46 for substitutes)

1 **pinch ground cloves**

1 **tablespoon coarse sea salt** (12 g)

1 **branch rosemary** (to use as a basting brush)

53. Spit-Roasted Hare

Roast Hare. Without washing it, lard it; and eat it with cameline [sauce] or *saupiquet*—that is, with the fat that falls into the dripping pan, and put in some thinly sliced onions, wine, and verjuice and a little vinegar, and pour it over the hare when it is roasted, or place it in the bowls. (VT Vat Scul 93)

Try this simple roast with a young, freshly killed hare. Contrary to what you hear about medieval tastes, game was not necessarily hung for a long time: "Note that the flesh of a freshly killed and promptly eaten hare is more tender than that of a hare that has been hung," we are told by the author of *Le Ménagier de Paris*. Furthermore, he writes that if killed in the depth of winter a hare will keep no more than eight days, and if in summer no more than four—and that only if stored out of the sun. If you are curious about how old your hare may be, the same author has a tip for you: "You may discover the age of a hare from the holes that are beneath the tail: for each opening, one year." Good luck!

1 young hare, skinned and cleaned

4 ounces fresh pork fatback (100 g)

1 medium onion scant ½ cup dry white wine (10 cl)

¼ cup verjuice (5 cl), or the juice of half a lemon mixed with a tablespoon of water

1 tablespoon good wine vinegar salt

Preheat the oven to 425 degrees F (220 degrees C).

With a thin-bladed, very sharp knife, carefully remove the shiny membrane that covers the meat; also remove any tough, stringy tissue (tendons and so forth) you may see, taking great care not to damage the meat.

Cut the pork fat into small strips and, using a narrow-bladed knife or a larding needle, evenly lard the entire hare.

Fix the hare to a spit and roast on a rotisserie with a dripping pan beneath, or place in a shallow roasting pan on a rack. Roast the hare for about half an hour, basting it frequently with the drippings. The meat should be just pink, at which point it will be at its juiciest and most tender.

While the hare is roasting, slice the onion very thinly, and when the meat has cooked for about 15 minutes add the onions to the roasting pan (or dripping pan if you are using a rotisserie). Five minutes before the hare is done, add the wine, the verjuice, and the vinegar to the pan.

When the hare is done, let it rest a few minutes, then carve it into serving portions; meanwhile, over medium heat, reduce the pan juices if necessary. Season the portions of hare and the sauce with salt to taste. Pour the sauce over the meat just before serving.

54. Roast Rib of Beef

Roast Beef. Roast of beef, taken from the ribs near the spine, is simply spit-roasted and served with boiled pepper. (Tr 388)

Search as you may through medieval cookery treatises, English or French, you will find not a trace of "roast beef." Their authors, and contemporary physicians, viewed beef as a "gross" meat good only for boiling: gross in the sense that it lacked the subtlety or finesse needed by nobles, who lived on poultry (which was considered the finest meat), and who lacked the digestive powers of peasants and others who engaged in heavy labor. With their frail constitutions, how could they safely digest so "cold" and "dry" a meat?

Yet curiously, we find the present recipe for an unmistakable roast beef among a long list of items for roasting: whole goose, loin of pork, shoulder of mutton, and so forth. Still, the author does not reject the opinion of the day: "In general," he writes, "all the meats that should be boiled in water are the flesh of pork, beef, and mutton." As was often true of spices, the sauce of boiled pepper was undoubtedly intended as a corrective, to make it easier for the diner to digest this "unhealthy" meat—which might not have tasted so terrible after all.

Trim the meat and fix it to the spit of a rotisserie, making sure it is well balanced on the spit, or place it on a rack in a broiling pan. Roast on the rotisserie, or cook under the broiler, not too close to the heat, for 20 to 30 minutes (or to an internal temperature of 120 degrees F/48 degrees C), turning from time to time.

1 rib roast of beef, bone-in, about 2¼ to 3 pounds (1 to 1.4 kg)
2 tablespoons black peppercorns
10 tablespoons (5 fl. ounces) water (15 cl)
   salt

Meanwhile, crush the peppercorns in a mortar or grind them coarsely in a spice grinder. Add them to the water, bring to the boil, and simmer for several minutes. Add salt to taste.

When the beef is done, let it rest for at least 5 minutes in a warm place (such as on the open door of the oven), so that the juices will be evenly distributed. Carve into even slices, sprinkle with salt and serve with the pepper infusion.

55. Round-Steak Rolls

Beef rolls.   Make thin slices of round, and wrap in them beef marrow and beef fat; then put them on the spit, roast them, and eat them with salt. (MP 177)

Nowadays, we generally use bottom round for stewing or boiling, so the notion of roasting or broiling it may seem surprising. But if the meat is sliced thin it has lots of flavor. Unless you are adept with the knife, much will depend on your butcher's willingness to slice the round and pound it thin for you. You can also use thin slices of sirloin or other steak. It's a nice—and delicious— change of pace.

Pound the meat very thin, as for veal scaloppine (or have the butcher do it for you). Cut the fat into 6 portions and pound it between sheets of waxed paper or plastic wrap until very thin. Slice the marrow into thin rounds.

Preheat the broiler.

Sprinkle the beef with salt; place a slice of fat on each slice of beef and arrange

6 thin slices bottom round
4 ounces beef kidney fat (or hard, white fat from the rib or loin) (100 g)
3 to 4 ounces beef marrow (80 to 100 g)
   salt

slices of marrow on top of the fat. Roll and fold each slice of beef into a little bundle and secure it with a wooden toothpick or bamboo skewer.

Broil for about 10 minutes, turning the beef rolls halfway through the cooking period.

Serve sprinkled with salt.

56. Roast Beef Tongue

Beef tongue.   Fresh beef tongue should be boiled, skinned, larded, and roasted, and eaten with cameline sauce.

Note: you should know that some say that the tongue of an old steer is better than the tongue of a young one; others say the opposite. (MP 177)

> A surprising, and excellent, recipe for roast tongue. The initial boiling tenderizes the flesh, then the roasting adds a great deal of flavor through browning. Larding prevents the meat from drying out and keeps it particularly succulent and flavorful. If you are fond of tongue and have a smoker or a big fireplace, the author of *Le Ménagier de Paris* suggests the Gascon technique of half-cooking some beef tongues, skinning them, salting them for a week, and then hanging them in the chimney for the whole winter. He says they will keep a long time in this way. To eat them, you boil the tongues in a mixture of water and wine and serve them with mustard. Try it and let us know the results!

1 **fresh beef tongue, about 3¼ pounds** (1.5 kg)

3 **to 4 ounces fresh pork fatback** (80 to 100 g)

salt

Trim the tongue and brush it under cold running water; soak it in cold water for about an hour.

Place the tongue into a large pan and add cold water to cover. Add about 2 teaspoons salt per quart of water. Bring to the boil, skimming any impurities that rise to the surface. Cover the pan, adjust the heat to a simmer, and cook for about an hour and 20 minutes, or about 25 minutes per pound. This will not completely cook the tongue, which generally takes about 35 minutes of simmering per pound.

Meanwhile, cut the fat into thin strips and keep in the refrigerator until needed.

Preheat the oven to 475 degrees F (250 degrees C).

Remove the tongue from the pot and let it cool until you can handle it comfortably. Skin it without damaging the meat, and remove all bones from the base.

With a narrow-bladed knife or a larding needle, pierce the tongue all over and insert the reserved strips of fat.

Place the tongue in a shallow roasting pan and bake for about 20 minutes, or until nicely browned. Slice and serve with either of our cameline sauces (recipe 106 or 107).

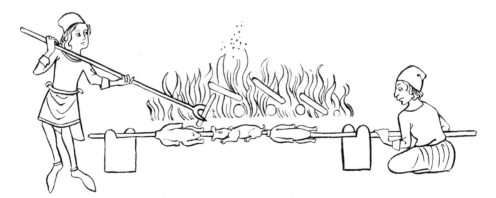

57. Roast Stuffed Quail

oasted little birds. Pluck them dry [that is, without first immersing them in hot water], then remove the crop and innards, and singe them over a smoke-free fire, and skewer them with slices of fat and bay leaves between them, and fill their cavities with fine rich cheese and beef marrow; eat them with fine salt, and bring them to table covered [to keep warm] between two bowls or plates. (VT Maz Scul 97)

> Our culinary treatises are often disappointing when it comes to the chapter on roasts, which is generally limited to a list of animals and cuts of meat that, it is understood, will be simply roasted. That is why this is a priceless recipe: it describes in great detail the preparation of birds, from plucking to roasting. It is nothing less than succulent prepared with quails: stuffed with rich cheese and marrow, interspersed with pork fat and bay leaves, their flavor and tender richness cannot be equaled with any other method of cooking.

alt and pepper the interior of the quails and stuff each one generously with a chunk of marrow and a piece of cheese. Place a bay leaf, then a slice of fat or prosciutto, on the breast and on the back of each quail, and fasten with toothpicks.

You can either skewer the quails or place them on a rack in a roasting pan. If you cook them on a skewer, be sure to place them over a dripping pan in order to catch the juices and melted cheese that will flow from the birds and that you will pour over them when they are served.

Cook them under the broiler or in a pre-

For one serving

2 **small or 1 large quail**

2 **ounces cream cheese (60 g)**

2 **walnut-sized chunks beef marrow from a fresh marrow bone**

4 **thin slices fresh pork fatback, salt belly of pork, pancetta, or prosciutto**

4 **fresh bay leaves**

   salt

   pepper

heated hot oven (400 degrees F/200 degrees C) for about 20 to 25 minutes, checking frequently to make sure they do not overcook, and turning them once about halfway through the cooking time. When they are nice and brown, serve them with the pan juices and sprinkled with salt. What a treat!

You can sew up the quails after stuffing them, to keep the melted cheese from flowing out, or you can leave them open: the cheese will add flavor and consistency to the pan juices.

58. Roast Goose

osling. Cut the gosling's or goose's throat; pluck it thoroughly and singe it; cut off the feet, remove the innards, and wash it well: then take verjuice and garlic, or, if you have none, take aromatic herbs soaked in vinegar, and sew up the cavity and put it on a spit, and roast it; and if it is not fat put some pork fat inside. Then put a little water in a dish and catch the fat that comes from within. And when it is properly cooked, take it off the fire and serve it with the juice of oranges, lemons, or sweet limes [*Citrus limettioides*]. (Za 30)

Tender, succulent goslings were highly esteemed in the Middle Ages, and they appear in the roast sections of all our treatises. On the other hand, there may have been less affection for fully grown geese, which were served at All Saints' Day in Italy and at the feast of Saint Martin in France. The *oyers* who sold and roasted geese in the Saint-Merri and Saint-Séverin quarters of Paris were famous for their skill with these fowl. They fattened them before roasting and they could carve them to perfection, but best of all they used the head, liver, wings, feet, and tripe to prepare a cold dish called *petit oie* ("little goose") which customers would munch on while they waited for their goslings to be cooked.

In French sources, roast goose is often accompanied by sauces featuring garlic, or garlic shoots, and pepper. This Italian recipe calls for citrus juice to be added to the juices in the dripping pan. But garlic is not neglected: it is among the aromatics that scent the bird as it roasts. Maître Chiquart recommends *jance* (recipe 111) with roast goose, a most popular sauce in its day; Chiquart's version is a perfect foil to the rich meat. Since goslings are hard to come by, you can also cook this dish with a nice, fat duck.

1 **young goose, 5½ to 6½ pounds (2.5 to 3 kg)**
1 **cup good wine vinegar (¼ liter)**
2 **juicy lemons or bitter oranges**
1 **bunch parsley**
3 **or 4 fresh bay leaves**
1 **sprig sage**
1 **sprig rosemary**
4 **or 5 cloves garlic**
   salt

Preheat the oven to 400 degrees F (200 degrees C).

Clean and truss the goose as you would any other poultry. Peel and lightly crush the garlic and roughly chop the herbs. Place the garlic and herbs in a bowl and add the vinegar; stir well.

Generously salt the cavity of the goose, and insert the vinegary garlic and herbs; sew up the vent and the neck. Roast on a rack for 14 to 17 minutes per pound for a young goose or 18 to 20 minutes per pound for an older, fatter bird.

When the goose is done, remove it to a platter and keep it in a warm place while you prepare the sauce. Put the roasting pan over medium heat (pour off some of the fat if there is a great deal), bring to the boil, and add about ⅔ cup (15 cl) water. As it returns to the boil, scrape the caramelized juices from the bottom of the pan with a wooden spoon and reduce the liquid by a third. Add the citrus juice and return briefly to the boil. Taste for salt and adjust the seasoning if necessary.

Carve the goose, and serve with the sauce.

59. Chicken with Orange Sauce

℟oast chicken. To prepare roast chicken, you must roast it; and when it is cooked, take orange juice or verjuice with rose water, sugar, and cinnamon, and place the chicken on a platter; and pour this mixture over it and send it to table. (Ma 127)

> How do you lend unexpected elegance to a simple roast chicken? By following Maestro Martino's advice to coat it with a fruity sweet-and-sour sauce when it comes out of the oven. If you have a guest who is apprehensive about medieval dishes, serve this one and you will make a convert. Chicken with Orange Sauce will also appeal to waist-watching epicureans: no fat is added either during the cooking or to the sauce.

℘reheat the oven to 425 degrees F (220 degrees C).

Wash and dry the chicken and salt the cavity. Place in a roasting pan and put in the oven, basting frequently with the pan juices, until golden brown and nicely cooked. Add the sugar and cinnamon to the bitter-orange juice or the verjuice/rose water mixture, and pour this over the roasted chicken (still in its roasting pan).

Place the chicken on a platter. Serve with the pan juices.

You can substitute normal orange juice for the bitter-orange juice, but in that case omit the sugar and add the juice of half a lemon.

1 free-range chicken, 3¼ to 4½ pounds (1.5 to 2 kg)
juice of 3 bitter oranges
or
10 tablespoons (5 fl. ounces) verjuice (15 cl) (or the juice of 2 lemons mixed with 6 tablespoons water) plus 1 tablespoon rose water
½ teaspoon sugar
1 pinch ground cinnamon
salt

60. Roast Capon with *Jance* Sauce

ℭapons, hens, *hétoudeaux.* Roasted, with grape-must sauce in summer or with *poitevine* sauce in winter, or with *jance*; and in winter you can make a sauce similar to grape must, i.e., with wine and sugar boiled together. (VT Vat Scul 90)

> *Hétoudeaux* were young capons or large chickens of an age at which they could be neutered. Fattened hens and, even more so, capons (which are neutered, fattened roosters) have exceptionally flavorful and succulent flesh. Medieval diners were particularly fond of capon, and its reputation did not flag in later centuries: it is a constant feature of cookery texts of the seventeenth and eighteenth centuries as well. To bring out all the merits of a capon, roast it.
>
> Capons are not easy to find, but you can order one from your butcher, especially around the fall and winter holidays (or see Mail-order Sources).

They are expensive, but worth the price: their moist, tender flesh will make you forget those sorry, dry holiday turkeys (which, we must recall, were unknown to our medieval cooks: the turkey did not make it to Europe until after the discovery of America).

1 **capon, 6½ to 9 pounds (3 to 4 kg)**

salt

jance **sauce** (recipe 111)

Preheat the oven to 400 degrees F (200 degrees C).

Rinse and dry the capon, and salt it inside and out. Truss it, place it in a shallow pan, and roast for about 15 to 18 minutes per pound, basting frequently with the pan drippings. If the oven temperature is too hot, the capon will brown too quickly and the flesh could dry out.

To check for doneness, pierce the thigh with a skewer or cooking fork. The juices should run perfectly clear; if they are even slightly pink, the capon is not fully cooked.

Carve into serving pieces, and salt lightly. Moisten with a spoonful of the pan juices.

Bring the remaining pan juices to the table in a sauceboat; serve the *jance* sauce in a second sauceboat.

Fish

 In the Middle Ages, "fish" implied various things. First and foremost, penitence: it replaced meat during times of abstinence. But eating fish was a real hardship only when it came down to the dried cod or herring that were imported from Nordic waters. And even they could be improved through clever cooking and saucing (see recipe 73).

It implied uncertainty. Even if municipal authorities worked hard to organize the sale of fish, supplies were unpredictable, freshness fragile, and transportation difficult. When the Friday market closed, the poor would collect the unsold fish that city regulations directed be left for them to prevent vendors from trying to sell them later on, when they were no longer fresh. Those who lived in the countryside at any distance from the coast would probably have seen nothing of sea fish. They aspired to eels, but most often they had to make do with roaches from nearby ponds.

Yet it also implied gourmandism: the very uncertainty heightened longing and fantasy.

We, of course, have no intention of forcing our readers to do penance. We want rather to gratify your gourmandism—not a difficult task, because culinary invention responds to this implication no less than to the others. Cooks knew their fish, and could use them in roasts (recipe 63), pies or pâtés (recipes 89 to 91), or *brouets/brodi* (recipe 62). They adapted sauces used for meats by adding a little extra fruit juice or spice to compensate for the "moist, cold" nature of this Lenten food. They also preserved fish in salt, in marinades, or in *escabèches,* to have them on hand for days of abstinence.

Today's market in fish has changed vastly as a result of refrigeration and speedier transportation. So take advantage of it.

61. Innkeeper's *Escabèche*

Jellied fish without oil. Boil wine with vinegar and put in the well-washed fish to cook; and when they are cooked, remove them and put them in another container. And into the wine and vinegar put onions sliced crosswise and boil it long enough to reduce by two-thirds: then put in saffron, cumin, and pepper and pour it all over the cooked fish and leave to cool. This is "Innkeeper's *Escabèche*." (Za 7s)

In taverns there was always some uncertainty about when a meal would have to be served, so their owners had to offer dishes that could be prepared quickly with preserved ingredients, such as *Carbonata* (recipe 43), or items that were ready to serve, such as *escabèches*. Preparing a fish as an *escabèche* both cooks and preserves it; the technique could also be applied to poultry, as in recipe 30, Chicken *Ambrogino* with Dried Fruit, which one menu lists as *Pollastri ad anbrosina aschibeci*. The style is generally defined by preliminary frying followed by maceration in an acidic liquid: wine and/or vinegar. Onions and saffron are often added. No particular fish is specified because of the preparation's function as a method of preservation and also because of how chancy supplies could be: there would always be surprises in the market, and cooks tended to buy whatever fish was available.

They still serve *scapece* in southern Italy and *escabeches* in Spain; Italian snack bars often offer little marinated anchovies, which are very similar, though not called by the same name.

As we said in "Histories and Tales from the Kitchen," that name, and the recipe itself, could well reflect a medieval European borrowing from Arab sources (the Arabic term is *sikbâj*).

4 **cups wine, either red or white depending on what color you want the dish to be** (1 liter)

1 **cup wine vinegar, the same color as the wine** (¼ liter)

1¾ **to 2¼ pounds fish, such as scrod, mackerel, or cod, on the bone, cut up if large** (800 g to 1 kg)

3 **medium-small onions**

6 **or 7 threads saffron**

½ **teaspoon cumin seed**

½ **teaspoon ground black pepper**

salt

In a nonreactive saucepan large enough to hold all the fish, combine the wine and the vinegar; salt lightly and bring to the boil. Add the fish, return to the simmer, and cook gently for barely 5 to 10 minutes, depending on the thickness of the pieces of fish. Meanwhile, cut the onions into ¼-inch (6-mm) slices.

Remove the fish with a slotted spoon or skimmer and transfer to a deep plate, preferably glazed pottery or glass.

Return the liquid to the heat, add the onions, and bring to the boil. Reduce over medium-low heat for about half an hour or until reduced by two-thirds. Then remove from the heat and add the saffron, cumin, and pepper. Check for salt.

Pour the liquid over the fish (do not strain it), and leave to cool; the liquid should gel. Serve cold.

62. Sweet-and-Sour Fish

Brodo of fish.   Take as much well-washed fish as you need: fry it in plenty of oil, then let it cool; then take onions sliced crosswise; fry them in the oil left from the fish; then take skinned almonds, raisins, dried elecampane, and prunes, and fry them together with the onions, and remove the excess oil. Take pepper, saffron, and other selected spices, finely pounded, and mix with the onions, and wine and vinegar; and when it is thoroughly blended put it on the fire until it boils; then take it off the fire, and put it into another container: put it in alternating layers with the fish. And if you like it sweet, add either boiled wine or sugar in the appropriate quantity. (Za 29)

> The mixture of ingredients here is a little disconcerting at first. But it is altogether characteristic of the Italian taste for sweet-and-sour flavors and of the lack of a clear line in medieval cooking between sweet and savory. This *brodo*, while differently named, falls into the category of an *escabèche*; the same text contains a recipe for a simplified Innkeeper's *Escabèche* (recipe 61). This, on the other hand, is a variation that is richer in sweet flavors: the sweetness of the onion is greatly increased by that of the dried fruits.
>
> In our version we have skipped the elecampane *(Inula helenium)*, because we have no idea which part of the plant would have been used.

Cut the fish into chunks and dry it thoroughly. Heat the olive oil in a skillet over medium-high heat. Add the fish and fry until just done. Remove the fish and reserve. In the same oil, fry the onions until they begin to turn golden, then add the almonds, raisins, prunes, spices, and salt to taste. Stir to combine, then add the wine and the vinegar. Simmer for about 20 minutes.

Place the fish and the sauce in alternating layers in a deep dish of glass, glazed pottery, or other nonreactive material.

Serve cold or lukewarm. At the last minute, for additional sweetness, you can pour over a glass of a sweet wine such as Muscat de Beaumes de Venise.

- 1¾ to 2¼ **pounds monkfish or other firm-fleshed fish** (800 g to 1 kg)
- 4 **medium-large onions, sliced**
- ⅔ **cup blanched almonds** (100 g)
- generous ½ **cup raisins** (100 g)
- 20 **prunes**
- 10 **tablespoons (5 fl. ounces) wine, red or white** (15 cl)
- 3 **tablespoons vinegar** (5 cl)
- 3 **tablespoons olive oil** (5 cl)
- 10 **threads saffron, approximately**
- ¼ **teaspoon ground black pepper**
- 1 **generous pinch ground ginger**
- 1 **generous pinch ground cardamom**
- **salt**

63. San Vincenzo's Day Grilled Eel

The priest's recipe: first, they skinned the eel with boiling water and removed its innards, and cut off the tail and the head, then washed it thoroughly in six changes of water, then made it into chunks of a *palmo* [hand's-breadth?] each, or less, and put them onto a skewer with bay leaves between the chunks to keep them from sticking together, and they gently roasted them thus. Then, having first put into a container some salt, vinegar, and a wee drop of oil, with four spices (i.e., half an ounce each of pepper, spice, cloves, and cinnamon) and, with a little branch of rosemary, they constantly basted the eel with this ginger water. And when it was nicely cooked and boned, they took an aspic dish and arranged the chunks in it; then they squeezed six pomegranates over it, with at least twenty oranges and with plenty of fine spices; then they covered it with a warm cake pan to keep it warm until it was brought to the table. (Sermini, *Novelle* 29)

You will have noticed the narrative style of this recipe. And in fact, we found it not in a cookbook but in a collection of tales by the early-fifteenth-century Sienese writer Gentile Sermini. Here is the tale:

Ser Meoccio was the parish priest of Pernina in the Montagnola, the hill that is the evening backdrop to Siena. He loved good food above all else, and he made his parishioners provide it in the form of offerings to God, for whom Ser Meoccio acted as surrogate. As he told his flock, God was the sole proper recipient of alms; it was improper to give to the poor, because they did not know how to use their wealth, or to prisoners, because they would not be in prison if they were not such dreadful people. So the credulous peasants heaped the altar with all the produce of their gardens, their farmyards, and their flocks. Ser Meoccio placed special stress on the value of offerings honoring a saint on his or her day.

That year Saint Vincent's Day, January 22, fell on a Friday, so one parishioner, named Vincenzo, bought the priest a beautiful eel weighing ten *libri* (six and a half pounds). He delivered it to Ser Meoccio's house, but the priest had already gone to celebrate mass. His cook was flustered, and took himself to the church; from the doorway he tried to catch the priest's attention by making broad gestures signifying the eel. The priest understood. He was in the middle of narrating the miracles and martyrdom of Saint Vincent, but he diverted the course of his sermon by means of a transition that, to tell the truth, was rather flimsy.

"Saint Vincent," he preached, "ate and drank in moderation; he was nothing like these hogs nowadays. In that connection, I shall tell you a tale, to which I myself was witness."

And he told of how his teacher and four of his friends ordered an enormous eel to be cooked; he himself served at table. The recipe thus was relayed to the cook from the pulpit by way of an exemplum: a true-to-life story a preacher would insert in his sermons to help convince his listeners. The priest continued with the rest of the menu, then finished with a hasty peroration: hasty because Ser Meoccio was in a hurry to get home and supervise the preparation of his feast. Sermini tells us that six priests stuffed themselves, while in a nearby hut Vincenzo and his family ate a meal of dried beans and bony little fish.

The tale might have ended there, but Sermini is on a roll.

The surfeited priests collapsed in ecstasy and chanted a *Te Deum*. Drawn by the shouting and the singing, Vincenzo and his family came running. To explain the immoderate caroling, Ser Meoccio concocted the story that Saint Vincent had materialized, bursting with gratitude for a feast he had not actually tasted. And, to reproduce the miraculous effect of an "odor of sanctity," the priest sprinkled the devout family with rose water.

But this was the fifteenth century, and opposition to a corrupt Church was on the rise. So the wicked priest was unmasked by one Lodovico Salerni, a city dweller who was more sophisticated than the peasants. Sermini had no sentimentality for either men of the cloth or men of the land. At the height of his attack, Lodovico grabbed the priest's breviary:

"It was full of recipes for every possible dish, every possible treat: how to cook them, what sauces to accompany them with, what time of year to prepare them."

It was, no doubt, that book that inspired this Saint Vincent's Day dish. So let us return to our recipe, leaving Ser Meoccio to his unhappy fate (in dread of the inquisitor and the bishop, he fled, but was abducted by pirates; he washed up near the mouth of the Tiber and was saved from penury and starvation only by the charity of . . . Lodovico Salerni).

Today, on the shores of Lake Trasimeno, eel is still prepared in this way. It is better to cook this dish on a grill than in the oven, because it is easier to baste the eel. Medieval oranges were not sweet, so we suggest a mixture of lemon juice and orange juice. If you can find unhybridized sour oranges or mandarins, by all means use them.

In our adaptation we have taken the generic term "spices" to mean ginger, because the author calls the basting liquid *zenezaverata*, or ginger water.

Have your fishmonger kill, skin, and clean the eels and cut them into 2-inch lengths.

Preheat the grill or broiler.

Thread the pieces of eel onto skewers, alternating them with bay leaves.

In a small bowl or measuring cup, combine the vinegar, the oil, and the pepper/clove/cinnamon/ginger mixture.

Squeeze the oranges, lemons, and pomegranate, and reserve the juice.

Grill the eels, not too close to the fire. Baste frequently with the spiced vinegar mixture, using the branch of rosemary as a brush. Be sure the eels do not overcook and fall apart.

When the eels are done, arrange them in a deep platter, pour the fruit juice over them, and sprinkle with the cardamom/ginger mixture. Allow to cool slowly to lukewarm and serve.

1 large or 2 medium eels, total weight 3¼ pounds (1.5 kg)
3 tablespoons to ½ cup vinegar (5 to 10 cl)
2 tablespoons oil
4 oranges
3 lemons
  half a pomegranate
1 branch rosemary
  about 20 fresh bay leaves
  salt
¼ teaspoon each of ground black pepper, ground cloves, ground cinnamon, and ground ginger, blended
¼ teaspoon each of ground cardamom and ground ginger, blended

64. Marinated Trout *in Carpione*

To prepare *carpione* of trout as you would cook a carpione, clean the trout well and gut them, then pierce them in many places all over with the point of a knife. Then make a brine with equal parts of water and vinegar, adding plenty of salt which you must dissolve thoroughly; and put the trout in for half a day or more. And when this is done, transfer them to a table, putting them under a weight for three or four hours, and fry them well in plenty of good oil, so that they are nicely cooked but not burnt. You can keep these trout for a month, refrying them if you like, and preparing them again as you would a carpione. (Ma 202)

This way of preparing trout is conceived in principle for the carpione *(Salmo trutta Carpio L.)*, a freshwater fish related to the salmon and the trout, today found only in Lake Garda. Even in Maestro Martino's day, this method seemed so perfectly suited to the carpione that the verb *carpionare* came to be used for this technique for cooking freshwater fish. Traces are still found in an 1863 book on Milanese cooking, in a recipe for a "marinade for carpione or any other freshwater fish." There is no question but that marinating adds flavor, aroma, and texture to the flesh of freshwater fish, which is often fine but a little mushy, quite apart from its function as a method of preservation.

The technique in this recipe is to marinate the food in a vinegary brine, then to fry it. The opposite technique—frying first, then macerating in an acidic liquid—is known today as *a scapece* or *schibezia*; in the middle ages it was known as *alla scapetia* (see recipe 61). In modern-day Piedmont, oddly enough, the two methods seem to have canceled each other out: in summertime they prepare all manner of cold dishes that are called *in carpione* but that are cooked as *escabèches*. None of the cooks we spoke with knew the meaning of the word *carpione*. It was only after a careful reading of Maestro Martino that we made the connection between his recipe and the delicious, refreshing dishes we were served in that little Piedmontese town—where we had gone precisely to prepare a medieval banquet inspired by Martino.

6 **tablespoons coarse sea salt or a generous ½ cup kosher salt (100 g)**

1¼ **cups water (30 cl)**

1¼ **cups white wine vinegar (30 cl)**

6 **trout**

4 **tablespoons olive oil**

Prepare a brine with the salt, water, and vinegar. Clean and wash the trout and prick them all over with the point of a sharp paring knife. In a glass or other nonreactive dish large enough to hold all the fish in one layer, marinate the trout in the brine, refrigerated, for about 3 hours. Pour off the brine and weight the trout for about 2 hours more: cover them loosely with plastic wrap, set a flat object (such as a pan lid or wooden board) on top of them, and place a 2-pound weight—a large can of tomatoes for example—on this surface.

Dry the trout carefully. Heat the oil in a large skillet, preferably nonstick, over medium-high heat. Quickly brown the trout on both sides, then lower the heat to medium-low and cook for 7 or 8 minutes on each side. They should be cooked thoroughly, but the skin must not burn. Serve hot or cold, as a first course.

65. Roast Shad

Shad. Fresh ones come into season in March. They should be gutted through the gills and scaled. . . .

Note: Prepare shad as above, but without scaling them, then roast them in the oven with parsley and half verjuice, half a mixture of wine and vinegar; in season from February to June. (MP 188)

> As the author of *Le Ménagier de Paris* reminds us, this freshwater fish (which can reach considerable size) is a seasonal delicacy. It still comes to market in springtime and is particularly prized for its roe. In France, it is especially popular in the Southwest. This preparation, with its sharp, clear flavors, goes well with the shad's fatty, succulent, and flavorful flesh. Terence Scully, editor of Taillevent's *Le Viandier* (which also contains a version of this recipe), notes that it is surprising in this period to find a fish being roasted in the oven, which in principle was set aside for bread, savory pies, and so forth. He describes it as an innovation: an innovation that had a great future before it.

Wash and dry the fish. Sprinkle with salt inside and out, and set aside for a few minutes. Preheat the oven to 400 degrees F (200 degrees C).

Combine the verjuice, vinegar, wine, and parsley and pour into a baking dish. Put the shad into the baking dish and roast for 20 to 25 minutes, depending on size, basting every few minutes with the flavorful pan juices. If you are using shad fillets, place them into the dish skin-side up.

Before serving, remove the crisp skin and baste one final time with the pan juices.

1 large shad, about 4½ pounds, whole or filleted (2 kg)
scant ½ cup verjuice (10 cl), or a mixture of 5 tablespoons cider vinegar and 3 tablespoons water
3 tablespoons white wine (5 cl)
3 tablespoons good-quality white wine vinegar (5 cl)
1 tablespoon chopped parsley
salt

If you have leftovers, by all means serve them cold the next day. Especially if you have used a whole fish, the sauce should set into a delicious, supple aspic.

66. *Chaudumé* of Pike

To make *chaudumé,* take some pike, scale them, and brown them, cut into pieces or whole, on the grill; grill some bread and soak it in the liquid from cooking dried peas; and then, when the bread is soaked, take some verjuice and white wine and some of the dried-pea liquid, and sieve the bread together with these; and when it has been strained, mix an *once* [about an ounce] of ginger into the broth along with a little saffron, and add the fish to the broth and some fresh or salted butter. (VT XV 179)

Cooking this recipe is child's play; it is conceived for pike, but is also delicious with salmon or any number of other fish more easily found in your local fish market. The moderately tart flavor of the sauce, ever so slightly softened by the butter, and its richness and bronzed color are a perfect match for the fine flesh of the fish.

1   slice country bread
1   scant cup broth from cooking
      dried peas or beans, or plain
      water (20 cl)
1   pike, about 2¼ pounds (1 kg)
10 tablespoons (5 fl. ounces) good
      white wine (15 cl)
      scant ½ cup verjuice (10 cl), or
      the juice of 1 lemon plus 3
      tablespoons water
1   teaspoon ground ginger or a
      thick slice fresh ginger minced
      to a puree
4   tablespoons (2 ounces) butter,
      cut into small cubes (50 g)
3   or 4 threads saffron
      salt

Preheat the grill or broiler. Grill or toast the bread, then cut it into pieces and soak it in the broth or water. Clean, wash, and dry the fish; salt it inside and out.

When the bread has softened, add the wine and verjuice (or diluted lemon juice). Puree it by forcing it through a sieve or in a food processor.

Grill or broil the fish, turning once.

While the fish is cooking, bring the bread sauce to the boil and simmer it gently for 10 or 15 minutes, or until it thickens slightly. Check for salt, then add the ginger and saffron. Off the heat, swirl in the butter to bind and smooth the sauce.

When the fish is done, transfer it into the pan with the sauce, and baste it. Reheat without boiling, and serve.

67. Grilled Mackerel

Mackerel.   Fresh mackerel comes into season in June, although it can be found as early as March. Gut it through the gills, then wipe it with a clean cloth; without washing it at all, roast it, then eat it with cameline sauce or fine salt. (MP 196)

This recipe specifies that the mackerel should not be split open or washed, but cleaned through the gills and wiped with a cloth. If you would rather wash it, be careful to dry it thoroughly before roasting. The mackerel is served either with salt—easy!—or with the famous cameline sauce, for which a wide range of recipes is to be found in both French and Italian sources. For this dish we have chosen the winter Tournai-style cameline (recipe 107). As you prepare the sauce, taste it for salt and sugar, but do not make a final judgment until you have tasted it together with the mackerel: its flavor may be unexpected, but remember that it will be served with a fish that it goes with very well indeed.

Prepare the sauce.
    Preheat the grill or broiler.
    Salt the fish and grill them about 7 inches from the heat, about 7 or 8 minutes on each side.
    Serve with the prepared sauce.

4   **very fresh medium-sized mackerel, cleaned, washed, and thoroughly dried**
    salt
    cameline sauce (recipe 107)

68. Inside-Out Stuffed Fresh Sardines or Anchovies

Stuffed anchovies and sardines.   To stuff anchovies or sardines, put them in hot water after having removed the heads and bones so that they are open along the back. Then grind marjoram, rosemary, sage, good spices, saffron, and the flesh of a few fish. Fill the anchovies or sardines with this stuffing so that the skin is next to the stuffing and the outside in. Then fry them in oil. They may be eaten with lemon juice. (Lc 415)

In your wildest culinary dreams did you ever imagine opening a fish from the back, removing the bones and head without piercing the belly skin, spreading the skin with a stuffing, and closing the fish so that the flesh is on the outside, and then frying it? Yet this is what the author of this recipe suggests—and other writers as well. Maestro Martino splits a suckling pig along the back-bone, turns it inside out like a sock, and then roasts it (see recipe 50); an eel is *renversée* in *Le Ménagier de Paris*, or *rovesciata* in Italian sources, then cooked flesh-side out.

    The recipe we have chosen here uses the same intimidating technique, but in this case for a rather smaller creature. Fish are often hard to identify on the basis of their names, which even today vary from region to region. In Nordic regions, it is generally herrings that go by the Latin name of *allex* or *hallex*. This and other recipes in the *Liber de coquina* link the terms *allectes* and *sarde* or *sardelle*; medieval Latin uses a number of words derived from *allex* and *allicium* for small fish of all kinds; modern Italian uses *alice* for anchovy: for all these reasons, we have adapted this recipe for sardines and anchovies. We believe that sardines were sold lightly salted to keep them better; this would explain why the recipe instructs us to place them in warm water before removing their heads and bones.

It is hard to know what benefits medieval cooks would have seen in a preparation of this kind, but it is certainly true that fatty flesh (and this inside-out technique is used only for suckling pig and fatty fish) will render some of its fat when exposed to direct heat. And the results are excellent from the standpoint of flavor.

We have not been entirely faithful to the original recipe: we remove the head and bones from the fish without soaking them in hot water, which would be pointless—indeed harmful—for fresh fish.

24	whole sardines or large anchovies, not cleaned by the fishmonger
10	ounces boneless meat of fatty fish such as sardines, herring, or mackerel (300 g)
1	teaspoon chopped fresh marjoram or oregano (or half as much dried)
1	teaspoon chopped fresh rosemary (or half as much dried)
2	leaves sage, chopped
¼	teaspoon ground ginger
¼	teaspoon freshly grated nutmeg
⅛	teaspoon freshly ground black pepper
3	or 4 threads saffron, crushed
	salt
2	tablespoons olive oil
	lemon wedges to serve

Using a thin-bladed, extremely sharp knife, cut into the back of each sardine or anchovy, cutting along either side of the backbone to free the backbone from the rib cage. At the same time remove the heads and the innards, being careful not to pierce the skin. This will yield 2 fillets joined by the skin of the belly.

With a pair of good tweezers remove the most obvious rib bones. Remaining bones will be very visible when the fish has been cooked and can be removed easily by each diner.

Wash the fish thoroughly and dry them with paper towels. Sprinkle them inside and out with salt and pepper and set them aside while you prepare the stuffing.

For the stuffing, puree the fish flesh, herbs, spices, and salt to taste in a food processor. Transfer to a bowl and refrigerate, along with the filleted fish, if you are not going to continue immediately; if your kitchen is warm, keep the stuffing on ice as you work.

It will be easier to stuff the fish if you sew each one partially closed, to form a pocket, skin-side in, flesh-side out. Stuff the fish and complete sewing each one up the back, leaving a little stuffing protruding from where the head used to be. To make this process even easier, put the stuffing into a piping bag with a small, plain tube, and pipe the stuffing into each fish.

Heat the olive oil over medium heat in a skillet, preferably nonstick. Sauté the fish for 3 to 4 minutes on each side, then cover the pan, lower the heat, and cook for another

30 seconds or so. Before serving, insert a knife into one of the fish and make sure the stuffing is cooked through.

Sprinkle with lemon juice and serve garnished with additional lemon wedges.

69. Grilled Fish with Herbs and Spices

Roast fish.   If you want fish roasted on the grill: take the fish, wash it, and then split it and sprinkle some salt over it. Take good spices, sprinkle them on the outside skin; gather it together so that the [edges] of the skin meet; put good aromatic herbs between the layers of skin, tie with a string, brush oil on the fish with a branch of sage, put it over smoke-free embers; turn it often, and remove. Serve either with sauce or with salt. (Gu 33)

> Another recipe that directs you to manipulate the fish so that the flesh is outside and the skin inside, as in recipe 68, Inside-Out Fresh Sardines or Anchovies. But in this case the original author is very stingy with details. Only someone who already knew the secret could figure out how these fish were to be prepared. The first step is to bone the fish, but this is never mentioned, as though the cook would obviously have this procedure under his belt. In any event, this recipe is absolutely delicious when prepared with ordinary mackerel. Exposing the flesh of a fatty fish to direct heat without the insulation of its skin indisputably yields excellent results. And the herbs and spices placed directly on the skin add an incomparable flavor.

Clean and wash the fish. Split them open at the belly and remove the backbone, taking care not to pierce the skin along the back, or ask your fishmonger to do this for you.

Preheat the grill or broiler. You will not want a very hot fire.

Pat dry with paper towels, sprinkle with salt inside and out, and set aside for 5 or 10 minutes. Generously sprinkle the skin with the spice mixture.

Arrange the fish skin-side up on your work surface, and lay a few sprigs of parsley and sage on each fish. Fold the fish over the herbs, so that the skin is on the inside. Tie each fish closed with string, or secure with toothpicks or bamboo skewers.

1   fatty fish per person (such as mackerel, horse mackerel, bluefish, or large sardine)
1   bunch parsley
1   bunch fresh sage
    olive oil
    salt

For the spice mixture
1   teaspoon ground ginger
½   teaspoon ground coriander
¼   teaspoon freshly grated nutmeg
¼   teaspoon freshly ground black pepper

Dip a sprig of sage in olive oil and spread some oil on each fish.

Gently grill or broil the fish for about 5 minutes per side; they should be lightly golden.

Serve immediately, with salt if needed.

70. Poached Fresh Tuna with Yellow Sauce

Tuna is a fish that is found in the sea or the marine ponds of the Languedoc, and which has no bones apart from the backbone, and has a tough skin; it should be cooked in water and eaten with *poivre jaunet*. (MP 196)

This recipe is extremely healthy by our modern lights. Simply cooked in salted water, tuna stays tender and has a very good flavor. The tart, aromatic, and fat-free sauce is a perfect accompaniment.

1¾ **pounds fresh tuna, thickly**
   sliced or in a single piece
   (800 g)
   sea salt or kosher salt
   yellow sauce, or *poivre jaunet*
   (recipe 109)

Wash the fish and pat it dry. Place it into a pan and add cold water to cover; add salt (about 1 heaping tablespoon per quart/liter). Bring to the boil, lower the heat, and simmer until done; begin checking after about 10 minutes. The tuna should be cooked through but still moist.

Arrange the fish on a warmed platter and top with *poivre jaunet* sauce. Serve immediately.

71. Dover Sole with Bitter Orange Juice

Soles.   They should be fried, and sprinkle over them a little fine salt, orange juice, or verjuice, and plenty of chopped parsley. (Ma 186)

Despite what many people think, you do not need to flour fish to prevent it from sticking to the pan, so long as you are careful to get the oil nice and hot before adding the fish. These soles will cook in just a few minutes, and the unusual and refreshing seasoning is a perfect match for the delicate flesh. If you can get bitter oranges, you need not bother with the lemon juice.

6 **small Dover soles, gutted and**
   skinned but not boned
3 **tablespoons olive oil**
   juice of 2 oranges
   juice of 1 lemon
3 **tablespoons finely chopped**
   parsley
   salt

Wash and dry the soles and salt them on both sides.

Heat the oil in a large skillet, preferably nonstick, over medium heat. When it is hot, brown the fish for 3 or 4 minutes per side. When they are done and golden brown, decrease the heat to very low, pour over the orange and lemon juices, and sprinkle with parsley. Serve immediately.

72. Skate with Garlic Sauce

Skate, or sea dog, is cooked in water after it has been cut into pieces; then drain it and remove the skin, and put it back into the water until it has cooked sufficiently. And eat it with garlic sauce. (Tr 390)

> Finally: a change from that bistro standby "Skate with brown butter" (and from the typically *nouvelle cuisine* "Skate wings on a salad of baby lettuces"). When you anoint it with this sauce of almond (or walnut) milk, infused with garlic, you will see skate in a whole new light.

Since nowadays skate is generally sold skinless, you will not need to parboil it, as the original recipe specifies, in order to remove the skin.

Put the skate into a nonreactive pan and add cold water to cover. Add ½ cup (12 cl) vinegar and a tablespoon of salt per quart (liter) of water.

4½ **pounds skate wings, skinned but not boned** (2 kg)
vinegar
sea salt or kosher salt
garlic sauce (recipe 100)

Bring to the boil, skimming any impurities that rise to the surface. Lower the heat and poach the skate for about 15 minutes; the motion of the simmering water should be barely visible.

Drain the skate and remove its cartilaginous bones. Spoon garlic sauce over and serve.

73. Salt Cod with Garlic Sauce

Salt cod is cooked in water and is served with mustard or with a garlic sauce prepared as follows: crush garlic and crumb of bread moistened with almond or walnut milk. And add this to onions fried in oil with the cod, and boil it for a while. (Tr 390)

> The Latin treatise from which this dish comes is of uncertain origin, but its author had high culinary ambitions (he announces that he has collected his recipes from the four corners of the world). This recipe for salt cod seems to be an ancestor of the Provençal *brandade de morue*. But you will find no cow's milk here, only almond (or walnut) milk: fish—and especially salt cod—was a symbol of abstinence and was prepared with vegetable products only.

18 ounces salt cod (bone in) (500 g)

2 small slices dry country bread, crusts removed (60 g)

2 cups almond milk (½ liter) (recipe 151)

3 cloves garlic

2 medium onions

olive oil

salt, if necessary

For the court bouillon

6 cups water

1 small onion

1 rib celery

1 carrot

a sprig of parsley

1 bay leaf

6 whole peppercorns

A day in advance soak the cod overnight in cool water, changing the water at least once.

The next day, prepare the court bouillon: combine all the ingredients, bring to the boil, and simmer for 30 minutes. Strain and let cool.

Cut the bread into small pieces and soak it in the almond milk. Peel the onions and cut them into small dice; sauté them in olive oil until they are light golden brown.

Poach the cod in the court bouillon over very low heat for about 20 minutes. Remove the cod to a plate and let it rest until it is cool enough to handle. Pick out the bones, and flake the flesh.

Put the bread and almond milk into a saucepan; mash the bread with a fork or an immersion blender to form a pulp. Over medium-low heat, add the onions. Peel and finely mince (or crush) the garlic, and add it

to the sauce. Add the flaked cod and simmer for about 15 minutes, stirring frequently. Check for salt, and serve.

74. Cuttlefish in Black Sauce

Cuttlefish. If you want cuttlefish prepared as mushrooms: take the cuttlefish, wash it well, split it open, remove the black sauce that is inside and, separately, the milk; and then wash it again and put it to boil. And when it has boiled awhile, remove it, chop it up like mushrooms, and put it into a skillet to fry with fresh oil; and add good herbs, and garlic, and chopped leeks, and good pounded spices; chop up the reserved milk and add it, and add the black sauce that was inside, and cook at high heat so that it is thoroughly cooked; and put it on hot *testi*, and stir frequently so that it does not stick. (Gu 34)

A *testo* comprises a base and a domed cover made of terra cotta or metal; these were a substitute for an oven, and were placed in the fireplace. In this case, clearly, the cooking pan is placed on the base, which functions as a cooktop. For more on *testi* see p. 133 and recipe 78.

In this recipe the anonymous Italian author displays thorough knowledge of his maritime resources—specifically, cephalopods such as cuttlefish—as well as irrefutable culinary learning. He instructs the reader, in cleaning the cuttlefish, to set aside both the ink sac and what he calls the "milk." Everyone knows that cuttlefish have a sophisticated defensive system that enables them to hide from aggressors behind a cloud of dark ink. But only a cook (or an ichthyologist) would know that hidden away in the cuttlefish's body is another sac containing a syrupy bluish-yellow substance, which is also used in this recipe. A number of modern Italian recipes we have seen also note that the cuttlefish contains two sacs. Their contents, so different in color, continue today to flavor and color the cuttlefish risotto that is popular in Roman cooking.

This is a delicious dish and deserves a try. If you happen upon some fresh cuttlefish (not, alas, an everyday occurrence—although you can use squid), you must not miss the opportunity to cook this recipe, even if it is a little time-consuming.

Clean the cuttlefish. Cut off the tentacles below the eyes, then gently pull the remainder of the head free from the body, taking care not to crush any of the internal sacs. Remove the cuttlebone by slitting the skin of the mantle with a knife. Cut open the body; remove the sacs and set them aside.

Remove the eyes and discard. Open and clean the remainder of the head. Pull the skin away from the head and the body, exposing the white flesh.

2¼ pounds whole fresh cuttlefish (or substitute squid) (1 kg)
1 very small leek, white part only a small handful each of fresh mint, parsley, and basil
2 leaves sage
2 tablespoons olive oil
1 teaspoon strong spices (recipe 150, variation C)
salt

Put the cuttlefish into a saucepan, cover with cold water, and add salt (about 1 tablespoon per quart/liter). Bring to the boil and simmer for about 15 minutes. Drain and set aside.

While the cuttlefish are simmering, trim and wash the leek and the herbs. Finely mince the leek and the herbs, to yield about ¼ cup.

When the cuttlefish are cool enough to handle, dry them and slice into very thin strips. Heat the olive oil in a saucepan, add the cuttlefish, and sauté until lightly golden brown.

Decrease the heat to very low, stir in the leek-herb mixture and cook for half a minute. Stir in the spices and salt to taste. Cover the pan and cook over very low heat for about half an hour, stirring from time to time to make sure the mixture does not stick:

add a couple of teaspoons of water occasionally if necessary. When the dish is nearly done, stir in the milky substance (if you have been able to find it as you cleaned the cuttlefish). Break one ink sac into the saucepan and immediately stir it in vigorously. The sauce will thicken and become quite black. Check for seasoning and serve immediately.

75. Grilled Oysters

ysters are cooked over hot coals, and when they open they are cooked and can be eaten thus. And if you want them in a different way, take them out of their shells and fry them a little in oil, and put on them some verjuice and strong spices. (Ma 189)

In the Middle Ages, oysters were most often cooked in a *civet*, and many sources contain such recipes. But we continue to place our trust in Maestro Martino, and it is from him that we learn a different method. These oysters, poached in their own essence with no culinary artifice, reach perfection. From the coals to the plate, they enter the mouth just as they are: warm, juicy, and tasting of the sea.

In the fireplace or on a wood or charcoal grill:

3 dozen large oysters

uild a fire, using wood or natural wood charcoal (not briquets). Wait until the embers are glowing under a layer of ash.

Brush the oysters clean and set them on a rack over the embers. After about 10 minutes or less you will hear a tiny sound of juices or steam escaping from the shells; this signals that the oysters are ready. Some of their shells will open slightly, but even if they do not, the upper shell will loosen and become very easy to remove.

Eat immediately: just lift the upper shell with a table knife. The oysters will be barely warmed and will have just begun to cook. A delight.

Under the broiler:

Lacking a live fire, you can set the oysters in a sheet pan, on a ½-inch (1-cm) bed of coarse salt to stabilize them.

Cook about 5 inches (13 cm) away from a hot, preheated broiler, for about 15 minutes or less; then follow the instructions above.

Pies and Tarts

In the Middle Ages, these sweet and savory preparations baked in a crust were the specialty of *pâtissiers*—who had no other functions, as wafers *(gaufres* and *oublies)* and cakes were the province of *oubloyers*. Things have changed: pastry is almost always a treat for dessert, and pâtés no longer have any relation to pies or tarts, except for the few that we now call *pâtés en croûte*.

We know that medieval cooks did not always have ovens, and they worked with *pâtissiers,* to whom they sometimes brought fillings of their own making for the *pâtissier* to place in a crust and bake. This explains why cookbooks intended for professional chefs were nearly silent about the ingredients of these pastry wrappings, but spoke only about consistency and thickness, and about the most suitable shapes. For his *pâtés nurriz,* Maître Chiquart requests his pastry-chef colleague to provide *croûtelettes petites et hautelettes*—"wee little crusts, a trifle high."

Still, medieval cooks might take a chance and cook a simple pie or tart on their own (see recipes 78, 79, 81, 82, and 94) by placing it in a shallow pan, covered with a lid and surrounded by live embers, whose progress they had to monitor very closely. The Italians had in fact developed an appliance known as a *testo* specifically to permit home baking. But again, there is not so much as a hint in the texts about the secret of its construction.

Eating a pie could sometimes be full of surprises: the crust might conceal not only tender, chopped fillings, but also unboned creatures, whole or cut into chunks. These were selected for their tenderness; they were sometimes larded with fat and often spiced. From time to time, different meats would be mixed: a pie containing six large quail, supported by three partridges, supported in turn by a dozen larks, is memorialized in a poetical recipe by Gaces de la Bugne, principal chaplain to Kings Charles V and Charles VI.

This wrapping had the additional role of protecting the precious juices of delicate flesh that could be harmed by an open fire or by the heat of the oven. In effect, the pastry became an oven, ensuring moderate heat thanks to its insulating properties. This is probably how a ground meat filling cooked in a pot or mold came to be called a pâté, even though it is not surrounded by any pastry *(pâte)* at all (see recipe 85, Crustless Lamb Pâté). In those days, the pot would have been a rustic article made of earthenware and of little value. It would not have been made to last, and its function here would have been that of a wrapping—just like a *pâtissier*'s crust.

So could it be that these pastry coverings were not necessarily eaten once they had done their job of containing and protecting the filling? If the goal was indeed to protect the meat effectively, as our authors inform us, a simple mixture of flour and water, applied in a thick layer, would serve as an excellent barrier during the cooking process. But it would be a real jawbreaker if you tried to eat it. For his part, Gaces de la Bugne considered that the wrapping should equal the filling in savor:

> *Si tu veux que du pâté tâte*   If you want a pie that's tasty
> *Fais mettre des oeufs en la pâte.* Have eggs put into the pastry.

Tourtes/torte were preferred with a thin crust laid into a generously greased shallow pan and then coated with lard or oil. The empty crust was sometimes put over the fire and allowed to harden slightly before filling. This would give flavor and richness to even the simplest of doughs.

The "Hungarian" *Torta* (recipe 88) is a magnificent example: its eighteen membrane-thin layers of dough are kept apart from one another by brushings of melted lard. This encloses a mixture of spiced meats whose appeal is enhanced by its flaky sheath. In concept and in execution, this unusual recipe foreshadows modern puff pastry, which we expect both to melt in the mouth and to protect its delicate filling.

SAVORY PIES AND TARTS
76. Garlic *Torta*.

Garlic *torta*.   Take the garlic cloves, and peel them and boil them; when they are cooked, put them to soak in cold water, and then pound them and add saffron and plenty of cheese, which should be fresh, and chopped pork fat, and sweet and strong spices, and moisten with eggs, and add raisins, and then make the *torta*. (Fr 55)

Among their numerous pies, most of our cookbooks include garlic, onion, and shallot preparations. The procedures in this recipe are utterly typical; as the garlic is completely cooked, it does not dominate. The flavors are elegant and well balanced among garlic, saffron, and cheese.

For the pâte brisée
1¾ **cups flour** (250 g)
9 **tablespoons butter** (125 g)
⅓ **cup water, approximately** (10 cl)
1 **scant teaspoon salt**

A few hours in advance, prepare the *pâte brisée* according to the instructions given in recipe 153 (variation B). Wrap in plastic wrap and refrigerate until needed.

Bring a pot of water to the boil. Meanwhile, break the garlic into cloves. Peel the garlic and add it to the boiling water; lower the heat to medium, and cook for 15 minutes. Drain and transfer to a bowl of cold water.

Grind the pork in a food processor or meat grinder, or chop it finely with a knife. Do not trim away the fat.

Preheat the oven to 400 degrees F (200 degrees C).

Drain the garlic thoroughly and puree it in a food processor or mortar and pestle. In a mixing bowl, add the cheeses, the ground pork, the spice mixture, the saffron (crushed between your fingers), the eggs, and the raisins. Add salt to taste and stir the mixture until smooth. If you are using salt pork belly, be very sparing with the salt.

Roll out two-thirds of the pastry and line a deep 9-inch (22-cm) tart pan. Add the filling, roll out the remaining pastry, and cover the pie, pressing the seams tightly shut. Put the tart pan on a baking sheet to catch any drips, and bake for 45 minutes to an hour.

For the filling

5 heads garlic

7 ounces fresh (or salt) pork belly (200 g)

6 ounces whole-milk farmer's cheese (165 g)

5 ounces cream cheese (135 g)

3 eggs
scant ½ cup raisins (80 g)

12 threads saffron
salt

For the spice mixture

⅓ teaspoon each ground cloves, freshly grated nutmeg, and ground ginger

1 teaspoon each ground cinnamon and freshly ground pepper

77. Onion or Shallot Tart

Torta of shallots, or of onions, etc.   If you want to make a *torta* of these two things, take whichever you like and boil it well. First thoroughly remove the water with a sieve, and then chop them fine, and take good pork fat and chop it well; take eggs and fresh cheese and saffron and chop them together, and make the *torta*. (Fr 54)

Unlike many other texts, this recipe does not say whether the *torta* should be covered with a pastry lid. We have decided to follow the letter of the recipe and interpret it as simply as possible. This tart is something like a *quiche lorraine*, but it is lighter and more elegant in flavor.

For the pâte brisée

1½ cups flour (200 g)

7 tablespoons butter (100 g)

3 tablespoons water, approximately

½ teaspoon salt

For the filling

1 generous pound onions or shallots (500 g)

4 ounces pancetta (125 g)

11 ounces fromage blanc, well drained, or whole-milk farmer's cheese, or ricotta enriched with a little heavy cream (300 g)

1 egg, beaten

4 or 5 threads saffron

salt

A few hours in advance, prepare the *pâte brisée* according to the instructions given in recipe 153 (variation B). Wrap in plastic wrap and refrigerate until needed.

Preheat the oven to 400 degrees F (200 degrees C).

Finely chop the pancetta in a meat grinder or food processor. Mince the onions. Combine the pancetta, onions, cheese, and egg. Crush the saffron between your fingers and stir into the mixture. Add salt to taste.

Roll out the pastry, and line a 10-inch (25-cm) tart pan. Line the pastry with aluminum foil, add dried beans or pie weights to keep it from rising, and bake, on a sheet pan, for 10 minutes. Remove the foil and beans, then bake for an additional 5 minutes. Remove from the oven, add the filling, and bake for 35 to 50 minutes, checking after 35 minutes to make sure the tart is not burning.

78. Mixed-Greens *Torta*

Green-Vegetable *Torta.* If you want to make a green-vegetable *torta* for twelve persons, take six large cheeses and take a large quantity of greens, that is, chard, parsley, spinach, mint, and two *libre* [about 1 pound 5 ounces, or 600 g] of salt pork fat, and eight eggs; take these greens, thoroughly cleaned and finely chopped, and take the fat which you have chopped as fine as you can, and take your eggs, and mix these things together and put it, between two crusts, in a *testo;* and color yellow the top crust of this *torta,* which should be rich with plenty of cheese and greens; and if you want to make it for fewer persons, use the ingredients in the same proportions. (Fr 50)

This is a close relative of the *Torta Bolognese* (recipe 81), although its ingredients differ. Here, mint leaves add a pleasant and unexpected note of freshness.

This *torta* was cooked in a *testo:* that is, under a terra cotta dome, or between two heat-proof slabs, placed in the hearth and covered with live embers. *Testi* were in wide use in the northern Italian countryside until the beginning of the twentieth century, and are still used for certain traditional dishes. In France, *tourtières,* which are mentioned in culinary sources from the beginning of the seventeenth century, were similarly employed to bake pies and tarts when no oven was available. In the Middle Ages, skillets and cooking pots were sometimes used, as in recipes 80, 93, and 94.

An hour or two in advance, prepare the *pâte brisée* according to the instructions given in recipe 153 (variation B). Wrap in plastic wrap and refrigerate until needed.

Wash the greens and herbs in several changes of cold water. Remove the stems and discard. Finely chop all the leaves and dry thoroughly in a towel, pressing to remove as much moisture as possible.

Preheat the oven to 425 degrees F (220 degrees C).

With a rubber spatula or wooden spoon, beat the cheeses together. Grind the pancetta in a food processor or meat grinder, and add it to the cheese mixture. Add the eggs and beat thoroughly to blend. Add salt to taste (bearing in mind that the pancetta is fairly salty).

Roll out about two-thirds of the dough and line a deep 9-inch (22-cm) tart pan. Add the filling, roll out the remaining pastry, and cover the pie, pressing the seams tightly shut. Paint the top crust with the egg yolk and saffron mixture.

Put the tart pan on a baking sheet to catch any drips, and bake for an hour, or until the top is golden brown and the bottom thoroughly baked.

For the pâte brisée

2¼ cups flour (300 g)

12 tablespoons (6 ounces) butter (150 g)

¼ cup water, approximately

generous ½ teaspoon salt

For the filling

generous 5 ounces chard leaves, approximately (150 g)

generous 5 ounces spinach, approximately (150 g)

½ cup parsley, loosely packed

½ cup mint leaves, loosely packed

8 ounces pancetta, not too lean (250 g)

6 ounces whole-milk farmer's cheese (165 g)

5 ounces cream cheese (135 g)

4 eggs

1 egg yolk beaten with a few threads of saffron

salt

79. Vegetable-Cheese *Tourte* from *Le Ménagier de Paris*

To make a *tourte*, take four handfuls of chard, two handfuls of parsley, a handful of chervil, a sprig of fennel, and two handfuls of spinach; and trim them and wash them in cold water, then chop them very fine; then, crush the two kinds of cheese, that is, soft and medium, and mix in some eggs, both yolks and whites, and beat them into the cheese; then put the herbs into a mortar and pound everything together, and also put in some fine powder [spices]. Or instead, pound two knobs of gingerroot in a mortar and then pound in your cheeses, eggs, and herbs, and then sprinkle some aged hard cheese, or other cheese, grated atop the herbs; and take it to the oven; and have a tart made and eat it hot. (MP 218)

As with other recipes, it is hard to know whether this pie would have had a top crust, as no instructions are given on that point. The instruction to "sprinkle some aged hard cheese . . . grated atop the herbs" gives the impression that the cheese forms a kind of gratin, which makes sense only if the pie has no top crust. Yet the order of the recipe's steps is not very clear: the author tells us first to "take it to the oven" and only then to "have a tart made." There are a couple of explanations: first, the order given in the recipe might be a mistake; or, secondly, the crust might have been prepared elsewhere by a professional pastry cook and all one had to make at home was the filling, since in any case the two elements would come together only when the pie was baked by the *fournier*—the oven-keeper. This could explain why "take it to the oven" mysteriously precedes "have a tart made," for oven-baking would always have to have been done outside the home of our Parisian bourgeois. In principle, an everyday pie such as this one could almost certainly have been prepared at home: the Bibliothèque Mazarine manuscript of *Le Viandier* contains a recipe (recipe 80, below) whose ingredients are very similar, but which is cooked, like its Italian kin that were baked in a *testo* (see recipe 78), in a deep dish set over the embers in the hearth and covered with another dish, and with fire "above and beneath."

The *poudre fine* ("fine powder") used in this pie, also known as *épices fines* ("fine spices"), was a blend of ground spices that could be purchased ready-made at the apothecary.

An hour or two in advance, prepare the pâte brisée according to the instructions given in recipe 153 (variation B). Wrap in plastic wrap and refrigerate until needed.

Wash the greens and herbs in several changes of cold water. Remove the stems and discard. Finely chop all the leaves and dry thoroughly in a towel, pressing to remove as much moisture as possible.

Preheat the oven to 425 degrees F (220 degrees C).

In a bowl, beat the cream cheese with a rubber spatula or wooden spoon until smooth; grate the raclette or tomme into the bowl, and add the chopped greens. Mix until smooth, then add the eggs, spice mixture, and ginger. Add salt to taste.

Roll out the dough and line a deep 9-inch (22-cm) tart pan. Line the dough with a sheet of aluminum foil and fill with baking weights or dried beans. Bake the shell for 8 minutes; remove the foil and weights and bake for another 5 minutes. Add the filling, sprinkle evenly with the grated cheese, and bake for an hour, or until the top is golden brown and the bottom thoroughly baked. If you find that the *tourte* is browning too quickly, lower the heat to 375 degrees F (190 degrees C).

For the pâte brisée

1½ cups flour (200 g)
7 tablespoons butter (100 g)
3 tablespoons water, approximately
½ teaspoon salt

For the filling

7 ounces chard leaves (200 g)
7 ounces spinach (200 g)
a handful of chervil
a handful of parsley
a handful of dill or fennel fronds
8 ounces cream cheese, softened (250 g)
5 ounces moderately rich, rather mild cheese such as raclette, or a very young tomme de Savoie or other tomme (150 g)
2 eggs, beaten
1 teaspoon fine spices (recipe 150, variation A)
1 teaspoon ground ginger
3 ounces freshly grated parmesan or Swiss gruyère cheese (80 g) (about ½ cup parmesan or ¾ cup gruyère, lightly packed)
salt

80. *Tourtel:* Herbed Egg Tart

Tourtel. Take parsley, mint, chard, spinach, lettuce, marjoram, basil, and pella-mountain, pound everything thoroughly in a mortar, moisten with clear water, and squeeze out the juice; break many eggs into the juice and add powdered ginger, cinnamon, and long pepper, and good-quality grated cheese, and salt, and beat it all together. Make your dough very thin to put into your pan: the same size as the pan so as to fit your pan well. Put some lard into the pan, then the pastry; put it over the coals and put some more lard atop the pastry; when this has melted, put your mixture into the pastry and cover with another pan, and put some fire both on top and on the bottom, and wait for the pie to dry slightly, then remove the upper pan and nicely top the pie with five egg yolks and fine powder [spices]; then cover with the pan and arrange it as before; let it cook gradually over a low charcoal fire, and check often so that it does not overcook; then put some sugar on top and serve. (VT Maz Scul 232)

This recipe is unique among the pies and tarts in our collection, because it does not use the greens themselves, but only their juice, which is mixed with water and beaten eggs. The result is a succulent dish of a magnificent jade-green color. The same technique is used (in recipe 121) for a brilliantly fresh-tasting herb omelette. We urge you to follow the recipe to the letter and, if you like, to make a plain, butter-free flour-and-water dough and roll it out very thin. The richness will come from greasing the tart pan with good lard and then spreading some more lard atop the pastry before filling it.

Pellamountain *(Menta pulegium)* is in the mint family; it is hard to come by nowadays. It appears that its flavor was similar to that of thyme.

For the pâte à foncer ordinaire

¾ **cup flour** (100 g)

about ¼ cup water (6 cl)

¼ **teaspoon salt**

Or for the pâte brisée

1½ **cups flour** (200 g)

7 **tablespoons butter** (100 g)

3 **tablespoons water, approximately**

½ **teaspoon salt**

For the filling

1 **handful each fresh parsley, mint, chard leaves, and spinach Several leaves flavorful lettuce (not iceberg)**

1 **tablespoon fresh marjoram leaves or 1 teaspoon dried marjoram or oregano**

1 **small handful fresh basil leaves**

6 **eggs, beaten**

3 **egg yolks**

2 **cups water** (½ liter)

good-quality lard (if using the flour-and-water dough)

¼ **cup lightly packed, freshly grated parmesan cheese** (40 g)

scant teaspoon ground ginger

scant teaspoon ground cinnamon

If using the *pâte à foncer ordinaire,* prepare the dough according to the instructions given in recipe 153 (variation A). Wrap it in plastic wrap and let it rest for about an hour. After you have prepared the filling (see below), preheat the oven to 425 degrees F (220 degrees C). Using flavorful home- or butcher-rendered lard, generously grease a 9-inch (22-cm) tart pan. Roll the dough out thin, and line the tart pan. Using a rubber spatula or, better, your fingers, spread some lard all over the pastry and bake for 8 minutes or until the pastry is partly cooked and the lard melted and glistening.

If you decide instead to use *pâte brisée,* prepare the dough several hours in advance according to the instructions given in recipe 153 (variation B). Wrap in plastic wrap and refrigerate until needed. After you have prepared the filling (see below), preheat the oven to 425 degrees F (220 degrees C). Roll out the dough, and line a 9-inch (22-cm) tart pan. You will not need the lard, as the butter in the dough serves the same purpose. Line the dough with a sheet of aluminum foil and fill with baking weights or dried beans. Bake the shell for 10 minutes; remove the foil and weights and bake for another 5 minutes.

To make the filling, stem and wash the greens and herbs. Puree them in a blender or food processor; add the water and continue to blend until thoroughly pureed. Over a mixing bowl, strain the puree through a fine strainer, pressing with a spoon to extract as much juice as possible. With a fork or whisk, blend in the beaten eggs, then the grated cheese, ginger, cinnamon, and long pepper.

When the crust has been prebaked, pour in the filling and return to the oven; check from time to time to make sure the tart is not overcooking. After about 40 or 45 minutes, lower the oven temperature to 375 degrees F (190 degrees C), beat together the egg yolks and the fine spices, and spread evenly over the tart, and return to the oven until done, about 15 minutes.

Cover the top with a light sprinkling of sugar and serve.

1 capsule long pepper, grated, or
   ⅓ teaspoon freshly ground
   black pepper
⅓ teaspoon fine spices
   (recipe 150, variation A)
   salt
   sugar

81. *Torta Bolognese,* or Herbed Swiss Chard and Cheese Pie

T̶orta bolognese. Take as much cheese as indicated above in the section on *torta bianca* [see recipe 94] and grate it. Note that the richer the cheese is in fat, the better; then take some chard, parsley, and marjoram; and when they are cleaned and washed, chop them very well with a knife, and mix them together with the cheese, combining and mixing with your hands so that they are well blended, and adding four eggs and enough pepper and a little saffron, as well as good lard or fresh butter, mixing and blending all these things very well, as I have said. And put this filling into a pan with a top crust and a bottom crust, and put on a moderate fire; and when it seems to you to be half cooked, so that it will look more attractive, color it yellow with an egg yolk beaten with a little saffron. And to know when it is cooked, remember that when the top crust comes away and rises, then it will be good, and you may remove it from the fire. (Ma 59)

> Here is a delicious pie with a delicate saffron-scented filling. If your guests do not like the distinctive flavor of saffron, you can omit it; but if you do decide to prepare the authentic version, you will need only 3 or 4 threads of saffron to perfume it.
>
> The pie was cooked in a pan placed on the embers, and there seems to be nothing that would cook the top crust, which is mentioned in the recipe and which is supposed to rise up when the pie is done. Perhaps we can infer that the pan is to be covered with a heated metal plate or a *testo,* as in other recipes (see, for example, recipe 78).

For the pâte brisée

1¾ cups flour (250 g)

9 tablespoons butter (125 g)

⅓ cup water, approximately (10 cl)

1 scant teaspoon salt

For the filling

1 pound raclette, young tomme de Savoie or other tomme, or cream cheese, softened (450 g)

7 ounces Swiss chard leaves (200 g)

1 handful fresh parsley

1 tablespoon fresh marjoram leaves, or 1 teaspoon dried marjoram or oregano

4 tablespoons butter, at room temperature (50 g)

4 eggs

1 egg yolk

saffron

black pepper

salt

A few hours in advance, prepare the *pâte brisée* according to the instructions given in recipe 153 (variation B). Wrap in plastic wrap and refrigerate until needed.

Preheat the oven to 400 degrees F (200 degrees C).

Grate or mash the cheese. Trim and wash the greens and herbs. Chop them finely in a food processor, then add the cheese and process until you have a smooth green mixture, scraping down the sides of the bowl as needed. Beat the whole eggs and blend them into the mixture. Add salt to taste, and plenty of freshly ground pepper. Crush 3 or 4 threads of saffron between your fingers and add them to the mixture along with the softened butter. Process until thoroughly blended.

Roll out about two-thirds of the dough and line a deep 9-inch (22-cm) tart pan. Add the filling, roll out the remaining pastry, and cover the pie, pressing the seams tightly shut. Set the tart pan on a baking sheet to catch any drips, and put in the oven. Crush a few threads of saffron between your fingers and add them to the egg yolk; beat well to blend and leave to infuse. When the pie has baked for 15 minutes, remove from the oven and paint the top crust with the egg yolk and saffron mixture. Return to the oven and bake for another 45 minutes to an hour.

82. Everyday *Torta*

Everyday *torta.*   Take some good cheese, with eight eggs and with good pork fat or veal fat, or butter, whole raisins, ginger, cinnamon, some breadcrumbs, with a little rich broth colored yellow with saffron, and to put it together do as indicated above for the *torta bianca.* (Ma 163)

> The preparation of this "everyday" pie is patterned on that of the *torta bianca* we give in recipe 94: it too uses a fine crust and is cooked in a *padella,* or shallow pan like a frying pan, heated from above and from below (see also recipes 78 and 80).

For the pâte brisée

1¾ cups flour (250 g)

9 tablespoons butter (125 g)

⅓ cup water, approximately (10 cl)

1 scant teaspoon salt

A few hours in advance, prepare the *pâte brisée* according to the instructions given in recipe 153 (variation B). Wrap in plastic wrap and refrigerate until needed.

Preheat the oven to 425 degrees F (220 degrees C).

Grate or mash the cheese and beat with a rubber spatula or a spoon until smooth. With a wire whisk, beat in the eggs, then the softened butter. Continue beating until the mixture is very smooth.

Stir in the raisins and the breadcrumbs. The mixture should be supple; if it is too stiff, crush the saffron into the water or broth and stir it in. If you do not need the extra liquid, crush the saffron directly into the cheese mixture. Mix in the spices. and salt to taste.

Roll out the pastry, and line a 10-inch (25-cm) tart pan. Line the pastry with aluminum foil, add dried beans or pie weights to keep it from rising, and bake, on a sheet pan, for 10 minutes. Remove the foil and beans, then bake for an additional 5 minutes. Remove from the oven, add the filling, and bake for about an hour or until the filling is lightly browned but the top not burnt, lowering the temperature to 375 degrees F (190 degrees C) after about 30 minutes.

For the filling

1½ pounds very young tomme de Savoie or other tomme or a mixture of farmer's cheese and cream cheese (700 g)

8 tablespoons (4 ounces) butter, softened (100 g)

generous ½ cup raisins (100 g)

1½ cups fresh bread crumbs (100 g)

3 eggs, beaten

3 tablespoons broth or water (if needed)

½ teaspoon ground cinnamon

½ teaspoon ground ginger

4 or 5 threads saffron

salt

83. Rabbit Baked in Pastry

Coney pies.   When they are old they must be cut into pieces, and young ones left whole; and with finely chopped pork fat on top; for spices: cloves, ginger, grains of paradise, and pepper. (VT XV 171)

The medieval French *connis* referred to a wild rabbit. The recipe we have chosen here is typical of medieval meat pies, or *pâtés en croûte*, where the crust envelops a whole piece of meat, bones and all. This casing was substantial, and was intended to function as a sort of enclosed oven in which the meat could gently roast.

This pie can be great fun. Select a nice fat rabbit and pose it in crouching position, like a hare on the *qui vive*. This will take some doing, and you will certainly need bamboo skewers to keep the head up. Enclose the rabbit in a firm dough that will cling to its contours, and use leftover dough to make ears and a tail. Insert a couple of dried black beans for eyes and bake until nice and brown. This sculpture should make quite an impression.

For the pâte à pâté

7   cups flour (1 kg)

9   ounces (2¼ sticks) butter (250 g)

1   egg
    about 1¾ cups water (40 cl)

1½ tablespoons kosher salt (20 g)

For the filling

1   young, tender rabbit, whole, with its liver and, if possible, with its head attached.

10 ounces salt pork (300 g)

1   pinch ground cloves

1   teaspoon ground ginger

1   teaspoon ground grains of paradise (see p. 46 for substitutes) **or black pepper**

1   scant tablespoon salt

2   dried black beans for decoration, optional

The day before, or at least a few hours in advance, prepare a fairly stiff *pâte à pâté* according to the instructions given in recipe 153 (variation C). Wrap in plastic wrap and refrigerate until needed.

Preheat the oven to 375 degrees F (190 degrees C).

Grind the salt pork in a meat grinder or (carefully) in a food processor. Mix the spices and salt in a small bowl and set aside.

Roll the dough out into a rectangle. It should be quite thick, a good half inch (1.5 cm). Lay it on a sheet pan. Trim the rabbit if necessary and coax it into a crouching position; if your rabbit still has its head attached, this should be raised vigilantly and held in place with bamboo skewers. Set the rabbit onto the third of the dough nearest you, leaving the larger portion of the dough free to fold over the rabbit.

Spread the chopped salt pork all over the rabbit and sprinkle generously with the spice-salt mixture. Fold the dough over the rabbit, sealing it carefully with water; press it closely against the body so that it clings to its contours. Trim away the excess dough and set aside.

With the back of a small knife, make a crease in the dough where the rabbit's mouth should be. Roll out the dough trimmings and cut out two ears and a tail; fasten these to the pie with water, in the appropriate places. Insert two dried black beans into the dough for eyes.

Bake for about 90 minutes, during which time the rabbit will cook to perfection. Overcooking will only dry it out. The pie is done when the crust is a deep brown.

Bring the whole pie to the table on a platter. Open it down the back and carve the meat as you would a roast rabbit. We recommend serving pieces of the crust only on request; there are those who would find it rather more than substantial.

84. Kid Pie

Another kid pie. Take a cut-up kid or jointed chickens, and fry with fresh pork fat and chopped onions and chopped aromatic herbs with saffron, and egg yolks; moisten well and mix with eggs, and put everything into a pan on the embers; stir frequently until it thickens. Add a good quantity of spices; color with egg yolk; and fill the mold with pastry and enclose everything. Cook and eat. (Za 57–58)

Italian sources contain excellent recipes for kid, which can be a little bland. This pie is no exception; it is highly flavored, and the cook must be lavish with the spices. Butchers with a large Muslim or Greek clientele will often be able to supply young kids.

A few hours in advance, prepare the *pâte brisée* according to the instructions given in recipe 153 (variation B). Wrap in plastic wrap and refrigerate until needed.

Bone the meat and grind it very coarsely or cut it by hand into ¼-inch (6-mm) dice. Cut the pork fatback into ⅛-inch (3-mm) dice. Chop the onions into small dice. In a large skillet, render the fat over low heat, then raise the heat to medium and add the meat, the onions, and a sprinkling of salt. Cook, stirring, until golden brown.

In a small bowl, beat together the egg yolks, the whole eggs, and the chopped herbs. Turn the heat under the skillet to very low and stir the egg mixture into the meat. Stir constantly until the mixture thickens. Remove from the heat and season with the spices and with salt. The mixture should be highly seasoned. Let the mixture cool.

Preheat the oven to 425 degrees F (220 degrees C).

Roll out about three-fourths of the pastry and line a 6-cup (1.5-liter) loaf pan (or a special *pâté en croûte* mold if you have one), leaving some dough hanging over the sides of the pan. Roll out the remaining dough to form a cover for the pie. Pack the filling into the mold, moisten the overhanging dough, and cover the pie with pastry. Seal well, and trim away the excess dough.

For the pâte brisée

2¾ **cups flour** (400 g)
11 **tablespoons butter** (150 g)
½ **cup water, approximately** (12 cl)
1 **teaspoon salt**

For the filling

2 **legs of young kid, to yield about 1¾ pounds of boneless meat** (800 g)
7 **ounces fresh pork fatback** (200 g)
10 **ounces onions (about 3 medium-small onions)** (300 g)
3 **egg yolks**
3 **eggs**
2 **tablespoons each chopped parsley, chervil, and chives**
salt

For the spice mixture

1 **teaspoon ground ginger**
½ **teaspoon ground cinnamon**
½ **teaspoon freshly ground black pepper**
½ **teaspoon freshly grated nutmeg**
1 **pinch ground cloves**

Bake for an hour or more, until the pie is nice and brown. Let the pie cool for 15 minutes before serving.

85. Crustless Lamb Pâté

Mutton pie cooked in a pot. Take some leg meat, and beef or veal fat or marrow, finely chopped, and finely chopped onions; bring it to the boil and cook in a tightly covered pot, with a very little meat broth or other liquid; then cook it with spices and a little vinegar to sharpen it, and serve on a platter. (MP 148)

> In principle, the word *pâté* referred in the Middle Ages to an item wrapped in dough (think of the English words "pasty" and "patty"), so the term *pasté en pot* comes as quite a surprise. And indeed, very few such recipes have come down to us. The phrase implies that the earthenware container for this special "pâté" fills the same function as a kind of pastry covering. In any event, this "pie in a pot" was to be served hot from the fire. Perhaps it is the ancestor of modern-day terrines: at some point in history, someone noticed that the left-overs were even better eaten cold. The meat for this crustless pâté is chopped with extra fat, then cooked slowly with very low heat: just like today's terrines. The present recipe, from *Le Ménagier de Paris*, is not explicit about this last point, but luckily Maestro Martino, cook to the Patriarch of Aquileia, is more forthcoming: in his recipe for a *pastello in una pignatta* he specifies that "the pot must be set on the embers far from the fire."
>
> So we suggest that you first taste this flavorful lamb pâté when it is hot and freshly cooked, but save some to eat cold with a good green salad. Because of its fine flavor, we have used veal fat in place of pork fat. Its delicacy is the ideal match for that of the lamb, and gives this easily prepared pâté an absolutely perfect texture.

11 ounces boneless lamb from the leg or the shoulder, trimmed of connective tissue and gristle (300 g)

7 ounces hard-textured veal fat, such as from the loin (200 g)

2 medium-small onions, about 4 ounces (100 g)

3 tablespoons good-quality wine vinegar

2 tablespoons water or meat broth

1 teaspoon ground ginger

1 teaspoon freshly ground black pepper

⅓ teaspoon freshly grated nutmeg

salt

Using the medium blade of a meat grinder, or a food processor, grind the lamb and the veal fat. If using a food processor, do this in batches and take care not to overprocess. Finely chop the onions. In a large bowl, mix the meat, the fat, and the onions. Add salt and mix again.

Turn this mixture into a small earthenware pâté mold fitted with a lid, or a similar container. Sir in the water or broth. Set the mold on a flame-tamer over very low heat, and simmer for about 45 minutes. Stir in the vinegar and the spices, and continue cooking for another 30 minutes.

Serve hot or cold.

86. Veal Pâté

Veal pies. Take veal and beef fat and finely chop them together; the appropriate spices are ginger and cinnamon; in wintertime, good cheese should be added. (VT XV 169)

This recipe says nothing of how the pie is to be assembled; like so many others, it is written in a laconic style. The ingredients are listed to jog the memory; it is assumed that the reader (most likely a professional cook) will already know the technique. The ingredients of this pie are uncomplicated; it is easy to make and is as good cold as it is hot.

A few hours in advance, prepare the *pâte brisée* according to the instructions given in recipe 153 (variation B). Wrap in plastic wrap and refrigerate until needed.

Using the fine or medium blade of a meat grinder, or a food processor, grind the veal and the fat. If using a food processor, do this in batches and take care not to over-process. In a bowl, mix the meat and the fat with your hands.

Add salt to taste and season with the ginger and the cinnamon. To make sure of the seasoning, fry a spoonful of the filling in a skillet, taste carefully, and adjust the seasoning if necessary.

Preheat the oven to 400 degrees F (200 degrees C).

For the pâte brisée

2¼ cups flour (300 g)
7 tablespoons butter (100 g)
¼ cup water, approximately
½ teaspoon salt

For the filling

1 pound 10 ounces boneless breast of veal (750 g)
9 ounces hard beef or veal fat, such as from the loin (250 g)
1½ teaspoons ground ginger
1 teaspoon ground cinnamon salt

Roll out about three-fourths of the pastry and line a 6-cup (1.5-liter) loaf pan (or a special pâté or terrine mold if you have one), leaving some dough hanging over the sides of the mold. Roll out the remaining dough to form a cover for the pie. Pack the filling into the mold, moisten the overhanging dough, and cover the pie with pastry. Seal well, and trim away the excess dough. With a paring knife, make a small slash in the center of the top crust, to vent the steam.

Bake for about two hours. Check for doneness by inserting a thin metal skewer into the center of the pâté. If the tip comes out hot, the pâté is done.

87. King Manfred's *Torta*

*T*he excellent and celebrated *torta Manfreda*. Take chicken gizzards and livers, and take pork belly, and chop them together with a knife, then add pepper. Take a deep pan and fry everything, then remove it and let it cool; then add eggs and make a crust, then put it in a pan and cook it gently. (Fr 57)

As there is no indication of quantities, we have adapted this recipe on the basis of texture, with a view to achieving a sort of *pâté en croûte*.

The name of the recipe is odd. Like the recipe that follows it in the manuscript ("King Manfred's Fresh Fava Bean *Torta*," Fr 56), it refers to the King of Sicily and illegitimate son of Emperor Frederick II. Dante imagines him in purgatory: "a handsomely patrician blond he was, although a sword wound cut through one eyebrow" (Dante, *Purgatory,* III.107–8).

Manfred was descended from German emperors and the Norman kings of Sicily, and was the defender of the Ghibellines, who were enemies of the Church of Rome. The pope condemned him as a heretic, and Manfred died excommunicate, tragically defeated and killed in 1266 at the battle of Benevento by the Guelph coalition under the pope and Charles, Count of Anjou and the brother of Saint Louis—Louis IX, King of France from 1226 to 1270. The Church would undoubtedly have consigned him to hell, but because of his loyalty to the empire, Dante gave him a place in purgatory, in the circle of good Christians who had perished without the opportunity to repent.

King Manfred is a tragic figure in Italian culture, and not solely because of Dante. What is more difficult to understand is his connection with fava beans or chicken livers. The two recipes that, in a way, are dedicated to him are both based on humble ingredients and relatively inexpensive spices. They seem hardly connected to the royal feasts at the court of Palermo, but rather to the uncertain diet of a warrior king who, like other commanders, would dispatch his men to raid local gardens and henhouses.

For the pâte brisée

1½ cups flour (200 g)
7   tablespoons butter (100 g)
3   tablespoons water, approximately
½   teaspoon salt

For the filling

generous ½ pound chicken livers (250 g)
generous ½ pound chicken gizzards, tough membranes removed (250 g)
generous ½ pound boneless fresh belly of pork (250 g)
2   tablespoons good lard
4   eggs
1   teaspoon freshly ground black pepper
salt

A few hours, or a day, in advance, prepare the *pâte brisée* according to the instructions given in recipe 153 (variation B). Wrap in plastic wrap and refrigerate until needed.

In a food processor, or a meat grinder using the fine or medium blade, chop all the meats. Mix together, season with salt and pepper, and sauté in the lard until lightly browned. Taste the mixture and adjust the seasoning if necessary. Allow to cool, then mix in the eggs one by one.

Preheat the oven to 425 degrees F (220 degrees C).

Roll out about three-fourths of the pastry and line a 4-cup (1-liter) loaf pan, a 9-inch (22-cm) round mold, or a special pâté or terrine mold if you have one, leaving some dough hanging over the sides of the mold. Roll out the remaining dough to form a cover for the pie. Pack the filling into the mold, moisten the overhanging dough, and cover the pie with pastry. Seal well, and trim away the excess dough.

Bake for 45 minutes to an hour. Serve hot or cold.

88. "Hungarian" *Torta*

Hungarian *torta* **for twelve persons.**   Take a nice, fat capon and take a large loin of pork, and two big onions, and half a *libra* of sweet fine spices, and take three *libre* of fresh fat that has not been salted, and take some flour, enough to make three loaves of bread, the best you can get; and take the capons and the pork loin, and cut them into small pieces; and fry these things in plenty of fresh lard, and those sweet spices and plenty of saffron and a little salt; and when it is well fried add a glass of water so that it will cook gently. Take the flour and mix it with fresh water, salted with a little salt, and knead it vigorously; when it is well kneaded, take a well-tinned copper *testo* and grease it with the fat. Take the dough, knead it, and flatten it with a large spoon and make it thin; two of you should stretch it thin, by the sheet, with the fat, and make as many as eighteen sheets; and then take the stuffing of capon and other ingredients and make a layer of it on half [of the sheets], then put the other sheets atop this layer, each one well greased with the fat; and make a top crust for protection. This *torta* requires a small fire below and a strong fire above, and you can make it for many or for few by using ingredients in these proportions. (Fr 59)

> This recipe is exceptional in its detail, an area where our authors are usually silent. Generally we never learn anything about the ingredients or methods for tart or pie crusts, but here we are told, to our surprise, to layer no fewer than eighteen ultra-thin sheets of dough with fat between them as the crust for a spiced meat and onion filling. This is nothing less than a kind of puff pastry, and the technique recalls that for a Moroccan pastilla—that wonderful pigeon pie with its heap of membrane-thin layers of pastry—or for southwestern French *croustades* or *tourtières,* those delicious armagnac-scented apple and prune pastries with their many translucent folds of crust.
>
> We know two versions of this recipe, both Italian, but we have been unable to discover why it is called "Hungarian."
>
> This "Hungarian" *torta* takes time and patience to prepare (although using ready-made strudel or phyllo dough makes things easier), but there is compensation in the admiration of your guests when you bring it to the table, golden brown and fresh from the oven.

One recipe *pâte à foncer ordinaire* (recipe 153, variation A), or **use ready-made strudel or phyllo dough**

1 small capon or a free-range chicken, about 4 pounds (1800 g)

1 generous pound boneless loin of pork (500 g)

2 medium onions

1 generous pound good lard, home- or butcher-rendered (500 g)

sweet spice mixture (recipe 150, variation B)

saffron

salt

Prepare the pastry dough an hour or two ahead of time; make sure it is nice and soft. It will need lengthy kneading to develop the gluten that will make it elastic and stretchable. Wrap in plastic and refrigerate until needed.

Remove the skin of the chicken and cut all the meat from the bones. Cut the chicken meat and pork into ⅛-inch dice; peel the onions and cut into ¼-inch dice.

In a casserole or deep skillet over medium heat, melt a little more than one-third of the lard. Add the meats and onions, season with salt, the spice mixture (about a tablespoon, or to taste) and a couple of pinches of saffron, and sauté until golden brown. Add ¾ cup of water and simmer for about 15 minutes. Remove from the heat and leave to cool. Taste, and adjust seasoning if necessary.

Melt the remaining lard in a small saucepan; set aside to cool.

Preheat the oven to 400 degrees F (200 degrees C).

If using *pâte à foncer,* divide the dough into eighteen equal pieces and roll each into a ball. Use a rolling pin to roll out each ball of dough as thin as possible. Then use your hands to stretch it until it is nearly transparent; take care not to tear the dough. Keep the dough and the rolled-out sheets under a damp towel to keep them from drying out. If using ready-made strudel or phyllo pastry, be sure it is completely defrosted, but still cold, before separating the sheets.

Using a brush and the cooled melted lard, grease a deep 11-inch (28-cm) tart pan. Line the pan with one sheet of dough, leaving the edges to overlap the sides of the pan, and brush it with lard. Add another sheet of dough, brush it with lard, and continue until you have nine layers.

Press the completely cooled filling into the prepared tart pan, and top with the remaining nine sheets of dough, each brushed with lard. Seal the edges by folding and pressing with your fingers. Generously brush the top of the pie with lard and bake for a good hour, or until nicely browned.

89. Eel and Spinach *Torta*

Eel pie. Skin the eel and cut it into pieces the size of two fingers, boiling them a little so that they are not fully cooked. And make some nice, white almond milk, straining the almonds along with some good verjuice and rose water through a sieve, so that the milk will be nice and thick, i.e., dense. Thoroughly pound a few raisins with three or four dried figs. Then take some spinach torn by hand into thin crosswise pieces, and fry it briefly in oil, adding a little finely chopped parsley; take an *oncia* of whole raisins and an *oncia* of shelled, cleaned pine nuts, and ginger and cinnamon and pepper and saffron in moderation, depending on the quantity you wish to prepare. And blend together this entire mixture, mixing very well by hand; put the bottom crust in the pan, and place the stuffing and the mixture into it, first making a layer on the crust, then a layer of eel; thus layer by layer, as many as you like: you can make as many as the mixture will allow; on top, put the other crust; cook it very slowly, with moderate fire below and above. And when it is half cooked, take a little verjuice and rose water, with some sugar; and make many holes in the top crust so that these things can penetrate when you put them on top; leave it on the fire for as long as it takes to be very well cooked. (Ma 165)

> In the Middle Ages, the eel was the most sought-after of fishes, or at least the most dreamed-about. Literature is full of references to eels, from the *Roman de Renart* to French verse tales *(fabliaux)* to Italian *novelle*. We have therefore included a number of eel recipes: San Vincenzo's Day Grilled Eel (recipe 63), plus several pies and pâtés. Could its snake-like appearance have evoked the sins for which we atone during Lent? Whatever the case, we have already noted that it was indissolubly linked with the clergy's good eating; and indeed, Maestro Martino, who cooked for a high prelate, includes quite a few eel recipes in his manuscript.
>
> This pie is complicated and takes time to prepare, but it is worth it. Your guests may be surprised to find bones in their slice of pie; the recipe does not instruct us to remove them. Besides, eel bones are easy to pick out, as they consist mainly of a very obvious backbone.
>
> Not every fish market in every town will carry eels, though you may be able to order them with a couple of days' notice. But live eels (and you *should* buy them live) can be found in many Asian and Mediterranean markets.

A few hours in advance, prepare the *pâte brisée* according to the instructions given in recipe 153 (variation B). Wrap in plastic wrap and refrigerate until needed.

Wash the spinach and put it in a colander or strainer to drain.

You will probably want to have your fishmonger kill, skin, behead, and clean the eels. Cut the cleaned eels into pieces about 1 to 1½ inches (3 to 4 cm) in length. Put

For the pâte brisée
1½ **cups flour** (200 g)
7 **tablespoons butter** (100 g)
3 **tablespoons water,**
  approximately
½ **teaspoon salt**

For the filling

1 to 4 eels, total weight 1½
   pounds (smaller eels will be
   better in this recipe) (700 g)
1 cup almonds (150 g)
1 scant cup (7 fl. ounces) verjuice
   (20 cl)
⅓ cup rose water (10 cl)
1 tablespoon sugar
   scant ⅓ cup raisins (50 g)
3 or 4 dried figs
1¾ pounds spinach (800 g)
2 tablespoons olive oil
1 bunch parsley
2 tablespoons pine nuts (25 g)
1 teaspoon ground ginger
1 teaspoon ground cinnamon
½ teaspoon freshly ground black
   pepper
   generous pinch saffron threads
   salt

them into a pan and add cold water to cover. Add salt, bring to the boil, and simmer for 10 seconds, then drain and reserve. Grind the almonds in a blender. Combine the verjuice and the rose water and add half of this mixture to the almonds; continue to blend until a smooth puree is formed. Put this puree through a fine strainer, pressing hard with a spoon to extract as much liquid as possible. In a food processor or a mortar and pestle, grind 2 tablespoons of the raisins and all the dried figs. Chop the parsley.

Tear the spinach into small pieces. In a large skillet heat the oil over high heat, then add the spinach and toss until the spinach is wilted but not completely cooked. Discard any excess liquid apart from a few tablespoonfuls. Stir in the parsley and set aside in a large bowl to cool. When cool, combine with the almond milk, the raisin-fig mixture, the remaining whole raisins, the pine nuts, the spices, and the saffron. Stir vigorously with a rubber spatula or wooden spoon until evenly mixed.

Preheat the oven to 425 degrees F (220 degrees C).

Roll out three-quarters of the pastry and line a 6-cup (1½-liter) soufflé mold. Spoon a layer of the spinach filling into the mold, then a layer of eel pieces; continue alternating layers until you have used all the ingredients. Roll out the remaining pastry and cover the pie, sealing the edges carefully. Bake for 25 minutes, then remove from the oven. Using a chopstick or large wooden knitting needle, poke holes all over the top, then pour the remaining verjuice and rose water mixture over the pie. Return to the oven and bake for another 20 minutes.

Serve hot.

90. Eel *Torta*

If you want to make a pie of fresh eels, take the eels, half-boil them, and cook with them parsley and mint and purslane[?], then cool and take them apart by hand. Discard the skin and the bones. Take good walnuts, skin them with boiling water, then crush them slightly. And take a *libra* of almonds, make them into milk, and cook it until it becomes very thick; and set it aside to cool; it will be a junket. Then put these things in a pan; make a crust; herbs should be chopped, and add strong spices, saffron, and twelve chopped dates. And when it is cooked, remove it; and if [the eels] were not fat, add good oil. (Gu 39–40)

Unlike the previous recipe, this one instructs us to remove the bones from the eels before putting them into the pie. It is therefore easier to eat, and you may prefer it if your guests are absentminded, lazy, too young, or very nearsighted.

On the basis of the text, we decided to put this filling directly into a soufflé mold without a bottom crust, but we seal the mold with a layer of pastry that serves as a cover.

Note the interesting reference to almond milk thickened to a *giuncada*— "junket." A *giuncada* is a fresh cheese put into a little basket woven of rushes— *giunchi*—to drain; the French equivalent is a *jonchée,* also from the word for rushes, or *jonc.* Many sources include Lenten junkets: vegetarian "cheeses" made of almond milk, like that used in this recipe. You will find that this dish reflects a real food-lover's approach to Lenten penitence.

A few hours in advance, prepare the *pâte brisée* according to the instructions given in recipe 153 (variation B). Wrap in plastic wrap and refrigerate until needed.

Following the instructions in recipe 151, prepare a rich almond milk. Over low heat, boil it for about 30 minutes to thicken it. Set it aside to cool. Coarsely chop the walnuts.

Put the eels into a pan and add cold water to cover. Add salt, the parsley, and the mint; bring to the boil, immediately turn off the heat and let stand for 3 minutes. Drain and reserve the eels and herbs.

Preheat the oven to 425 degrees F (220 degrees C).

When the eels have cooled enough to handle, remove the skin and bones, then, in a large bowl, break up the flesh with your fingers. Chop the parsley and the mint, as well as the dates; add to the eels along with the walnuts. Brush a 4-cup (1-liter) soufflé mold with olive oil and add the eel mixture. Pour the thickened almond-milk "cheese" over the filling and sprinkle with the saffron and the spices.

Roll the pastry dough into a circle about an inch larger than the diameter of the mold; moisten the edge of the mold and cover with the pastry, pressing to seal. With a paring knife, make a steam hole in the center of the pastry.

For the pâte brisée

1 cup flour (150 g)
6 tablespoons (3 ounces) butter (75 g)
2 tablespoons water, approximately
¼ teaspoon salt

For the filling

1 to 4 eels, to yield 1½ pounds of meat (smaller eels will be better in this recipe), cleaned, but not skinned (700 g)
1 bunch fresh mint
1 bunch parsley
12 walnuts, shelled
12 dates
10 threads saffron, approximately
1 teaspoon freshly ground black pepper
1 pinch ground cloves
¼ teaspoon freshly grated nutmeg
salt
olive oil

For the almond milk

1⅓ cups almonds (200 g)
1 cup water (¼ liter)

Bake for 30 to 45 minutes, or until the pastry is nicely browned and the filling bubbling hot.

91. Eel and Roe Tart

Eel pie. The eel should be skinned and cleaned, or you may choose another fish, also trimmed and cleaned; cut it into pieces the thickness of two fingers; you should also have good fat or fish roe; cut it small and add it to the pieces [of eel]. Also take a little very finely chopped mint and parsley. Take an *oncia* of raisins, some cinnamon, ginger, pepper, and cloves, all pounded. Mix all these things very well and combine them. Take your pastry, nicely made and rested; put this mixture inside it; put a little good oil on top and put it to cook, and when it is nearly cooked, take two ounces of skinned, well-pounded almonds mixed with verjuice and put through a sieve, and add this, pouring it on top of the pie, also adding a little saffron; and let it boil again, and cook everything together a little longer until it is very well cooked, for that is how it should be. Note that when it is permitted to eat eggs, you can take two egg yolks and add them to the verjuice at the same time as the other mentioned items; this will go very well, and can only be an enhancement. (Ma 169–70)

The best eels and fish roes come to market in the winter; fortunately, parsley and mint are now available year-round, but remember that they will still be at their best in the summer, grown in your own garden or purchased at a farmers' market. The ideal size eels for this dish are those weighing between 5 and 7 ounces (150 and 200 g); if they are even smaller they will not have enough flesh on their bones, while if very large they can be fatty. In the Middle Ages the eel was among the most sought-after of fish but, like today, it was not always easy to find, so the author offers the alternative of using another fish (perhaps mackerel) in its place, which will make it all the easier for you to try this recipe.

Note that the recipe does not instruct us to bone the eels before cooking.

For the pâte brisée
1½ **cups flour** (200 g)
7 **tablespoons butter** (100 g)
3 **tablespoons water,**
    approximately
½ **teaspoon salt**

For the filling
1 **to 4 eels, total weight 1½**
    pounds (smaller eels will be
    better in this recipe) (700 g)
    Roe from 1 large or 2 small
    soles or flounders, or other fish
    depending on availability, about
    2 ounces (50 g)
1 **bunch fresh parsley**

A few hours or a day in advance, prepare the *pâte brisée* according to the instructions given in recipe 153 (variation B). Wrap in plastic wrap and refrigerate until needed.

You will probably want to have your fishmonger kill, skin, behead, and clean the eels. Cut the cleaned eels into pieces about 1 to 1½ inches (3 to 4 cm) in length. Put them into a bowl with the roe, cut up into small pieces.

Preheat the oven to 425 degrees F (220 degrees C).

Chop together the herbs and the raisins; add the spices, apart from the saffron, and combine this mixture with the fish. Add salt to taste.

Roll out the dough and line a deep 8-inch (20-cm) tart pan. Add the fish mixture and sprinkle with the olive oil (note that there is no top crust). Put into the oven.

Meanwhile, grind the almonds in a blender; add the verjuice and blend until pureed together. Strain through a fine strainer into a small bowl, pressing to extract as much liquid as possible. Beat in the egg yolks and saffron.

When the tart has baked for 25 minutes, remove from the oven and pour over the almond milk and egg yolk mixture. Lower the heat to 375 degrees F (190 degrees C). Bake for another 20 to 25 minutes. Serve hot.

1   bunch fresh mint
    scant ¼ cup raisins (30 g)
1   teaspoon ground cinnamon
1   teaspoon ground ginger
½   teaspoon freshly ground black pepper
¼   teaspoon ground cloves
6   or 7 threads saffron
3   tablespoons olive oil
    generous ⅓ cup blanched almonds (60 g)
    generous ¾ cup verjuice (20 cl)
2   egg yolks
    salt

92. Trout in Pastry

Dry pasties made with fresh fish: Take the cleaned and trimmed fish, and slit it a little on either side next to the backbone, and season the whole fish very well, inside and out, with salt and good spices mixed together. Then take a somewhat thick pastry and arrange the fish sealed inside it, and cook it well in the oven, slowly, so it will be well cooked. (Ma 170)

This recipe says nothing about what kind of fish to use. We tried trout, with excellent results. Maestro Martino's intent here is to cook the fish wrapped in pastry to encourage it to take on all the flavors and aromas of the spices and to keep it from drying out. It is indeed fair to assume that the pastry envelope, like most others encasing whole animals, was used for those purposes only and would not have been eaten. You could therefore use a simple flour-and-water dough for this dish, although if your appetite is driven by a lust for pastry you can certainly sheathe your trout in a good, buttery *pâte brisée*, as we propose in our version. Like the fish itself, it will be delicious.

For the pâte brisée

2¾ cups flour (400 g)

14 tablespoons, or 1¾ sticks butter (200 g)

½ cup water, approximately (12 cl)

1 teaspoon salt

For the fish

4 fresh trout

1 tablespoon salt

1 tablespoon ground ginger

1 teaspoon freshly ground black pepper

1 pinch ground cloves

½ teaspoon freshly grated nutmeg

A few hours in advance, prepare the *pâte brisée* according to the instructions given in recipe 153 (variation B). Wrap in plastic wrap and refrigerate until needed.

Preheat the oven to 425 degrees F (220 degrees C).

Clean the trout, and wash and dry them thoroughly. In a small bowl, mix the salt and spices.

With a thin-bladed, very sharp knife, cut a 3-to-4-inch slit along either side of the back of each trout, following the backbone with the blade.

Sprinkle plenty of the salt-spice mixture into these slits, as well as all over the inside and outside of each fish. Do not be afraid to season generously.

Divide the pastry into four pieces and roll each one into a rectangle large enough to hold one of the fish. Wrap each fish in pastry to form a boat shape; leave a small opening at either end.

Arrange the fish on a sheet pan and bake until golden brown, about 20 minutes. Serve hot from the oven.

Sweet Pies and Tarts
93. Pumpkin or Winter Squash Tart

Pumpkins. Take pumpkins and peel them carefully, and grate them as you would grate cheese, and boil them a little in good broth, or in good milk. And take as much fresh cheese as indicated in previous sections, adding and mixing in a little good aged cheese. And take a *libra* of good pork tripe or a calf's head boiled very well and chopped fine with a knife. And if you like, you can replace these two things, using butter or lard if you prefer, adding half a *libra* of sugar, a little ginger, and cinnamon, with a glass of milk and six eggs. And when the pumpkins appear to be cooked, remove them from the water and put them through a sieve; and color this mixture yellow with *sesanime* [unidentified ingredient] then put it into a pan with only one thin bottom crust and no top crust, and when it seems half cooked, top with very fine *lasagne* in place of a crust. And when it is fully cooked, top it with a layer of good sugar and rose water. (Ma 160)

This sweet tart from Italy tastes exquisite and has a lovely marmalade color. Make everyone guess the ingredients; we bet no one will detect the parmesan cheese.

The appeal of this tart is the perfect combination of the delicate flavor of the sweetened pumpkin scented with rose water, the spiciness of the cinnamon and ginger, the richness of the butter, and the hint of pungency from the parmesan cheese. The *lasagne* arranged on top of the half-baked tart are not the broad noodles we know today, layered with cheese and sauce, and baked in the oven; the word refers here to their shape. Rich pastry is rolled out thin and cut into narrow ribbons, which are placed attractively on top of the tart as a covering. This terminology evolved: later sources refer to putting "bands" or "grill marks" on a pie.

A few hours in advance, prepare the *pâte brisée* according to the instructions given in recipe 153 (variation B). Wrap in plastic wrap and refrigerate until needed.

Peel the pumpkin or squash, cut it into chunks, and cook it in the milk (supplemented with water if necessary to cover) for about 15 minutes, or until tender.

Preheat the oven to 475 degrees F (250 degrees C).

Beat together the butter and the farmer's cheese until smooth. Add the parmesan, the ½ cup of sugar, the eggs, and the spices and salt to taste. Puree the pumpkin in a food mill or food processor and beat into the cheese mixture.

Roll out three-quarters of the pastry dough and line a deep 9-inch (22-cm) tart or pie pan. Fill with the pumpkin mixture and bake for about 20 minutes. Meanwhile, roll out the remaining pastry and cut it into ⅜-inch (1-cm) strips. Remove the partially baked tart from the oven and lay the strips over it in a lattice pattern; lower the temperature to 400 degrees F (200 degrees C) and return the tart to the oven to finish baking, about 40 minutes. If the tart is browning too quickly, cover it with a piece of aluminum foil.

When the tart is done, remove it from the oven and sprinkle with sugar and rose water. Serve barely warm.

For the pâte brisée

1¾ cups flour (250 g)
9 tablespoons butter (125 g)
⅓ cup water, approximately (10 cl)
1 scant teaspoon salt

For the filling

1¾ pounds pumpkin or winter squash (750 g)
1 cup milk (¼ liter)
11 ounces whole-milk farmer's cheese, drained if necessary, at room temperature (300 g)
14 tablespoons (7 ounces) butter, softened (200 g)
½ cup sugar (100 g)
⅓ cup (2 ounces) freshly grated parmesan cheese (50 g)
4 eggs, beaten
½ teaspoon ground ginger
½ teaspoon ground cinnamon salt

For the topping

2 tablespoons sugar
2 tablespoons rose water

94. *Torta Bianca:* White Tart

White tart. Take a *libra* and a half of good fresh cheese and cut it up fine, and pound it very well; take twelve or fifteen egg whites and blend them very well with this cheese, adding half a *libra* of sugar and half an *oncia* of the whitest ginger you can find, as well as a half *libra* of good, white pork lard, or instead of lard, good, fresh butter, and some milk, as much as needed; this will be a good third of a *boccale*.[1] Then make the pastry, or crust, [put it] into the pan, as thin as it ought to be, and cook it nicely with fire both below and above; and make sure that the top is a little colored from the heat of the fire; and when it seems cooked, remove it from the pan and put fine sugar and good rose water on top. (Ma 158)

In the Middle Ages, the color white evoked purity and asceticism; this white tart is one of Maestro Martino's greatest gastronomic achievements. People always request it when we prepare our medieval dinners, and it seems to be especially popular with women. *Torta bianca* makes a very strong case for restoring rose water to its rightful place in pastry-making. Its subtle floral overtones are a perfect match for the hint of ginger and the barely sweetened richness of the cheese.

For the pâte brisée

1¾ cups flour (250 g)
9 tablespoons butter (125 g)
⅓ cup water, approximately (10 cl)
1 scant teaspoon salt

For the filling

generous 10 ounces cream cheese, softened (300 g)
6 egg whites
scant ⅔ cup sugar (125 g)
9 tablespoons butter, softened (125 g)
¾ teaspoon ground ginger
1 cup milk (¼ liter)
salt

For the topping

2 tablespoons sugar
1 teaspoon rose water

A few hours in advance, prepare the *pâte brisée* according to the instructions given in recipe 153 (variation B). Wrap in plastic wrap and refrigerate until needed.

Preheat the oven to 425 degrees F (220 degrees C).

With a rubber spatula or wooden spoon, or in a food processor or electric mixer, cream the sugar, the ginger, and a pinch of salt with the butter and the cream cheese. Whip the egg whites briefly with a fork, just to break them up, and beat into the cheese mixture. Beat in some milk, until the mixture has the consistency of a thick cream.

Roll out the dough and line a deep 8-inch (20-cm) tart pan. Line the pastry with aluminum foil, add dried beans or pie weights to keep it from rising, and bake for 10 minutes. Remove the foil and beans, then bake for an additional 5 minutes. Remove from the oven and lower the heat to 375 degrees F (190 degrees C). Pour the filling into the partially baked shell and bake for about an hour. Monitor the baking: while the crust must be thoroughly baked, the top must be only lightly colored—this is, after all, a "white" tart. If it seems to be browning too quickly, protect it with a sheet of aluminum foil.

When the tart is done, remove from the oven and sprinkle the top with sugar and rose water.

1. A *boccale* could equal anywhere from about half a quart (liter) to more than two, depending on the region.

95. Crustless "Sienese" Tart

Sienese tart. Take twenty almonds and blanch them thoroughly, and pound them as fine as possible. Then take half a *libra* of sugar, twelve eggs, and a *fogletta* [about a cup] of milk, two *quatani* of cinnamon, and the proper amount of salt, and half a *quarto* of fresh probatura cheese, pounded until it need be pounded no more. Then spread a mold with butter, and then flour it, and put the mixture on top. And set the mold or pan far from the fire, covered, with a moderate fire. And note that you can put into the mixture a ladleful of *lasagne* cooked in good broth. And when it is cooked, put sugar and rose water on top. (Bü 49v–50)

> We chose this recipe because it is the only one in any of our sources to be called "Sienese." Although it is called a *tartara*, like many pies and tarts in this Neapolitan collection, it is very similar to a crustless flan or quiche. We can find nothing like it in the cooking of modern Siena, and, as we have noted (see recipe 8), provatura cheese comes from southern Italy.

Preheat the oven to 325 degrees F (160 degrees C).

Grind the almonds in a clean spice or coffee grinder, or in a blender, together with the sugar and cinnamon. Place the ground almond mixture into a bowl; beat in the softened cheese, then the eggs one by one, and the milk. Taste the mixture and add salt as needed.

Butter and flour a 6-inch (15-cm) soufflé dish or other ovenproof mold, and pour in the mixture. Bake for about 45 minutes and set aside to cool.

When cool, you may unmold it (carefully: it is fragile) or serve it from the dish. Before serving, sprinkle with sugar and rose water.

10 **almonds, blanched**
    scant ½ cup sugar (80 g)
6 **eggs**
1 **cup milk** (¼ liter)
2 **tablespoons cream cheese, softened**
1 **teaspoon ground cinnamon**
    a pinch salt

For the topping

3 **tablespoons rose water** (5 cl)
1 **tablespoon sugar**

96. *Dariole,* or Custard Tart

Diriola. Form the dough into the shape of a deep pie and fill it completely with flour so it will keep its shape; cook it in a pan until it is somewhat dry. And when this is done, remove the flour and take some egg yolks, milk, sugar, and cinnamon. When these things are made into a mixture, put it into the pastry, cooking it like a tart, moving it from time to time and stirring with a spoon. And when you can see it starting to set, pour on some rose water and stir well with a spoon. And when it has set completely it is cooked. Note that it should not cook too much, and that it should quiver like a junket. (Ma 172)

French kitchenware stores still sell *dariole* molds: deep, flared molds, shaped rather like drinking glasses. Until very recently, every general French cookbook or baking book would include recipes for these little milk or almond custards with various flavorings.

The *dariole,* in short, was a classic of traditional French *pâtisserie.* But as to the Middle Ages, we learn nothing about it from French sources. Its name barely appears in a handful of the menus set out in *Le Ménagier de Paris,* and the only French recipe is the incomprehensible text found in the fifteenth-century edition of Taillevent's *Le Viandier.* Still, the author of *Le Ménagier de Paris* repeats as a truism that "*darioles* are suitable for French weddings."

On the other hand, the English texts all include a variety of instructions on how to prepare "darioles," "darials," or "daryols." Italian authors seem to have had no idea of the *dariole's* existence—apart from the great Martino, of course, whose recipe we have chosen here; it yields exceptionally good results and is unusually detailed: how to prebake the crust filled with flour to prevent it from collapsing; how to know when the *dariole* is done (it should, he tells us, quiver like a junket—in other words, its consistency should be that of a freshly made cheese in its little draining basket, woven of rushes (*giunche* in Italian and *jonc* in French, hence the word "junket"). Note too that Martino's *diriola* is a single large tart; the word had not yet come to mean individual confections.

For the pâte brisée

1¾ cups flour (250 g)

9 tablespoons butter (125 g)

⅓ cup water, approximately (10 cl)

1 scant teaspoon salt

For the filling

3 cups milk (75 cl)

6 egg yolks

1½ cups sugar (300 g)

1 teaspoon ground cinnamon

2 to 3 tablespoons rose water

A few hours in advance, prepare the *pâte brisée* according to the instructions given in recipe 153 (variation B). Wrap in plastic wrap and refrigerate until needed.

Preheat the oven to 425 degrees F (220 degrees C).

Roll out the pastry and line a 9-inch (22-cm) pie or tart pan at least 2 inches (5 cm) deep. Line it with aluminum foil and fill with pie weights or dried beans (or you could try flour, as Maestro Martino suggests). Bake for about 15 minutes, remove the weights and foil, and return to the oven for a further 5 minutes. Lower the temperature to 350 degrees F (175 degrees C).

Meanwhile, whisk the egg yolks and sugar with the cinnamon and a pinch of salt until smooth and glossy, then slowly beat in the milk.

Pour the egg mixture into the partly baked shell, return to the oven, and bake for about an hour or until set but still soft enough to quiver slightly when moved. If the top is browning too quickly, cover it with aluminum foil.

When done, remove from the oven and sprinkle with rose water.

Note that we have strayed from Martino, who instructs us to stir the mixture as it cooks. The closed oven of the modern kitchen makes this impractical—and its even heat makes it unnecessary.

97. Whole-Pear Pie

Pies of raw pears.   Stand three large pears in a pie and fill the gaps with about a *quarteron* [about 4 ounces/120 g] of sugar, cover well, and glaze with eggs or saffron, and put in the oven. (VT XV 175)

> While quite simple to prepare, this dish was probably fairly costly judging by the amount of sugar required: the quantity required to fill all the gaps between the pears would be lavish indeed.
>
> When the pears are baked enclosed in pastry, their juice combines with the sugar to form a sweet, almost caramelized essence that is absolutely luscious. But your masterpiece is all too likely to collapse when you unmold it: the syrup that is produced during the baking is such a powerful glue that it is difficult to prevent the pears and their cocoon from going their separate ways when you try to serve the pie, although a nonstick mold helps.

A few hours in advance, prepare the *pâte brisée* according to the instructions given in recipe 153 (variation B). Wrap in plastic wrap and refrigerate until needed.

Preheat the oven to 400 degrees F (200 degrees C).

Generously butter, then flour two loaf pans (preferably nonstick) just large enough to hold snugly 3 pears each, side by side.

Divide the dough in two and roll each piece into a rectangle large enough to line a loaf pan with enough overhanging dough to fold over the filling; it should be just under ¼ inch (about ½ cm) thick.

For the pâte brisée

3½ **cups flour** (500 g)

9 **ounces (18 tablespoons) butter** (250 g)

⅔ **cup water, approximately** (20 cl)

1 **heaping teaspoon salt**

For the filling

6 **large pears**
   about 1¼ cups sugar, preferably superfine (250 g)

1 **egg, beaten, for glazing**

Peel the pears, leaving the stems attached. Arrange 3 pears in each loaf pan, side by side, and fill the remaining space with sugar. Fold the dough over the pears and seal well, but let the stem ends of the pears protrude through the dough: this will provide steam vents. Glaze the top of each pie with beaten egg.

Bake for about 90 minutes.

Let cool completely before unmolding.

98. Tiered Dried-Fruit Pie

Tiered *torta* for twelve persons.   Take the whitest flour you can get, three *libre* in quantity, and take two *oncie* of sugar and take a *libra* of almonds, and thirty-six good walnuts, and half a *libra* of raisins, and twenty-five dates, and half a *quarto* of cloves; and take a good quantity of almond milk; take the flour, moistened with water to make it very thick, and take the pan and grease it well with oil; make a crust from the flour with crushed sugar and the aforementioned spices; take the walnuts, then the chopped dates and well-washed raisins, and the red cloves; and put a crust between each layer, and put a crust on top of all these things to make a *torta*. (Fr 53)

This layered pastry unquestionably belongs in our category of sweet desserts. Because it is full of dried fruit, which medieval doctors viewed as the healthiest kind, it has great strengthening qualities. Because it is so solid, you need serve only a small portion. It is particularly apt for winter meals; this is also when the best dried fruits from the previous summer are available.

This is a great recipe; besides giving quantities for nearly all the ingredients, it yields a result that is always extremely popular.

For the pâte brisée
generous 3 cups flour (450 g)
14 **tablespoons (1¾ sticks) butter** (200 g)
scant ⅔ cup water, approximately (18 cl)
1 **teaspoon salt**

For the almond milk
1 **cup almonds** (150 g)
1 **quart water** (1 liter)

For the filling
2 **tablespoons sugar** (25 g)
⅓ **teaspoon ground cloves**
scant ½ cup raisins (75 g)
18 **walnuts, shelled**
13 **dates**

A few hours in advance, prepare the *pâte brisée* according to the instructions given in recipe 153 (variation B). Wrap in plastic wrap and refrigerate until needed.

Prepare the almond milk according to the instructions given in recipe 151. Note that you will probably not need the full amount for this pie.

Preheat the oven to 425 degrees F (220 degrees C).

Divide the dough into thirds. Roll the first third into a circle large enough to line a deep 9-inch (22-cm) tart pan. On your work surface, sprinkle the pastry with some of the sugar and the cloves and press them into the dough with the rolling pin. Line the tart pan and arrange the walnuts on the sugared pastry. Sprinkle liberally with almond milk.

Divide the second third of the dough in

half, and roll one piece into a thin circle that will fit into the tart; sprinkle with sugar and cloves, and press them into the dough. Place this on top of the walnuts.

Coarsely chop the dates and arrange them on top of this layer of dough; sprinkle liberally with almond milk.

Roll out and sugar the other small piece of dough as before, and place it on top of the dates.

Arrange the raisins on top of this layer and sprinkle liberally with almond milk. Roll out the remaining dough and cover the pie, sealing the edges well.

Bake for at least an hour.

Sauces

Sauces provide savor, and in Italian the two words—*salsa* on the one hand and *sapore* or *savore* on the other—were synonymous. The liquid of a *brouet/brodo* could be given the same name as a sauce because it comprised the liquids (wine, almond milk, fruit juice, and so forth) and the spices that defined and flavored the dish: we find both *brouets/brodi* and sauces listed under the same titles, such as *poivrade/peverada, cameline/camelino,* and *sarrasine/saracenico.*

But the present chapter is devoted to sauces pure and simple, which performed no culinary role until the moment when the diner, seated at the table, chose one of them to flavor a slice of roasted or boiled meat or fish—just as we today might choose between mustard and horseradish.

These sauces are lovely both in color and in texture; they are vivid in flavor—often sweet and sour—and they can really rouse a weary palate.

We have already spoken of the aesthetic functions of sauces, but we must not forget their dietary role: they were most often thickened with no fats other than the oil found in the almonds; and, fruity and spicy, they added the "warmth" necessary for good digestion.

99. Garlic Sauce

Garlic sauce for all meats: take the garlic and cook it in the embers, then pound it thoroughly and add raw garlic and crumb of bread, and sweet spices, and broth; and mix everything together and boil it a little; and serve hot. (Fr 2)

Garlic sauces were commonly served with boiled meat and poached fish. The late-fourteenth-century poet Folgore da San Gimignano, whose cycle of sonnets, *The Months,* depicted the Tuscan year in verses alive with horse races, hunts, and tournaments, all accompanied by banquets, suggests *agliata* in July (for those who like it) with young kid and boiled capon—after the aspics, the roast partridges, and the young pheasants. In other words, garlic was by no means banned from the aristocratic table, so long as it was moderated through careful preparation: in other contexts, its odor signified "peasant."

This garlic sauce is simpler than the others we have included. It has a vivid flavor and goes well with heartier meats such as beef and venison.

20 cloves garlic
½ cup dry breadcrumbs (40 g)
1 cup broth (¼ liter) (recipe 152)

For the spice mixture
¼ teaspoon ground ginger
¼ teaspoon ground cinnamon
1 pinch ground cloves
   salt

Preheat the oven to 400 degrees F (200 degrees C).

Wrap 18 of the cloves of garlic, unpeeled, in aluminum foil and bake for 30 minutes (you can do this in the embers of your fireplace, if they are aglow).

Soak the breadcrumbs in about one-third of the broth until softened. Peel all the garlic, cooked and raw.

In a mortar or a blender, puree the garlic, blend in the soaked breadcrumbs, and add the spices and enough broth to create a creamy sauce. Pour into a small saucepan, add salt to taste and bring to the boil. Simmer for a few minutes, thinning with additional broth if necessary. Serve hot.

100. White Garlic Sauce

White garlic sauce. Take carefully skinned almonds and pound them, and when they are pounded halfway, add as much garlic as you like, and pound them very well together, adding a little cool water to prevent them from becoming oily. Then take crumb of white bread and soften it in lean meat or fish broth depending on the calendar; this garlic sauce can be served and adapted at will for meat days and days of abstinence. (Ma 157)

> Cooks could—and still can—modify the flavor of garlic sauces by controlling the amount of garlic, adapt them to the religious calendar by choosing the appropriate broth, and even change their color for purely aesthetic reasons (see recipe 101). In this case, almonds are used to soften the intensity of the garlic. You could prepare this sauce to serve with poached chicken or boiled beef, by using the cooking broth, skimmed of excess fat.

½ cup almonds (70 g)
3 cloves garlic, peeled
1 slice sandwich bread, made into crumbs
1¾ cups meat broth, completely defatted (40 cl) (recipe 152)
   salt

Blanch the almonds and dry them thoroughly. Grind them finely in a mortar or a blender, then add the garlic, one clove at a time, continuing to blend.

Soak the breadcrumbs in about a third of the broth and, when softened, whisk until smooth; blend in the almond-garlic mixture.

Whisk in additional broth until the mixture forms a creamy sauce. (The entire preparation could also be done in the blender.) Check for salt before serving.

101. Pink Garlic Sauce

Pink garlic sauce.   Follow the instructions in the previous chapter, except that you must not add broth, but take black grapes and crush them very well with your hands into a pot or other container; boil them for half an hour; then strain this grape must, with which you will moisten the garlic sauce; the same can be done with cherries. This garlic sauce can be served on meat days or fish days, as desired. (Ma 157)

> Chapter 3 of Maestro Martino's manuscript gives 23 recipes for sauces and often includes a number of variations under a single general title. This pink garlic sauce differs from the white version (recipe 100) not only in color: the grape juice, concentrated by boiling, adds a subtle contrasting sweetness to the sauce.

Stem the grapes, put them into a stainless steel or other nonreactive pan and crush them thoroughly with your hands. Alternatively, you can puree them coarsely in a food processor. Bring to the boil and simmer for 30 minutes, then strain, pressing to extract the maximum possible juice.

1	**generous pound red grapes** (500 g)
½	**cup almonds** (70 g)
3	**cloves garlic, peeled**
¼	**cup fresh breadcrumbs** **salt**

Meanwhile, blanch the almonds and dry them thoroughly. Grind them in a mortar or in a blender, along with the garlic.

Soak the breadcrumbs in about ½ cup of the reduced grape juice and, when softened, whisk until smooth; blend in the almond-garlic mixture.

Whisk in additional grape juice until the mixture forms a creamy sauce. (The entire preparation could also be done in the blender.) Check for salt before serving.

102. Walnut-Garlic Sauce for Fish

Garlic Sauce.   Here is how to make garlic sauce: crush garlic and crumb of bread, and moisten with almond or walnut milk. (Tr 390)

This wonderfully smooth sauce is a fine accompaniment for fish. The *Tractatus* manuscript pairs it with skate and salt cod (see recipes 72 and 73).

1⅓ **cups walnut meats** (160 g)
  1 **slice good white bread, crust removed**
  1 **cup warm water** (¼ liter)
  3 **cloves garlic**
     salt

In a blender, grind the nuts to a fine powder. Add the water and blend until you have a smooth paste. Squeeze through a kitchen towel or several layers of strong cheesecloth into a bowl to obtain a rich walnut milk.

Break up the bread and soak in the walnut milk until soft. Peel the garlic and crush it to a fine puree.

Mash the bread until smooth; beat in the garlic and add salt to taste. This sauce should be quite thick; if it is too thick, you may thin it with some water; if too thin, add some additional moistened bread.

103. Summertime Cerulean Blue Sauce

Sky-blue sauce for summer.   Take some of the wild blackberries that grow in hedgerows and some thoroughly pounded almonds, with a little ginger. And moisten these things with verjuice and strain through a sieve. (Ma 156)

Toward the end of summer, when blackberries are at their best, this cerulean blue sauce will add zest to your September meat dinners. The pectin in the berries helps the sauce set to a lovely midnight-blue jelly that is a visual foil and a delicious accompaniment to white meats such as veal and chicken.

  1 **quart blackberries** (1 liter)
  ⅓ **cup unblanched almonds** (50 g)
  ⅔ **cup verjuice, or a mixture of two parts cider vinegar to one part water**
  ¼ **inch slice ginger, peeled**
     salt

Puree the blackberries in a food processor or food mill, and strain the juice, pressing to extract as much liquid as possible. In a mortar or in a blender, grind the almonds and ginger, then mix with the blackberry juice. Contact with the air will turn the mixture a dark blue.

Add the verjuice and strain once more. Season with salt to taste.

104. Green Sauce

reen sauce. Here is how to make green sauce: take ginger, cinnamon, pepper, nutmeg, cloves, parsley, and sage. First grind the spices, then the herbs, and add a third of the sage and parsley, and, if you wish, three or two cloves of garlic. Moisten with vinegar or verjuice. Note that to every sauce and condiment salt is added, and crumb of bread to thicken it. (Tr 394)

> Green sauce is one of the great classics of medieval cooking. All of our sources include a recipe for it. Like mustard, it was sold ready-made by *traiteurs*—the vendors of prepared foods—and was extremely popular. It always includes a variety of aromatic green herbs (hence its name) and an acidic liquid such as vinegar or verjuice.
>
> The closing sentence of the original recipe recalls the necessity, when making medieval sauces, of including bread as a thickener and salt as a seasoning. This is interesting because it shows that these treatises were often written as reminders for professional cooks, who needed only the essential outlines and who knew perfectly well that all sauces had to contain bread and salt.

oak the bread in the water. When it has softened, mash it with a fork and put it into the container of a blender. Add the herbs, the spices, and the garlic if desired, and blend thoroughly to bring out the flavor of the herbs and to create a smooth puree. Gradually add the vinegar. Add salt to taste. This can also be done in a mortar. Press through a sieve, and serve with roast meat, such as leg of lamb.

1   slice dry country bread
5   tablespoons finely chopped parsley
2   leaves fresh sage, finely chopped
1   pinch freshly ground black pepper
1   pinch ground cloves
1   pinch freshly grated nutmeg
¼   teaspoon cinnamon
¼   teaspoon ground ginger
3   tablespoons wine vinegar
2   cloves garlic, pureed (optional)
     scant ½ cup water (10 cl)
     salt

105. Green Sauce for Boiled Meats

reen sauce for kid and other boiled meats. Take parsley, ginger, cloves, cassia buds, and a little salt and pound everything together, and moisten with good vinegar; make it not too strong; and it should not be left to stand, because it will spoil. (Fr 44)

> This green sauce is for boiled meat, particularly for kid—actually mentioned in the title, which is unusual enough for us to highlight it. Unlike recipe 104,

this one, from our "Venetian" text, does not specify a bread thickening, but we know that this could have been understood by the reader. In this case, however, we have decided to follow the instructions to the letter by pureeing all the ingredients without adding moistened bread or straining the sauce. When we used a mortar and pestle to crush the chopped parsley with salt, we ended up with a smooth puree that we thinned with vinegar and flavored with spices. When pressed out by pounding, the parsley juices infused all their taste and aroma into the sauce, whereas a mere mixture of chopped parsley, vinegar, and spices has only an overwhelmingly vinegary flavor. As the author of the original recipe rightly observes, the color of this extraordinary sauce quickly darkens, so it should be prepared just before serving.

4 tablespoons good wine vinegar
3 tablespoons finely chopped
   parsley
⅛ teaspoon ground ginger
⅛ teaspoon ground cinnamon
1 pinch ground cloves
1 pinch coarse sea salt

In a mortar, pound the parsley with the coarse salt until you have a juicy puree. Add the spices, continuing to mix and pound with the pestle. Stir in the vinegar. The sauce will have a reasonable consistency, but not as though it had been thickened.

Serve with any hot or cold boiled meat.

106. An Excellent Cameline Sauce

Excellent cameline sauce. To make an excellent cameline sauce, take skinned almonds and pound and strain them; take raisins, cinnamon, cloves, and a little crumb of bread and pound everything together, and moisten with verjuice; and it is done. (Fr 48)

Cameline was a medieval standard; along with garlic sauces and mustard, it was a nearly obligatory accompaniment to roasted or boiled meat in France, England, Italy, Catalonia, and elsewhere. The name "cameline" could be connected with "cinnamon"—*cannelle* in French—or with the sauce's "camel's hair" color: sauces were often named either for their predominant spice or for their color. But, as is the case with blancmange (see comments on recipe 130) it is difficult to pinpoint a unifying ingredient in the many recipes for this sauce, apart from cinnamon. Italian camelines combine it with cloves, while French recipes use ginger. The English and Catalans used a wider variety of spices, including cloves, ginger, and nutmeg, but always in addition to cinnamon.

This is a sweet-and-sour cameline; in order to allow the cinnamon to prevail, you must be very careful with the cloves.

lump the raisins in warm water for about an hour.

In a mortar or a blender, grind the almonds finely, add about ¾ cup warm water, and continue blending until thoroughly combined. Strain through a fine sieve, pressing with a spoon to extract the maximum possible almond milk.

Moisten the bread with a little water and let stand until softened.

½ cup blanched almonds (70 g)
¼ cup raisins (40 g)
½ cup dry breadcrumbs (40 g)
1¼ cups verjuice, or 3 parts cider vinegar to one part water
1 teaspoon ground cinnamon
¼ teaspoon ground cloves
salt

Puree the raisins in a blender, together with the spices and the bread. Add the almond milk, then the verjuice. Blend until well combined, then add a little salt; taste for seasoning.

This should be quite a loose sauce, of a strong tan color.

107. Tournai-style Cameline Sauce

ameline.   Note that at Tournai, to make cameline they pound ginger, cinnamon, saffron, and half a nutmeg, moistened with wine then removed from the mortar; then take crumb of white bread, without grilling it, soaked in cold water and pounded in the mortar, moisten with wine and strain; then boil everything, and finish with brown sugar: this is a winter cameline. In summer, they do the same, but it is not boiled at all. (MP 230)

> Here is an example of a French cameline sauce, from *Le Ménagier de Paris*. Our medieval experiments have often shown Italian camelines to be superior to their French counterparts, perhaps because they often contain something sweet, which is lacking in other versions. Nonetheless, this Tournai-style cameline is perfect for grilled mackerel, and we highly recommend it for that fish. Perhaps this is because, unlike most French camelines, it does indeed contain a little sugar.

ut up the bread and leave it to soak in 1 cup (¼ liter) of water. Stir the wine into the spices.

When the bread has softened, squeeze out excess water and mash with a fork or a pestle, then stir in the spiced wine mixture. Press through a sieve into a small stainless steel or other nonreactive saucepan. Bring to the boil and simmer for a few minutes, until the sauce thickens. Add salt and brown sugar to taste.

Serve with grilled fish.

½ slice country bread
1¼ cups white wine (30 cl)
½ teaspoon ground ginger
1 teaspoon ground cinnamon
a few threads saffron
⅛ teaspoon freshly grated nutmeg
2 to 3 teaspoons light brown sugar
salt

108. Black Sauce, or *Poivre Noir*

Black *poivre*.   Crush ginger and charred bread and pepper, moisten with vinegar and verjuice, and boil. (VT BN Scul 227)

The simplest of sauces: so that its appearance lives up to its name, we recommend thickening it with nearly burnt bread. We have found this sauce to be particularly popular with grilled steak.

1 slice country bread
⅓ cup verjuice (10 cl), **or equal parts cider vinegar and water**
1 tablespoon wine vinegar
1 scant teaspoon freshly ground black pepper
¼ teaspoon ground ginger
salt

Toast or grill the bread until very dark. In a small stainless steel or other non-reactive pan, soak it in the verjuice and the vinegar until it has completely fallen apart.

Mash the bread with a fork and stir in the spices. Slowly bring to the boil and simmer until thickened. Add salt to taste. If you want a smoother sauce, you can press it through a fine strainer.

109. Yellow Sauce, or *Poivre Jaunet* or *Aigret*

Yellow or Sour Sauce.   Take ginger and saffron, then take grilled bread soaked in meat broth (or even better, meatless cabbage water) and boil; when it boils, add vinegar. (MP 232)

Despite its name, *Poivre,* this sauce from *Le Ménagier de Paris* contains no pepper at all, though it is certainly *jaunet*—yellow. As in recipe 108, the word *poivre* simply means "sauce." *Poivre jaunet* is among the standard boiled sauces mentioned in all the French medieval treatises. We recommend it particularly with fatty meats: it brings out their flavor and seems to make them more digestible.

1 generous slice country bread, crust removed
10 tablespoons (5 fl. ounces) meat broth (recipe 152) or cabbage cooking liquid, or water (15 cl)
3 tablespoons good white wine vinegar (5 cl)
½ teaspoon ground ginger
1 pinch saffron threads
salt

Grill or toast the bread, and, in a small saucepan, leave it to soak in the broth. When it is very soft, mash it thoroughly, add the spices, and bring to the boil. When it comes to the boil, add the vinegar and simmer until thickened. Add salt to taste and adjust the seasoning if necessary. For a smoother result, you can force this sauce through a fine strainer.

To serve, spoon over the meat or fish.

110. A *Peverada* That Does Not Mention Pepper

everada. Take grilled bread, a little saffron that does not add color, spices, and livers, chopped and pounded in the mortar, and moisten with vinegar or wine and the above-mentioned broth; make it sweet or sour as you wish. And this *peverata* can be served with meat, game, or fish. (Za 42)

> The title of this entry is somewhat tantalizing; the generic ingredient, *spezie*, "spices," certainly could include pepper, which is very frequently used elsewhere in the text. Still, it is surprising that it is not explicitly mentioned. This makes this *peverada* quite different from that described in the *Liber de coquina,* which contains pepper and saffron but no liver. We have found no explanation for the term "saffron that does not add color." Could it be a different spice? Or an indication that the saffron is used in this recipe for its flavor and aroma rather than for its color? In any event, we have used normal saffron. This sauce is slightly bitter and is a good match for strongly flavored meats.

reheat the oven to 375 degrees F (190 degrees C). Wrap the chicken livers, or the cubed pork liver, in aluminum foil and bake for 10 to 15 minutes, or until cooked through. Toast or grill the bread.

In a food processor, chop together the liver, bread, and spices; add the wine and broth and continue processing to yield a smooth, fairly fluid puree. Add salt and check for seasoning. If you wish, you can add a little sugar or sweet wine (such as a sweet muscat or grenache).

2 slices country bread
6 ounces chicken livers, or pork liver (150 g)
3 tablespoons red wine (5 cl)
3 tablespoons broth (5 cl) (recipe 152)
5 or 6 threads saffron
1 pinch ground cinnamon
1 pinch freshly grated nutmeg
1 pinch freshly ground black pepper
  salt

111. *Jance*

Jance. To instruct anyone who wishes to make *jance*: take a quantity of nice, good-quality table bread according to what you wish to make, and grate it well and neatly over a nice cloth; then take a fine, clean pot and pour in rich beef and mutton broth, and note that it should not be too salty; and then take eggs and mix them with the bread, and then gently put this into the broth, constantly stirring with a nice wooden spoon; and also add spices, that is, white ginger, grains of paradise, a little pepper, and saffron to give it color, and then verjuice to heighten the flavor; and bring it all to the boil, and serve. (Ch 182)

> *Jance* is a light-colored French sauce; it always contains ginger, but the other ingredients could vary quite a bit. *Le Ménagier de Paris* gives a version based on cow's milk, which amounts to an egg sauce spiced with ginger. Here, Chiquart's *jance* uses a number of spices, but the dominant flavor is that of saffron, which also tints the sauce a brilliant golden color. The unusual flavor goes well with grilled meats.

2   large slices dry country bread
1   egg, beaten
1   cup broth (25 cl) (recipe 152)
3   tablespoons verjuice (5 cl), or equal parts cider vinegar and water
½   teaspoon ground grains of paradise (see p. 46 for substitutions)
¼   teaspoon ground ginger
¼   teaspoon freshly ground black pepper
1   large pinch saffron threads
     salt

In a food processor, or using a grater, break the bread into fine crumbs; add the beaten egg, process or stir to combine, and leave to stand for a minute. Add the broth and spices, then the verjuice, and process or stir to combine. Place in a small saucepan and bring to the boil over medium heat, stirring constantly, until thickened. Add salt to taste, and serve hot.

112. Sauce for Roast Goose or Suckling Pig

Sauce for crane. Take the crane's liver and roast it on the embers; then take good spices, marjoram, saffron, and the liver, and pound everything well together; and add two egg yolks to this, and moisten with good wine and a little vinegar; then add a little boiled grape must, so that it will be sweet and sour.

Sauces for geese and suckling pigs

Do as indicated above, apart from the boiled wine. And add to the sauce the fat that runs from the goose. Do the same for roast piglet; if you do not want to make this sauce, make green sauce. (Za 80)

This sauce can be adapted to any roast meat. The recipe indicates how adaptable culinary practice could be and how much attention was devoted to finding just the right flavors: sweet and sour for crane, and sour alone for goose and suckling pig. The recipe's final comment also points to the flexibility of dining habits. Note that the manuscript from which we took this recipe does not contain a recipe for green sauce; in recipe 104 we give one from another collection, and the principle of green sauces was always the same: herbs, pounded and then moistened with an acidic liquid.

It is altogether possible that you will not find any crane in your local supermarket, so we have adapted this sauce for roast goose.

When you roast your goose, put the liver in the cavity to cook along with the bird.

Grind the cooked liver, and combine with the wine, the egg yolk, the vinegar, and about 2 tablespoons of goose fat from the roasting pan. Add the marjoram and the spices, and salt to taste. Pour into a sauceboat and serve with the roast goose.

the liver and some rendered fat from a roast goose
1 egg yolk
3 tablespoons red wine (5 cl)
1 teaspoon red wine vinegar
½ teaspoon chopped fresh marjoram or ¼ teaspoon dried
5 or 6 threads saffron
1 pinch ground cinnamon
1 pinch freshly ground black pepper
salt

113. Black-Grape Sauce

Grape sauce.   Take good black grapes and crush them very well into a bowl, breaking in a bread or half a bread depending on the quantity you wish to prepare; and add a little good verjuice or vinegar so that the grapes will not be so sweet. And boil these things over the fire for half an hour, adding cinnamon and ginger and other good spices. (MA 155)

According to Martino, sauces could be made from most of the juicy fruits known in the Middle Ages. But grapes were the most commonly used. The amount of bread you use will determine the thickness of the sauce; bear in mind that it will get much thicker as it cools.

1 slice country bread or ¼ cup dry breadcrumbs (20 g)

2¼ pounds black or red grapes (1 kg), or 3 cups freshly pressed black or red grape juice (¾ liter)

scant ½ cup verjuice or vinegar (10 cl)

⅓ teaspoon ground cinnamon

⅓ teaspoon ground ginger

1 pinch freshly ground black pepper

1 pinch ground cardamom

salt

*J*f using fresh grapes, puree them in a food processor or put them through a food mill with the fine grill. You may also use a juicer. Add the verjuice or vinegar and strain through a fine sieve, pressing with a spoon to extract as much juice as possible. If you are using juice, do not use the excessively sweet dark purple beverage much loved by children: prepare or purchase juice freshly extracted from table grapes.

Pour ¼ cup of the juice over the bread and leave to soften, then beat with a wire whisk until smooth. Stir in the spices and gradually whisk in the remaining liquid. Add salt to taste.

In a stainless steel or other nonreactive saucepan, bring this to the boil and simmer for 30 minutes, stirring constantly with a wooden spoon to prevent the bread from sticking to the bottom of the pan. Check for seasoning and serve.

114. Prune Sauce

*D*ried-plum sauce.   Take prunes and put them to soak in red wine, and remove the pits; pound them very well with a few unskinned almonds and a little roasted or grilled bread soaked in the wine where the prunes had been. And pound all these things together with a little verjuice and the above-mentioned wine and a little boiled grape must, or sugar, which would be much better; mix and strain, adding good spices, especially cinnamon. (Ma 154)

This dried-fruit variant of Maestro Martino's fruit sauces is excellent with roasted white meats, most particularly rabbit.

12 medium prunes

⅓ cup unblanched almonds (50 g)

1 slice country bread, toasted or grilled

1 cup red wine (25 cl)

3 tablespoons verjuice (5 cl) or equal parts lemon juice and water

1 heaping tablespoon sugar

For the spice mixture

1 teaspoon ground cinnamon

1 pinch ground ginger

1 pinch ground cardamom

salt

*S*everal hours in advance, put the prunes into a bowl with the red wine and leave them to soak.

Grind the almonds in a blender. Pit the prunes and mash them. Break up the bread and put it into the wine in which the prunes had soaked; when softened, mash the bread.

Combine the almonds, bread, and prunes; add the sugar and spices, and enough wine and verjuice to result in a good consistency. Press through a fine strainer and add salt to taste.

The entire sauce can also be made in the blender.

115. Mustard

Mustard.   If you want to prepare a supply of mustard to keep for a long time, make it from fresh grape must at harvest time. And some say that the must should be boiled. Item: if you want to make mustard in a village[?], in a hurry, crush mustard seed in a mortar and moisten with vinegar, and put through a sieve; and if you want to use it as soon as it has been strained, put it into a pot near the fire. Item: and if you want to make it well, and taking the proper time, put the mustard seed to soak overnight in good vinegar, then crush it in a mill and add vinegar little by little; and if you have spices left over from making aspics, *claré,* hypocras, or sauces, grind them along with this and let it mature. (MP 229)

Mustard was the most popular condiment in the Middle Ages, and the most ancient and widespread as well. It remains so: worldwide, more mustard is produced than any other condiment. This recipe from *Le Ménagier de Paris* holds the etymological key to the word "mustard," or *moutarde,* which literally means *moût ardent,* or "fiery grape must": and mustard, the condiment, was long made by grinding mustard seed and grape must. But "mustard" refers also to the seed itself: either white mustard *(Brassica alba* or *Sinapis alba)* or black mustard *(Brassica nigra).* Even though they differ in degree of pungency—black mustard being fiery and white mustard merely hot—they are often confused; today's commercial French-style mustards are commonly a blend of the two seeds, whose individual characteristics counterbalance each other.

White mustard comes originally from the coastal areas of the Mediterranean, while the tiny black seeds of *Brassica nigra* probably come to us from Persia and Asia Minor. But both have long been cultivated in Western Europe; mustard was a very popular condiment in Roman times.

You can use either seed for this recipe; both are available from spice merchants and South Asian groceries (see Mail-order Sources), and even supermarkets. But the yellowish seeds of white mustard are easier to work with: black mustard is harder and more difficult to soften and crush. Whichever you choose, once you have crushed the seeds and mixed them with the vinegar and spices, you must let your mustard rest for eight to ten days before tasting it, sealed tightly in a container and kept out of the light, preferably in the refrigerator, which in our view is the best place to store it. Mustard seeds contain crystalline glucosides known as sinigrin (in black mustard) and sinalbin (in white), which on contact with water give up their essential oils, which are the source of mustard's hotness and flavor; initially, these oils are bitter and need a few days of aging to soften.

We have followed the advice in *Le Ménagier de Paris* to make excellent mustard with vinegar and spices, using white mustard seeds. Note, incidentally, that the thrifty author of *Le Ménagier,* always with an eye to the efficient management of his household, recommends using spices left over from other preparations: aspics, spiced wine drinks, and sauces.

1½ cups white mustard seeds
(250 g)
about 1¾ cups excellent-
quality white wine vinegar
(40 cl)
1 teaspoon strong black spices
(recipe 150, variation C)
salt

Soak the mustard seeds overnight in vinegar to cover by about ¼ inch. The following day, make sure the seeds have swelled and softened; you should be able to crush them between your fingers. Strain them, reserving the vinegar.

In a blender, grind the mustard to a very thick paste, then blend in a little vinegar. If the seeds are not all broken, continue to blend. Gradually add additional vinegar until the consistency is neither too thick nor too thin. Add the spices and some salt. Taste, and add more salt if necessary: the mustard should be fairly salty.

Scrape into a glass or glazed ceramic jar with a tight lid. Close the jar and store in the refrigerator for a week or ten days before using.

Eggs

Here are some egg recipes, collected in a chapter of their own. They should not be neglected, because, as they are today, eggs were an important household resource; judging by the literature, home cooks often improvised on the egg theme.

Remember too that eggs were used as binders in most pies and tarts—meat or fish, sweet or savory—and in a number of sauces. It must have been difficult to get through the most rigorous of penitential days, when all animal products, including eggs, were forbidden. That was *real* penitence.

Medical and agricultural writings of the time ascribed many virtues to the chicken egg. Owing to the distinction between their yolks and their whites, they possessed balance, and were suitable for nearly everybody; they preserved sexual potency. But it was important to select the right cooking method: an egg cooked over the coals was seen as better than one cooked buried in the embers, and poaching was superior to frying.

116. Eggs in Red Wine, or Civet of Eggs

Civet of eggs. Poach some eggs in oil, then take onions, cut into circles and cooked, and fry them in oil, then boil them in wine, verjuice, and vinegar, and boil everything together; then put three or four eggs in each bowl and pour the *brouet* over; it should not be thick. (MP 174)

> Here is a fine change of pace from those unending fried eggs. This recipe is surely the ancestor of *oeufs en meurette*, that famous, hearty Burgundian dish of eggs in red wine sauce. The ruby-red onion "jam" spooned over the sunny side of the fried eggs is a feast for the eyes. And this combination does not lose sight of flavor: the smooth richness of the egg yolk is a perfect companion for the sweet-and-sour flavor of the onion sauce.

179

4 extremely fresh eggs
2 medium onions
2 cups good, light-bodied red
   wine, such as a Beaujolais or
   other gamay (½ liter)
1 tablespoon good red wine
   vinegar
3 tablespoons verjuice (5 cl), or
   the juice of half a lemon plus 2
   tablespoons water
   olive oil
   salt

Peel the onions and cut them into ¼-inch slices. Steam or poach them for 5 to 7 minutes. Drain well.

Over medium heat, warm 2 tablespoons of olive oil in a small saucepan; add the cooked onion slices and sauté for about 10 minutes, or until lightly golden. Add the wine, the verjuice, and the vinegar, bring to the boil, and cook at a gentle boil until the mixture has reduced by three-fourths and the onions have formed a somewhat loose "jam." Add salt to taste.

When the onions are nearly done, fry the eggs in olive oil, sunny-side up, being careful not to break the yolks. Drain them well, and place them on heated plates. Spoon the onion sauce over the eggs.

117. Eggs with Mustard Sauce

Sippets in mustard. Take eggs, poached whole in oil without their shells, then take some of that oil, wine, water, and onions fried in oil, all boiled together; take slices of bread browned on the grill, then cut them into square pieces and put them to boil with the other ingredients; then remove the broth and dry your sippets of bread, then put it on a platter; then add mustard to your broth and boil; then put the sippets into your bowls and pour it over. (VT BN Scul 150)

There are several versions of this French recipe, but none of them indicates whether the "eggs, poached whole in oil" are actually a part of the dish. We decided in our adaptation to set the eggs on top of the bread—the *soupes* or sippets, grilled and then soaked in sauce—even though we are not explicitly instructed to do so. Otherwise, what are we supposed to do with the eggs once we have used their cooking oil to make the sauce? It is hard to imagine throwing them away and keeping only their oil as a sauce base. But it also depends on whether this recipe is for a *potage* with bread (as its title would suggest) or for an egg dish. After some indecision, we decided that it would be more interesting among the egg preparations, and devised our version to yield relatively little sauce.

peel and slice the onions, then sauté until golden in a little olive oil. Reserve.

Fry the eggs, sunny-side up, in 3 generous tablespoons of olive oil; reserve on a warm plate.

To the same pan add the sautéed onions, the wine, the water, and a little salt, and boil until the raw wine flavor has disappeared and the sauce is somewhat reduced. Dip both sides of the bread into this sauce; the bread should absorb some of the liquid but not become sodden. Place one slice of bread on each plate. Now stir the mustard into the sauce, bring to the boil, and remove from the heat.

Set one fried egg on each slice of bread and top with some of the mustard sauce.

For two servings

4   very fresh eggs
2   slices dry country bread, grilled or toasted
2   medium onions
1   cup red wine (¼ liter)
5   fl. ounces water (15 cl)
1   tablespoon homemade mustard (recipe 115), or Dijon or Meaux mustard
    olive oil
    salt

118. Stuffed Eggs

Eggs: to prepare for stuffing.   To make stuffed eggs, cut each one in half when it has been well cooked and [is] thus hard. Then remove the yolk and take marjoram, saffron, and cloves and mix with the yolks of those eggs; and mash it thoroughly, adding a little cheese. For each eight eggs, add one raw egg. This done, fill the egg whites with this mixture. And fry in good pork fat, and eat with verjuice. (Lc 412)

This simple recipe is found, with minor differences, in all the sources. In the Latin collection from which we have chosen it, it is the first of seven methods of cooking eggs. We find the same preparation in the Tuscan manuscript edited by Zambrini in 1868, which offers no other egg recipes, saying that "there is no need to speak of fried, roasted, and scrambled eggs, because everyone knows how to make them." This shows how commonplace eggs were; remember too that eggs were frequently used to bind sauces and pie fillings.

The Tuscan version of the recipe does not use the normal word for verjuice, *agresta*, but substitutes *il savore che si dice verzuso francioso*—"the sauce known as French verjuice." Is this a case of the same linguistic contamination found in the fourteenth-century text edited by Frati in 1899, whose language is similar to Venetian? That manuscript indiscriminately uses both *verzuso* and *agresta*. Or does it refer to a kind of custard, like Maestro Martino's *Verzuso in Quadragesima* (Ma 149)?

9 eggs

2 ounces cheese such as Swiss gruyère or French comté (60 g)

5 fl. ounces verjuice or equal parts of cider vinegar and water

7 ounces good lard (200 g)

1 sprig fresh marjoram or ½ teaspoon dried marjoram or oregano

6 or 7 threads saffron

⅛ teaspoon ground cloves

salt

Hard boil eight of the eggs. Grate the cheese. Finely chop the marjoram, if using fresh. Shell the hard-boiled eggs, cut them in half lengthwise, and remove the yolks to a bowl.

Mash the yolks and mix them with the remaining whole, raw egg. Add the cheese, the marjoram, the spices, and salt to taste (salt with care because of the cheese). Blend to a smooth mixture with a spatula or a wooden spoon.

Divide the mixture into sixteen, and stuff the cavities of the hard-boiled whites.

Heat the lard in a deep skillet, and fry the stuffed eggs on all sides, turning very carefully so as not to dislodge the stuffing.

Sprinkle with verjuice before serving.

119. Poached Eggs in Custard Sauce

Thickened cow's milk. Take best-quality milk, as indicated above in the chapter on *potages*; bring it to the boil then remove from the fire; then put through a sieve many egg yolks, their filaments removed, and then crush a knob of ginger and some saffron and add them; and keep warm near the fire; then take eggs poached in water and put two or three poached eggs in each bowl and pour the milk over them. (MP 175)

You will long remember the richness and incomparable delicacy of these eggs in custard sauce. They are, obviously, a substantial dish and would be enough for a whole meal. Or you can serve them to athletic, hungry teenagers.

The *cloche* ("bell") of ginger means a chunk of the rhizome; perhaps ginger bought by the piece and pounded at home would be softer and fresher than the powdered ginger sold by the spice merchant.

Ingredients for two servings

2 cups milk (½ liter)

4 very fresh eggs

4 egg yolks

¼-inch slice fresh ginger, peeled, or, if unavailable, 1 teaspoon ground ginger

1 pinch saffron threads

salt

Bring the milk just to the boil, and salt lightly. Grate or puree the ginger.

Bring a pan of water to the simmer (for poaching the eggs).

Beat the four yolks and put them through a fine strainer into a bowl; salt lightly. Whisk a little of the hot milk into the yolks, then pour the yolk mixture into the saucepan with the remaining milk. Cook over very low heat, stirring constantly, until the mixture becomes slightly thick. Overheating will cause the sauce to curdle. Add the ginger and saffron, and check for salt.

Poach the four remaining eggs in barely simmering water for about 4 minutes. Serve, immediately, two per portion in soup plates, with the sauce spooned over.

120. Egg Ravioli

Eggs in the form of ravioli.   Make a dough as for lasagne, neither too thinly rolled nor too soft, and break onto it fresh eggs, sprinkling them with sugar and sweet spices and a little salt; enclose these eggs one by one in the dough so as to form ravioli; boil or fry them as you prefer. But they are better fried. (Ma 183)

> This takes some skill, but it is an entertaining dish. It reminds us of making Tunisian *brik*, which involves breaking eggs into very thin pastry and then frying them. The present recipe is sweet, rather startling to modern tastes.

On a board or in the food processor, make a somewhat firm dough using the flour, a pinch of salt, and as much water as required. Knead well, wrap in plastic and let rest for 30 minutes.

Divide the dough into six, and roll out each piece into a thin circle. Set a piece of dough into a small, lightly floured bowl, and break an egg into the hollow. Sprinkle with salt, a teaspoon of sugar, and a pinch of spices, and fold the dough over the egg, pressing hard to seal tightly. Do the same for each egg.

6 **eggs**
2 **cups flour** (300 g)
2 **tablespoons sugar**
sweet spices (recipe 150, variation B)
salt
vegetable oil for deep frying

Heat the oil to about 350 degrees F (175 degrees C) and fry the ravioli until golden. (If the oil is too hot, they will burn.) Drain on paper towels and serve.

121. Green Omelette

Frittata.   Beat the eggs very well, and add a little water and a little milk to make them a little softer; add a little good grated cheese and cook in butter so it will be richer. Note that for it to be good it should not be turned over or overcooked. And to make it green, also take the above-mentioned ingredients, adding the juice of these herbs: chard, lots of parsley, borage, mint, marjoram, and a little sage, straining the juice; then strain out the very finely chopped herbs. And to make an omelette with herbs in another way, take the above-mentioned herbs, chopped fine, fry them a little in good butter or oil; mix them with the eggs and other above-mentioned ingredients and make the omelette; cook it quickly so that it is properly done and not overcooked. (Ma 180)

Here are two versions of an omelette with herbs and greens. The first is made with only the vegetable juices and is a bright jade green; the other has a lovely marbling of green running through the yellow of the eggs. We suggest trying both and serving them together on the same plate: a very pretty presentation. If you like, you can use half of the ingredients for each, yielding two smaller omelettes. We were drawn to this recipe among all the many medieval omelette recipes, because it is the closest to a modern French omelette: cooked in butter and still runny in the center. Today, the Italian *frittata* is a sort of thick egg pancake cooked until well done, while Maestro Martino's is cooked on one side only and remains very soft—just like a good French omelette. In French texts, most of these dishes are called *alumelles*, a word that developed into the modern "omelette." But herb omelettes have the lovely name of *arboulastres*, which probably derives from the word *herbes*.

We have substituted spinach for the borage, but obviously this omelette can be made with any herbs or leafy greens that are in season or that you grow in your own garden. The flavor will be determined by their proportions.

For either version

6   very fresh eggs

5   fl. ounces milk (15 cl)

3   tablespoons water (5 cl)

2   tablespoons freshly grated parmesan, Swiss gruyère, or French comté cheese

4   tablespoons (2 ounces) butter (50 g)

1   small handful young Swiss chard, leaves only

1   small handful young spinach, leaves only

1   small handful parsley

4   fresh sage leaves

4   or 5 fresh mint leaves, to taste

5   or 6 sprigs fresh marjoram salt

Variation A

Beat the eggs together with the milk, water, and cheese. Salt (but lightly, because of the cheese).

Trim, wash, and thoroughly dry the greens and herbs. Chop finely by hand or in a blender or food processor, until nearly pureed. Transfer to a mortar, add a little coarse salt, and pound until you have a juicy puree. Alternatively, the entire process can take place in a blender. Strain through a fine sieve into the beaten eggs, pressing with a spoon to extract as much juice as possible. Beat into the eggs, which should now be an even green color.

Melt the butter over medium-low heat; when it begins to color, pour in the egg mixture and cook as you would any omelette. Let the bottom turn golden, but the top should remain very soft. Fold the omelette and slide it onto a serving plate.

Variation B

Beat the eggs together with the milk, water, and cheese. Salt (but lightly, because of the cheese).

Trim, wash, and thoroughly dry the greens and herbs. Chop finely with a knife. Over medium-low heat, melt the butter in a skillet and, when it begins to color, add the greens and herbs, sprinkle with salt and sauté for 7 or 8 minutes. Stir in the eggs, and cook as you would any omelette. Let the bottom turn golden, but the top should remain very soft. Fold the omelette and slide it onto a serving plate.

122. Orange Omelette for Harlots and Ruffians

How to make an orange omelette. Take eggs and break them, with oranges, as many as you like; squeeze their juice and add to it the eggs with sugar; then take olive oil or fat, and heat it in the pan and add the eggs. This was for ruffians and brazen harlots. (Bo 738)

> Johannes Bockenheim (or Buckehen) was cook to Pope Martin V and in the 1430s wrote a brief but highly original cookbook recently edited by Bruno Laurioux (see bibliography). This German, who lived at Rome, wrote as a professional, with telegraphic terseness and little detail; yet he was careful to specify the destined consumer of each recipe, pigeon-holed by social class—from prostitutes to princes—or by nationality: Italian, French, German from any of various provinces, and so forth.
>
> We cannot see why this omelette, which contains no meat and no seasoning other than sugar, should be particularly well suited to debauchees. Surely, it is flesh (further fired by spices) that enflames the flesh. This omelette can be safely tasted without running the risk of moral turpitude.
>
> Since medieval oranges were bitter, we suggest a blend of oranges and lemons. The sugar and the acidity of the juice prevent the eggs from completely setting, so this is more of a custardy cream that makes an unusual and very pleasant dessert.

Juice the oranges and the lemon. Beat the eggs, add the juice, the sugar, and salt to taste, and cook the omelette in olive oil. Serve warm.

6 eggs
2 oranges
1 lemon
2 tablespoons sugar
2 tablespoons olive oil
salt

Entremets, Fritters, and Golden Bread Treats

Of all the French culinary terms that have remained in the language since the Middle Ages, the word *entremets* is undoubtedly the most confusing. Today it retains almost nothing of its etymological roots or its medieval meaning. Modern French dictionaries define it as a sweet dish served after the cheese course: it has thus become nearly synonymous with "dessert." Yet (without having to go back as far as the fourteenth century) as recently as the turn of the twentieth century the word still meant a course that marked the progression from roast to dessert, and referred also to the delicate dishes, both sweet and savory, that comprised that course, such as seasonal vegetables, flavored gelatin preparations, creams, and fruit compotes. Modern habits gradually eliminated that course from the menu, and thus stripped the word *entremets* of its meaning. The savory dishes that used to be served as a separate course were shifted to one side of the meat plate, and the sweet ones to the dessert course. The Robert dictionary—to French what Webster's or the *Oxford English Dictionary* is to English—seeks to clarify the evolution of the word, and in its usage note indicates that "today, *entremets* refers only to sweet dishes. These dishes are most often served after the cheese course, not before, and are confused with dessert and are often improperly called by that name."

Of course, there is nothing "improper" about this at all: it simply reflects changes in practice and in taste.

But what were *entremets* in the Middle Ages? As the word indicates, they were served between two courses—*entre deux mets*—and functioned as a divider. Yet, depending on the context, the word could have differing connotations—a point in time, an entertainment, or a dish—and it would be pointless to try to impose a single accepted meaning. In Italy, the *intermezzo* was an entertainment, not something to eat. In fifteenth-century France, at great feasts, it referred both to the interval between the roast and the dessert, and to the entertainment offered to the guests during that interval, which could be theatrical or culinary: *tableaux vivants;* scenic paintings; vast, extraordinary edible sculptures; sumptuously decorated arrangements of food; unusual birds served clothed in their own plumage; tinted gelatin preparations; stuffed poultry; grain dishes; and much more. In culinary treatises emanating from royal households, notably Maître Chiquart's *Du Fait de Cuisine*, culinary and artistic feats are described in the greatest detail: the *Château d'amour* ("Castle of Love") had crenelated walls and four

187

towers defended by little soldiers, who were repelling a naval assault on a fish-filled sea painted on fabric. At the foot of the towers, guests were tempted by an enormous pike cooked in three ways, a bear's head, a roast swan covered in its own plumage and positioned to appear poised for flight, and a glazed suckling pig—all these creatures breathing fire. In the middle of the castle's courtyard, a Fountain of Love flowed with unlimited quantities of rose water and spiced wine; and a multitude of perfectly roasted birds tumbled from the galleries of a dovecote. And so forth.

In simpler texts such as *Le Ménagier de Paris*, *entremets* are merely things to eat. Some could be elegant, or decorated, or tinted, but they were never on Chiquart's level of extravagance. Presumably, a genuine *entremets*, in all the senses of the word, would have been arranged only for a magnificent feast. But dishes described as *entremets* in *Le Ménagier* could well have formed part of the third or fourth course of a more ordinary banquet, toward the end of the meal.

Our choice of recipes for this chapter anticipates the evolution of the category: it includes a high proportion of sweet dishes to match our expectations for a dessert. But we have not contravened the order of a medieval menu, because we have chosen dishes that would all have been served at the close of a dinner or supper.

123. Meats in Aspic

For Jelly, take calves' legs or feet, whichever you can get, and boil them in white wine, with their meat. Then, when the calves' legs or feet are about half cooked, take pork cut into pieces and young chickens cut in half and well cleaned and washed, and young rabbits if you can get them. Then take ginger, grains of paradise, a little mace, plenty of saffron, and a reasonable amount of vinegar. And when the meat is cooked, take the broth and put it in a pot over a charcoal fire. If the aspic is too fatty, take egg whites and add them to the broth when it is on the point of boiling; and when it boils, have a cloth ready through which to pour it; when it has been strained, put the meat into dishes—the pork, rabbit, and chicken—and when the meat is arranged in the dishes, put it into the cellar and pour the broth over the meat in each dish. (VT XV 156)

> Every medieval cookery text includes recipes for jellied meat and fish. The large quantities of ingredients suggest that these were dishes of high standing, prepared for important occasions. These aspics were perfectly clear, having been clarified with egg whites, colored golden with saffron, or tinted blue or red, and they were one of the main attractions at a feast. Maestro Martino goes into great detail about the delicate construction of a layered, multicolor gelatin creation, and about a chicken imprisoned in jellied broth inside a basket that was to be borne to the table by its handles. Aspics and other jellied

dishes gave cooks the chance to show off their talent as artists and sauce-makers.

These aspics were made with wine or vinegar and with quantities of many spices; they also served to preserve the meats they coated. Flavorings varied from text to text; in Italy they might have included bay leaves and *spico—espic* or *aspic* in French, which gives us the English word "aspic" and which refers to lavender or to Indian spikenard *(Nardostachys jatamansi)*, an aromatic rhizome known and highly esteemed since ancient times. Bay and *spico*, used together with cassia buds, pomegranate seeds, white violets, or vermilion-colored sugared almonds, were among the decorations used to embellish these dishes when they were brought to the dining room. This focus on the artistic underscores the important place of aspics.

The modern cook may be surprised by the mixture of pork, rabbit, and chicken, but the combination is found in all French sources.

The calves' leg or feet seem to be used only to gel the broth, and their meat is not used in the finished dish.

The recipe can be prepared in two ways: either the pieces of meat can be left whole with their bones and covered in the jellied broth, or the meat can be boned and cut into small pieces and served in the form of a jellied loaf or cake (like a headcheese). The original recipe seems to point to the first method, but we have also tried the second.

If you are using a calf's foot, clean it thoroughly before using. Put the calf's foot or veal shank into a stainless steel or other nonreactive pot with the wine, bring slowly to the boil, and simmer for 90 minutes, skimming as necessary.

Cut the pork, the rabbit, and the chicken into serving pieces, then wash and dry thoroughly. Add to the pot with the foot or shank. Wrap the gingerroot, grains of paradise, mace, and saffron in a piece of cheesecloth and tie it with kitchen twine or white cotton thread; add to the pot along with the vinegar. Salt lightly. Gently simmer for about another hour, until the pork, rabbit and chicken are all tender.

Turn off the heat, and remove all the meats from the broth and reserve; discard the bundle of spices. As the broth stands off the heat, whisk the egg whites in a bowl until they are just frothy. Continue to whisk as you slowly add about a cup of hot broth; return to the pot containing the broth, whisking constantly as you pour. Return to

1 calf's foot or veal shank (whole or cut up by the butcher)

14 ounces boneless loin of pork, not too lean (400 g)

1 small rabbit, 2¼ to 2¾ pounds (1 to 1.2 kg)

1 small chicken, just over 2 pounds (1 kg)

2 egg whites

4 bottles white wine (3 liters)
scant ½ cup good white wine vinegar (10 cl)
a piece of gingerroot about the size of a walnut

2 tablespoons whole grains of paradise (20 g) (see p. 46 for substitutions)

2 heaping tablespoons unground mace blades (10 g)

⅓ teaspoon saffron threads
salt

the heat and bring back to the boil, continuing to whisk the broth. Reduce the heat to very low and simmer undisturbed for 15 to 20 minutes. The egg white, distributed throughout the liquid, will eventually coagulate and collect all the impurities.

When you can see clarified broth beneath the raft of coagulated egg whites and impurities, turn off the heat and slowly strain through a sieve lined with a cotton or linen kitchen towel or three layers of rinsed cheesecloth.

While the broth is simmering with the egg whites, arrange the bones-in meat in a deep serving dish, or remove the bones, cut the meat into bite-sized pieces, and place it in a pâté mold or loaf pan; do not pack it tightly.

Taste the clarified broth for seasoning, especially for salt. Pour over the meat and put into the refrigerator. By the next day, the broth will have set into a lovely amber-colored aspic.

124. Trout in Aspic

Fish in jelly. Take good wine and a little vinegar, and, when it has been skimmed upon boiling, put in the fish, and, when they are cooked, remove them, and boil the wine so that it reduces to one-third; then add saffron and other spices, with bay leaves; then when the wine has been strained, add lavender and leave to cool; then put it over the fish in a deep dish. (Za 28)

> This is one of the simplest of recipes for fish in aspic, but it sets out the basic principles for preparing such dishes. Another of our authors, Maestro Martino, tells us that a good fish aspic must contain as little water as possible, and that it will last longer if it is made only of flavored wine or vinegar. The only appropriate fish are those that *Le Viandier* refers to as *poisson[s] a lymon*—fish with oily skins and covered with a mucus-like natural oil. Like Maestro Martino, the author of the Vatican manuscript of *Le Viandier* instructs us to skin the fish after cooking and to add the skins and trimmings to the broth and to reduce it separately. That is the best way to achieve a good aspic: the gelatinous elements of fish are located mainly in the skin and bones. Moreover, the Vatican manuscript of *Le Viandier* is very precise about the choice of spices and about how to use them: it recommends wrapping the bay leaves and lavender in the cloth that has been used to strain the broth from cooking the fish and that still holds the residue of the spices from that process. Such refinement!

In a stainless steel or other nonreactive pan large enough to hold the trout, bring the wine and the vinegar to the boil; skim if necessary, then remove from the heat and leave to cool. Cooling can be speeded up by setting the pan in a large bowl of ice water.

Wash and clean the trout, then dry them with paper towels. Salt them generously inside and out and set aside for about 10 minutes.

Wrap each fish in a piece of rinsed cheesecloth and tie with kitchen twine or cotton thread. Do not tie too tightly, because the fish will swell as they cook and this would leave unattractive indentations.

When the wine mixture is nearly cold, add the fish; the liquid should barely cover them. Bring to the boil, reduce the heat to very low, and simmer gently; the total cooking time should be about 10 minutes. Turn the fish over after 5 minutes.

6	medium trout
5	cups white wine, approximately (1¼ liters)
5	fl. ounces good white wine vinegar (15 cl)
½	teaspoon ground grains of paradise (see p. 46 for substitutions)
⅓	capsule long pepper, ground, or ⅓ teaspoon freshly ground black pepper
1	scant teaspoon ground cinnamon
1	pinch ground cloves
3	bay leaves
7	or 8 threads saffron
1	teaspoon lavender blossoms, fresh or dried
	salt

When done, remove the trout from the poaching liquid. When they are cool enough to handle, unwrap them, then skin and filet the trout and add the heads, skin, bones, and other trimmings to the poaching liquid. Bring this to the boil and add the saffron. Line a small strainer with two layers of rinsed cheesecloth and put the ground spices into the cloth. Holding the strainer over the pot, ladle some of the stock over the spices. Add the bay leaves to the cloth and tie it into a small bundle. Add the bundle to the broth, and cook over medium heat, uncovered, until it has reduced by two-thirds. When it is done, add the lavender blossoms and check for seasoning. Let the broth cool; again, this can be hastened with an ice-water bath.

Arrange the trout on a serving platter. When the broth is cool but not yet set, pour it over the fish, reserving about 3 tablespoons. Put the platter and the reserved broth into the refrigerator. When the broth begins to gel, brush the reserved broth over the fish to give them a lustrous coating of aspic.

It can be difficult to get this broth to gel, because the fish cook for such a short time. That is why it is so important to reduce the broth with the skin, bones, and trimmings of the fish. In fact, when you buy the trout, try to get your fishmonger to give you some heads and bones of other freshwater fish; you can make these into a rich broth and, after the trout have been poached, add it to the cooking liquid for the final reduction.

125. Marrow Fritters

Marrow fritters.   Whoever wants to make fritters from marrow should plump it in the proper way[*], then take flour and egg yolks and make a batter; take each piece of marrow and fry it in lard.

[*] Beef marrow that is plumped: that is, put the marrow into a pierced spoon, and put the pierced spoon with the marrow into broth in a pot where the meat has boiled, and leave it there as long as you would leave a plucked spring chicken in hot water to firm it up; and then put it in cold water, then cut up the marrow, and roll it into pieces like large *jabets* [birds' crops(?)] or little balls. (MP 223)

Scholars do not know what the text means by *jabets*. We think it might refer to the crops of certain birds. Beef marrow was a medieval delicacy. The author of *Le Ménagier de Paris*, the source of these fritters, tells us that "at the court of lords such as Monseigneur de Berry, when they killed an ox, they made the rissoles out of the marrow." Those without the wherewithal to buy an ox had to make do with less luxurious rissoles made of ground pork and eggs. Rabelais too, when he saw how greedy his dog became when faced with a marrow bone, came to the conclusion that there was no more perfect food in the whole world.

When you can get some fresh marrow, try these fritters, if only as an entertaining novelty. They are lovely, and will be a treat for anyone who, like Rabelais's dog, loves to dig the marrow out of the *osso buco*.

For the batter

- ⅞ **cup flour** (125 g)
- 2 **egg yolks**
- 7 **fl. ounces white wine** (20 cl)
- ¼ **teaspoon salt**
- 7 **ounces fresh beef marrow** (200 g)
- 4 **cups broth or water** (1 liter)
- **salt**
- **lard or oil for frying**

An hour in advance, make the batter: beat together the flour, egg yolks, and salt until smooth, then gradually whisk in the wine.

Bring the broth or water to the boil, then lower the heat. Put the marrow into a strainer and lower it into the simmering liquid for a few seconds. Do not let it actually cook, or it will fall apart; all you want to do is slightly soften the surface. Remove the marrow and plunge it into a bowl of ice-cold water.

When the marrow has cooled, drain it on paper towels and cut it into pieces about half the size of a walnut, or shape it with your fingers into little balls: it will be malleable, like modeling clay.

Heat the lard or oil in a deep fryer or other pan to about 360 degrees F (180 degrees C).

Put the pieces of marrow into the bowl of batter, then fry them five or six at a time until golden. Serve immediately.

126. *Cheese Fritters*

Pipefarces. Take egg yolks and flour and salt, and a little wine, and beat them together vigorously, and take cheese cut into thin slices, and then put the slices of cheese into the batter, and then fry it in an iron pan containing lard. (MP 227)

> What a nice name these fritters have! Children will love them: warm, melting cheese oozing into the mouth from within a golden crust. But be careful not to overcook them: the cheese could melt, burst through the crust, and flow into the frying fat. Fritters like these are still popular in parts of southern Italy, where they are prepared with a mild version of provolone, *provolone dolce*.

Prepare the batter about an hour in advance. Cut the cheese into sticks about ⅜ inch thick and 1¼ to 1½ inches long.

Heat the oil or lard in a deep fryer or other pan to 375 degrees F (190 degrees C). Dip the cheese sticks into the bowl of batter

Batter (see recipe 125)
14 ounces mild cheese such as raclette (400 g)
lard or oil for deep frying

and fry them five or six at a time until golden on all sides (about a minute). Drain, and serve hot. Do not pile these fritters up on the platter, or they will quickly get soggy.

127. *Syrup-dipped Fritters*

Mistembec is made thus: take as much [risen][1] wheat dough as you wish, and a little starch dissolved in tepid water; with this, thin the dough to the consistency of sorbet. Put it into a dish with holes pierced through its bottom and sides, and drop it into hot oil or pork fat in various shapes as you please. When they are cooked and crisp and still hot, put them in syrup made of sugar or honey, and remove them immediately. (Tr 391)

> What could this strange word mean? It has nothing of Latin about it, and we have searched in vain through dictionaries of old French. This is certainly not a case of "kitchen Latin" either, because the author of the *Tractatus* uses rather refined language (which is not to say that he never includes vernacular words). No other treatise, Latin, French, or Italian, has any information on *mistembec*. For Marianne Mulon, the editor of the *Tractatus*, the word is evocative: *mis en bec*, "put in the mouth," is what *mistembec* means for her. Yet it makes sense to connect *misembec* with the *myncebek* or *nysebek* found in English texts, which are also fritters made with yeast batter. Some English and American scholars suggest that this odd-sounding and incomprehensible word could come from Arabic. And *mistembecs*, glossy with honey or sugar syrup, do rather remind us of the tempting window displays of neatly stacked sweets in the Middle Eastern groceries that sometimes seem so out of place under the gray skies of our home city, Paris.

1. The Latin reads *lavata*, or washed, but we suspect a mistake for *levata*, or raised. "Washed" does not make much sense, but "raised" with yeast accords well with the general sense of the recipe.

For the batter

2 teaspoons active dry yeast, or
⅔ ounce cake yeast (20 g)
1¼ cups tepid water (30 cl)
¾ cup flour (100 g)
⅔ cup wheat starch (if
   unavailable, potato or corn
   starch may be substituted)
   (150 g)
salt
oil for deep frying

For the syrup

1 cup sugar (200 g)
scant ½ cup water (10 cl)

issolve the yeast in about ½ cup of the water and let stand for 10 minutes. Mix in the flour to form a smooth dough, and knead for 7 or 8 minutes. Put the dough into a bowl covered with a cloth and let rise for an hour.

Gradually whisk the remaining water into the starch; add a good pinch of salt. Combine the starch mixture with the yeast dough (this can be done in a stand mixer or a food processor, or with a wooden spoon); this should yield a thick batter. Let rise in a covered bowl for at least an hour; the surface of the batter should be riddled with small bubbles.

Combine the sugar and water in a small saucepan and boil gently for about 8 minutes, or until the syrup thickens slightly.

In a deep fryer or other pan, heat the oil to 360 degrees F (180 degrees C). Drop the batter into the hot oil by heaping teaspoonfuls and fry in batches until golden brown. Drain on paper towels, then add to the hot syrup. Turn them once in the syrup, immediately remove them with a fork or skimmer, and arrange on a serving platter.

128. Fruit Patties

rdinary rissoles. These are made of figs, raisins, roasted apples, and peeled walnuts to resemble *pignolat*, and spice powder; and the dough should be well flavored with saffron, then fried in oil. If they need thickening, starch will bind them, and so will rice. (MP 225)

The apple and cinnamon flavor of these little patties recalls certain Middle Eastern or Viennese pastries. Plump and inflated like little balloons, they are delightful—almost enough to make us forget about how few medieval desserts have come down to us. We have no medieval recipes for the *pignolat* mentioned in the text, but Nostradamus described it in the sixteenth century as a light nougat made with pine nuts.

Several hours ahead of time, bake the apple until cooked through, and make the pastry. For the pastry, infuse the saffron in the water until nicely colored; cut the butter into the flour, then add the saffron-infused water and a good pinch of salt. Form into a ball, wrap in plastic wrap, and refrigerate until needed.

For the filling, remove the peel and core from the baked apple. Coarsely chop the apple flesh, the raisins, the figs, and the walnuts. Add the spices and combine well. If the filling seems too moist, add the rice flour.

Roll the dough out thin and, using a round cutter or drinking glass, cut circles about 2½ inches (6 cm) in diameter. Put a tablespoon of stuffing onto each circle, lightly moisten the edges of the dough with water, and fold over to form little turnovers. Seal the edges with the tines of a fork.

In a deep fryer or other pan, heat the oil to 350 degrees F (175 degrees C). Fry until golden. Drain on paper towels and sprinkle with sugar. Serve cold.

For the pastry
(for 25 to 30 small patties)

1¾ cups flour (250 g)
9 tablespoons butter (125 g)
5 fl. ounces water (15 cl)
5 threads saffron
  salt

For the filling

1 large apple
3 tablespoons raisins (30 g)
  scant 4 ounces dried figs (100 g)
½ cup walnut meats (60 g)
¼ teaspoon ground ginger
¼ teaspoon ground cinnamon
1 pinch ground cloves
1 teaspoon rice flour (if needed)
  oil for deep frying
  sugar

129. The Emperor's Fritters

The Emperor's Magnificent Fritters. If you want to make the Emperor's fritters, take egg whites and slices of fresh cheese, and beat them together with the egg whites, and add a little flour and hulled pine nuts. Take a pan with plenty of fat, bring it to the boil, and make the fritters. When they are cooked, sprinkle them with plenty of sugar and keep them hot, etc. (Fr 14)

The golden color of these fritters evokes the riches of empire, and the white of the sugar the dazzling brilliance of dominion. A French cook would have dedicated them to the king. Perhaps naming the emperor in a manuscript which elsewhere invokes the memory of King Manfred of Sicily (illegitimate son of the great Emperor Frederick II—see also recipe 87) reflects the author's imperial sympathies in the ongoing conflict that split medieval Italy: the clash between those two Roman and universal powers, the Church and the empire.

This recipe makes about 15 small fritters.

4 ounces cream cheese (110 g)

5 ounces farmer's cheese, drained if necessary (150 g)

3 egg whites

1½ tablespoons pine nuts (40 g)

5½ tablespoons flour (50 g)

oil for deep frying

sugar

Mash the two cheeses and beat in the egg whites; mix until smooth. Stir in the flour until well blended, and add the pine nuts.

In a deep fryer or other pan, heat the oil to 360 degrees F (180 degrees C). Gently add the cheese mixture to the oil by tablespoonfuls and fry until golden. Drain on paper towels, sprinkle with sugar, and serve immediately.

130. An Italian Blancmange in Catalan Style

Blancmange in Catalan style. To make ten portions, take a *libra* [about 10 ounces, or 300 g] of carefully skinned, well-pounded almonds, and moisten them with rich chicken broth or other good broth; putting them through a sieve, boil them in a very clean pot, adding two ounces of rice flour mixed into and strained with the almond milk; let it boil for an hour, moving it and stirring it constantly with a spoon, adding half a *libra* and a finely chopped and pounded breast of capon, which had been cooked from the beginning in that milk. And when the entire mixture is cooked, add a little rose water, when you serve it, top it with sweet spices. (Ma 152)

British readers especially will probably recoil at the very word "blancmange," thinking of the quivering, gelatinous puddings forced upon them in childhood. Yet the blancmange marked a nearly indispensable stage in medieval banquets throughout Europe. It was most commonly served in deep plates and, at least in Italy, at the beginning of the meal. But relax: medieval blancmange does not at all resemble the childhood bogey we have just described. First and foremost is the word *blanc* ("white"), which ordained the use of ingredients of that color, such as rice, rice flour, chicken breast, milk, almond milk, and sugar. As a rule, blancmanges were mildly spiced, and doctors therefore prescribed them for invalids. And since diners could never get enough of them, cooks also devised Lenten versions, where white-fleshed fish replaced chicken or capon.

But there are no absolutes in cooking, and blancmange could also be highly spiced, or entirely without sugar, such as in the present recipe, drawn from Maestro Martino.

But there is a problem with this apparent lack of sugar: the odd passage "half a *libra* and a finely chopped and pounded breast of capon." The word "sugar" could have been dropped by the scribe. But the same omission is found in both of the two known manuscripts: the one edited by Emilio Faccioli in 1966 and the one that Bruno Laurioux unearthed in the Vatican library. We have therefore kept to the letter of the text. We venture to confess that this suited us, as not adding sugar to the chicken meat is more in keeping with modern tastes.

Martino himself describes three other blancmanges; rose water is the only ingredient common to all four. One is for Lent, and uses the cooking liquid from dried peas in place of chicken broth, and the flesh of pike, if available. Two are strongly seasoned with ginger: a white spice. Two of them are thickened with crumb of bread rather than rice and given zest with verjuice. This shows clearly that the names attached to dishes are not to be trusted unquestioningly, all the less since one of Martino's blancmanges, intended as a sauce for capon, could be yellow: "If you want this dish to be of two colors, take an egg yolk and some saffron; mix these things into one portion of the blancmange and add some verjuice to make it sourer than the white one. In this form it is called *ginestra* [after the color of the flowers of the broom plant]. And if you have two capons, you can cover one in the white and one in the yellow" (Ma 136).

Nor can one necessarily have much faith in the "national" designations attached to many recipes: Martino twice gives "Catalan" blancmanges, including the present adaptation, but neither bears any particular resemblance to this genuinely Catalan recipe from the *Libre de Sent Sovi*:

Qui parla con sa deu ffer manjar blanch. Si volls ffer manyar blanch, prin gualines e cou-les, e puys, can les auràs ben cuytes, prin del blanch dell pits e de les ales, so és lo blanch, e talle-tu ben manut, e puys, can les auràs ben cuytes, prin del blanch dell mol-lo axi con a ffarina. E ages let d'amelles destrempades ab lo brou de les gualines, e mescla-y hom de l'arros en guissa che torn espès; e après lo blanch de les galines, e quant sia cuyt. E vol-se coura a bresquet de braces, per pahor de ffum. E no'n deu hom pertir la mà, per raho con tem molt. Puys prin hom dell sucre blanc e mescla-u hom mentre que cou. E quant és espès a fur de morteroll, leve-u hom del ffoch. E va cempre en escudelles. E prin hom del sucre, e met-ne hom per scudelles axi con a polvora. E axi-ll mengès. (Grewe, *Libre de Sent Sovi*, 93)

[Chapter 38,] Which speaks of how to make blancmange. If you want to make blancmange, take chickens and cook them, and then, when you have cooked them well, take some of the white flesh of the breast and the wings, that is, the white meat, and cut it very fine, and then, when you have cooked it well, take some of the white meat and pound it with flour. And make some almond milk soaked in the chicken broth. Mix in some rice to thicken it, and then the white of the chickens when it is cooked. The cooking should be done on a brazier of coals for fear of smoke; you must not cease stirring so that it does not stick to the pan. Then take a little white sugar and add it during the cooking, and when it is as thick as a *morterol* [a hash made of ground meat], remove it from the fire for a while, and always serve it in bowls. And take a little sugar and sprinkle a little on the plates. That is how you eat it.

So were there national styles of blancmange? Jean-Louis Flandrin has tried to identify these. But it is better to speak of "preferences" than "differences." The French used less sugar and preferred whole rice; the Italians used rice flour and tended to add more spices than others; and the English often decorated each plate with almonds, as you can see from this recipe, which you can try adapting on your own:

For to make blank maunger. Put rys in water al a nyght, and at morowe waisshe hem clen. Afterward put hem do the fyre fort that they berts, & not to mych. Sithen take brawn of capouns, or of hennes, soden, & drawe it smale. After take mylke of almaundes and put in to the rys & boile it. And whant it is yboilet, put in the brawn & alye it therwith that it be wel chargeaunt, and menge it fynelich wel that it sit not to the pot. And whan it is ynowhg & chargeaunt do therto sugur gode part, put therin almandes fried in white grece, & dresse it forth. ("Forme of Cury," *Curye on Inglysch*, 143–44)

To make blancmange. Put rice in water overnight, and in the morning wash it clean. Afterward, put it on the fire until they burst, but not too much. Then take flesh of capons or chickens, boiled, and chop it fine. Then take almond milk, add it to the rice and boil it. And when it is boiled, add the meat and mix together until thickened; stir it well so that it does not stick to the pot. And when it is done and thickened, add a good amount of sugar, add almonds fried in white fat, and serve.

The recipe we have chosen to adapt is Maestro Martino's excellent "Catalan" version, which is unusual in that it is unsweetened.

1   cup almonds (150 g)
2   tablespoons rice flour (25 g)
1   small chicken breast, about 5 ounces, taken from the chicken used to make the broth, or freshly purchased (150 g)
2   cups chicken broth (½ liter) (recipe 152)
    about 3 tablespoons rose water (5 cl)
    sweet spice mixture (recipe 150, variation B)
    salt

As you are making the broth, remove the meat from one chicken breast when done, about 20 minutes into the simmering. Alternatively, poach a small chicken breast in salted water or broth. Mince the chicken finely, or chop in a food processor.

Blanch the almonds and grind them in a blender or in a mortar. Stir in the rice flour, then add the warm chicken broth. Strain to obtain almond milk. In a heavy saucepan, bring the almond milk to the boil and add salt to taste. Add the minced chicken and simmer, stirring constantly, until the mixture reaches the consistency of a thick custard. When done, add the rose water. Serve warm in deep dishes, sprinkled with sweet spices.

131. An Italian Blancmange from Foreign Parts

Blancmanges.   Take cooked breasts of chicken and put them on a table and shred them into the finest fibers you can. Then wash the rice and dry it, and make it into flour, and put it through a sieve; then moisten this rice flour with goat's, sheep's, or almond milk, and boil it in a well-washed and clean pan; and when it begins to boil, add those shredded breasts, with white sugar and fried white pork fat; and keep it away from the smoke and let it boil gently without excessive fire, so that it becomes as thick as the rice should be. And when you serve it, top it with crushed or pounded sugar, and fried pork fat. If you like, you can make it with whole rice, moistened and prepared with goat's milk, in the foreign style; and when you serve it, top it with almonds fried in pork fat and sliced white ginger. (Za 46–47)

> We chose this recipe because it sets out two styles of blancmange: one Italian, possibly Tuscan, and one that is either German or French *(a modo oltramontano)*; our adaptation is French. We use cow's milk when we cannot find any goat's milk, although farmers' markets and many supermarkets now sell goat's milk.

Shred the chicken. Cut the fatback into ⅛-inch (3-mm) dice; sauté half of it in a small skillet until lightly golden and crisp.

Bring the milk to the boil and sprinkle in the rice. Boil for a few moments, stirring constantly, then add the chicken, two-thirds of the sugar, and the fried fatback, drained. Lower the heat and simmer, stirring from time to time, until the rice is tender and can be easily crushed between your fingers.

Meanwhile, sauté the remaining fatback together with the almonds. Peel some ginger and cut it into paper-thin slices.

Serve warm or cold, decorated with the sautéed fatback and almonds and with slices of ginger.

2 **ounces cooked chicken breast meat, possibly from making broth (about a third of a medium chicken breast) (60 g)**
2 **heaping tablespoons arborio or other round-grain rice (30 g)**
2 **cups goat's milk, or cow's milk (½ liter)**
2 **ounces fresh pork fatback**
2 **tablespoons sugar (30 g)**
10 **blanched almonds**
 fresh gingerroot for garnish
 salt

132. Frumenty: Wheat-berry Porridge

Frumenty.   First, you should hull your wheat as is done to make hulled barley; for ten platefuls you need a *livre* of hulled wheat, which is sometimes found at the spice merchant's already hulled at a cost of one *blanc* per *livre*. Clean it and cook it in water in the evening, and leave it overnight, covered, near the fire, in warm water, then drain and clean it. Then boil some milk in a pan, and do not stir it because it will curdle: and immediately, without waiting, put it in a pot that has no metallic bronze odor; and when it is cold, skim the cream from the top so that it does not make the frumenty curdle, and then bring the milk to the boil again with a little wheat, but hardly any wheat; then take egg yolks and add them—for each *sextier* [about two gallons or 7½ liters] of milk, a hundred eggs—then take the boiling milk and beat the eggs with the milk, then remove the pot [from the fire], cast in the eggs, and mix; and if you see that it is about to curdle, put the pot into a basin full of water. On fish days, use milk; on meat days, meat broth; and you can add saffron if the eggs do not make it yellow enough; also, half a knob of ginger. (MP 210)

Medieval cooking texts contain a number of recipes for groats: rye, barley, or millet. These porridges made from hulled grain are generally listed under foods for invalids and often contain sugar—which here serves as much as a medication as a sweetener. Frumenty was a hulled-wheat porridge that does not seem to have been only for invalids. To the contrary, it appears on menus alongside game, as the classic French pairing of *venaison et fromentée*—game and frumenty—attests. And the author of *Le Ménagier de Paris* reminds us that "salted wild boar is eaten with frumenty."

As our recipe shows, frumenty could be prepared with milk for days of abstinence, or with good broth for meat days; we have chosen the second option. To enjoy frumenty at its best, we recommend serving it with a richly flavored meat stew.

You can buy wheat berries in health food stores, but be careful not to buy wheat used for sprouting, which still has its outer shell, or pericarp, which would remain tough no matter how long you cooked it.

7 **ounces wheat berries (about 1 cup) (200 g)**
4 **cups chicken or meat broth (1 liter) (recipe 152)**
2 **egg yolks**
¼ **teaspoon ground ginger**
    salt

A day in advance, put the wheat berries in a heavy pan with 3 cups of salted water. Bring to the boil, and simmer for about an hour, or until the water is nearly absorbed and the wheat berries begin to burst open. Cover the pan and leave the wheat in a warm place, such as on a radiator or near a range-top pilot light, overnight.

The next day, drain the wheat berries, discarding any remaining water. Pick through the wheat for any foreign bodies, and remove them.

Put the wheat and the broth into a heavy pan, bring to the boil, reduce the heat, and simmer for about 2½ or 3 hours, until the grain and liquid begin to meld into a very thick porridge.

Check for salt and stir in the ginger. Remove from the heat.

Beat the egg yolks in a small bowl, then stir in a ladleful of porridge. When thoroughly blended, add the egg mixture to the pot and, still off the heat, stir to blend. Serve hot.

133. Rice Pudding with Almond Milk

The best rice.   If you want to make rice in the best possible way, for twelve persons, take two *libre* of rice and two *libre* of almonds, and half a *libra* of sugar. Then take the rice, well cleaned and well washed, and take the almonds, well skinned and well washed and well ground and well sieved. Take the rice and put it on the fire in clean water, and when it has reached a full boil and has been well skimmed, drain it immediately and add a quantity of almond milk; and cook it at a distance from the fire, and stir it around often in such a way as not to break [the grains]. And when it has become dry, again add a quantity of almond milk; and when it is nearly cooked, add a quantity of sugar. This dish should be white and very thick. And when it is cooked, put sugar over the bowls. If you want to make it for more persons, or for fewer, use the ingredients in these proportions. (Mo 22)

This is a simple rice pudding, but using almond milk instead of cow's milk. Doctors, who were leery of rice as a heavy, binding food, advised tempering it with almond milk and sugar. So this recipe would certainly have been recommended for invalids, especially as it uses no "spice" other than sugar—which was indeed classified as a spice, because it was sold by spice merchants and signified a certain quality of life.

This dish also denotes culinary refinement: the Sienese writer Gentile Sermini was scandalized at seeing a peasant at a banquet "eating rice with sugar, filling his bowl with huge slabs of bread and churning it over and over again, exactly as they do with cabbage in the countryside" (Sermini 2: 521).

This rice pudding was intended not only for nourishment: it combined flavor with a startling whiteness, as in blancmanges, which themselves almost always contained rice, sugar, and almonds.

In our adaptation, we can guarantee authentic flavor, since this recipe gives exact proportions for all ingredients apart from the water. You may find it a little bland, though it will have great finesse if you take care to use very fresh almonds, plus one or two bitter almonds or a few drops of almond extract.

You can also give it a lift by serving it with a plum mousse (recipe 142).

Wash the rice in several changes of cold water. Make a fairly rich almond milk according to recipe 151.

Put the rice into a large, heavy pan of cold water, bring to the boil, skim, and drain. Return the rice to the pan and add just enough almond milk to cover. Bring to the boil, and simmer, stirring constantly with a wooden spoon.

¾ **cup arborio or other round-grain rice** (150 g)
scant ¼ **cup sugar** (40 g)

For the almond milk (recipe 151)
1 **cup blanched almonds** (150 g)
4 **cups water** (1 liter)

As the rice absorbs the liquid, add more almond milk, half a cup at a time, until it is used up, as though you were making a risotto. The rice should be thoroughly cooked and should have the consistency of normal rice pudding. If more liquid is required and you have run out of almond milk, you can use water. When the rice is done, add three-quarters of the sugar and bring to the boil for a final time. Sprinkle each serving with some of the remaining sugar.

134. *Taillis*: Dried-Fruit Pudding

Taillis.   Take figs, raisins, boiled almond milk, *échaudés*, wafers, and crusts of white bread cut into little squares, and boil your milk, with saffron to give it color, and with sugar, and then boil everything together until it is thick enough to cut; serve in bowls. (VT Vat Scul 118)

There are a number of French versions of this thick pudding made from almond milk and dried fruits. The name *taillis* probably comes from the verb *tailler,* "to cut," and means that the final product is firm enough to be cut into pieces with a knife. Could this recipe have some sort of northern inspiration? It bears similarities to a number of fifteenth-century English sources, but is entirely absent from the Italian repertory. *Échaudés*, wafers, and crusts of white bread are used here to thicken the *taillis*. Unfortunately, we do not know what went into these wafers, and can only guess at how *échaudés* were made. They are often mentioned in our texts. Had they already taken the form of the little yeast cakes, first poached in water then dried in the oven, whose recipes survive in a number of French regional cuisines (such as that of Aveyron)?

For the almond milk

4   cups water (1 liter)
1   cup blanched almonds (150 g)
    the crusts from 8 to 10 slices stale sandwich bread, completely dry
1   scant cup raisins (150 g)
5   ounces high-quality dried figs (150 g)
    generous ¼ cup sugar, preferably superfine (60 g)
6   or 7 threads saffron

Prepare the almond milk according to the instructions in recipe 151. Using a grater, or in a food processor, make the bread crusts into coarse crumbs. Thoroughly rinse the raisins and figs.

Bring the almond milk to the boil in a heavy saucepan; add the saffron, the sugar, and the breadcrumbs. Over low heat, simmer, stirring constantly, until the breadcrumbs soften and the mixture begins to thicken. Add the dried fruit and continue to cook over very low heat for about 15 minutes, stirring frequently and making sure the thickening mixture does not burn.

When the mixture is quite thick, turn it out into a deep dish, such as an 8- or 9-inch (20 or 22 cm) glass pie plate. Serve when completely cooled.

135. Almond Pudding

Cooked almond pudding.   If you want to make cooked almond pudding for twelve persons, take three *libre* of almonds and half a *libra* of sugar; then take the almonds, well washed, well skinned and well pounded, mixed with a little clear water and well strained, and put them to boil in a pan; boil until it becomes thick; put sugar onto each serving. If you want to make it for a greater or smaller number of persons, use the ingredients in the same proportions. (Mo 22)

> This pudding takes a long time to cook, but the results will surprise you: a subtle, creamy, fresh, light, barely sweetened reduction of almond milk. Its flavor will be better if you take the time to soak the almonds in cool water over-night.

A day in advance, leave the almonds (and bitter almonds, if using) to soak in cool water.

The following day, rinse and drain the almonds and, in batches, grind them with the water to a homogeneous mixture in a blender. Strain through a kitchen towel or several layers of cheesecloth, squeezing to extract as much liquid as possible. This almond milk should be quite rich and thick. Add the almond extract, if using.

2⅔ cups blanched almonds (400 g)
 2 or 3 bitter almonds or a few
     drops of almond extract
 8 cups water (2 liters)
 5 tablespoons sugar, preferably
     superfine (70 g)

In a heavy saucepan, reduce this mixture by half over very low heat. This should take 2 to 3 hours. Serve cool, sprinkled with sugar.

136. Marzipan Tart

Marzipan. Skin the almonds very well and pound them as finely as possible, be-cause they will not be put through a sieve. Note that to make the almonds whiter, more flavorful, and sweeter in the mouth, they should be put to soak in fresh water for a day and a night, or even longer, so that they can be skinned by pressing them between your fingers. When you pound them, dampen them with a little rose water so that they do not become oily. And if you want to make this *torta* good, use equal weights of sugar and almonds, that is one *libra* of one and one of the other, or more or less as you prefer; and also use one or two *oncie* of good rose water; and mix all these things together thoroughly. Then take *cialdoni* or *nevole* made with sugar and first moistened with rose water; arrange them on the bottom of the pan, and on top put the aforementioned mixture or filling. And when you have spread it and flattened it, you should moisten it again with a little rose water, also putting on top some good pulverized sugar. And when the sugar is spread evenly over all, cook it in the oven, or over the fire, very slowly as with other *torte*, taking great care to keep the fire moderate and to check it often so that it does not burn. Remember that such marzipan *torte* should be low and thin rather than high and thick. (Ma 168)

> Here Maestro Martino gives us one of the very earliest recipes for what is still called marzipan, or almond paste. Much consideration has been given to the origin of the word: "marzipan" in English and German, *massepain* in French, and *marzapane* in Italian. In several vernacular versions we find the word used

in the 1340s, both in Italy and in Provence, to mean both the box in which sweetmeats were kept, and the sweetmeats themselves. Is this a borrowing from Arabic, as some have suggested? That is not impossible, as this tart contains three of the ingredients most typical of medieval Arab-Persian pastry-making: sugar, almonds, and rose water. And Martino is not stingy with the sugar, either: it is used in equal proportion to the almonds. This is quite different from the miserly way the author of *Le Ménagier de Paris* uses that ingredient.

We have to stress Martino's mastery in the way he sets out this recipe. He knows what he is talking about. Cooking the almond paste at the right temperature is critical to success, and Martino is well aware of this as he instructs us to take care to keep the fire moderate. An overcooked marzipan tart will not only look unappetizingly murky but will become dry and hard.

On one point, adapting this tart was problematical: the almond mixture is spread over a base made up thin wafers, *cialdoni* in Italian, which were probably the same as the French *oublies*, for which we know neither the ingredients nor the medieval method of preparation. But, in our opinion, these wafers are there only to protect the filling from the heat and add little by way of flavor. And like the wafer or rice paper used today as the base of nougat, they make it easier to handle this rather sticky mixture. So we offer several options: for those who have a *pizelle* or *gaufrette* iron, we suggest a recipe for wafers; if not, you can use baker's rice paper or even communion wafers (unconsecrated, of course) from a church supply store.

A huge marzipan tart was served at the Bandinelli banquets in Siena, of which we spoke above (see p. 6).

For the cialdoni
generous ½ cup flour (80 g)
2 **tablespoons sugar, preferably superfine (30 g)**
7 **tablespoons ice water**
1 **pinch salt**

For the marzipan filling
1⅔ **cups unblanched almonds (250 g)**
1¼ **cups sugar (250 g)**
about ½ cup rose water
enough *cialdoni*, or baker's rice paper or communion wafers, to line your tart mold
sugar for topping

One day in advance, pour boiling water over the almonds to cover. When it is cold, pour it off and rinse the almonds in several changes of water until the water runs clear. Soak the almonds overnight, which will make it easy to pop them out of their skins.

To make the *cialdoni*, if you are using them, mix the flour, salt, and sugar, then stir in ice water until you have a fairly thin batter. Heat your *pizelle* or *gaufrette* iron and pour a small amount of batter onto the bottom plate (a tablespoon, or more depending on the size of the iron). Close the iron and cook according to the manufacturer's instructions until the wafer is a dark golden brown. Remove from the iron and repeat until you have enough wafers to line a 10-inch (25-cm) tart pan.

Slip the soaked almonds out of their skins, then grind them to a fairly smooth puree in a blender (in batches if necessary) or food processor with 3 tablespoons of rose water.

Add the sugar and an additional 3 tablespoons rose water, and process or stir by hand until the mixture is smooth.

Preheat the oven to 250 degrees F (130 degrees C).

Line the tart pan with *cialdoni* or rice paper (or communion wafers), overlapping to cover the entire bottom; sprinkle sparingly with rose water. Turn the almond mixture into the tart pan and spread evenly over the wafers. Sprinkle with a little rose water and sprinkle evenly with sugar.

Bake for about an hour, until the top is lightly golden. Check from time to time to make sure the tart does not become too brown. Cool completely before serving.

137. Marzipan Sweetmeats: *Caliscioni*

To make *caliscioni*, take a filling or mixture similar to that for the aforementioned marzipan *torta*, and make your dough, which you should make with sugar and rose water; and roll out that dough as though you were making ravioli, and put on this filling, making them big, medium-sized, or small, as you prefer. And if you have an elegantly carved wooden mold, mold them, pressing it onto their tops; they will be nicer to look at. Then cook them in a shallow pan, like marzipan, taking great care that they do not burn. (Ma 169)

There is no doubt that this recipe for *caliscioni* is one of the earliest known sources for the diamond-shaped almond cakes for which the town of Aix-en-Provence is known: *Calissons d'Aix*. Unlike today's *calissons*, these *caliscioni* contain no candied fruits, but their name and the way they are formed in a particular shape are indications of their possible relationship. Yet interpreting this recipe is not altogether straightforward. At first glance, it seems to be for ravioli stuffed with almond paste—not at all like modern-day *calissons*. But in fact, Maestro Martino does not say that the filling should be wrapped in dough, as he does, for example, in his recipe for meat ravioli (recipe 7). He says only that you should roll out the dough "as though" you were making ravioli, add the filling, and make them in whatever size you like. The mold he recommends seems to have only a decorative function, as it is to be elegantly carved to stamp a design on the *caliscioni*; being made of wood, it would not have been used to cut the shapes like a cookie cutter. Thus, these *caliscioni* would be very similar to modern-day *calissons*: small almond-paste sweetmeats on a thin pastry base, cut into a specific shape and stamped on top with a design. Nor should we forget Nostradamus, who was best known in the sixteenth century as a sorcerer, but who was in fact a physician from Saint-Rémy-de-Provence; he wrote a treatise on preserves in which he describes the preparation of *tartes de massapan*: "You should make it into little cakes or little round tarts spread out on top of *oublies* . . . and you can make little squares in that shape on those *oublies*." We can surely detect *calissons* in these tartlets in the shape of little squares.

It is by marrying this recipe with the instructions for marzipan (recipe 136) that we come very close indeed to today's *calissons*. The marzipan recipe gives us the basic ingredients: sugar, almonds, and a sugar and rose-water topping (which in today's *calissons* has evolved into a glaze of royal icing, made of confectioner's sugar and egg whites). And from the other we learn to make individual sweetmeats in a particular shape.

That is how we have adapted this recipe here, although for a medieval-style banquet given at Siena in 1981 we interpreted these *caliscioni* as a kind of sweet ravioli. Those chubby little purses, barely browned, were excellent, and conveyed to perfection the elegance of the almonds and rose water. It has been our experience that women are particularly fond of *caliscioni*.

marzipan filling (recipe 136)

For the sweet pasta dough
generous ½ cup flour (80 g)
2 tablespoons superfine sugar (30 g)
about 2 to 3 tablespoons rose water
1 pinch salt

Combine the flour, sugar, and salt, and knead in enough rose water to form an elastic dough; it should be fairly soft, but should not stick to your fingers. Set the dough aside to rest for 30 minutes, wrapped in a damp towel or in plastic wrap.

While the dough is resting, make the marzipan filling as described in recipe 136. Preheat the oven to 250 degrees F (130 degrees C).

On a lightly floured surface, roll out the dough into a nearly transparent sheet, and dot it with scant tablespoons of the marzipan filling, evenly spaced about 1½ inches (4 cm) apart. With a knife or pastry wheel, cut the dough into squares, with a portion of filling centered on each square. Using the bottom of a drinking glass or other smooth object, evenly flatten the marzipan filling on each *caliscione*, leaving it reasonably thick. If you have a carved wooden butter or cookie stamp, press to decorate the top of each one.

Line a sheet pan or cookie sheet with parchment or other nonstick paper, or use a nonstick pan. Bake the *caliscioni* for about an hour; the point is to dry them, like meringues, rather than actually to cook them. Check them often to make sure they are not baking too quickly and that they barely begin to turn golden. Cool completely before serving.

138. Crêpes

Crêpes. Take some flour, and moisten it with eggs, as many yolks as whites, with the filaments removed, and mix with water and add salt and wine, and beat everything together for a long time; then put some lard on the fire in a little iron pan, or half lard and half fresh butter, and let it bubble; and then take a bowl pierced with a hole as wide as your little finger, and then put the batter in the dish; beginning with the center, let it flow all over the pan; then put it in a plate with powdered sugar on top. And that iron or bronze pan should hold three *chopines*, and have a rim half a finger's-breadth high and should be as broad at the top as at the base, neither more nor less; there is a good reason for this. (MP 226)

Crêpes seem to be a French specialty. Neither the *crispa* and *crispelli* found respectively in Latin and Italian texts nor the "cryspes" in English sources are really similar to what we think of as crêpes: a mixture of flour, eggs, and liquid (milk or cream nowadays; water and wine in the Middle Ages) made into thin pancakes in a shallow pan. There is indeed every reason to think that this preparation is specific to France, where it was already being prepared in the pan known as a *galettière*, judging by the description in *Le Ménagier de Paris* of a low-rimmed skillet with perpendicular, not flared, sides ("as broad at the top as at the base"), which is the shape of a *galettière*.

On the other hand, *crispa* and *crispelli* were made of a leavened dough and were deep fried. While "cryspes" were indeed cooked in the same way as crêpes, they were made of only flour and egg whites.

We recommend these crêpes highly; thanks to the absence of milk and cream, they are particularly light, digestible, and delicious.

Add the salt to the eggs, beat them with a wire whisk, then gradually beat in the flour. Add the wine and the water, and whisk to combine. Leave to rest for one hour.

Heat a crêpe pan or nonstick skillet over medium heat; add ½ teaspoon each of butter and lard. When sizzling, add a small ladleful of batter, swirling the pan to spread the batter evenly over the entire surface. When golden brown, turn the crêpe over and lightly brown the second side. Pile the finished crêpes on a warmed plate, and sprinkle each with sugar.

¾ **cup flour** (100 g)
3 **eggs**
6 **tablespoons white wine** (10 cl)
6 **tablespoons water** (10 cl)
¼ **teaspoon salt**
butter and good-quality lard for frying
sugar for sprinkling, preferably superfine

139. Medieval Italian "French Toast"

Gilded sippets. Take slices of white bread, trimmed so that they have no crusts; make these slices square and slightly grilled so that they are colored all over by the fire. Then take eggs beaten together with plenty of sugar and a little rose water; and put the slices of bread in this to soak; carefully remove them, and fry them a little in a frying pan with a little butter and lard, turning them very frequently so that they do not burn. Then arrange them on a plate, and top with a little rose water colored yellow with a little saffron, and with plenty of sugar. (Ma 174)

This medieval version of what amounts to French toast seems to have been popular throughout Europe. But everyone seems to have had his own name for the dish: Maestro Martino and some English authors called it *suppe dorate* and *soupys yn dorye* respectively, while French writers favored *tostées dorées*, reserving the word *soupe* for slices of bread soaked in a *potage* (which gives rise to the expression *trempé comme une soupe*, the French equivalent of "soaked to the skin"). Eventually, as we know, the word "soup" would come to mean the actual liquid in which these *soupes* were soaked. Other English sources surprisingly call this dish *payn purdyeu,* clearly the same as today's French name, *pain perdu.* And of course the modern English term is "French toast": what goes around comes around.

In England and in Italy, these golden brown bread slices were served with game meats and with peacocks and other grand birds. We do not know exactly how they were used in France even though there are several otherwise undefined menu references to *venaison aux soupes,* "game meat with sippets."

In any event, we have once again thrown in our lot with Maestro Martino, because his recipe is the most polished of them all, using rose water where no one else thought to do so. Still, some of the English recipes are not without delicacy, specifying that the butter for frying the toast should be clarified (gently boiled to separate out its impurities, which prevents burning) and that the bread should be soaked not in whole eggs but in beaten egg yolks that have been put through a sieve to make them perfectly smooth and creamy.

6 slices excellent-quality white sandwich bread, somewhat stale

6 eggs

1 tablespoon sugar

3 tablespoons rose water

6 threads saffron
butter for frying (4 to 8 tablespoons) (60 to 120 g)
sugar for sprinkling over the toast

Trim the crusts from the bread to create square slices. Toast or grill the bread very lightly.

Beat the eggs with 1½ tablespoons of rose water and 1 tablespoon of sugar, and pour this mixture into a dish large enough to hold the bread in one layer. Soak the bread slices in the egg mixture for about 10 minutes, but be sure to remove them earlier if they threaten to become mushy.

Meanwhile, crush the saffron in a mortar or with your fingers, and add the remaining rose water; leave to steep until needed.

Over medium-low heat, melt some butter in a skillet, and gently fry the bread until golden on both sides. How much butter you need will depend on the size of your pan and whether you need to cook the bread in several batches.

When the toasts are done, arrange them on a serving platter and sprinkle them with the saffron-colored rose water. Just before serving, sprinkle generously with sugar.

140. Cherry Pudding

Chireseye. To make chireseye, take cherries at the Feast of St. John the Baptist and remove the pits. Grind them in a mortar, and then press them hard through a sieve to extract all their juice; and put this in a pot and put in good fat or butter and good white bread, plenty of sugar, and some wine. And when it is thick and served up on plates, stud it with cloves and sprinkle with sugar. (Ds HB 77)

There are few sweet dishes in our French sources, and even they contain only miserly amounts of sugar. But while in fourteenth-century France this "spice" performed a therapeutic function in dishes for invalids, it was already counted among the standard ingredients in Italy and, especially, in England. Hence, we offer this cherry pudding from an English source. Its lovely translucent red color and its texture helped us to understand the Anglo-Saxon taste for the brightly colored, quivering gelatin desserts that Britons and Americans enjoy to this day. But unlike those startling feats of modern chemistry, this creamy pudding is absolutely delicious. We have prepared it with normal dark cherries and red wine, but it could also be made with sour cherries; in that case, use a little extra sugar and a good-quality rosé wine so as not to darken their bright color.

Stem and pit the cherries, puree them in a blender or food processor, then strain in a fine sieve, pressing hard to extract as much juice as possible.

1½ pounds ripe cherries
 2 slices dry white bread
    scant ½ cup sugar (100 g), plus
    1 tablespoon for garnish
1½ tablespoons butter (20 g)
 5 fl. ounces good red wine, such
    as a Bordeaux or other
    cabernet sauvignon (15 cl)
    whole cloves for garnish

Remove the crusts from the bread, and cut the bread into small dice. In a heavy saucepan, combine the bread, cherry juice, wine, sugar, and butter. Bring to the boil and simmer over low heat for 10 to 15 minutes, until the mixture thickens and the bread falls apart and swells, binding the dessert into a creamy pudding. Turn into a serving bowl and chill well. Stud the top with cloves, forming a design of your own choice. Refrigerate until served. Just before serving, sprinkle the top with sugar.

Don't forget to warn your guests that the cloves are there for decoration only. Some people will eat anything rather than insult the cook!

141. Apple Mousse with Almond Milk

Apple Sauce. To explain it to whoever will make it, he should take good barberine apples depending on the quantity to be prepared. Then he should peel them carefully and cut them into pieces into fine gold or silver platters. He should take a good earthenware pot, very clean, and boil some pure water over good bright coals, then add the apples. He must also have good, sweet almonds, in large quantity depending on the quantity of apples being cooked; he should skin them and wash them well, then crush them in a mortar that has no garlic odor; when they are very well crushed, he should moisten them with the liquid in which the apples are cooking, and when the apples are sufficiently cooked he should remove them to a nice clean surface, and strain the almonds with this water, making a good, thick milk, and return it to the boil over bright, clean, smoke-free coals, with a tiny bit of salt. And while it is boiling, he should chop the apples finely with a small, clean knife; when they are chopped, he should add them to the milk and add a great deal of sugar, as required for this applesauce; then, when the physician calls for it, he should serve it in fine bowls or dishes made of gold or silver. (Ch 194)

> Here is an dish for invalids that modern food-lovers will enjoy even if they are in the pink of good health. The delicacy of the almond milk accords to perfection with the mild acidity of the cooked apples. This almond-milk applesauce is made without spices and is sweetened with "a great deal" of sugar, as indicated for those who, because of a passing illness, need a lift. This recipe is remarkably precise and demonstrates Maître Chiquart's near obsession with hygiene: he wants the cook to be sure that pots, dishes, and work surfaces are impeccably clean; even the mortar must be free from anything that would remind us of past contents: *Mortier sent toujours l'ail*—"A mortar always smells of garlic"—was probably no empty phrase in the Middle Ages! But we can see meticulous professionalism in this storm of details; there is no doubt but that the cook to the Duc de Savoie genuinely plied his trade, and was no mere chronicler of recipes, as some of our authors were.
>
> The French name for this dish, *Emplumeus*, is rendered as "appulmoy" or "appulmos" in English sources, where the dish is not specifically aimed at invalids and contains spices or meat broth. And Terence Scully speaks of a possible German origin: *Apfelmus*, which is quite close to "apple mousse."

1¾ pounds apples (a variety that does not disintegrate when cooked, such as golden delicious) (800 g)

3½ cups water (80 cl)

1⅓ cups unblanched almonds (200 g)

4 bitter almonds or a couple of drops almond extract

4 tablespoons sugar (50 g)

Pour boiling water over the almonds and soak them for 15 minutes; then skin them. Alternatively, pour boiling water over the almonds; when it has cooled, replace it with fresh cool water and soak overnight. This long soaking softens the almonds and makes them more tender.

Peel and core the apples and cut them into large chunks.

Bring the water to the boil in a stainless steel or other nonreactive pan. Add the apples and cook until very tender but not falling apart, about 10 to 15 minutes. Drain the apples, reserving the cooking liquid.

Grind the almonds in a blender or food processor, gradually adding the apple-cooking water to yield a thick, white liquid. Strain through three layers of cheesecloth or a clean kitchen towel. Squeeze the almonds with your hands to extract as much liquid as possible. The resulting almond milk should be thicker than usual.

Chop the apples with a knife or (carefully) in a food processor; they should be finely chopped, but not pureed. Bring the almond milk to the boil and add the chopped apples and the sugar. Whisk to combine, and simmer for about 15 minutes, stirring frequently. Serve cold.

142. Spiced Plum Mousse with Honey

Erbowle. Take plums and boil them with wine, then put them through a strainer; put them into a pot. Clarify some honey and add it, with strong spices and rice flour. Salt it and garnish with white anise seeds, and serve. (Fc HB 119)

> Here is another very nice English recipe: a puree of plums cooked in wine, thickened with a little rice flour, sweetened with excellent honey, and flavored with spices. Yellow plums and white wine yield a golden-colored mousse, while purple plums and cabernet sauvignon form a quite different but nonetheless harmonious marriage. Make both and serve them with Rice Pudding with Almond Milk (recipe 133): the heraldic effect of gold and red on a field of white even *looks* medieval.
>
> Candied anise seeds can be purchased inexpensively in Indian groceries or, at great cost, in fancy French groceries as *anis de Flavigny.*

Wash and pit the plums. Meanwhile, bring the wine to the boil in a stainless steel or other nonreactive pan. Add the plums and simmer for about 5 minutes. Drain, reserving the wine.

Puree the plums in a food mill or press them through a sieve into a heavy saucepan. Place this saucepan over low heat and stir in the honey. Stir the rice flour into ¼ cup of the reserved cooking liquid, then stir this mixture into the plum puree and add the salt and spices.

Cook over low heat for about 10 minutes, until thickened. Pour into a serving bowl and cool before serving. Just before serving, decorate with the candied anise seeds.

3¼ **pounds yellow plums (such as mirabelles), or other ripe plums (1.5 kg)**

4 **cups white wine (or red if using purple plums) (1 liter)**

2 **tablespoons acacia honey or other high-quality honey**

1 **tablespoon rice flour**

1 **pinch salt**

1 **pinch strong spices (recipe 150, variation C)**

1 **tablespoon candied anise seeds, preferably white**

143. Poached Pears in Spiced Syrup

Pears in syrup.   Boil pears so that they are quite tender; peel them and cut them into pieces. Take a great deal of cinnamon; put it through a sieve three or four times with good wine, into a pot. Add a great deal of sugar, anise, cloves, and mace and, if you like, chopped dates and currants. Put it on the fire; when it boils add the pears; let them boil together. When it has boiled enough, make sure it is brown with cinnamon, and add a great deal of powdered ginger; make sure it is rather sweet, and serve. (Hi 65)

Our English manuscripts include excellent recipes for pears cooked in wine with spices; these are not found in French texts of the period. Indeed, there is little mention of this fruit in French, Latin, or Italian culinary sources. There was a clear distinction between pears to be eaten raw and those to be cooked. Some of the latter were used as vegetables—in the words of the author of *Le Ménagier de Paris*, "like turnips." Although several French and Italian menus refer to "Pears with Hypocras"—cooked in spiced wine—not until the fifteenth-century edition of *Le Viandier* of Taillevent do we find a recipe for this. Candied pears were served at the end of the meal every day at the series of banquets organized at Siena in 1326 for the knighting of Francesco Bandinelli (see above, p. 6).

2¼ **pounds firm pears, just ripe (1 kg)**

3 **cups good red wine (75 cl)**

4 **tablespoons sugar (50 g)**

1 **tablespoon ground cinnamon**

½ **teaspoon whole anise seeds**

3 **pieces blade mace**

2 **cloves**

½ **teaspoon ground ginger**

⅓ **cup currants or raisins (optional) (60 g)**

12 **dates, pitted and coarsely chopped (optional, but not recommended)**

Poach the pears in simmering water just until they begin to become tender. Peel them, cut them into quarters, remove the cores, and reserve.

Whisk the cinnamon into the wine and leave to steep for about 10 minutes. Strain through a very fine sieve into a stainless steel or other nonreactive saucepan. Add the sugar, the anise, the mace, and the cloves. If you are using the raisins and/or dates, add these as well. Bring to the boil, skimming if necessary, then lower the heat. Add the pears and simmer until completely tender and beginning to turn translucent and amber-colored. Add the ginger, remove from the heat, and allow to cool before serving.

If you use a softer variety of pears, do not precook them, but peel, core, and quarter them raw before adding to the spiced wine mixture. The reason we do not recommend using dates is that their skins come off during the cooking, making the dish look rather unattractive.

144. Pears in Greek-Wine Syrup

ears in syrup. Take pears and peel them thoroughly. Take good red wine and some mulberries [blackberries] or sandalwood, and put in the pears, and when they are done remove them. Make a syrup of Greek wine or vernage with white powder or white sugar and powdered ginger, and put the pears in it. Boil it briefly and serve. (Fc HB 129)

> During this period, "vernage"—*vernaccia* in Italian—was produced in the southeastern Mediterranean, on the Tyrrhenian islands and in Liguria. Today it is one of the best known wines of Sardinia. It is made in sweet versions that can, like Tokay, attain 15 or 16 percent alcohol, and in dry versions. It is similar in flavor to sherry. This vernaccia should not be confused with Vernaccia di San Gimignano, a dry white wine made, in relatively small quantities, of a different but identically named grape.
>
> Wild berries, early-season pears, and good wine, all simmered together; the cooked pears, translucent and glazed in sweet wine syrup, mounded in a pyramid: this is a lordly dessert. Bright red, amber, and dark red merge as the fruit is glazed. Here hue is as important as aroma and flavor, and the blackberries are used more for their color than for their taste; indeed, the recipe offers the alternative of sandalwood, a common medieval "artificial" coloring (see p. 26).

eel the pears, leaving them whole. In a stainless steel or other nonreactive saucepan, simmer them in the red wine together with the blackberries, about 30 minutes or until a needle can pierce the pears easily to the core; they should become slightly translucent.

Meanwhile, in another saucepan, combine the muscat, sugar, and ginger. Bring to the boil and reduce by half; the reduced wine should be syrupy.

2¼ **pounds pears, ripe but still firm** (1 kg)
⅔ **cup blackberries** (about 120 g)
1 **bottle good red wine** (75 cl)
1 **bottle Greek muscat of Sámos or other sweet muscat wine**
4 **tablespoons sugar** (50 g)
1 **teaspoon ground ginger**

Add the cooked pears to the muscat syrup and leave to cool.

To serve, pile the pears in a pyramid and top with the muscat syrup.

Other Sweetmeats and Basic Preparations

In France *épices de chambre*—"parlor spices"—were served at the end of the meal. These were certainly the equivalent of the *confetti* served in Italy before and after eating. *Confetti* were spices or fruits candied in sugar in the same way that modern glacé fruits are made, or covered in a sugar coating, like sugared almonds. These things were generally purchased ready-made at the spice merchant's, and medieval cooks, who obviously knew where to buy them, have left us no recipes. Items such as nougat, candied orange peel, and quince and apple pastes were, however, sometimes made at home, implying a more painstaking preparation than one would want to entrust to outside suppliers.

To accompany these *confitures* ("preserves") and spices, flavored wines such as hypocras or sweet wines such as malvoisie/malvasia were drunk; these were considered so necessary to good health that municipal leaders saw to it that they were available in case of epidemics.

The word "confetti" is now used for the little flecks of colored paper tossed into the air at parties; the Italian word for these is *coriandoli*, which clearly comes from "coriander," and the *confetti* served at medieval banquets did indeed include candied coriander seeds. It would have been amusing to throw these at the end of a banquet in the same way that rice is thrown after a wedding ceremony; today's paper confetti is but a pale imitation!

145. *Cotignac,* or Quince Jelly Candies

To make *cotignac,* take quinces and peel them, then cut them into quarters and remove the core and seeds, then cook them in good red wine and then put them through a sieve; then take some honey and boil it for a long time, and skim it; then put in your quinces and stir very well; boil long enough that the honey reduces by at least a half; then add hypocras powder and stir until it is completely cold; then cut into pieces and store. (MP 247)

> This is one of the first French recipes for these quince jellies, which, as *pâte de coings*, would later be a specialty of the town of Orléans. Here they are made with honey, like all the "preserves and sweets" described in *Le Ménagier de Paris*—and this is further evidence of the bourgeois origins of that text: its author would never have dreamed of using that precious commodity, sugar. He saves it for rather fancier purposes, such as "The Duke's Powder," a sweet-

ened spice mixture. Still, this recipe is not without interest, for cooking the fruit in red wine rather than in water adds a fine color and a slightly acidic, winey flavor, which balances the sweetness of the quinces and the musky undertone of the honey.

The name *cotignac* is related to the words for "quince": *condougn* in Provençal and *mela cotogna* in Italian. Etymologists tell us that this refers to the city of Cydonia (now Canea) in Crete, whose Latin name was Cotonea. In his first-century A.D. *Natural History*, Pliny the Elder refers to Cotonea in connection with the quince trade.

4½ **pounds very ripe quinces** (2 kg)

4 **cups good red wine, or more as needed** (1 liter)

4¼ **cups honey, approximately** (1.5 kg)

1 **teaspoon hypocras powder (recipe 149), or more to taste**

Peel and core the quinces, then cut into chunks. Place in a heavy stainless steel or other nonreactive saucepan and add wine to cover. Bring slowly to the boil, and simmer until the quinces are tender, about 15 to 20 minutes from when the wine comes to the boil. Drain completely, and put the fruit through a sieve or the fine blade of a food mill, or puree in a food processor until smooth.

Weigh the puree, and for every pound (450 g) of puree add a scant 10 ounces (270 g) (a generous ¾ cup) honey, previously brought to the boil and skimmed of any impurities. Simmer over very low heat (too high a heat will cause the mixture to burn and stick), somewhat reducing the puree until it forms a slightly translucent jelly. To check for doneness, drop half a teaspoonful of the mixture onto a plate; if it sets quickly, it is ready.

When the jelly is done, stir in the hypocras powder, and pour the mixture into a rectangular glass baking dish to a thickness of about ⅝ inch (1.5 cm). Let cool, and then leave to cure for several days, covered with plastic wrap, before cutting into bite-sized pieces.

To serve *cotignac* as part of a medieval banquet, cut it into diamond shapes and arrange them on a bed of fresh bay leaves. But for everyday use, coat each piece in granulated sugar and set it into a little paper candy cup.

146. Apple Jelly Candies

Preserve of Apio apples or Paradise apples.   If you wish to make this as soon as they are grated, you may do so as you prefer. Take the apples and peel them, then grate them; make sure the seeds do not fall into the grated flesh; and let them macerate for two days. Leave the juice from the apples together with the apples; put the grated apples through a sieve, and for every three *libri* of apples, add three *libri* of honey, and leave the apples and honey for two days; then, boil them, stirring constantly, with spices until the apples are cooked; remember that the spices should be added when the preserve is nearly cooked, as for that of quinces. Then spread it on a table or on a moistened board and make it into a sheet thinner than half a fingersbreadth; then let it cool, and cut it like a chess board into little pieces, and put it into a box adding, with the other hand, bay leaves beneath and then on top; keep adding these sheets layer by layer; and if you want to put spices between the sheets, this will be very good. Remember that this should boil for a good hour at least, perhaps two, stirring constantly and protecting it from smoke. (Fr 71)

> Even lacking the specified apples—*mele apio* (which could be like the modern lady apple) or *pome paradiso*—these jellies are delicious, and are very easy to make with ordinary apples, such as a mixture of local varieties from your farmers' market, or even golden delicious and Granny Smith. They are even better eaten at the end of a medieval dinner (or any other meal) with a little glass of hypocras (recipe 149). At the very beginning of the seventeenth century, Giacomo Castelvetro, an Italian nobleman who had fled from Venice to England to escape the prisons of the Inquisition, wrote about the greatest specialties of his homeland; these included "paradise apples." He tells us that they were found only in Italy and that their skin was yellow marked with blood-red dots, and that their aroma was so fine that they were used to perfume linen. Ah, where are the paradise apples of ages past?

Finely grate the apples or puree them in a food processor, then put through a fine strainer to yield a very smooth puree. Combine with the honey in a heavy saucepan and simmer over low heat, stirring frequently with a wooden spoon or spatula, for an hour or 70 minutes. Add the spices

1¾ **pounds apples, peeled and cored** (800 g)
2⅓ **cups honey** (800 g)
1 **teaspoon sweet spice mixture** (recipe 150, variation B)

about 15 minutes before cooking is complete. The jelly mixture is done when it is a translucent amber in color and when a drop of the mixture holds its shape when spooned onto a plate. Be careful as the mixture simmers, as it has a tendency to spurt out of the pan—and it is very hot. Use a pan that is larger than you might think necessary, and for safety's sake use a long-handled spoon for stirring.

When the jelly mixture is done, spread it out in a rectangular glass baking dish in an even layer a scant half inch (1 cm) thick. It will set quickly. Cool, then leave to cure for several days covered in waxed paper or plastic wrap. When it is dry, cut it into diamond shapes and serve on a bed of fresh bay leaves.

147. *Nucato*, or Spiced Honey Nut Crunch

Of honey boiled with walnuts, known as *nucato*. Take honey, boiled and skimmed, with slightly crushed walnuts and spices, boiled together: wet the palm of your hand with water and spread it out; let it cool, and serve. And you can use almonds or filberts in place of walnuts. (Za 77)

> This *nucato* is related to the delicious *nougat noir* ("black nougat") still made in the southern French town of Sisteron. But here, there is an additional pleasant surprise when you taste it: the perfumed bite of spices. This is a perfect treat for Christmastime.

For once we advise departing from the technique described in the recipe: unless you happen to have asbestos skin, it would be very dangerous to spread the burning-hot mixture with your bare hands, even if you did wet them first. Better to use the cut surface of a halved lemon instead.

3 cups honey (1 kg)
2¼ pounds shelled almonds, hazelnuts, or walnuts (1 kg)
1 lemon for spreading the mixture

For the spice mixture
1 teaspoon ground ginger
1 pinch freshly ground black pepper
1 rounded teaspoon ground cinnamon
⅓ teaspoon ground cloves

Gradually bring the honey to the boil, skimming off any impurities that may rise to the surface. Very coarsely chop the nuts and add to the honey along with 1 teaspoon of the spice mixture. Cook over low heat, stirring constantly, for 30 to 45 minutes. The mixture is done when you can hear the almonds beginning to "pop" from the heat of the honey. Take care not to let the nuts burn and turn dark and bitter. When done, stir in the remaining spice mixture.

When the *nucato* is done, pour it out onto a sheet pan or cookie sheet lined with parchment paper; spread it into an even layer with the cut surface of a halved lemon. Cool completely before serving.

148. Candied Orange Rind

To make *orengat*, cut the peel of an orange into five segments and, with a knife, scrape off the white pith that is inside. Then soak them in nice, fresh water for nine days, and change the water every day; then boil them in fresh water until it comes to the boil, then spread them on a cloth and let them dry thoroughly; then put them in a pot with enough honey to cover them completely, and boil over a low fire, and skim it; and when you think that the honey is done (to see if it is done, put some water into a bowl and drop into that water a drop of the honey, and if it spreads it is not cooked; and if that drop of honey holds its shape in the water without spreading, it is done); then, remove your orange peel, and make a layer of it and sprinkle ginger powder on top, then another layer, and sprinkle, etc., ad infinitum; leave for a month or longer before eating. (MP 265)

> This is one of the first recipes for a candy that would have an ever larger place on menus as time passed. Yet for candying the rind of his oranges (a precious commodity in Paris), the author of *Le Ménagier de Paris* uses honey, a locally produced, everyday ingredient. It was not for another century that Nostradamus would offer the choice between honey and sugar in his recipe for candied orange rind. By the mid-sixteenth century, the crystallized juice of the cane plant—sugar—had conquered all of Europe; and its success has continued to grow to this day.

sing a vegetable peeler, remove the zest from the orange, leaving behind all the white pith. Alternatively, peel the oranges by hand and use a sharp paring knife to remove the pith. Cut the zest into ¼-inch (60 mm) strips.

2 organically grown, pesticide-free oranges: a thick-skinned variety such as navel oranges

1¾ cups honey (600 g)

ground ginger

Soak the zest overnight in a bowl of cold water; the following morning change the water. Repeat this process seven times over the course of seven days.

Bring a quart (liter) of water to the boil. Add the soaked orange zest and return to the boil. Drain immediately, and dry the strips of zest on a clean towel.

Place the strips of zest into a small, heavy saucepan and add the honey, which must completely cover the zest. Over medium-low heat, bring to the boil, then reduce the heat to very low. Simmer until a drop of the honey, when spooned into a glass of water, holds its shape as it falls to the bottom of the glass. This should take about 10 or 15 minutes of simmering.

Put the strips of zest onto a rack to cool; let them dry for several hours. Store in a cookie tin or other airtight container, sprinkled with ground ginger. Keep in a cool place for one month before eating.

149. Hypocras, *Claré*, and Hypocras Powder

To make a lot of good hypocras, take an *once* of *cinamonde*, known as long tube cinnamon, a knob of ginger, and an equal amount of galangal, pounded well together, and then take a *livre* of good sugar; pound this all together and moisten it with a gallon of the best Beaune wine you can get, and let it steep for an hour or two. Then strain it though a cloth bag several times so it will be very clear. (MP 273)

Like other measures, the *lot* varied from place to place. North of the Loire, it was generally the equivalent of four *pintes*, and at Paris a *pinte* amounted to 93 centiliters. One *lot* was thus almost the exact equivalent of a United States gallon. An *once* was one sixteenth of a Paris *livre*; at just over 30 g, it was the very close equivalent of a modern ounce.

Hypocras and *claré* (made with red wine and white wine respectively) were both spiced wines sweetened with honey or sugar, served mainly at the end of the meal along with preserves, candies and wafers (see "Some Menus"). Either can be used today as a before- or after-dinner drink. Be careful not to overdo them: they are strong. But we can assure you that there is nothing like a little glass of hot hypocras to clear up a bad cold.

Hypocras and *claré* should be made well in advance, and should be kept refrigerated; otherwise they could ferment.

The original recipe is for a gallon, or about five 75-cl bottles; our adaptation is for one quart (liter) of either hypocras or *claré*. If you like it, all you need to do next time is multiply the quantities by the number of quarts you want to make.

4   cups good red wine (or dry white wine, such as sauvignon blanc, for *claré*) (1 liter)

¾   cup sugar (150 g)

For the hypocras powder

1   rounded teaspoon ground cinnamon

1   rounded teaspoon ground ginger, or a small piece of dried gingerroot

1   small piece dried galangal or dried gingerroot

Grind the spices if necessary, and mix with the sugar in a glass or stainless steel bowl. Gradually stir in the wine; mix well to combine. Let the mixture stand for about two hours, stirring occasionally.

Strain the wine through a double layer of cheesecloth; repeat several times until clear. Store in a corked bottle in the refrigerator for a few days before drinking.

150. Spice Mixtures

A. *Fine Spice Mixture*

Fine spices for all foods.   Take an *onza* of pepper and one of cinnamon and one of ginger, and half a quarter [*onza*] of cloves and a quarter of saffron. (Fr 40)

It is a good idea to have this mixture ready for those times when you feel like cooking medieval. The text edited by Frati is from the Venice region, but not necessarily from Venice itself, so we cannot be sure of the exact equivalent of the *oncia*, or *onza* in the usage of the source. We have done our best, however, to retain the correct proportions.

Fine Spice Mixture

2 rounded tablespoons freshly ground black pepper (16 g)

2 rounded tablespoons ground cinnamon (16 g)

2 rounded tablespoons ground ginger (16 g)

1½ tablespoons saffron threads, loosely measured, crushed to a powder in a mortar or with your fingers (4 g)

¾ teaspoon ground cloves (2 g)

B. *Sweet Spice Mixture*

Sweet spices for many good and fine foods.   The best sweet spices you can make are good for lamprey in pastry and for other good freshwater fish cooked in a crust, and to make good *brodetto* and good sauces. Take a quarter of cloves and an *onza* of good ginger, and take an *onza* of fine cinnamon, and take the same quantity of leaf; and pound all these spices together as you like; if you want to make more, use the ingredients in the same proportions; this is wonderfully good. (Fr 40)

This recipe has one problem: the "leaf." The same term appears in French medieval recipes and commercial records, but it has not been identified. Bay leaves are unlikely, because these do not appear on lists of costly imported spices; and cinnamon leaf was not used in the Asian regions from which spices were imported. Another theory is that it refers to a sort of Indian mint leaf related to patchouli. This will need to be pursued. In the meantime, we suggest using bay leaves, which is the only kind of "leaf" you are likely to find.

2 rounded tablespoons ground
ginger (16 g)
2 rounded tablespoons ground
cinnamon (16 g)
2 heaping tablespoons powdered
bay leaves, or dried bay leaves
ground to a powder in a spice
grinder to yield 2 heaping
tablespoons (16 g)
1½ teaspoons ground cloves

C. *Strong Black Spice Mixture*

Black, strong spices to make sauces: take half a quarter of cloves and two *onze* of
pepper, and take the same amount of long pepper and two nutmegs; this will serve
for all spices. (Fr 40)

¼ cup freshly ground black
pepper (30 g)
¼ cup ground long pepper
(or additional black pepper)
(30 g)
¾ teaspoon ground cloves
1 whole nutmeg, grated

151. Almond Milk

Almond milk was essential in the medieval kitchen, because it could replace
cow's or sheep's milk during Lent and on fish days, when all animal products
were forbidden.

Do not be intimidated by the thought of blanching a batch of almonds; it
is child's play. In fact, your children will be delighted to help you. Your efforts
will be rewarded a thousandfold when you taste this elegant, digestible liquid.
You need not confine it to medieval cooking either: try it in your coffee, or in
creamy desserts. The results will not disappoint you.

Still, if you haven't got the energy to blanch and grind your own almonds,
you can try using ground almonds from the baking section of the supermarket.
The result will be nowhere nearly as good, but it won't be bad either.

Any time you use almonds, once they are blanched you should soak them
overnight in clean water, or at least for a few hours. They will swell very
slightly and will regain much of their fresh-picked fragrance.

If you require a thicker almond milk, you can increase the proportion of
almonds to water.

o blanch the almonds, place them in boiling water, return to the boil, and immediately drain in a strainer. Run cold water through the almonds until cool. One by one, pinch each almond between thumb and forefinger; the nut will easily slide out of its brown skin. And that's it: you are blanching almonds! It will take you only 10 minutes or so to blanch the whole batch—less, if you use both hands.

generous ¾ cup almonds, shelled but not blanched (120 g), or 6 ounces ground almonds (150 g)

4 cups warm water (1 liter)

If time permits, soak the blanched almonds in cool water overnight or for a few hours.

Put half the almonds (or half the commercially ground almonds) and 2 cups of warm water into a blender and blend for quite some time, until a smooth, white liquid forms. Reserve, and repeat with the remaining almonds and water. Line a strainer with a double layer of strong cheesecloth, washed and squeezed dry. Strain the almond milk, pressing lightly to extract as much liquid as possible. The result will be a magnificently rich milk ready to use in any way you can imagine. The remaining ground almonds can be used in baking or in a soup such as cream of chicken.

Note: when almond milk is heated and brought to the boil, it can separate slightly; generally this will not affect the result, as it is used in combination with other ingredients.

152. Broths

A. *Chicken Broth*

lean and truss the chicken, and place it in a large pot along with the giblets. Add cold water to cover generously. Cover the pot and slowly bring to the boil over medium heat. As soon as the water comes to the boil, reduce the heat to a very low simmer. Continue to skim carefully as impurities rise to the surface.

1 chicken, 2¾ to 3¼ pounds, and its giblets, but not the liver (1.3 to 1.5 kg)

3 or 4 carrots

2 or 3 small turnips

4 or 5 small leeks, or 2 large leeks

1 medium-large whole onion, peeled and studded with 4 cloves

1 teaspoon whole black peppercorns

2 bay leaves
   salt

Peel and wash the vegetables, and add them to the pot. Add a very little salt, the peppercorns, and the bay leaves. Simmer for 90 minutes to 2 hours.

Remove the chicken from the pot and set aside. You can eat it with a medieval garlic sauce (recipes 99 to 101), or another sauce from the period.

Strain the broth and let it cool. Refrigerate until cold, preferably overnight. The fat will solidify on the surface of the broth, and you can remove it easily with a fork or spoon.

B. *Beef Broth*

1¾ pounds beef neck bones or shin
      of beef (800 g)
2   pounds short ribs or flanken
      (900 g)
4 or 5 carrots
3 or 4 small turnips
7 or 8 small leeks, or 3 large leeks
1   large stalk celery, including the
      leaves
1   small bunch parsley
1   large whole onion, peeled and
      studded with 4 cloves
3   bay leaves
1   scant tablespoon whole black
      peppercorns
      salt

Put the meat into a large pot and add cold water to cover generously. Bring to the boil over medium heat. As soon as the water comes to the boil, reduce the heat to a very low simmer. Skim carefully as impurities rise to the surface; continue until no more scum rises.

Peel and wash the vegetables, and add them to the pot along with the parsley. Add a very little salt, the peppercorns, and the bay leaves. Simmer over very low heat for about 3½ hours.

Remove the beef, saving it for use in other dishes, or to be eaten with one or more medieval sauces.

Strain the broth and let it cool. Refrigerate until cold, preferably overnight. The fat will solidify on the surface of the broth, and you can remove it easily with a fork or spoon.

153. Doughs for Pâtés, Pies, and Tarts

A. *Flour-and-Water Dough, or* Pâte à Foncer Ordinaire

This simple dough is typically used for covered pies, although if rolled very thin it can also be used for open tarts. If the filling is a moist one, you can certainly partly bake this crust unfilled (or "blind") to prevent it becoming soggy, shortening the baking time for the filled pie. Even if the recipe does not mention it, you must generously grease your mold with olive oil or lard before lining it with this pastry.

1¾ cups flour (250 g)
5   fl. ounces water, approximately
      (15 cl)
1   tablespoon olive oil
1   scant teaspoon salt

Combine all the ingredients and knead vigorously until a smooth, somewhat elastic and rather soft dough is formed. If the dough is too moist, you can knead in a little additional flour. Wrap in a moist towel, and leave to rest in the refrigerator for at least an hour before using.

B. *Rich Pastry Dough,* or Pâte Brisée

The delicate, fragile, and crisp pastry has infinite uses. It is suitable for all the pies, tarts, and pâtés in this book, rolled thicker or thinner as the recipe specifies. The basic proportions given here may vary from recipe to recipe.

Cut the butter into small pieces, and rub or cut it into the flour until the mixture has the consistency of sawdust. Dissolve the salt in half of the water, and add to the flour mixture. Combine quickly with your fingertips, without overworking, just until the dough comes together. If necessary, add more water as required. Form into a thick disk, wrap in plastic wrap or waxed paper, and leave to rest in the refrigerator at least 2 hours before using.

1¾ cups flour (250 g)
9 tablespoons cold butter (125 g)
⅓ cup water, approximately (10 cl)
1 scant teaspoon salt

C. *Dough for Pâtés,* or Pâte à Pâté

This is a flavorful, substantial dough. It will form a sturdy casing for all manner of savory pâtés. It should be made a day in advance and left to rest in the refrigerator.

Cut the fat into the flour. Dissolve the salt in 1 cup of the water, then add to the flour mixture along with the egg. Work with your fingers until a smooth dough forms, adding more water as required. Shape into a thick disk, wrap in waxed paper or plastic wrap, and refrigerate for 12 hours or overnight before using. A large pâté will require you to double the recipe.

3½ cups flour (500 g)
9 tablespoons butter or good lard (125 g)
1 egg
1¾ cups water, approximately (40 cl)
2 scant teaspoons salt

The Medieval Texts

1. Cretonnée de pois nouveaulx ou fèves nouvelles

Cuisiez-les jusques au purer, et les purez, puis prenez lait de vache bien frais, et dictes à celle qui vous le vendra qu'elle ne le vous baille point s'elle y a mis eaue, il tournera. Et icelluy lait boulez premièrement et avant que vous y mettez rien, car encore tourneroit-il: puis broiez premièrement gingembre pour donner appétit, et saffran pour jaunir: jàsoit-ce que qui le veult faire lyant de moieulx d'oeufs filés dedans, iceulx moieulx d'oeufs que de lioison de pain et du saffran pour colourer. Et pour ce, qui veult lier de pain, il convient que ce soit pain non levé et blanc, et sera mis tremper en une escuelle avec du lait ou avec du boullon de la char, puis broyé et coulé par l'estamine; et quant vostre pain est coulé et vos espices non coulées, mettez tout boulir avec vos pois; et quant tout sera cuit, mettez adonc vostre lait et du saffren. Encores povez-vous fair autre lioison, c'est assavoir des pois mesmes ou des fèves broyées, puis coulées; si prenez laquelle lioison que mieulx vous plaira. Car quant est de lioison de moieulx d'oeufs, il les convient batre, couler par l'estamine, et filer dedans le lait, après ce qu'il a bien boulu et qu'il est trait arrière du feu avec les poix nouveaulx ou fèves nouvelles et les espices. Le plus seur est que l'en preigne un petit du lait, et destremper les oeufs en l'escuelle, et puis encores autant, et encores, tant que les moieux soient bien destrempés à la cuillier avec foison de lait, puis mettre ou pot qui est hors du feu, et le potage ne se tournera point. Et se le potage est espois, allayez-le de l'eaue de la char. Ce fait, il vous convient avoir poucins escartelés, veel, ou petite oé cuit, puis frit, et en chascune escuelle mis deux ou trois morceaulx et du potage pardessus. (MP 159)

2. Menestra d'herbette

Togli le foglia di viete, et un pocha di borragine et fagli dare un boglio in acqua chiara bogliente quando le mitti dentro; dapoi cacciale fore et battile molto bene col coltello. Et togli un pocho de petrosillo, et di menta cruda, et similmente le batti co le ditte herbe. Dapoi macinale bene nel mortale, et mittile in una pignatta con brodo grasso et falle bollire un pocho. Et se ti pare mettevi un pocho di pepe. (Ma 146)

3. Congordes

Pour congordes, pelés les et deccopés par rouelles, et ostés la graine dedans, s'il en ya, et les mettés pourbouilir en une poelle, et puis les purés, et mettés de l'eaue froide par dessus, et les espregnés et hachés bien menu; et puis les assemblés avec boullon de beuf et d'autre char, et y mettés du lait de vache, et destrampés demy douzaine de moyeux d'oeufz, passés par l'estamine parmy le boullon avec le lait, et, au jours maigrez, de purée de poys ou de lait d'amandes, et du beurre. (VT XV 181)

4. Brodo de ciceri rosci

Per farne octo menestre: togli una libra et meza di ciceri et lavali con acqua calda et poneli in quella pignatta dove gli vorrai cocere et che siano sciutti et mettevi meza oncia di farina, cioè del fiore, et mettevi pocho olio et bono, et un pocho di sale, et circha vinti granelli di pepe rotto, et un pocha di canella posta, et mena molto bene tutte queste cose inseme con le mani. Dapoi ponivi tre bocali d'acqua et un pocha di salvia, et rosmarino, et radici di petrosillo, et fagli bollire tanto che siano consumati a la quantitade di octo menestre. Et quando sono quasi cotti mittivi un pocho d'oglio. Et se lo brodo si facesse per ammalati non gli porre né oglio né spetie. (Ma 147)

5. Per fare zanzarelli

Per farne dece menestre: togli octo ova et meza libra de caso grattugiato, et un pane grattato, et mescola ogni cosa inseme. Dapoi togli una pignatta con brodo di carne giallo di zafrano et ponila al focho; et como comincia a bollire getta dentro quella materia, et dagli una volta col cocchiaro. Et como te pare che sia presa toglila dal focho, e fa'le menestre, et mittivi del le spetie di sopra. (Ma 137–38)

6. De lasanis

Ad lasanas, accipe pastam fermentatam et fac tortellum ita tenuem sicut poteris. Deinde, divide eum per partes quadratas ad quantitatem trium digitorum. Postea, habeas aquam bullientem salsatam, et pone ibi ad coquendum predictas lasanas. Et quando erunt fortiter decocte, accipe caseum grattatum.

Et, si volueris, potes simil ponere bonas species pulverizatas, et pulveriza cum istis super cissorium. Postea, fac desuper unum lectum de lasanis et iterum pulveriza; et desuper, alium lectum, et pulveriza: et sic fac usque cissorium uel scutella sit plena. Postea, comede cum uno punctorio ligneo accipiendo. (Lc 412)

7. Ravioli in tempo di carne

Per farne dece menestre: togli meza libra di caso vecchio, et un pocho d'altro caso grasso et una libra di ventrescha di porcho grassa overo una tettha di vitella, et cocila allesso tanto che sia ben disfatta. Dapoi battila bene et togli di bone herbe ben battute, et pepe, garofoli, et zenzevero; et giongendovi il petto d'un cappone pesto serebe migliori. Et tutte queste cose distemperarle inseme. Dapoi fagli la pasta ben sottile, et liga questa materia ne la pasta como vole essere. Et questi ravioli non siano maiori d'una meza castagna, et ponili accocere in brodo di cappone, o di carne bona, facto giallo di zafrano quando bolle. Et lassali bollire per spatio de doi paternostri. Dapoi fanne menestre, et mettili di sopra caso gratto et spetie dolci mescolate inseme. Et simili raffioli si posson fare di petto di fasani et starne et altre volatile. (Ma 144)

8. Ravioli bianchi

Piglia de bona probatura fresca he pistala molto bene poi azonze pistando un pocho de butiro, zenzevero he canella. Et per una probatura azonze tre ghiari d'ova ben batuta et del zucaro honestamente. Et incorpora tute queste cose insieme. Poi fa li ravioli longhi he grossi uno dito. Poi imbratelli in bona farina. Et nota che questi voleno esser senza pasta. [marginal annotation in the manuscript: et se cum pasta li vorrai, falli.] He falli bollire adasio che non si rompano. Como hano levato uno buglore levali fora he meteli in scutelle cum zucaro, canella, he li poi far ghialdi de zaffrano. (Bü 5rv)

9. Se vuoi i gnocchi

Togli lo cascio fresco e pestalo: poscia togli la farina et intridi con tuorla d'uova a modo di migliacci. Poni il paiuolo al fuoco con acqua e quando bolle, poni lo triso in su in uno taglieri, fallo andare colla cazza nel paiuolo, e quando sono cotti, poni sopra li taglieri e getta su assai cacio grattugiato. (Gu 33)

10. Souppe despourveue

Aiez du percil et frisiez en beurre, puis gettez de l'eaue boulant dessus et faites boulir: et mettre du sel, et dréciez vos souppes comme en purée.

Aliter, à jour de char, prenez du chaudeau de la char, et aiez pain trempé ou maigre de l'eaue de la char, puis broyez, et six oeufs: puis coulez et mettez en un pot avec de l'eaue grasse, espices, vertjus, vinaigre et saffran; faictes boulir un bouillon, puis dréciez par escuelles. (MP 145–46)

11. Lait d'amandes

Pourboulez et pelez vos amandes, puis les mettez en eaue froide, puis les broyez et destrempez de l'eaue ou les oignons auront cuit et coulez par une estamine: puis frisiez les oignons, et mettez dedans un petit de sel, et faites boulir sur le feu, puis mettez les souppes. Et se vous faites lait d'amandes pour malades, n'y mettez aucuns oignons, et ou lieu de l'eaue d'oignons pour destremper les amandes et dont dessus est parlé, mettez-y et les destrempez d'eaue tiède nette et faites boulir, et n'y mettez point de sel, mais succre foison au boire. (MP 241)

12. Porée blanche

Porée blanche est dicte ainsi pour ce qu'elles est faite du blanc des poreaux, à l'eschinée, à l'andoulle et au jambon, ès saison d'automne et d'iver, à jour de char; et sachez que nulle autre gresse que de porc n'y est bonne.

Et premièrement, l'en eslit, lave, mince et esverde les poreaux, c'est assavoir en esté, quant iceulx poreaux sont jeunes: mais en yver quant iceulx poreaux sont plus viels et plus durs, il les convient pourboulir en lieu esverder, et se c'est à jour de poisson, après ce que dit est, il les convient mettre en un pot avec de l'eau chaude et ainsi cuire, et aussi cuire des oignons mincés, puis frire les oignons, et après frire iceuls poireaux avec les oignons qui jà sont fris; puis mettre tout cuire en un pot et du lait de vache, se c'est en charnage et à jour de poisson; et se c'est en karesme l'en y met lait d'amandes. Et se c'est à jour de char, quant iceulx poreaux d'esté sont esverdés, ou les poreaux d'iver pourboulis comme dit est, l'en les met en un pot cuire en l'eaue des saleures, ou du porc et du lart dedans.

Nota que aucunesfois à poreaux, l'en fait lioison de pain. (MP 139–40)

13. Porrata bianca

Se vuoli fare porrata bianca per XII persone, togli due libre di mandorle e una oncia di gengiove fine bene pesto, e togli IIII maçi di porri, e mettigli a lessare; e quando sono bene cotti, pure il bianco, scolali dall'acqua e battigli. E togli le mandorle ben lavate e ben monde e stemperate con acqua poca e bene colate; e mettile a bollire col porro, e fallo bene cuocere, e mettivi del detto gengiove che tu ai. Questa vivanda vuol esere biancha e bene spessa; e poni spetie sopra scodella. (Mo 21)

14. Porée de bettes

Porée de bettes qui est lavée, puis mincée et pourboulie, se tient plus vert que celle qui premièrement est pourboulie et puis hachée. Mais encores est plus verte et meilleur celle qui est esleue, puis lavée et puis mincée bien menu, puis esverdée en eaue froide, puis changer l'eau et laissier tremper en autre eau, puis espraindre par pelottes et mettre au pot boulir ou boullon avec le lart et de l'eaue de mouton; et quant elle a un petit bouli et l'en le veult drécier, que l'en mette dedens du percil esleu, lavé et haché, et un petit de fanoul jeune, et boulir un boullon seulement. (MP 141)

15. Porée verte à jour de poisson

Soit eslite, mincée, puis lavée en eaue froide sans pourboulir, puis cuite au verjus et pou d'eaue, et mettre du sel, et soit drécée toute boulant bien espoisse sans cler, puis l'en mettra dedans, au fons de l'escuelle, dessoubs la porée, du beurre salé ou frais qui veult, ou frommage ou frommagée ou vertjus viel. (MP 142)

16. Porée de cresson en karesme au lait d'amandes.

Prenez votre cresson et le mettez parboullir et une pongnée de bettes avec hachées, et les friolez en huile puis la mettez boullir en lait d'amandes; et en charnage, friolez au lart et au beurre tant qu'il soit cuit, puis destrempez de l'eaue de la char; ou au frommage et dressiez tantost, car il roussirait. Toutesvoies, se l'en y met precil, il ne doit point estre esverdé. (MP 140)

17. Porée noire

Porée noire est celle qui est faite à la ribelette de lart; c'est assavoir que la porée est esleue, lavée, puis mincée et esverdée en eaue bouland, puis fritte en la gresse des lardons; et puis alaier d'eaue chaude frémiant . . . , puis convient mettre sur chascune escuelle deux lardons. (MP 142)

18. Tredura

A ffare tredura, toy lo bianco delli porri e mitilo a lessare intriego e poy li batte con coltello ben trito; poy lo frizi con lo grasso della carne che tu coxi; toy pan e gratillo e mitilo a moglo in acqua calda; toy una peza de carne e bati lo pan e la carne con coltello, poy to ove batute e zafarano assay el bati in sema e miti su quelli porri fritti cum specie assay e serà bon. (Fr 62)

19. Delle foglie minute

Togli spinacci e triplice biete; scielglili bene e fà bollire. Poi le cava, e battile col coltello fortemente: poi togli petroselli, finocchi, anesi, cipolle, e battile e tritale col coltello e soffriggi con olio bene; e prendi altre erbe minute e soffriggile insieme e mettivi uno poco d'acqua e lassa bullire, e mettivi del pepe e de le specie; e dà mangiare.

In questo modo si possono ponere dentro ova dibattute, polpa di pesce senza spine, carne di castrone e di porco; o carne insalata, e diversificare secondo pare a la discrezione di buono cuoco; e torre maggiorana, trasmarino, petrosello con bone spezie, cum garofani; e di queste erbe, peste forte nel mortaro cum pesce o carne battuta, porestine fare mortadelli, comandelli e molte altre cose; a questo modo puoi torre erbe domestiche, ovvero salvatiche, se d'orti non si potesseno avere.

Del medesmo mangiare con borraggine
Togli borraggine, spinacci e biete trepice e simili; poni in acqua fredda a bullire; poi gitata via l'acqua, s'attritino forte col coltello; poi rimetti a cuocere con latte d'amandole e, messovi dentro battuto di tinca, potrai dare la quaresma al Signore, con le specie e con zaffarano, messovi del zuccaro.

Del predetto
Anche tollendo finocchio intero, bullito, cotto con cennamo, pepe e zaffarano, e mettivi ova perdute e carne di polli, o altra carne o quello che tu vuoli.

Del predetto
Anche tollendo erbe minute odorifere, bullite, battute, cotte col petto de la gallina, peste nel mortaro, et aggiunte de le foglie, si possono dare al Signore, o al'infermo per avere soluzione di ventre.

Del predetto
Togli finocchio bianco trito minuto e poi lo fà friggere con un poco di bianco di porro trito minuto, con ovo, o lardo, e ponvi uno poco d'acqua e zaffarano e sale, e fà bullire, e ponvi ova dibattute, se vuoli, dentro.

Del predetto
Togli finocchio ben lavato, poi fà allessare, e gittata l'acqua, friggilo con oglio, o lardo, sale e dà mangiare. (Za 3–6)

20. De li sparaci
Togli li sparaci, e fàlli bollire; quando sieno bolliti, ponili a cocere con oglio, cipolle, sale e zaffarano, e spezie trite, o senza. (Za 8)

21. Fungi di monte
Toglie fungi di monte, e lessali: e gittatene via l'acqua, mettili poi a friggere con cipolla tritata minuto, o con bianco di porro, spezie e sale e dà a mangiare. (Za 24)

22. Fave fresche con brodo di carne
Piglia le fave et mondale con l'acqua calda come se fanno le amandole, et poi le mitti a bollire in bon brodo. Et quando ti pareno cotte mette con esse un pocho di petrosillo et menta battuta facendogli bollire etiandio de bona carne salata. Et questa menestra volle essere un pocho verde che pare più bella. Et similmente poi fare i peselli, et ogni altro leghume frescho, ma nota che non voleno essere mondati con l'acqua calda como le fave, ma lasciali pur cosi con quella sua scorza sottile. (Ma 149)

23. Fève fresé en potaige
Metz ta fève fresé, bien nettoyée et lavée, emprès le feu, et quand commencera à boullir, exprimis l'eaue et la metz hors du pot, et y en metz de rechef de fraiche par autant que surmonte quelque deux doyz et y metz du sel à ton advis, et fais bouillir ta potée bien couverte loing de la flambe, pour cause de la fumée, et ce jusques ta dicte potée sera bien cuyte et redigée forment en paste. Après, la mettras au mortier et agiteras, et mesle-

ras icelle très bien, et la réduyras en ung corps, puis, de rechief, la tourneras à son dict pot et le feras chauffer. Et quand vouldras faire tes platz ou escuelles, confiras ta viande en ceste composte qui sensuit. Et cuyras, premièrement, des oignons decoupez bien menu en huyle fervent dedans ung pot, y mettras de la saulge, des figues ou des pommes, decoupées bien menu à petits loppins. Et ceste confection toute boulant et fervente infondiras, et mettras dedans tes platz ou escuelles où sont tes dictes fèves, et présenteras sur table; aulcuns y veulent par dessus inspargir des espices. (VT XV 206)

24. Lenti altramente

Togli le lenti bene lavate e nette da le pietre, et poni a cuocere con erbe odorifere, oglio, sale e zaffarano. E quando saranno cotte, tritale bene; e messovi su ova dibattute, e cascio secco tagliato, dà mangiare. (Za 22–23)

25. Cocer zucche

Mondale como vogliono essere, et poi cocile con brodo di carne, overo con acqua et mettevi un pocha de cipolla secundo la quantità che tu vorrai fare. Et quando parerà cotta cacciala fore, et passa ogni cosa per le cocchiara straforata, overo pistale molto bene, et metteli accocere in una pignatta con brodo grasso, e con un pocho d'agresto. Et siano un pocho gialle di zafrano; et quando sono cotte toglile dal focho et lasciale un pocho refredare. Dapoi togli di rossi d'ova secundo la quantità et sbattili con un pocho di caso vecchio et gittagli in le ditte zucche menando continuamente col cocchiaro accio che non si prendano: et fà le menestre et mectevi sopra spetie dolci. (Ma 148)

26. De la insaleggiata di cipolle

Togli cipolle; cuocile sotto la bragia, e poi le manda, e tagliale per traverso longhette et sottili: mettili alquanto d'aceto, sale, oglio, e spezie, e dà a mangiare. (Za 90)

27. Civé de lièvre

Premièrement, fendez le lièvre par la poictrine: et s'il est de fresche prise, comme d'un ou de deux jours, ne le lavez point, mais le mettez harler sur le greil, id est roidir sur bon feu de charbon ou en la broche; puis aiez des oignons cuis et du sain en un pot, et mettez vos oignons avec le sain et vostre lièvre par morceaulx, et les friolez au feu en hochant le pot très souvent, ou le friolez au fer de la paelle. Puis harlez et brûlez du pain et trempez en l'eaue de la char avec vinaigre et vin: et aiez avant broyé gingembre, graine, giroffle, poivre long, noix muguettes et canelle, et soient broyés et destrempés de vertjus et vinaigre ou boullon de char; requeilliez, et mettez d'une part. Puis broyez vostre pain, deffaites du boullon, et coulez le pain et non les espices par l'estamine, et mettez le boullon, les oignons et sain, espices et pain brûlé, tout cuire ensemble, et le lièvre aussi; et gardez que le civé soit brun, aguisé de vinaigre, attrempé de sel et d'espices.
    Civé de connins: comme dessus. (MP 169)

28. Civeri di lepore e altre carni

Smembra il lepore tutto e, con poco lavare, cuocilo in acqua; poi togli il fegato e polmone cotto, pestalo bene nel mortaio, e poi che fia cotto il detto lepore, togli spezie, pepe e cipolla, e soffriggi nel lardo col detto polmone e pane arrostito: e poi che sono tutte cose insieme bullite, dà a taola. Nota che tu dei, il fegato e polmone cotto, tritare e pestare nel mortaio con spezie e pane abbrusciato, e distemperallo con buono vino, e un poco d'aceto. E poi che fie cotto e soffritto il lepore con la cipolla, gitta il detto savore sopra'l lepore, e lassa freddare che sia tiepido, e dà mangiare. E tal modo si pò fare per le pernici, cioè starne. (Za 43)

29. Per fare civero de salvaticina

Per fare civero de carne salvacina in prima coci la carne in aqua miscolata con altrec-tanto aceto, et come è cotta cavala fori del brodo, azio che se sciucchi. Asciutta che serrà frigila in bono lardo; et volendo fare duo piatelli del dicto civero, togli una libra de uva passa, et mezza libra de amandole senza mondarle, et pista bene queste chose. Dapoi togli una libra de pane tagliato in fette, et siccato al foco, ma non troppo brusco-lato, et ponilo a mollo in uno poco de vino roscio, et pistalo con le predicte chose, poi distemperale col brodo de la dicta carne, et passale per la stamigna in una pignatta, et ponila su la brascia longi dal foco, facendola ben bollire per spazio de meza hora; dapoi vi metti zenzevro, et cannela assai, che sia dolce o forte secundo el commune gusto, o del tuo Signore. Dapoi tolli una cipolla, et cocila in una pignatta et macinala molto bene, et ponila insieme col lardo, nel quel è cocta; et metti ogni chosa in la pignatta ne la qual sono le chose predicte, lassandola bollire anchora un poco più; poi fa li piatelli de la prefata carne, et de sopra gli metti de questo civero, et mandali a tabula. (Ma 122)

30. Se vuoi ambrogino di polli

Togli li polli, ismembrali, poi li soffriggi col lardo fresco et uno poco di cipolla tagliata a traverso. Quando è a mezzo cotto, togli latte di mandorle et istempera con buglione et uno poco di vino, e metti con questi polli e iscema in prima del grasso s'egli è troppo, e mettivi cennamo trito col coltello e pochi garofani. E quando s'apparecchia, mettivi susine secche, datteri interi, alquante noci moscate tritate et uno poco di midolla di pane abbrusciata, bene pesta e stemperata con vino e con aceto. Questa vivanda vuole essere agra e dolce, e guarda li datteri che non si rompano. (Gu 20)

31. Polli infinocchiati

Togli li polli, ismembrali, falli soffrigere e quando sonno sofritti, si vi metti acqua, quella che ti piace; poi togli le barbe dei finocchi, barbe di petroselli e mandorle che non siano monde e queste cose fa bene macinare e stemperare con l'acqua di questi polli e fae bollire ogni cosa e colale con stamigna. Metti con questi polli e mettivi le migliori spezie che si possono avere. (Gu 45)

32. De la gratonata di polli

Polli smembrati, friggili con lardo e con cipolle; e, mentre si friggono, mettivi uno poco d'acqua, sì che si cocano bene nella pentola, e volgili spesso eziandio con la mescola: mettivi su spezie, zaffarano e succhio d'uva agresta, e fà bullire; e per ciascuno pollo togli quattro tuorla d'ova, e distempera coll'agresto, e fà bullire crudo, e sbatti insieme nel catino, e insieme, coll'arte de polli, fà oni cosa bullire; e, bullito, levalo dal foco, e mangia. (Za 69)

33. De limonia

Ad limoniam faciendam, suffrigantur pulli cum lardo et cepis. Et amigdale mundate terantur, distemperentur cum brodio carnis et colentur. Que coquantur cum dictis pullis et speciebus. Et si non habentur amigdale, spissetur brodium cum uitellis ouorum. Et si fuerit prope horam scutellandi, pone ibi succum limonum uel limiarum uel citrangulorum. (Lc 402)

34. De romania

De romania, suffrigantur pulli cum lardo et cepis et terantur amigdale non mondate et distemperentur cum succo granatorum acrorum et dulcium. Postea, colletur et ponantur ad bulliendum cum pullis et cum cocleari agitetur. Et ponantur species.

Potest tamen fieri brodium viride cum herbis. (Lc 402)

35. Brouet de chapons

Cuisiez vos chapons en eaue et en vin, puis si les despeciez par membres et frisiez en sain, puis broiez les braons de vos chapons et les foies et amandes, et deffaites de vostre boullon et faites boulir, puis prenez gingembre, canelle, girofle, garingal, poivre long et graine de paradis, et deffaites de vinaigre et faites boulir; et au dressier, mettez vostre grain par escuelles, et dressiez le potage sus. (MP 149)

36. Del brodo saracenico

Togli capponi arrostiti, e i fegati loro con le spezie, et pane abbrusticato, trita nel mortaio; e distempera nel mortaio buono vino bianco e succhi agri, e poi smembra i detti capponi, e metti a bollire con le predette cose in una pentola, e mettivi su dattali, uve grece, prugne secche, amandole monde intere, e lardo sufficiente; e dà a mangiare. Simile modo fà de' pesci marini; pome e pere puoi ponere nei detti brodi. (Za 32)

37. Se vuoi pippioni in istufa

Togli li pippioni, ismembrali, mettili nella pentola col lardo battuto, mettivi spezie et uno poco di cipolla tagliata minuta, poni sulla bragia, soffrigi sino a mezzo cotto e mettivi entro XXX mandorle colle corteccie et XXX monde. Togli li fegatelli lessi, pestali bene con uno poco di pane arrostito, stempralo con vino, colalo, metti in su pippioni e metti poi sopra le scodelle ispezie e zuccaro. (Gu 24)

38. Gravé d'oiselets ou d'autre char

Soient plumés à sec, puis aiez du gras du lart décoppé comme par morceaulx quarrés, et mettez au fer de la paelle et en traiez la graisse et là les frisiez; puis mettez cuire ou boullon de la char, puis prenez pain hallé sur le gril ou chappelleures de pain trempées ou boullon de la char et un petit de vin; puis prenez gingembre, girofle, graine et fleur de cannelle et les foies, et les broyez; et puis coulez vostre pain et boullon par l'estamine et les espices broyées à fin et sans couler; et mettre boulir avec vos oiselets et un petit de verjus;

item, qui n'a boullon, si mette purée de pois;

item, ne doit point estre trop lyant, mais claret; doncques ne convient-il que le pain ou les foies pour lier. (MP 150)

39. Gravé ou seymé

Gravé ou seymé est potage d'hiver. Pelez oignons et les cuisiez tout hachiés, puis les frisiez en un pot; or convient avoir vostre poulaille fendue sur le dos et hallée sur le grill au feu de charbon, ou se c'est veel, aussi; et qu'ils soient mis par morceaulx soit veel, on par quartiers se c'est poulaille, et les mettez avec les oignons dedans le pot, puis avoir pain blanc harlé sur le gril et trempé au boullon d'autre char: et puis broyez gingembre, clou, graine et poivre long, deffaire de verjus et de vin, sans couler, mettre d'une part: puis broyer le pain et couler par l'estamine et mettre au brouet, et tout couler ensemble et boulir; puis drécier. (MP 151)

40. Héricot de mouton

Despeciez-le par petites pièces, puis le mettez pourboulir une onde, puis le frisiez en sain de lard, et frisiez avec des oignons menus minciés et cuis, et deffaites du boullon de beuf, et mettez avec macis, percil, ysope et sauge, et faites boulir ensemble. (MP 148)

41. Mouton ausoerre

Despeciez le mouton par pièces, puis lavez et mettez cuire en eaue, puis broyez foison percil et pain, et coulez, et mettez en pot avec espices. (MP 148–49)

42. De sardamone di carne

Togli carne di castrone, del petto: taglia minuto, e fà bullire forte; e quando sirà bullita, acciò che non sapia di beccume, leva via l'acqua e friggi la carne col lardo; poi mettivi su abbastanza di quella acqua, in tanto che poco rimagna di quello brodo; e quando siranno cotte, mettivi su coriandoli e carote bene trite con spezie e zaffarano abbastanza. E se non avessi coriandoli, mettivi del comino, e mangia. (Za 69)

43. Per fare carbonata

Togli la carne salata che [sia] vergellata di grasso et magro inseme, et taglia in fette, et ponile accocere ne la padella et non le lassare troppo cocere. Dapoi mittele in un piatello et gettavi sopra un pocho di zuccharo, un pocha di cannelia, et un pocho di petrosillo tagliato menuto. Et similmente poi fare de summata o presutto, giongendoli in scambio d'aceto del sucho d'aranci, o limoni, quel che più ti piacesse, et farratte meglio bevere. (Ma 131)

44. Dei tomacelli ovvero mortadelle

Togli il fegato del porco, e lessalo: poi lo cava, e tritalo sulla taola col coltello fortemente e spesso; o vero tu il gratta colla grattusia al modo del cascio secco. Poi abbi maggiorana e altre erbe odorifere, bene peste col pepe, e detto fegato, e nel mortaio distempera con l'ova, tanto che sia spesso. Poi abbi rete di porco e, a modo di monticelli tondi, li copri, e spartitamente li friggi nella padella col lardo; e cotti, cavali e poni in una pentola nova. E prese spezie con zaffarano e pepe, distemperato con bono vino, gettato sopra essi nella pentola, e falli bullire competentemente, e mangia.

De li fegatelli
Togli il fegato, taglialo a pezzi e arrostili nel spiedo; e quando non seranno bene cotti, involgi sopra essi la rete del porco, e fa cocere. E, cotti, mettili in una pentola nova e

falli su il savore come detto è di sopra; e involgendolo ciascuno fegatello per sè in la rete del porco, è migliore. (Za 73–74)

45. Encor, une vinaigrete

Et pour donner entendement a celluy qui fera la vinagrete si prenne des foies de porcs et si les lave et puis les mecte sur le gril sur belles brases jusques que il soit assez cuit; et quant il sera cuit si le mecte sur belles postz et puis le trenche par minuz dez; et puis prenne des oignions grant foison et les plume et lave et trenche tresbien minuz et tout cela souffrise tout ensemble en de bon et beau lart. Et pour le potaige de ladicte vinaigrete si prenne de tresbon vin claret du meilleur qu'il pourra avoir selon la quantité dudit potaige et y mecte du boullon du beuf on du mouton ce qui sera necessaire; et puis prenne de beau pain blanc et le trenche par belles trenches et mecte roustr sur le gril jusques atant qu'il soit bien rousselet, et puis le mectés tremper audit vin et boullon; et quant il sera trempé si prennés d'espices: gingibre blanc, granne de paradis, poyvre et non pas tropt, cynamomy grant foyson ce que en sera necessayre, et du sel aussi, puis tout cela passer et coler par l'estamine bien nectement et appoint, et puis le mectés bullir; et, estre boullir, si lacés ledit grein souffrit dedans. Et puis en servés quant s'en devra servir. (Ch 181)

46. Capretto arrosto in sapore

Piglia un quarto di capretto et concialo molto bene come vole essere arrosto, et inlardalo et ponevi per dentro assai aglio in spichi mondate a modo se volesci impillottare o inlardare. Dapoi togli de bono agresto, doi rosci d'ova, doi spichi d'aglio ben piste, un pocho de zafrano, un pocho di pepe, et un pocho di brodo grasso, et mescola tutte queste cose inseme et ponile in un vaso sotto il capretto quando s'arroste, et bagnalo qualche volta con questo tal sapore. Et quando è cotto poni il quarto del capretto in un piatto et ponivi di sopra il ditto sapore et un pocho di petrosillo battuto menuto. Et questo quarto di capretto vole essere ben cotto e magnato caldo caldo. (Ma 130)

47. Mouton rosti au sel menu ou au vertjus et vinaigre

L'espaule soit première embrochée et tournée devant le feu jusques à ce qu'elle ait getté sa gresse, puis soit lardée de percil: et non plus tost pour deux causes, l'une car adonc elle est meilleur à larder, l'autre car qui plus tost la larderoit, le percil s'ardroit avant que l'espaule fust rostie. (MP 177)

48. Armus arietis

Armus arietis lardatur et in ueru ponitur et assatur et sal super aspergitur; inciditur et cum salsa uiridi comeditur. (Tr 388)

49. Pourcelet farci

Le pourcelet tué et acouré par la gorge soit eschaudé en eaue boulant, puis pelé: puis prenez de la char meigre de porc, et ostez le gras et les issues du porcelet et mettez cuire en l'eaue, et prenez vint oeufs et les cuisez durs, et des chastaignes cuites en l'eaue et pelées: puis prenez les moyeux des oeufs, chastaignes, fin fromage vieil, et char d'un cuissot de porc cuit, et en hachez, puis broyez avec du saffran et pouldre de gingembre grant foison entremellée parmy la char; et se vostre char revient trop dure, si l'alaiez de moyeux d'oeufs. Et ne fendez pas votre cochon parmy le ventre, mais parmy le cousté le plus petit trou que vous pourrez: puis le mettez en broche, et après boutez vostre farce dedans, et recousez à une grosse aiguille; et soit mengié ou au poivre jaunet se c'est en yver, ou à la cameline se c'est en esté.

Nota que j'ai bien veu pourcelet lardé, et est très bon. Et ainsi le fait-l'en maintenant et des pigons aussi. (MP 178)

50. Porchetta

Per aconciare bene una porchetta. Fa' in prima che sia ben pelata in modo che sia biancha et netta. Et poi fendila per lo deritto de la schiena et caccia fore le interiori et lavala molto bene. Et dapoi togli i figatelli de la ditta porchetta et battili bene col coltello inseme con bone herbe, et togli aglio tagliato menuto, et un poco di bon lardo, et un pocho di caso grattugiato, et qualche ovo, et pepero pesto, et un pocho di zafrano, et mescola tutte queste cose et mettele in la ditta porchetta, reversandola à modo che si fanno le tenche, cioè ponendo quello di dentro di fori. Et dapoi cusila inseme et legala bene et ponila accocere nel spedo, o vero su la graticula. Ma falla cocere adascio che sia ben cotta cosi la carne como etiamdio il pieno. Et fa una pocha di salamora con aceto, pepero et zafrano, et tolli doi o tre ramicelle de lavoro, o rosmarino; et gitta spesse volte di tal salamora sulla porchetta; et simile si po fare de oche, anatre, gruve, capponi, pollastri, et altri simili. (Ma 127)

51. Cormaryc

Take colyaundre, caraway smale grounden, powdour of peper and garlec ygrounde, in rede wyne; medle alle thise togyder and salt it. Take loynes of pork rawe and fle of the skyn, and pryk it wel with a knyf, and lay it in the sawse. Roost it whan thou wilt, & kepe that that fallith therfro in the rostyng and seeth it in a possynet with faire broth, & serve it forth with the roost anoon. (Fc HB 109)

52. Bourbier de sanglier frez

Premièrement il le convient mettre en eaue boullant et bien tost retraire et mettre rostir et baciner de saulse faicte d'espices, c'est assavoir gingembre, canelle, giroffle, grainne de paradis—et mieulx qui peult, du pain bruslé destrempé de vin et de verjus et de vinaigre, et l'en baciner; et puis quant il sera cuit, si bacinez tout ensemble; et soit clairet et noir. (VT Vat Scul 94)

53. Lyevres en rost

Sans laver, lardez-le; et le mengez à la cameline ou au saupiquet, c'est assavoir en la gresse qui en chiet en la lechefricte, et y mettez des ongnons menuz couppez, du vin et du verjus et ung pou de vinaigre, et le gectez sur le lièvre quant il sera rosti, ou mettez par escuelles. (VT Vat Scul 93)

54. Assatura bouina

Assatura bouina, cum costis iuxta dorsum acceptum, simpliciter in ueru assatur et cum bullito pipere administratur. (Tr 388)

55. Alloyaux de beuf

Faictes lesches de la char du trumel, et enveloppez dedans mouelle et gresse de beuf: puis embrochiez, rostissiez et mengiez au sel. (MP 177)

56. Langue de beuf

Langue de beuf fresche soit parboulie, pelée, lardée et rostie, et mengée à la cameline.

Item, est assavoir que la langue du vieil vault mieulx que la langue de jeune beuf, si comme aucuns dient; autres dient le contraire. (MP 177)

57. Menus oysaulx en rolz

Plumey les a sec, puis ostés les gavions et les brouailles et le bruler à feu sans fumer et les hastés et la ribelette de lart entredeux et des feulles de loriez, et emplisiez les ventres de fin froumaige fondant et miole de beuf; et se mainge a sel menu, et se servent à couvert entre deux escuelles ou entre deux plas. (VT Maz Scul 97)

58. Del paparo

Taglia la gola al paparo o oca; pelalo bene e bruscia; taglia i piedi, cavali l'interiori e lava bene: poi togli agresto, aglio, e se tali cose non poi avere togli erbe orodifere, bagnate in aceto, e ricusci di sotto, e poni in spiedo, e arrostilo; e se non fosse grasso, mettivi dentro del lardo. E poni un poco d'acqua in una scudella, e togli il grasso che esce d'inde. E quando serà assai cotto, levalo dal fuoco, e dà mangiare col succo d'aranci, o di limoncelli, o di lumie. (Za 30)

59. Pollastro arrosto

Per fare pollastro arrosto si vuole cocere arrosto; et quando è cotto togli sucho di pomaranci overo agresto con acqua rosata, zuccaro et canella, et mitti il pollastro in un piattello; et dapoi gettavi questa tal mescolanza di sopra et mandalo ad tavola. (Ma 127)

60. Chapons, gelines, hettoudeaulx

En rost, à la saulce de moulst en esté, ou à la poitevine en yver, ou à la jance; et si fait l'en bien celle saulce comme de moulst en yver, c'est à savoir, de vin et de succre bolu ensemble. (VT Vat Scul 90)

61. De la gelatina di pesci senza oglio

Metti a bullire vino con aceto, e mettivi dentro a cocere i pesci bene lavati; e, cotti, cavali e poni in un altro vaso. E in lo detto vino e aceto metti cipolle tagliate per traverso, e fà tanto bullire, che torni alla terza parte: poi mettivi dentro zaffarano, comino e pepe, e getta tutto sopr'al pesce cotto, e lassa freddare. Questa è schibezia da tavernaio. (Za 7s)

62. Del brodo del pesce

Pesce ben lavato, quanto si conviene: friggilo con l'oglio abbundantemente, poi lassa freddare: poi abbi cipolle tagliate per traverso; friggile con oglio rimanente del pesce: poi prendi amandole monde, uva secca, ienula secca e prugne, e friggi con le dette cipolle insieme, e leva via l'oglio che avanza, e togli pepe e zaffarano, e altre spezie elette, bene *trite, e distempera con le cipolle predette, e vino e aceto; e, distemperato fortemente, metti a fuoco fino che bolla: poi levalo dal fuoco, e poni in altro vaso, e mettilo ordinatamente a solaio col pesce predetto. E se 'l volessi dolce, ponvi o vino cotto, o zuccaro competentemente.* (Za 29)

63. Ricetta del prete

Prima pellaro quella anguilla con l'acqua bollita e cavaro quello dentro, e mozzaro la coda e la testa, poi lavaro bene a sei acque, poi ne fecero rocchij agugliati d'uno palmo l'uno o meno, e miserli in uno spedone con frondi d'alloro in mezzo tra' rocchij acciocché non s'attaccassero insieme, e così temperatamente l'arrostiro: e avendo prima messo in una conchetta sale, aceto e uno gocciolino d'olio, con quattro speziarie dentro, cioè pepe, specie, garofani e celamo fino, di ognuno di questi una mezza oncia, e con una rametta di osmarino, sempre di questa zenezaverata l'andavano ognendo: e quando fu bene cotta e spolpata, la trassero in una conca da gelatina, e ivi i rocchj assettaro; poi su vi premettero sei melegrane con bene vinti aranci, e con molto fine specie sopra essa, poi con una teglia da migliacci caldetta la copersero, acciocché calda si mantenesse infine che fossero a tavola. (Sermini, *Novelle* 29)

64. Carpionar trutte al modo di carpioni

Netta le trutte molto bene et cavane fora l'interiori, pugnendole in molti lochi con la punta del coltello da ogni parte, et farai una salimora d'acqua et aceto tanto dell'uno quanto dell'altro, mettendogli del sale assai, el quale farai strugere molto bene, et dentro gli mettirai le trotte per un mezo giorno o più. Et facto questo le cavarai sopra una tavola mettendole in soprescia per tre o quattro hore, et frigerale bene in olio bono et assai, che sian ben cotte et non arse. Et queste trutte poterai conservare un mese frigendole dell'altre volte se ti piacera et refacendole a modo di carpioni. (Ma 202)

65. Aloze

La fresche entre en saison en mars. La convient appareiller par l'oreille, escharder . . .

Item aloze appareillée comme dessus, sans escharder, puis rostir au four avec percil et moitié verjus, l'autre moitié vin et vinaigre; et est en saison depuis Février jusques en Juin. (MP 188)

66. Pour faire chaudumé

Prenés brochet, et les eschardés, et les mettés par pièces ou tous entiers hallés sur le gril, et halés du pain, et le mettés tramper avec purée de poys; et puis quand le pain sera trampe, prenes du vert jus et du vin blanc, et de la purée, et passés vostre pain tout ensemble; et quand il sera passé, pour quatre platz destrampés une unce de gingembre dedens le boullon, et ung peu de safran parmy, et mettés le poisson avec le boullon, et du beurre frais ou salé. (VT XV 179)

67. Maquerel

Maquerel frais entre en saison en Juin, jàsoit-ce que l'en en treuve dès le mois de Mars. Affaitiez par l'oreille, puis l'essuiez d'un net torchon, et sans laver aucunement soit mis rostir, puis mengié à la cameline ou à sel menu. (MP 196)

68. De allectibus et sardis implendis

Ad implendum allectia uel sardellas, ponantur in acqua calida remotis dapitibus et spinis, ita quod sint diuisa per dorsum. Postea, tere maioranam, ros marinum, saluiam, bonas species, crocum et pulpas alicorum piscium. Et imple de predicta impletura allectia uel sardellas, ita quod corium siue cutis sit es parte impleture, et pars exterior sit interius; et coniunge dictas partes insimul, ita quod dicta impleta sit in medio. Postea, frige cum oleo. Et possunt comedi cum succo citrangulorum. (Lc 415)

69. Pesce arrostito

Se vuoi pesce arrostito in su gradella. Togli lo pesce, lavalo e poi lo fendi e getta su della salina. Togli buone spezie, getta sulla buccia di fuori, ripiegala si che le buccie stiano insieme, metti buone erbe ollienti tra buccia, legalo con un filo, ungi lo pesce con frasuccia di salvia, ponlo in su brascia senza fumo, volgi spesso e togli o' vuoi salsa o vuoi salina. (Gu 33)

70. Ton

Ton est un poisson qui est trouvé en la mer ou estans marinaulx des parties de Languedoc, et n'a aucunes areste fors l'eschine, et a dure pel, et se doit cuire en eaue et se mengue au poivre jaunet. (MP 196)

71. Soglie

Vogliono essere fritte, e di sopra gli buttarai un poco di sal trito, di suco di naranci o dell'agresto, et del petrosillo tagliato pure assai. (Ma 186)

72. Rax

Rax uel canis marinus perfrustra incisus aliquantulum in acqua dequoquitur; post, deponitur et a pelliculis mundatur; et iterum in acqua monda dequoquitur donec satis fit. Et cum aleata comeditur. (Tr 390)

73. Morua

Morua in aqua dequoquitur et cum synapi comeditur uel cum aleata, hoc modo: teruntur allea et mica panis et cum lacte amigdalarum uel nucum distemperatur. Et ponitur in cepis in oleo frixatis cum morua et aliquantulum bulliri permitatur. (Tr 390)

74. Seppie

Se vuoi seppie fate come funghi. Togli la seppia, lavala bene, fendila, tranne fuori lo savore nero che v'e entro, e lo latte per se, e poi la lava anche e mettila a bollire: e quando hae bollito uno buono bollore, trae fuori, minuzzala come funghi e mettile nel pentolo a soffrigere coll'olio dolce, e metti buoni erbucci e alietti e porro trito e pesta buone spezie: minuzza il latte che ne traesti, mettivil entro e mettivi lo savore che v'era entro nero e fa cuocere forte, imperò c'hae gran cocitura; e ponvi su li testi caldi e mesta spesso sì che non s'appicchi. (Gu 34)

75. Ostriche

Ostriche si cocono sopra la brascia viva et quando s'aprono sonno cotte, et così si possono magnare. Et se lo voli altramente cavale fora di quella sua cortice, et frigile un pochetto in l'olio, et metterali di sopra dell'agresto et de spetie forti. (Ma 189)

76. Torta d'agli

Toy li agli e mondali e lessali; quando sono cocti metili a moglio in aqua freda e poy pistali e metili zafarano e formazo assay che sia fresco e lardo batuto e specie dolze e forte e distempera con ova e mitili ova passa e poy fa la torta. (Fr 55)

77. Torta de schalogne o de cepolle, etc.

Se tu voy fare torta de queste do cosse, toy quale tu voy e fay ben allessare. Pone prima l'aqua fuora ben con stamegna e po' le bati finalmente e toy lardo fino e batillo bene; toy l'ova e caxo freschο e zafarano e bati insiema e fay la torta. (Fr 54)

78. Torta de herbe

Se tu voy fare torta de herbe per XII persone, toi VI cassi grandi e toy granda quantità de herbe zoè blede, petrosemolo, spinaze, menta, e do libre de lardo salato e octo ova; toy queste herbe ben necte e ben batute e ben spremute del sugo, toy il caxo e trialo con herbe bene grosso tagliato e toy lo lardo che tu ay ben batuto al più che tu poy e toy l'ova che tu ay e mescola questo cosse insema e miti dentro do croste in el testo e fay zalla la crosta de sovra questa torta molto vole essere grasso e assay caxo e molte herbe e voy essere voa e se voy per men persone, toy le cosse a questa mesura. (Fr 50)

79. Pour faire une tourte

Prenez quatre pongnées de bettes, deux poignées de percil, une pongnée de cerfueil, un brain de fanoil et deux pongnées d'espinoches, et les eslisez et lavez en eau froide, puis hachiez bien menu: puis broyez de deux paires de frommages, c'est assavoir du mol et du möien, et puis mettez des oeufs avec ce, moyen et aubun, et les broyez parmi le frommage; puis mettez les herbes dedans le mortier et broyez tout ensemble, et aussi mettez-y de la pouldre fine. Ou en lieu de ce aiez premièrement broyé au mortier deux cloches de gingembre, et sur ce broyez vos frommages, oeufs et herbes, et puis gettez du vieil frommage de presse ou autre gratuisé dessus celles herbes, et portez au four, et puis faites faire une tartre et la mengez chaude. (MP 218)

80. Tourtel

Prener perresi, mente, bedtes, espinoches, letuees, marjolienne, basilique et pilieux, et tout soit broyer ensemble en ung mortiez et destranmper d'aigue clère et espreignez le jus; et rompez oeuf grant foison avec le jus et y mecter poudre de gigimbre, de cannelle et poivre long et fin fromaige gratusiez, et du sel, tout batez ensemble; et puis faicte vostre paste bien teine pour mectre en vostre bacin, et la grandeur du bacin et puis chassez bien vostre bacin, et puis y mecter du sain de porc dedans et puis vostre paste après dedans le dit bacin, et mecter vostre bacin sur les charbons et remecter dedans le paste du sain de porc; et quant il sera fonduz, mectez vostre grain dedans vostre paste et le couvrez de l'aultre bacin et mecter du feu dessus comme dessoubz et lessez vostre tourtel ung pol sechiez, puis descouvrés le bacin dessus, et mecter sur vostre torte par bone manière V moyeux d'euf et de la fine poudre, puis remecter vostre bacin dressez comme devant et le lessez po à pol cuire et à petit feu de charbon, et regarder souvent qu'elle ne cuise tropt; puis mecter du succre dessus a dressiez. (VT Maz Scul 232)

81. Torta bolognese

Pigliarai altretanto cascio como è ditto nel capitolo di sopra de la torta biancha, et grattalo. Et nota che quanto è più grasso il cascio tanto è meglio; poi habi de le vietole, petrosillo et maiorana; et nettate et lavate che l'avrai, battile molto bene con un coltello, et mittirale inseme con questo cascio, menandole et mescolandole con le mani tanto che siano bene incorporate, agiongendovi quattro ova, et del pepe quanto basti, et un pocho di zafrano, item di bono strutto overo botiro frescho, mescolando et incorporando tutte queste cose molto bene inseme como ho ditto. Et questo pieno mettirai in una padella con una crosta di sotto et una di sopra, daendoli il focho temperatamente; et quando ti pare che sia meza cotta, perché para più bella, con un roscio d'ovo battuto con un pocho di zafrano la farai gialla. Et acconoscere quando ella è cotta ponerai mente quando la crosta di sopra si levarà et alzarà in suso, che allora starà bene et poterala levare dal focho. (Ma 59)

82. Torta comune

Habi di bon caso con octo ova et con bon grasso di porcho o di vitello, overo del buttiro, dell'uva passa integra, del zenzevro, de la cannella, et un pocho di pan gratato, con un pocho di brodo grasso che sia giallo de zafrano et conciare la farai como di sopra è ditto de la torta bianca. (Ma 163)

83. Pastés de connis

Quand sont vieulx, doivent estre mis par pièces, et les jeunes entiers, et du lart menu haché dessus; et pour espices, clou, gingembre, graine et poyvre. (VT XV 171)

84. Del pastello dei capretti

Altramente
Togli uno capretto minuzzato, o polli smembrati, e friggili col lardo fresco e cipolle minuzzate, e erbe odorifere trite con zaffarano, e tuorla d'ova, e distempera fortemente, e mesta con ova, e metti tutto in uno vaso sopra la bragia, e volgi spesso, fine che sia spesso: giongivi spezie abbastanza; colorarlo con tuorla d'ova, e fà la forma de la pasta, e rinchiudi tutto: fà cuocere, e mangia. (Za 57–58)

85. Pasté en pot de mouton

Prenez de la cuisse, et gresse ou mouelle de beuf ou de veel haché menu et oignons menus hachiés, et faictes boulir et cuire en un pot bien couvert a bien petit de boulon de char ou autre eaue, puis mettez boulir dedans espices, et un petit de vinaigre pour aiguiser, et dréciez en un plat. (MP 148)

86. Pastés de veau

Prenés veau et gresse de beuf, et hachés tout ensemble bien menu, et les espices qui appartiennent sont gingembre, synamome; et, en façon d'hyver, y soit mis fromage fin. (VT XV 169)

87. Torta manfreda bona e vantagiata

Toy ventre e figatelii de polli e toy panza de porcho e pesta insiema con coltello, poy mitige pever; habii uno lavezo e fali frizer, poy tray fuora, faili arefredare, poy mitige ova e fay la crosta, poy mitila in la padella e faila coxere adassio. (Fr 57)

88. Torta ungaresca per XII persone

Toy uno capone ben grasso e toy uno lombolo de porco grande e do cepole grosse e meza libra de specie dolze e fine e toy tre libre d'onto fresco che non sia salato e toy tanta farina che sia tre pani, la migliore, che tu poi avere; e toy lo caponi e'l lombolo del porco [e] fane morselletti e de le do cepole fane morselletti e meti queste cosse a sofriger in lo songiazo fresco [in] quantità; e de le dite dolze e zafarano assay e un poco de sala; e quando è ben sofrito mitige un bichiero d'aqua ch'el se coca senza compimento, e toli la farina e destruta con aqua fresca insalata con un pocho de salina e menala molto forte, e quando è ben menato, toy uno testo de ramo ben stagnato e onzilo ben de quasto lardo fresco che tu ay. Toy la pasta e menala e sotiliala con una mescola e fala sotille, e siate due a trae sotile a foglio con lardo e fane infina a XVIII fogli, et postea toy questo batuto de capon e de altre cosse fane uno solo suso questa metà, e poni altre tante fogle sopra quasto solo ben inaffiato ziaschuno pe si de lardo e fa una crosta de sopra per vardia. Questa torta vole poco foco sotto e bon foco di sopra, e poy fare per più, o per men, toiando le cosse a questa mesura. (Fr 59)

89. Torta di anguille

Scorticarai l'anguilla et tagliaraila in pezoli larghi doi dita, facendola un pocho lessare, che non sia troppo cotta. Et farai del lacte di amandole bello et biancho, passando le ditte amandole con bono agresto et con acqua rosata per la stamegna, et che 'l ditto lacte sia ben spesso, cioè stritto. Et pistarai un pocha de uva passa molto bene con tre o quattro fiche secche. Poi prenderai de li spinaci rompendoli menuti con le mani per traverso, et frigerali un pocho nell'oglio, agiongendovi un pocho di petrosillo tagliato menuto, item una oncia di uva passa integra, et una oncia di pignoli mondi et necti e del zenzevero et de la canella et del pepe et del zafrano discretamente secundo la quantità che voli fare. Et tutta questa compositione mescolando con le mani incorporarai molto bene inseme et mettirai la crosta di sotto in la padela, et dentro li concirai questo tal pieno et compositione facendone prima un solo sopra la ditta crosta, et poi un altro solo de anguilla; cosi di grado in grado, piacendoti, poterai fare tanto che sia fornita questa compositione; et di sopra gli metterai l'altra crosta facendola cocere molto adagio, dandoli il focho temperatamente di sotto et di sopra. Et quando serà meza cotta pigliarai un pocha de agresta et d'acqua rosata con del zuccharo; et fa' de molti buchi in la crosta di sopra perche queste cose possino penetrare, li metterai di sopra lasciandola anchora tanto al focho, che sia molto ben cotta. (Ma 165)

90. Se vuoi torta d'anguille fresche

Togli l'anguille, lessale a mezzo e mettivi a cuocere con esse pretisemoli e menta e persa, poi fa affreddare e poi le fila con mano. Getta via il cuoio e le spine. Togli noci fine, mondale coll'acqua bollita, poi le pesta uno poco. E togli una libra di mandorle, fanne latte e cuocilo tanto che sia bene ispesso e ponlo a freddare e sia giuncada. Poi metti queste cose in tegghie, fa crosta e l'erbe siano battute, e metti su spezie forti, zaffarano e XII dattari tritati. E quando è cotta, trannela; e se non fossono grasse, mettivi olio fine. (Gu 39–40)

91. Pasticcio d'anguilla

Habi l'anguilla scorticata e netta, et volendo altro pesce simelmente concio et netto, et tagliarane pezoli larghi doi deta; habi anchora di bon grasso et lacte di pesce, et tagliato menuto lo mettirai con li sopra ditti pezoli. Item prenderai un pocha di menta et di petrosillo tagliati ben menuti. Item una oncia de uva passa, de la canella, zenzevero, del pepe, et di garofani pesti. Et tutte queste cosè molto bene mescolarai et incorporarai inseme. Poi habi la pasta sua ben fatta et stascionata, et dentro mettirali questa tale compositione; agiognendoli sopra un pocho di bon oglio il metterai a cocere, et quando è presso che cotta habi doi once d'amandole nette et ben piste, distemperate con agresto et passate per la stamegna, et mettendole dentro vi sopragiognerai nel sopra ditto pastello mettendogli ancora un pocho de zafrano; et anchora di novo lassarai bollire et cocere un pocho più tutte queste cose inseme, tanto che sia cotto molto bene, che così vole essere. Et nota che in tempo di magnare ova poterai mettere et distemperare con l'agresto, inseme con l'altre cose sopra dicte, doi rosci d'ova che gli dirando molto bono et non serà niente piggiore. (Ma 169–70)

92. Pastelli secchi

Pastelli secchi facti con pesce sano. Piglia lo pesce netto et concio, et findilo d'ogni lato presso a la schina un pocho, et con sale et bone spetie mescolate inseme salerai molto bene tutto questo pesce dentro et di fora. Poi haverai una pasta un pocho grossa et dentro gli conciarai et ligarai il ditto pesce, et cocilo nel forno bene ad ascio che sia ben cotto. (Ma 170)

93. Zucche

Habi le zucche et mondale molto bene, et grattale como gratti il cascio, et farale un pocho bollire in un bono brodo, overo in bon latte. Et pigliarai tanta quantità di cascio frescho quanto e ditto in li sopra ditti capitoli, giongendovi con esse et miscolandovi un pocho di cascio vecchio che sia bono. Et pigliarai una libra di bona ventresca di porco, overo una tetta di vitella cotta molto bene allessa et battuta assai col coltello. Et volendo poterai in loco de queste doi cose sopra ditte, se più ti piace, usare il butiro, overo il strutto, giongendovi meza libra di zuccharo, un pocho di zenzevero et di cannella, con un bicchieri di lacte, et sei ova. Et como ti pare che le predditte zucche siano cotte, tirale fora dell'acqua, et passale per la stamegnia; et farai gialla questa compositione col sesanime; poi la mitterai in una padella solo con una pasta sottile di sotto et non di sopra, et darali il focho temperatamente di sotto et di sopra, et quando ti pare meza cotta gli gitterai di sopra, in loco de la crosta, de le lasagne ben minute. Et quando serà cotta abastanza vi metterai suso di bono zuccharo et acqua rosata. (Ma 160)

94. Torta bianca

Piglia una libra et meza di bono cascio frescho, et taglialo menuto, et pistalo molto bene, et piglia dodici o quindici albume o bianchi d'ova, et macinali molto bene con questo cascio, agiogendovi meza libra di zuccharo, et meza oncia di zenzevero del più biancho che possi havere, similemente meza libra di strutto di porcho bello et biancho, o in loco di strutto altretanto botiro bono et frescho, item de lo lacte competentemente, quanto basti, che serà assai un terzo di bocchale. Poi farai la pasta overo crosta in la padella, sottile come vole essere, et mectiraila a cocere dandoli il focho a bell'agio di sotto et di sopra; et farai che sia di sopra un pocho colorita per el caldo del focho; et quando ti pare cotta, cacciala fore de la padella, et di sopra vi metterai del zuccharo fino et di bona acqua rosata. (Ma 158)

95. Tartara alla senese

Piglia vinti amandole e falle ben bianche he pistale quanto se po. Da poi habi meza libra de zucaro, XII ova he una fogletta di latte he doi quatani de canella he sale asufficientia he mezo quarto de probatura fresca tanto pistata che piu non bisogna pistarla. Dapoi inbrata una tiela de butiro he poi infarinala he desopra gli ponerai la dita compositione. Et pone la tiella sive padella lontano dal foco, coperta, cum foco moderato. Et nota che in la predita compositione ci potrai ponere uno ramaiolo de lasagne cote in bono brodo. He como sia cotto pone desopra zucaro he aqua rosata. (Bü 49v–50)

96. Diriola

Conciarai la pasta in forma d'un pastello et impiela ben di farina che stia deritta cocendola in la padella tanto che sia un poco secca. Et facto questo cava fora la ditta farina et prendirai alcuni rosci d'ova, de lo lacte, del zuccaro, et de la cannella. Et facta di queste cose una compositione la mettirai in la dicta pasta facendola cocere al modo de una torta, movendola tutta volta et volgendola spesso col cocchiaro. Et como tu vidi che incomincia a pigliarsi sopragiogneli un poca d'acqua rosata, et volta bene collo cocchiaro. Et quando serà fornita di prendere, serà cotta. Et nota che non vole cocere troppo et vole tremare como una ionchata. (Ma 172)

97. Pastés de poires crues

Mises sur bout en pasté, et emply le creux de sucre à trois grosses poires comme ung quarteron de sucre, bien couverte, et dorée d'oeufz ou de saffran, et mis au four. (VT XV 175)

98. Torta in balconata per dodeze persone

Toy farina più biancha che tu poy avere in quantità de tre libre e toy do onze de zucharo e toy una libra de mandole e XXXVI noce bone e meza libra de uva passa e XXV datali e mezo quarto de garofali e toy bona quantità de late de mandole, toy la farina che tu ay destruta con aqua sì che sia ben spesso e toy la padella e onzella ben de olio e de questa farina fassi crosta ad una polverizata de zucaro e delle dite specie, e toy la noce possa li datali minuzati e l'uva passa ben lavata e garofali russi e tute queste croste su chaschauna la suva parte e poni crosta sopra tute queste cose e sì che sia torta. (Fr 53)

99. Agliata

Agliata a ogni carne, toy l'aglio e coxilo sotto la braxa, poi pestalo bene e mitili aglio crudo, e una molena de pan, e specie dolçe, e brodo; et maxena ogni cossa insema e fala un pocho bolire e dala chalda. (Fr 2)

100. Agliata bianca

Piglia de le amandole monde molto bene et falle pistare, et quando sonno mezze piste metti dentro quella quantità d'aglio che ti pare, et inseme le farai molto bene pistare buttandogli dentro un pocha d'acqua frescha perché non facciano olio. Poi pigliarai una mollicha di pane bianco e mettirala a mollo nel brodo magro di carne o di pesce secundo i tempi; et questa agliata poterai servire et accomodare a tutte le stagioni grasse et magre como ti piacerà. (Ma 157)

101. Agliata pavonazza

Sequirai l'ordine del capitolo sopra scripto, excepto che non bisogna gli metti brodo, ma pigliarai dell'uva negra et con le mani la romperai molto bene in una pignatta, o altro vaso; et faralo bollire per meza hora; poi collerai questo mosto, col quale distemperarai l'agliata; et il simele si pò fare con le cerase. Et questa agliata si pò dare al tempo di carne, o di pesce, como si vole. (Ma 157)

102. Aleata

Aleata, hoc modo: teruntur allea et mica panis et cum lacte amigdalarum uel nucum distemperatur. (Tr 390)

103. Sapor celeste de estate

Piglia de li moroni salvatiche che nascono in le fratte, et un poche de amandole ben piste, con un pocho di zenzevero. Et queste cose distemperarai con agresto et passarale per la stamegnia. (Ma 156)

104. Salsa viridis

Salsa viridis hoc modo fit: accipe zinziber, cinamomum, piper, nucem muscatam, gariofilos, petrosillum atque salviam. Terantur primo species, post herbe et ponatur tertia pars salvie et petrosilum, et qui voluerit 3 uel 2 spice de aleis. Distemperentur aceto vel agresta. Nota quod in omni salsamento et condimento, sal est apponendum, et mica panis ad inspissandum. (Tr 394)

105. Salza verde a capretto e ad altre carni alesse

Toy petrosemolo e zenzevro e garofali e fiore de canella e un poco de sale e pista ogni cossa inseme e distempera con bono aceto; fay che sia temperato e non vole stare che se guasta. (Fr 44)

106. Savore camelino optimo

A ffare savore camelino optimo, toy mandole monde e masenale e colali, toy uva passa e canella e garofani e un pocho de molena de pan e masena ogni cossa in seme e distempera con agresta ed è fato. (Fr 48)

107. Cameline

Nota *que à Tournay, pour faire cameline, l'en broye gingembre, canelle et saffren et demye noix muguette: destrempé de vin, puis osté du mortier; puis aiez mie de pain blanc, sans bruler, trempé en eaue froide et broyez au mortier, destrempez de vin et coulez, puis boulez tout, et mettez au derrain du succre roux: et ce est cameline d'yver. Et en esté la font autelle, mais elle n'est point boulie.* (MP 230)

108. Poivre noir

Broiés gingembre et pain brullé et poivre, deffaites de vin aigre et de verjus et faites boullir. (VT BN Scul 227)

109. Poivre jaunet ou aigret

Prenez gingembre, safren, puis preignel'en pain rosty deffait d'eaue de char (et encores vault mieux la meigre eaue de choulx), puis boulir, et au boulir mettre le vinaigre. (MP 232)

110. De la peverada

Togli pane abbrusticato, un poco di zaffarano che non colori, spezie e fegati triti e pesti nel mortaio, e distempera con aceto o vino e bruodo predetto, e fàllo dolce o acetoso, come tu vuoli. E tale peverata si può dare con carne domestica, salvatica e con pesce. (Za 42)

111. Une jensse

Pour donner entendement a celluy qui fera ledit jensse si prenne de beau et bon pain de bouche grant quantité selon ce qui en vouldra fayre et si le gratuse bien et appoint sur ung beau mantil; puis prenne une oulle belle clere et necte et coulle dedans du boullon gras du beuf et du mouston, et advise qu'il ne soit tropt salé; et puis prenne des oefs et mesle avecques ledit pain et puis cela mecte dedans ledit boullon doulcement en menant tousjours a une belle cuillier de bois; et aussy mecte ses espices dedans, c'est assavoir gingibre blanc, grane de Paradis, et ung pou de poyvre, et du saffran pour luy donner couleur, et si l'agouste de verjust; et si face tout ce boullir ensemble et puis en drece. (Ch 182)

112. Del savore con la grua

Togli il fegato de la grua e arrostilo sulla bragia; poi piglia bone spezie, maggiorana, zaffarano e il detto fegatello, e pesta bene ogni cosa insieme, e due tuorla d'ova metti con essi, e distempera con buono vino e un poco d'aceto; poi mettivi un poco di mosto cotto, acciò che sia acro dolce.

Savori per papari et per porchetta
Fa come detto è di sopra, eccetto il vino cotto. Et il grasso che cola del paparo, mettilo nel savore. Simile fa colla porcella arrostita; e se non vuoli fare tale savore fà salsa verde. (Za 80)

113. Sapor de uva

Habi de la bona uva negra et rompila molto bene in un vaso, rompendo con essa un pane o mezo secundo la quantità che voi fare, et mettevi un pocho di bono agresto, overo aceto, perché l'uva non sia tanto dolce. Et queste cose farai bollire al focho per spatio di meza hora, agiongendovi de la cannella et zenzevero, et altre bone spetiarie. (Ma 155)

114. Sapor de progna secche

Habi le progne e mittile a moglio nel vino rosso, et cavagli fora l'ossa, et pistarale molto bene con un poche de amandole non mondate, et un pocho di pane rostito, o bruschulato, stato a moglio nel preditto vino dove erano le progne. Et tutte queste cose pistarai inseme con un pocho d'agresto, et de questo vino sopra ditto, et un pocha di sapa, overo zuccharo, che serrebe molto meglio, distemperarai et passarai per le stamegnia mettendovi dentro di bone spetie, spetialmente de la cannella. (Ma 154)

115. Moustarde

Se vous voulez faire provision de moustarde pour garder longuement, faites-la en vendenges de moulx doulx. Et aucuns dient que le moust soit bouly. Item, *se vous voulez faire moustarde en un village à haste, broyez du senevé en un mortier et deffaictes de vinaigre, et coulez par l'étamine; et se vous la voulez tantost faire parer, mettez-la en un pot devant le feu.* Item, *et se vous la voulez faire bonne et à loisir, mettez le senevé tremper par une nuit en bon vinaigre, puis le faites bien broyer au moulin, et bien petit à petit destremper de vinaigre: et se vous avez des espices qui soient de remenant de gelée, de claré, d'ypocras ou de saulces, si soient broyées avec et après la laissier parer.* (MP 229)

116. Civés d'oeufs

Pochez oeufs à l'uille, puis aiez oignons par rouelles cuis, et les friolez à l'uille, puis mettez boulir en vin, vertjus et vinaigre, et faite boulir tout ensemble; puis mettez en chascune escuelle trois ou quatre oeufs, et gettez vostre brouet dessus, et soit non liant. (MP 174)

117. Soupe en moustarde

Prennés des oeufs pochiés en huille tous entiers sans esquaille, puis prennés d'icelle huille, du vin, de l'eau, de oingnons fris en huille, boullés tout ensemble; prennés lèches de pain halé sur le gril, puis en faites morssiaux quarrés, et metés boulir aveques; puis hastés vostre boullon, et ressuiés vostre soupe; puis la verssés en un plat; puis de la moustarde dedans vostre boullon, et la boullir; puis metés vos souppes en vos escuelles, et metés dessus. (VT BN Scul 150)

118. De ovis, primo de implendis

Ad faciendum ova plena, findas unumquodque per medium, dum fuerint bene cocta et hoc integra. Tunc extrahe rubedi nem et, acceptis maiorana, safrano, gariofilis, distempera cum rubedine predictorum ovorum; et pista fortiter, adiuncto parum de caseo. Per singula octo ova, distempera unum ovum crudum. Hoc facto, de isto sapore imple albedines ovorum. Et frige cum bono lardo; et cum agresta comede. (Lc 412)

119. Lait de vache lyé

Soit pris le lait à eslite, comme dit est cy-devant ou chappitre des potages, et soit bouly une onde, puis mis hors du feu: puis y filez par l'estamine grant foison de moieux d'oeufs et ostez le germe, et puis broyez une cloche de gingembre et saffren, et mettez dedans, et tenez chaudement emprès le feu; puis ayez des oeufs pochés en eaue et mettez deux ou trois oeufs pochés en l'escuelle, et le lait dessus. (MP 175)

120. Ova in forma de raffioli

Farai una pasta al modo de le lasagne che non sia sottile né molto tenera, et rompevi dentro dell'ova fresche, buttandogli sopra del zuccharo et de le spetie dolci con un pochetto di sale, ad uno ad uno ligarai queste ova ne la ditta pasta al modo che faresti i raffioli, et falle allessare o frigere como ti piace. Ma meglio seranno fritte. (Ma 183)

121. Frictata

Battirai l'ova molto bene, et inseme un poco de acqua et un poco di lacte per farla un poco più morbida, item un poco di bon caso grattato, et cocirala in botiro perché sia più grassa. Et nota che per farla bona non vole esser voltata né molto cotta. Et volendola fare verde, prendirai similmente le cose sopra ditte giognendovi del suco de queste herbe, cioè vieta, petrosillo in bona quantità, borragine, menta, maiorana, salvia in minor quantità, passando il ditto suco; poi cavarai piste le herbe molto bene per la stamegna. Et fare in un altro modo frittata con herbe, prendirai le sopra ditte herbe et tagliate menute le frigerai un poco in un bon botiro o oglio, mescolandole con l'ova et l'altre cose sopra ditte farai la frittata et cocirala diligentemente che sia bene staionata et non troppo cotta. (Ma 180)

122. Sic fac fritatem de pomeranciis

Recipe ova percussa, cum pomeranciis ad libitum tuum, et extrahe inde sucum, et mitte ad illa ova cum zucaro; post recipe oleum olive, vel segimine, et fac califieri in patella, et mitte illa ova intus. Et erit pro ruffianis et leccatricibus. (Bo 738)

123. Pour gelée

Prenés gigotz ou piez de veau ce que pourrés finer, et les mettés bouillir en vin blanc et du grain qui y appartient. Après quant les gigotz ou piez de veau seront comme demys cuitz, prenés cochons par pièces, et poussins par moytiers, et bien nectoyés, et lavés, et jeunes lappereaulx, qui en pourra finer. Puis prenés gingembre et graine, ung peu mastis, et foyson saffran, et vin aigre par raison. Et quant le grain sera cuit, vous prendrés le boullon, et le mettrés en ung pot sur le feu de charbon. Se la gelée est trop grasse, prenés aulbins d'eufz et les mettés au boullon, quant il vouldra boullir; et, quant il bouldra, ayés toille toute preste pour le faire couler; tandis qu'elle coulera, vous mettrés le grain en platz, c'est à dire le cochon, le lapereau et la poulaille, et puis quant le grain sera mys en plats, vous les mettrés en une cave, et getterés le boullon sur le grain en chescun plat. (VT XV 156)

124. De la gelatina di pesce

Togli buono vino con un poco d'aceto, e, sciumato che sia quando bolle, mettivi dentro il pescie, e, cotto, cavalne, e fà bullire il vino tanto, che torni a la terza parte: poi mettivi dentro zaffarano e altre spezie, con alloro: poi colato il vino, mettivi spico, e lassa che sia freddo; poi metti, sopra'l pesce, nel catino. (Za 28)

125. Buignets de mouelle

Et qui en veult faire buignets de mouelle, convient la reffaire en la manière[*], puis prendre de la fleur et des moyeux d'oeufs et faire la paste, prendre chascun morcel de mouelle et frire au sain. (MP 224)

[*] Mouelle de beuf qui est reffaite, c'est à dire que l'en met icelle mouelle dedans une cuillier percée, et met-l'en icelle cuillier percée avec la mouelle dedans le bouillon du pot à la char, et l'y laisse-l'en autant comme l'en laisseroit un poucin plumé en l'eaue chaude pour reffaire; et puis la met-l'en en eaue froide, puis couppe-l'en la mouelle et arrondis-l'en comme gros jabets ou petites boulettes. (MP 223)

126. Pipefarces

Prenez des moyeux d'oeufs et de la fleur et du sel, et un pou de vin, et batez fort ensemble, et du frommage tranchié par lesches, et puis toulliez les lesches de frommage dedans la paste, et puis la frisiez dedans une paelle de fer et du sain dedens. (MP 227)

127. Mistembec

Mistembec hoc modo fit: accipe de pasta tritici lavata, quantum voleris, et aliquantulum de amido in aqua tepida dissoluto; de quo distemper predictam pastam ut fiat ad modum sorbitii; et facias descendere per scutellam in fundo et in latere foramen habende, et fac descendere in oleo fervido vel sagimine porci, diversas formulas ad placitum pertrahendo. Quibus per decoctionem induratis, et ad hoc calidis existentibus, proice in syrupo de zuccaro aut de melle facto, et protinus remove. (Tr 391)

128. Rissoles au commun

L'en les fait de figues, roisins, pommes hastées et noix pelées pour contrefaire le pignolat, et pouldre d'espices: et soit la paste très bien ensaffrenée, puis soient frites en huille. S'il y convient lieure, amidon lie et ris aussi. (MP 225)

129. Fritelle da Imperadore Magnifici

Se tu voy fare fritelle da Imperadore, toi la chiara de l'ova e fete de formazo frescho, e batille cum la chiara de l'ova, e mitige un pocho di farina e pignoli mondi. Toy la padella cum assay onto, falo bolire e fay le fritelle. Quando sono cocte, polverizali ben zucharo e tienli caldi, etc. (Fr 14)

130. Bianco mangiare al modo catalano

Per farce dece menestre habi una libra de amandole ben monde et ben piste, le quali distemperate con brodo di pollo grosso, o altro bon brodo, passandole per la stamegnia le mectirai à bollire in un vaso ben netto, agiongendovi doi once di farina de riso stemperata et passata con il lacte dell'amandole; et lassarai bollire per spatio de una hora movendo et menando sempre con il cocchiaro, agiongendovi una meza libra e un petto di cappone ben ben trito et pisto, il quale sia stato cotto dal principio nel dicto lacte. Et quando tutta questa compositione serà cotta tu ve agiongerai un pocha d'acqua rosata, et facendo le menestre tu mettirai di sopra de le spetie dolci. (Ma 152)

131. De' blanmangieri

Togli petti di galline, cotti, e, posti sopra una taola, falli sfilare piu sottili che puoi. Intanto lava il riso e sciugalo, e fànne farina, e cernila con setaccio o stamigna; poi distemperala detta farina del riso con latte di capra o di pecora o d'amandole, e metti a bollire in una pentola ben lavata e netta; e quando comincia a bollire, mettivi dentro i detti petti sfilati, con zuccaro bianco e lardo bianco fritto; e guardalo dal fumo, e fàllo bullire temperatamente senza impeto di fuoco, si che sia ispesso, come suole essere il riso. E quando tu menestrarai, mettivi suso zuccaro trito o pesto, e lardo fritto. Se tu vuoli, puolilo fare col riso intero da per sè, apparicchiato e ordinato col latte di capra, a modo oltramontano; e, quando tu il dai, mettivi su amandole soffritte nel lardo, e zenzovo bianco tagliato. (Za 46–47)

132. Froumentée

Premièrement, vous convient monder vostre froument ainsi comme l'en fait orge mondé, puis sachiez que pour dix escuelles convient une livre de froument mondé, lequel on treuve aucunes fois sur les espiciers tout mondé pour un blanc la livre. Eslisiezle et le cuisiez en eaue dès le soir, et le laissiez toute nuit couvert emprès le feu en eaue comme tiède, puis le trayez et eslisez. Puis boulez du lait en une paelle et ne le mouvez point, car il tourneroit: et incontinent, sans attendre, le mettez en un pot qu'il ne sente l'airain; et aussi, quant il est froit, si ostez la cresme de dessus afin que icelle cresme ne face tourner la froumentée, et de rechief faites boulir le lait et une petit de froument avec, mais qu'il n'y ait guères de froument; puis prenez moyeux d'oeufs et les coulez, c'est assavoir pour chascun sextier de lait un cent d'oeufs, puis prenez le lait boulant, et batre les oeufs avec le lait, puis reculer le pot et getter les oeufs, et reculer; et se l'en veoit qu'il se voulsist tourner, mettre le pot en plaine paelle d'eaue. A jour de poisson l'en prend lait: à jour de chair, du boullon de la char; et convient metter saffran se le oeufs ne jaunissent assez: item demie cloche de gingembre. (MP 210)

133. Riso nella migliore maniera

Se vuoli fare riso nella migliore maniera che fare si puote per XII persone, togli due libre di riso e due libre di mandorle, e meça libra di çucchero. E togli il riso bene mondo e bene lavato, e togli le mandorle bene monde e bene lavate e bene macinate e bene colate con istamigna. Togli il riso, e metti a fuoco in acqua chiara, e quando è levato buono bollore e bene schiumato, colane di fuori l'acqua incontanente, e mettivi suso quantitade di latte di mandorle; e fallo cuocere in sulla brascia da la lunge, e mestalo spesso intorno che non si rompa. E quando s'asciuga, arrogivi suso del latte delle mandorle, e quando è presso che cotto, mettivi suso quantità di çucchero. Questa vivanda vuol essere biancha e molto spessa. E quando è cotta, poni çucchero sopra le scodelle. Se vuoli fare per più persone o per meno, togli le cose a questa ragione. (Mo 22)

134. Tailliz

Prenez figues, roisins et lait d'amendes bouly, eschaudez, galettes et crouste de pain blanc couppé menu par petiz morceaulx quarrez et faictes boullir vostre lait, et saffren pour luy donner couleur, et succre, et puis mettez boullir tout ensemble tant qu'il soit bien lyant pour taillier; et mettre par escuelles. (VT Vat Scul 118)

135. Mandorlata cotta

Se vuoli fare mandorlata cotta per XII persone, togli tre libre di mandorle e meça libra di çucchero; et togli le mandorle ben lavate e bene monde e bene macinate e stemperate con acqua chiara, poca, e bene colate, e mettile a bollire in uno vasello che bolla tanto che torni spesso; e metti per scodelle çucchero. Se vuoli fare per più persone o per meno, togli le cose a questa medesima ragione. (Mo 22)

136. Marzapane

Monda l'amandole molto bene, et pistale quanto più sia possibile perché non fanno a passare per la stamegna. Et nota per fare le ditte amandole più bianche, più gustose et più dolci a la bocca, se vogliono tenere a mollo nell'acqua fresca per un dì et una nocte o tanto più, che da se stesse premendole con le ditte se mondino. Et pistandole le bagnarai con un pocha d'acqua rosata, perché non facciano olio. Et se vol fare bona la ditta torta, metteragli a peso equale tanto zuccaro siano quanto amandole, cioè una libra dell'uno et una dell' altro, o più o mancho como ti piace, et metterali anchora una oncia o doi d'acqua rosata bona; et tutte queste cose incorporarai molto bene inseme. Poi pigliarai di cialdoni o nevole fatte col zuccaro, et bagnate prima con l'acqua rosata; distemperarale sopra el fondo de la padella, et dentro gli mettirai questa compositione o pieno sopra ditto. Et disteso et spianato che l'haverai, un'altra volta si vole bagnare un pochetto con l'acqua rosata, sopragiogendoli ancora di sopra di bono zuccharo spolverizato. Et spianato bene per tutto con il zuccharo la farai cocere nel forno overo al focho come l'altre torte molto ad ascio, havendo bona avertenza a dargli il focho temperato et di rivederla spesso perché non s'abrusciasse. Ricordandoti che simile torta di marzapane più tosto vole essere un pocho bassetta et sottile, che troppo alta et spessa. (Ma 168)

137. Per far caliscioni

Prenderai simil pieno o compositione quale è la sopraditta del marzapane, et apparichiarai la sua pasta, la quale impastarai con zuccharo et acqua rosata; et distendi la ditta pasta a modo che si volesse fare ravioli, gli metterai di questo pieno facendoli grandi et mezani o piccioli como ti pare. Et havendo qualche forma de ligno ben lavorata con qualche gentileza et informandoli et premendoli di sopra pariranno più belli a vedere. Poi li farai cocere in la padella come il marzapane havendo bona diligentia che non s'ardino. (Ma 169)

138. Crespes

Prenez de la fleur et déstrempez d'oeufs tant moyeux comme aubuns, osté le germe, et le deffaites d'eaue, et y mettez du sel et du vin, et batez longuement ensemble; puis mettez du sain sur le feu en une petite paelle de fer, ou moitié sain ou moitié beurre frais, et faites fremier; et adonc aiez une escuelle percée d'un pertuis gros comme vostre petit doit, et adonc mettez de celle boulie dedans l'escuelle en commençant ou milieu, et laissiez filer tout autour de la paelle; puis mettez en un plat, et de la pouldre de succre dessus. Et que la paelle dessusdite de fer ou d'arain tiengne trois choppines, et ait le bort demy doy de hault, et soit aussi large ou dessus comme en bas, ne plus ne moins, et pour cause. (MP 226)

139. Suppa dorata

Habi de le fette di pane bianco mondato che non habia corteccia, et fa' le ditte fette siano quadre, un pocho brusculate tanto che da ogni parte siano colorite dal foco. Poi habi dell'ove battute inseme col succaro assai et un poca d'acqua rosata; et mettirali a mollare dentro le ditte fette di pane; et cavatile fora dextramente le mettirai a frigere un pochetto in una padella con un poco di butiro o de strutto, voltando molto spesso che non si ardino. Poi le conciarai in un piatello; et di sopra gli mettirai un pocha d'acqua rosata fatta gialla con un pocho zafrano, et del zuccaro habundantemente. (Ma 174)*

140. Chireseye

For to make chireseye tak chiryes at the fest of Seynt Iohn the Baptist, & do awey the stonys. Grynd hem in a morter, & after frot hem wel in a seue so that the ius be wel comyn owt; & do than in a pot & do therein feyre gres or boter & bred of wastel ymyid, & of sugur a god party, & a porcioun of wyn. & wan it is wel ysodyn & ydressyd in dyschis, stik therin clowis of gilofre & strew theron sugur. (Ds HB 77)

141. Emplumeus de pomes

Pour donner entendement à celluy qui le fera sy prennés de bonnes pomes barberines selon la quantité que l'on en vouidra faire et puis les parés bien et appoint et les taillés en beaulx platz d'or ou d'argent; et qu'il hait ung beau pot de terre bon et nect, et y mecte de belle eaue necte et mecte bouillir sur brase belle et clere et mecte bouillir ses pomes dedans. Et face qu'il ait de bonnes amendres doulces grant quantité selon la quantité des pomes qu'il ha mis cuire, et les plume, nectoie et lave tresbien et mectés broyer au mortier qui ne sante point les aulx, et si les broie tresbien et les arouse du boullon en quoy cuisent lesdictes pomes, et quant ledictes pomes seront assés cuictes si les tirés dehors sur belle et necte postz, et de celle eaue colle ses amendres et en face lait qui soit bon et espés, et le remecte boullir sur brase clere et necte sans fumee, et bien petit de sel. Et entretant que il bouldra si hache bien menut ses dictes pomes à ung petit et nect coutel et puis, estre hachiés, si les mecte dedans son lait, et y mecte du succre grant foison selon ce que il y a desditz emplumeus de pomes; et puis, quant le medicin le demandera, si le mectés en belles escuelles ou casses d'or ou d'argent. (Ch 194)

142. Erbowle

Take bolas and scald hem with wyne, and drawe hem thorow a straynour; do hem in a pot. Clarify hony, and therto with powdour fort and flour of rys. Salt it & florissh it with whyte aneys, & serve it forth. (Fc HB 119)

143. Perys in syrip

Boyle wardons that they be somdell tendyr; pare hem, cut hem yn pecys. Take canell, a grete dele; draw hit thorow a streynour III or IV tymys with good wyn in a pott. Do therto sygure, a grete dele; anneys, clovis & macys, and yf thu wilte, datys mynsyd & reysons of coraunce. Set hit on the fyre; when it boyleth cast yn the perys: lete hem boyle togedyr. When hit is boyled ynowghe, loke it be broun of canell, & put therto poudyr of gynger, a grete dele; loke hit be somedele doucet, & serve hit forth. (Hi 65)

144. Peeres in confyt

Take peeres and pare hem clene. Take gode rede wyne & mulberies, other saundres, and seth the peeres therin, & whan thei buth ysode take hem vp. Make a syryp of wyne greke, other vernage, with blaunche powdur, other white sugur and powdur gynger, & do the peres therin. Seeth it a lytel & messe it forth. (Fc HB 129)

145. Pour faire condoignac

Prenez des coings et les pelez, puis fendez par quartiers, et ostez l'ueil et les pépins, puis les cuisiez en bon vin rouge et puis soient coulés parmi une estamine: puis prenez du miel et le faites longuement boulir et escumer, et après mettez vos coings dedans et remuez très bien, et le faites tant boulir que le miel se reviengne à moins la moitié; puis gettez dedans pouldre d'ypocras, et remuez tant qu'il soit tout froit, puis taillez par morceaulx et les gardez. (MP 247)

146. Confetti de melle apio o de pome paradiso

Se le voy fare subito chomo è gratate le poy fare come ti pare. Toy la mella e mondala, poy la grata; varda che non vada le granelle dentro la gratitura e lassala sugare per dui iorni. El sucho che fa la mella lassalo pur con la mella; passa le pome gratate e per ogni tri libre de pome meti libre tri de mele e lassale stare dui zorni le pome chomo el mele; poy fale bolire sempre menandole con speçie tanto che le mele sia cocte, abi a mente le spezie voleno essere messe quando l'è quasi cocto el confetto, cossi quelle de chodogni. Poy la distendi suso una tavola o suso una pietra bagnata e fay a modo di foio grosso men de mezzo dido; poy lassala refredare e fane a modo de schachieri in pezetti picholi e reponile in una schatolla con foie de laurano de sotto e poy de sopra dall'altra mano va metando foie de suolo in suolo; et se voi mettere spezie tra foio e foio serà molto bono. Agi a mente ch'el vol per lo men bolire una hora grossa e forsi dui sempre menandole bene e guardale dal fumo. (Fr 71)

147. Dele mele bullito co le noci, detto nucato

Togli mele bullito e schiumato, con le noci un poco peste e spezie cotte insieme: bagnati la palma de la mano coll'acqua et estendilo: lassa freddare a dà a mangiare. E puoi ponere mandole e avellane in luogo di noci. (Za 77)

148. Pour faire Orengat

Mettez en cinq quartiers les peleures d'une orenge et raclez à un coustel la mousse qui est dedans, puis les mettez tremper en bonne eaue doulce par neuf jours, et changez l'eaue chascun jour: puis les boulez en eaue doulce une seule onde, et ce fait, les faictes estendre sur une nappe et les laissiez essuier très bien, puis les mettez en un pot et du miel tant qu'ils soient tous couverts, et faites boulir à petit feu et escumer, et quant vous croirez que le miel soit cuit (pour essaier s'il est cuit, ayez de l'eaue en une escuelle, et faites dégouter en icelle eaue une goutte d'icelluy miel, et s'il s'espant, il n'est pas cuit: et se icelle goute de miel se tient en l'eau sans espandre, il est cuit); et lors devez traire vos peleures d'orenge, et d'icelles faites par ordre un lit, et gettez pouldre de gingembre dessus, puis un autre, et getter etc., usque in infinitum; et laissier un mois ou plus puis mengier. (MP 265)

149. Pour faire ung lot de bon ypocras

Prenez une onches de cinamonde nommée longue canelle en pippe, avec une cloche de gingembre et autant de garingal, bien estampé ensemble, et puis prenez ung livre de bon çuquere: et tout cela broyés ensamble et destrempés avec ung lot du milleur vin de Beaune que pourrés finer et le laissir tremper ungne heure ou deux. Et puis coullés parmy ung chause par plusieurs fois tant qui soit bien cler. (MP 273)

150. Specie fine a tutte cosse

Toy una onza de pevere e una de cinamo e una de zenzevro e mezo quarto de garofali e uno quarto de zaferanno. (Fr 40)

Specie dolce per assay cosse bone e fine

Le meior specie dolze fine che tu fay se vuoi per lampreda in crosta e per altri boni pessi d'aque dolze che se faga in crosto e per fare bono brodetto e bon savore. Toi uno quarto de garofali e una onza de bon zenzevro e toy una onza de cinamo leto e toy arquanto folio e tute queste specie fay pestare insiema caxa como te piaxe, e se ne vo' fare più, toy le cosse a questa medessima raxone et è meravigliosamente bona. (Fr 40)

Specie negre e forte per assay savore

Specie negre e forte per fare savore; toy mezo quarto de garofali e do onze de pevere e toy arquanto pevere longo e do noce moscate e fa de tute spece. (Fr 40)

Bibliography

PRIMARY SOURCES

Aldobrandino da Siena, *Le régime du corps de maître Aldebrandin de Sienne: Texte français du XIIIe siècle,* edited by Louis Landouzy and Roger Pépin, Paris, Champion, 1911; reprinted Geneva, Slatkine, 1978.

Benefitiali di Ser Lorenzo Tani (1356–83). Manuscript in Archivio Arcivescovile, Florence.

Castelvetro, Giacomo, *The Fruit, Herbs, and Vegetables of Italy,* edited by Gillian Riley, London, Viking, British Museum, Natural History, 1989.

Chiquart, Maître, *Du fait de cuisine,* edited by Terence Scully in *Vallesia. Bulletin annuel de la Bibliothèque et des Archives cantonales du Valais, des Musées de Valère et de la Majorie* 40 (1985): 101–231. (Published also in book form with an English translation: *Chiquart's "On Cookery": A Fifteenth-century Savoyard Culinary Treatise,* American University Studies series, edited and translated by Terence Scully. New York, Peter Lang Publishing, 1986.)

Contes pour rire: Fabliaux des XIIIe et XIVe siècles, selected and presented by Nora Scott. Paris, 10/18 publishers, 1977.

Cronache Senesi, in *Rerum italicarum scriptores, nuova serie, t. XV, parte VI,* edited by Fabio Jacometti and Alessandro Lisini. Bologna, Zanichelli, 1931–36.

Dante, *The Divine Comedy,* translated and edited by Mark Musa, in *The Portable Dante.* New York, Penguin, 1995.

"Diversa Servicia," in *Curye on Inglysch: English culinary manuscripts of the fourteenth century,* edited by Constance Hieatt and Sharon Butler. London, Oxford University Press, 1985.

Folgore da San Gimignano, *Sonetti,* edited by Giovanni Caravaggi. Turin, Einaudi, 1965.

"Forme of Cury," in *Curye on Inglysch: English culinary manuscripts of the fourteenth century,* edited by Constance Hieatt and Sharon Butler. London, Oxford University Press, 1985.

Frati, Ludovico, ed., *Libro di cucina del secolo XIV.* Livorno, 1899; reprinted Bologna, Forni, 1970 ("Testi Antichi di Gastronomia," 7).

Guerrini, Olindo, ed., *Frammento di un libro di cucina del sec. XIV edito nel dì delle nozze Carducci-Gnaccarini.* Bologna, Nicola Zanichelli, 1877.

Hieatt, Constance, ed., *An Ordinance of Pottage: An Edition of the Recipes in Yale University's ms Beinecke 163.* London, Prospect Books, 1988.

Journal d'un bourgeois de Paris, edited and presented by Colette Beaune. Paris, Le Livre de poche, 1990.

Lami, Giovanni, *Sanctae ecclesiae Florentinae monumenta* III (1251, 1384). Florence, 1758.

Liber de coquina, edited by Marianne Mulon, in "Deux traités inédits d'art culinaire médiéval," *Bulletin philologique et historique* 1 (1971), *Les problèmes de l'alimentation,* Actes du 93e Congrès national des Sociétés savantes tenu à Tours (1968): 396–420.

Martino, Maestro, *Libro de arte coquinaria,* edited by Emilio Faccioli, in *Arte della*

257

cucina, *Libri di ricette: Testi sopra lo scalco, il trinciante e i vini dal XIV al XIX secolo.* Milan, Il Polifilo, 1966, 1: 115–204.

Le Ménagier de Paris, edited by Jérôme Pichon. Paris, Crapelet, 1846; reprinted Geneva, Slatkine, 1970.

Morpurgo, Salomone, ed., *LVII ricette di un libro di cucina del buon secolo della lingua.* Bologna, Nicola Zanichelli, 1890.

New York, Pierpont Morgan Library, MS Bühler 19; unpublished manuscript.

Nice, Musée Masséna, Bibliothèque de Cessole, ms. 226. Published edition: Giovanni Rebora, ed., in *Miscellanea storica ligure* XIX (1987), "Studi in onore di Luigi Bulferetti," 1530–60.

Prudenzani, Simone, "Il Saporetto," edited by S. Debenedetti, in *Giornale storico della letteratura italiana,* supp. 15 (1913): 91–188.

"Le 'Registre de Cuisine' de Jean de Bockenheim, cuisinier du pape Martin V," edited by Bruno Laurioux, in *Mélanges de l'École française de Rome (Moyen Age, Temps modernes)* 100, no. 2 (1988): 709–60.

Samminiato de'Ricci, *Il manuale di mercatura,* edited by A. Borlandi. Genoa, 1963.

Sercambi, Giovanni, *Le Novelle,* edited by Giovanni Sinicropi, 2 vols. Bari, Laterza, Scrittori d'Italia, 1972.

Sermini, Gentile, *Le Novelle,* edited by Giuseppe Vettori, 2 vols. Rome, Avanzini e Torraca, 1968.

Tables florentines, nouvelles de Franco Sacchetti, translated and presented by Jacqueline Brunet and Odile Redon. Paris, Stock, 1984.

Tractatus de modo preparandi et condiendi omnia cibaria, edited by Marianne Mulon, in "Deux traités inédits d'art culinaire médiéval," *Bulletin philologique et historique* 1 (1971): 380–95.

The Viandier of Taillevent, edited by Terence Scully, Ottawa: University of Ottawa Press, 1988.

Le Viandier de Guillaume Tirel dit Taillevent, edited by Jérôme Pichon and Georges Vicaire. Paris, Leclert & Cormuau, 1892; reprinted Geneva, Slatkine, 1967; also reprinted Luzarches, Daniel Morcrette, no date.

Zambrini, Francesco, ed., *Libro della cucina del secolo XIV,* Bologna, Gaetano Romagnoli, 1863; reprinted, Bologna, Forni, 1968.

SECONDARY SOURCES

Bec, Christian, *Les Marchands écrivains, affaires et humanisme à Florence, 1375–1434.* Paris, Mouton, 1967.

Dion, Roger, *Histoire de la vigne et du vin en France des origines au XIXe siècle.* Paris, Flammarion, 1990 (first edition, Paris, 1959, published by the author).

Flandrin, Jean-Louis, "Internationalisme, nationalisme et régionalisme dans la cuisine des XIVe et XVe siècles: Le témoignage des livres de cuisine," in *Manger et boire au Moyen Age,* edited by Denis Menjot. Paris, Les Belles Letters, 1984, 2: 75–91.

Grewe, Rudolf, *Libre de Sent Soví: Receptari de cuina.* Barcelona, Editorial Barcino, 1979.

Lachiver, Marcel, *Vins, vignes et vignerons: Histoire du vignoble français.* Paris, Fayard, 1988.

Lafortune-Martel, Agathe, *Fête noble en Bourgogne au XVe siècle; Le banquet du Faisan (1454): Aspects politiques, sociaux et culturels.* Cahiers d'études médiévales, no. 8. Montréal, Bellarmin-Vrin, 1984.

Laurioux, Bruno, *Le Moyen Age à table.* Paris, Adam Biro, 1989.

Menjot, Denis, ed., *Manger et boire au Moyen Age*. Actes du Colloque de Nice, 15–17 October 1982. Paris, Les Belles Lettres, 1984.

Nourritures. Special issue of *Médiévales* 5 (1983).

Plants, mets et mots. Special issue of *Médiévales* 16–17 (1989).

Montanari, Massimo, *L'Alimentazione contadina nell'alto Medioevo*. Naples, Liguori editore, 1979.

———, *Alimentazione e cultura nel Medioevo*. Rome, Laterza, 1988.

Pelner Cosman, Madeleine, *Fabulous Feasts: Medieval Cookery and Ceremony*. New York, George Braziller, 1976.

Rodinson, Maxime, "Romania et autres mots arabes en italien," *Romania* 71 (1950): 433–49

Renouard, Yves, *Etudes d'histoire médiévale*, 2 vols. Paris, SEVPEN, 1968. See especially the articles on the wine trade in the Middle Ages, 1: 223–359.

Stouff, Louis, *Ravitaillement et alimentation en Provence aux XIVe et XVe siècles*. Paris, Mouton, 1970.

Recipes by Manuscript Source

The number at the left margin refers to the recipe number in this book; the number following the name of the recipe refers to the page or folio number in the source. Full citations of the sources appear in the Bibliography.

Le Ménagier de Paris (MP)

Maestro Martino, *Libro de arte coquinaria* (Ma)

2. Herb Soup *(Menestra d'herbette)* 146
4. Chickpea Soup *(Brodo de ciceri rosci)* 147
5. Zanzarelli *(Zanzarelli)* 137
7. Meat Ravioli in Broth *(Ravioli in tempo di carne)* 144
22. Fresh Fava Beans with Herbs *(Fave fresche con brodo di carne)* 149
25. Pumpkin or Winter Squash Soup *(Cocer zucche)* 148
29. Sweet and Sour Civet of Venison *(Civero de salvaticina)* 122
43. *Carbonata (Carbonata)* 131
46. Roast Kid with Sauce of Gold *(Capretto arrosto in sapore)* 130
50. *Porchetta*, or Inside-out Suckling Pig *(Porchetta)* 127
59. Chicken with Orange Sauce *(Pollastro arrosto)* 127
64. Marinated Trout *in Carpione (Carpionar trutte)* 202
71. Dover Sole with Bitter Orange Juice *(Soglie)* 186
75. Grilled Oysters *(Ostriche)* 189
81. *Torta Bolognese*, or Herbed Swiss Chard and Cheese Pie *(Torta bolognese)* 159
82. Everyday *Torta (Torta comune)* 163
89. Eel and Spinach *Torta (Torta di anguille)* 165
91. Eel and Roe Tart *(Pasticcio d'anguilla)* 169
92. Trout in Pastry *(Pastelli secchi facti con pesce sano)* 170
93. Pumpkin or Winter Squash Tart *(Torta di zucche)* 160
94. *Torta Bianca*: White Tart *(Torta bianca)* 158
96. *Dariole*, or Custard Tart *(Diriola)* 172
100. White Garlic Sauce *(Agliata bianca)* 157
101. Pink Garlic Sauce *(Agliata pavonazza)* 157
103. Summertime Cerulean Blue Sauce *(Sapor celeste de estate)* 156
113. Black-Grape Sauce *(Sapor de uva)* 155
114. Prune Sauce *(Sapor de progna secche)* 154
120. Egg Ravioli *(Ova in forma de raffioli)* 183
121. Green Omelette *(Frictata)* 180
130. An Italian Blancmange in Catalan Style *(Bianco mangiare al modo catalano)* 152
136. Marzipan Tart *(Marzapane)* 168
137. Marzipan Sweetmeats: *Caliscioni (Caliscioni)* 169
139. Medieval Italian "French Toast" *(Suppa dorata)* 174

Le Viandier de Guillaume Tirel dit Taillevent (VT XV)
(Edited by J. Pichon from fifteenth-century editions)

3. Winter Squash or Pumpkin Soup *(Congordes)* 181
23. Puree of Dried Young Fava Beans *(Fève fresé en potaige)* 206
66. *Chaudumé* of Pike *(Chaudumé)* 179
83. Rabbit Baked in Pastry *(Pastés de connis)* 171
86. Veal Pâté *(Pastés de veau)* 169
97. Whole-Pear Pie *(Pastés de poires crues)* 175
123. Meats in Aspic *(Pour gelée)* 156

The Viandier of Taillevent (VT Scul)
(Edited by T. Scully from manuscript sources)

52. *Bourbelier* of Wild Boar in Spiced Sauce *(Bourbier de sanglier)* Vat 94
53. Spit-Roasted Hare *(Lyevres en rost)* Vat 93

A Few Mail-order Sources

This is not intended to be an exhaustive list and is limited to companies with which the translator has had good experiences. There are many other vendors throughout the country, and the reader is encouraged to seek out local sources.

BREAD AND FLOUR

Poilâne
8, rue du Cherche-Midi
75006 Paris, France
International access code plus (33) 1 44 39 20 94 (After-hours answering machine message in English)
E-mail: commerce@poilane.fr

Lionel Poilâne bakes his sourdough loaves from organic flour in hardwood-fired ovens and now sends them by express delivery service to addresses in the United States. Because of the shipping costs, this is expensive bread, but it is also extremely good and long-lasting, especially if you cut each 2-kilo (4.4-pound) loaf into quarters and freeze them. It can be a good option if your local baker cannot supply a true, plain sourdough country loaf.

Great Valley Mills
1774 Country Lane Road
Barto, PA 19504
(800) 688–6455
Fax: (610) 754–6490

Great Valley Mills does not have organic certification, but sells excellent unbleached wheat flours, some stone-ground, others not, but all fresh and flavorful.

King Arthur Flour
The Baker's Catalogue
P.O. Box 876
Norwich, VT 05055
(800) 827–6836
Fax: (800) 343–3002
Web site: http://www.kingarthurflour.com

King Arthur Flour sells an enormous variety of flours, some organic, some not. The descriptions in their catalogue are complete and helpful.

Walnut Acres Organic Farms
Penns Creek, PA 17662
(800) 433–3998
Web site: http://www.walnutacres.com

As the name of the company indicates, all their products are certified organic.

POULTRY AND GAME

Free-range poultry, capons, and game (wild and farm-raised) are available from:

D'Artagnan
399 St. Paul Avenue
Jersey City, NJ 07306
(201) 792–0748
(800) DARTAGN

SPICES

Adriana's Caravan
409 Vanderbilt Street
Brooklyn, NY 11218
(800) 316–0820
(718) 436–8565
Fax: (718) 436–8565

Adriana's Caravan publishes two catalogues: one that lists only the more usual products, and a far longer one that covers the more exotic items you may want to buy for the recipes in this book, such as grains of paradise and cubeb. If a spice is available in the United States, it is probably in the Adriana's Caravan catalogue.

Penzey's, Ltd.
P.O. Box 1446
Waukesha, WI 53187
(414) 574–0277
Fax: (414) 574–0278

Penzey's is run by extremely knowledgeable people who publish an informative and entertaining catalogue. They are unlikely to have the more arcane spices (although it would pay to ask them), but what they do have is fresh and of very high quality indeed.

Foods of India
121 Lexington Avenue
New York, NY 10016
(212) 683–4419

Kalustyan's
123 Lexington Avenue
New York, NY 10016
(212) 685–3416

Both of these shops are in one of New York's South Asian neighborhoods and their stock reflects this; Kalustyan's also sells a variety of Middle Eastern products, including good rose water.

Dean and Deluca
560 Broadway
New York, NY 10012
(800) 221–7714
(212) 431–1691
Web site: http://www.ishops.com/dd

Dean and Deluca is a rather ritzy shop in New York's SoHo district. In addition to a good selection of spices and other groceries, dried beans are something of a specialty.

VERJUICE

Sour grape juice can sometimes be purchased in Middle Eastern groceries (see Kalusty-an's above), but a number of American wine growers are now producing verjuice and will sell it by mail order. Two sources are:

Navarro Vineyards
P.O. Box 47
Philo, CA 95466
(800) 537–9463

Bonny Doon Vineyard
10 Pine Flat Road
Santa Cruz, CA 95060
(408) 425–3625

Index

Note: *References in bold indicate pages on which recipes occur.*